Fundraising for Social Change

Readers are invited to view and download the supplementary Instructor's Manual for *Fundraising for Social Change*. The manual includes a course description and syllabus, with week-by-week questions for discussion, writing assignments, small-group exercises, and case studies of ethical dilemmas. It also describes in detail the eight-week field placement component of the class.

The Instructor's Manual is available FREE on-line.

If you would like to download and print out an electronic copy of the manual, please visit www.wiley.com/college/fundraisingforsocialchange.

Thank you,

Kim Klein

THE CHARDON PRESS SERIES

Fundamental social change happens when people come together to organize, advocate, and create solutions to injustice. Chardon Press recognizes that communities working for social justice need tools to create and sustain healthy organizations. In an effort to support these organizations, Chardon Press produces materials on fundraising, community organizing, and organizational development. These resources are specifically designed to meet the needs of grassroots nonprofits— organizations that face the unique challenge of promoting change with limited staff, funding, and other resources. We at Chardon Press have adapted traditional techniques to the circumstances of grassroots nonprofits. Chardon Press and Jossey-Bass hope these works help people committed to social justice to build mission-driven organizations that are strong, financially secure, and effective.

Kim Klein, Series Editor

JB JOSSEY-BASS

Fundraising for Social Change

FIFTH EDITION,

REVISED & EXPANDED

Kim Klein

John Wiley & Sons, Inc.

Published by Jossey-Bass
A Wiley Imprint
989 Market Street, San Francisco, CA 94103-1741   www.josseybass.com

Jossey-Bass books and products are available through most bookstores. To contact Jossey-Bass directly, call our Customer Care Department within the U.S. at 800-956-7739, outside the U.S. at 317-572-3986, or fax 317-572-4002.

Jossey-Bass also publishes its books in a variety of electronic formats. Some content that appears in print may not be available in electronic books.

Library of Congress Cataloging-in-Publication Data

Klein, Kim.
  Fundraising for social change / Kim Klein. - 5th ed., rev. & expanded.
         p. cm. - (Chardon press series)
  Includes bibliographical references and index.
  ISBN-13: 978-0-7879-8455-7
  ISBN-10: 0-7879-8455-8
  1. Fund raising-United States. 2. Nonprofit organizations-United States-Finance. I. Title
  HV41.9.U5K57 2007
  361.7068'1-dc22
                                                            2006029100

Printed in the United States of America
FIFTH EDITION
PB Printing   10 9 8 7 6 5 4 3 2 1

CONTENTS

For everyone I have met during the past thirty years who believes that the world can be a better place and who finds joy and meaning in working toward that end.

When I line up all the editions of *Fundraising For Social Change* since the first one in 1988, I am amazed at how much longer each one is. Does this mean each one has that much more knowledge, or am I just getting to be a windbag? I hope the former, and my hope is bolstered by how much fundraising has changed over these decades.

Every chapter in this edition has been significantly changed to reflect new and expanded technology—e-mail, the Web, online giving, cell phones, blogs. Some of these technologies did not exist when the Fourth Edition came out in 2000, but they are now part and parcel of organizational life. I have added chapters on ethics, on working across cultural lines, and on how to create opportunities for fundraising more systematically. I have also greatly expanded the chapters on major gifts, capital, and endowment campaigns. Needing much more information on large campaigns reflects the fact that many grassroots organizations have become institutions and are able to project their work decades into the future.

Some things that have changed since this book was first published—and which have changed exponentially since the last edition—are not positive. The gap between rich and poor is the largest it has ever been. In the United States, this chasm is caused in great part by the recent tax changes that have made already wealthy people more wealthy while driving millions into poverty. The minimum wage is not enough keep a family out of poverty. Homeless shelters are full of people who work full time but can't afford housing. Meanwhile, the federal taxes we do pay fund a military budget supporting bloody and pointless wars around the world and a "war on terror" at home that is more about suppressing dissent than concern for safety. Moreover, public schools, parks, arts programs, and the like are no longer truly "public" because they must raise large amounts of money privately to do their job.

This book is designed to help small organizations raise money effectively by building a broad base of individual donors. But private-sector giving cannot take the place of government funding, and the nonprofit sector cannot solve the many social problems created or exacerbated by public policies more commonly associated with oligarchies than democracies. Nonetheless, an organization that is financed by a broad base of individual donors is in the strongest position to advocate for the structural changes our society must make. The late management guru Peter Drucker said, "Every important idea for social change has come from the nonprofit sector." For these ideas to become reality, they must be supported by the time and money of dozens, hundreds, or thousands of people. For organizations serious about social change, the number of donors you have is as important as the amount of money you raise, and to state the obvious, the more donors you have, the more money you will raise. In this book, I assume you are already working as hard as you can; I suggest ways for you to work smarter. Then you can find and reach the donors you need to get the money you deserve.

Oakland, California   Kim Klein
August 2006

ACKNOWLEDGMENTS

A humbling fact for any writer is how much of the work of getting one's writing in print depends on other people. As a how-to writer, I am further humbled by the number of people I have learned from and from whose ideas and experiences this book borrows heavily. If I were to be completely truthful in these acknowledgments, I would have to list and thank all the people I have met in trainings, at conferences, and in my work as a development director for their thoughts, their stories, and their willingness to try new things.

Some of the information in this book appeared first in article form in the *Grassroots Fundraising Journal,* a bimonthly periodical that I have been publishing since 1981. The *Journal* is the best expression of my commitment to capturing in writing the vast oral tradition that is grassroots fundraising. The letters that are sent to me every month, which become the basis of my e-column, "Dear Kim," also inform the content of this book. I am able to see what people want to know and focus on those requests.

Stephanie Roth, my life and business partner, provides unflagging help and feedback through all my writing and never fails to make me laugh on a daily basis.

Thank you as always to my dear friend, Nancy Adess, who has edited everything I have written since 1981. Her ability to make all concepts clearer and more accessible is extraordinary. Thanks also to Maria Mottola, Mal Warwick, Joan Flanagan, and an anonymous reader for their honest and candid feedback on the previous edition of this book. Many of the improvements in this edition are a credit to them. I also thank Allison Brunner and the team at Jossey-Bass who take care of the hundreds of details that go into a book of this size with patience, good humor, and constant encouragement while dealing with dozens of other authors.

Ann Holder and Frances Kunreuther provided technological help in finishing this manuscript while I was in New York City staying with them. Without Ann's help in the final stages of editing, the book would have been badly delayed.

My dog, Brooklyn, her sister, Gracie, who lives next door, and my cats, Ruby and Jack, couldn't care less about fundraising and won't feel the least bit flattered that their names are included here. They and all their animal colleagues remind me that while my work is important, it is not everything.

—K. K.

THE AUTHOR

Kim Klein is widely credited for helping to document, define, and develop the field of fundraising for grassroots organizations and for people and groups working for social change. She founded the *Grassroots Fundraising Journal* in 1981 and served as its publisher until 2006. She is also the author of *Fundraising for the Long Haul, Fundraising in Times of Crisis,* and *Ask and You Shall Receive;* she is coeditor, with her partner, Stephanie Roth, of *Raise More Money: The Best of the Grassroots Fundraising Journal.* She is the featured writer for the e-newsletter, *Grassroots Fundraising,* with her column—"Dear Kim"—of answers to questions posed by readers.

Klein is a member of the Building Movement Project and leads workshops on tax policy and the importance of the "commons"; she is a regular contributor to the project's Web site. She travels and lectures widely and has provided fundraising training and consultation in all fifty United States and in twenty-one countries. She lives in Berkeley, California.

INTRODUCTION

This is a how-to book. Its goal is to provide organizations that have budgets of less than two million dollars (including much less than that) with the information they need to establish, maintain, and expand a successful community-based fundraising program. Building a broad base of individual donors gives organizations maximum freedom to pursue their mission. They can then use foundation, corporate, or government grants for special programs, start-up costs, technical assistance, capital or endowment projects, or other time-limited needs.

Organizations with small budgets, particularly those working for social change, need to keep in mind that the context in which their fundraising efforts take place is different from that of large, established organizations such as universities.

First, the name of your group is not a household word. And even when they hear about you, many people will not understand what you are trying to do. Many of those who do understand may disagree with you, particularly if you are trying to challenge the status quo. Even those in sympathy with your mission may think your aims are hopelessly naïve or idealistic; you may often be told to "face reality."

Second, you probably have little or no front money and not enough staff and you are often either just holding your own financially or falling behind.

Third, your board of directors, volunteers, and staff are likely to be unfamiliar with fundraising strategies and may not be comfortable with the idea of asking for money.

For grassroots groups such as yours, traditional fundraising strategies need to be rethought and translated into workable terms. This book does that. All of the strategies explained and recommended here have been successful for small groups. Not every strategy will work for every group, but the discussion of each strategy will allow you to decide which strategies will work for your group and how to expand the strategies you are already using.

Fundraising without planning, without a strong, committed group of volunteers to help, without a workable organizational structure, or without understanding the basic components of all fundraising plans is practically impossible. The appropriate staff, whether paid or unpaid, of every organization should read the first two sections of this book to learn the context for successful fundraising.

The next sections present detailed descriptions of how to carry out strategies to acquire, retain, and upgrade donors to your organization. These proceed from the most impersonal—direct mail appeals and special events—to the most personal—solicitation by telephone and in person. The book gives special attention to the difficulties most people have asking for money and offers concrete ways to overcome these difficulties. Finally, the book covers how to create a budget and a fundraising plan and the rudiments of setting up a fundraising office, keeping records, working with an executive director, and hiring fundraising staff or consultants. Special circumstances for fundraising are also discussed, such as raising money in rural communities or raising money for a coalition of groups. There are many fundraising strategies that are not covered in this book, and readers are encouraged to explore them. However, all successful fundraising strategies are, at the end of the day, about people. Corporate giving is about knowing someone in the corporation who will shepherd your cause through their system. Service clubs, houses of worship, foundations, and so on are also about knowing someone. So even though this book doesn't cover that specifically, it does cover what you need to know to pursue any strategy you want to pursue.

If you find this book helpful, I encourage you to buy my other books and to subscribe to the *Grassroots Fundraising Journal*, a bimonthly publication that will help you keep up with fundraising strategies and developments in the field. I also encourage you to buy my training videotapes and use them with your board. All that helps me, and it will help you.

But ultimately, after you have read about how to raise money and gone to workshops on how to do it, the only thing left is to do it. Like driving a car or learning to swim, all the theory and explanation will not help until you get behind the wheel or into the pool and try it for yourself.

Few people give money without being asked. Make this your motto: "Today somebody has to ask somebody for money."

 **PART ONE**

Fundraising Framework

When I hand out the agenda for a fundraising workshop, participants are often surprised to see that the section on personal solicitation is in the afternoon. Many have said, "I came to learn how to identify prospects and ask for money, not how to create a case statement or build a board of directors." Successful fundraisers know, however, that fundraising doesn't start with asking for money; it starts with understanding how fundraising and philanthropy work and what an organization needs to have in place in order to be successful in asking for money. This first section starts with what, for me, are the two most important facts I have ever learned about fundraising: the bulk of money given away to nonprofits comes from individuals, and the majority of people who give are not rich. The corollary to these facts is this: fundraising starts with who you know, and you already know all the people you need to know to begin your fundraising efforts. The section continues by describing what a group should have in place before it can begin asking for money in earnest and finishes with a discussion about the group of people who are going to be key to a successful fundraising effort: the board of directors.

Philanthropy in America

The word *philanthropy* comes from two Greek words meaning "love of people." In modern times this goodwill, or humanitarianism, is often expressed in donations of property, money, or volunteer time to worthy causes. Similarly, the word *charity* comes from a Latin word meaning "love" in the sense of unconditional lovingkindness, compassion, and seeking to do good. The roots of these words remind us of the fundamental reasons for the work of most nonprofit organizations.

The United States has the largest system of organized private philanthropy in the world. In this country, nongovernmental organizations have been created—and funded through private sources—to provide services that countries with greater government commitment to social welfare provide directly and fund through taxation. If nonprofits in the United States were a single industry, they would rank as the nation's largest industry, accounting for just under 10 percent of the workforce and about 5 percent of the gross domestic product. As of 2005, more than 1.5 million organizations have been recognized by the Internal Revenue Service as tax exempt. Several million more small, grassroots organizations that are doing important charitable work are not registered with the government and have no formal tax status. These groups include organizations just getting started; organizations using a fiscal sponsor; organizations that use very little money, such as neighborhood block clubs; organizations that come together for a one-time purpose, such as cleaning up a vacant lot or protesting something; and those that don't wish to have a structural relationship with the state or federal government.

Because of the size and growing sophistication of the nonprofit sector, it has increasingly drawn the attention of the government, researchers, academics, and many members of the general public. Although nonprofits are increasingly regulated by federal, state, and local government, public awareness, coupled with the role of individuals in funding nonprofits, means that voluntary compliance with accepted ethical standards of accounting, personnel, and fundraising practice provides an added, and usually sufficient, layer of self-regulation. Nonprofit status is a public trust and tax exemption is, in effect, a public expense. Even if an organization has no formal tax status, if it seeks to raise money from the public it has the same moral duty as registered nonprofits to operate ethically, be truthful with donors, and provide the highest quality of services to clients.

THE FOUNDATION-CORPORATE GIVING MYTH

As with many endeavors that are critically important and use the resources of millions of people, it is not surprising that a number of misconceptions have grown up about philanthropy and charities.

The most serious misconception for fundraising is many people's belief that most money given to nonprofits comes from foundations and corporations. The truth is far different. Of all the income of all nonprofits, about half is earned income: fees for service, tuition, products for sale, and the like. About 30 percent of nonprofit income is derived from government programs (collectively known as "the public sector"). Extensive cutbacks in government funding starting in the 1980s and continuing to this day have reduced government funding a great deal, but it remains a significant source of income for many organizations. The final 20 percent of nonprofit income is from the private sector: individuals, foundations, and corporations. For most of the organizations using this book, the private sector will provide the majority of your funding. Surprising to most people is the fact that gifts from individuals make up the bulk of private-sector funding, far more than all foundation and corporate money combined. This book focuses almost entirely on how to raise money from that enormous market of individual donors.

There is now an enormous body of research on philanthropy, both in the United States and in other countries, and determining who gives what to whom and why comprises a lot of it. The most widely used report is *Giving USA,* compiled yearly by the Giving USA Foundation AAFRC Trust for Philanthropy. Every year since 1935, the authors have calculated just how much money was given away to nonprofits and by whom. They have identified four general sources of gifts from the private (nongovernmental) sector: living individuals, bequests (cash or other donations an individual arranges to be given to a charity on their death), foundations, and corporations. Their research shows that the proportion of giving from each of these sources remains constant, varying from year to year by only two or three percentage points, with gifts from individuals (living or deceased) exceeding the rest by an impressive ratio of nine to one.

For the year 2005, the latest for which figures are available, giving from these sources totaled $260.68 billion.

Sources of Contributions, 2004		
Contributions From	**Amount in Billions**	**Percentage of Total**
Individuals	$187.92	75.6
Bequests	$19.80	8.0
Foundations	$28.80	11.6
Corporations	$12.00	4.8

Source: *Giving USA*, 2006.

Given these facts, an organization should have no trouble knowing where to go for money: individuals provide the vast bulk of private support to nonprofits.

WHO GIVES AWAY MONEY?

The logical follow-up question—Who are these people?—is more difficult to answer because there are many complex variables. Not only does the answer vary by which methods are used in doing the research, but there are also many aspects of giving that it is difficult for researchers to learn about. The bottom line is that, although the *Giving USA* figures presented above are probably fairly accurate in terms of foundation and corporate giving—which is easier to measure—giving by individuals is probably even greater than those statistics can measure. Here's why.

There are some formal ways that estimates of individual giving are made: by analyzing the tax returns of people who itemize their giving and extrapolating from them, by surveying a random sample of the population about their giving and extrapolating from their answers, and by comparing the results of either or both of these methods with what charities report of their income, either in their own tax filing statements (known by the name of the IRS form, 990) or in polls and surveys. The data collected in any of these ways can then be further analyzed by demographic breakdowns, such as the age or income of the donor, or by looking at the giving patterns of a particular set of donors over several years. Further information can be learned by comparing the characteristics of donors with those of nondonors or by conducting focus groups on why (and to what) people give or don't give.

There are a few well-known, established sources of research on who gives away money, how much, and to what. Perhaps the best known is *Giving USA,* cited above. Independent Sector, a leadership forum for nonprofits that also reports on giving in the United States, publishes a biannual report, *Giving and Volunteering in the USA,* based on written and phone surveys. The Center on Philanthropy at Indiana University surveys giving and volunteering by the same households over time as families and reports its findings in its Center on Philanthropy Panel Study (known as COPPS). Other researchers include the Center on Wealth and Philanthropy at Boston College, the Foundation Center, the National Center for Charitable Statistics, the NewTithing Group, and empty tomb, inc. (for research on religion).

Each of these institutions uses slightly different methods of counting philanthropic giving, with correspondingly disparate results. No matter what method is used, however, chances are that charitable giving by individuals is underreported because of the limitations of the information available.

For research that uses tax returns to estimate giving, as with *Giving USA,* it's important to note that only 30 percent of Americans file an itemized return. The 70 percent of Americans who file a "short form" receive no tax benefits from their giving because their giving doesn't exceed the standard deduction. Extrapolating what nonitemizers give is done with an econometric model. Though there is no reason to think the results from this model are wildly inaccurate, the estimates are probably conservative and thereby likely undercount a lot of giving.

For those who do report giving on their tax forms, we are confronted with the fact that people tend to understate their income and exaggerate their giving. By how much? Hard to say. When people are surveyed by phone about their giving, might they exaggerate their generosity? Probably. By how much? Hard to say. Certainly, people often forget how much they have given to charity when they have no incentive, such as a tax deduction, to help them remember. Possibly the exaggerators cancel out the underreporters. Add to that mix that rules about what is tax deductible and what is not are confusing even to nonprofits, and we can safely assume that it is difficult to say with great accuracy exactly who gives away money and how much they give away every year.

Here are some other variables that make knowing who gives away money difficult:

Although the majority of people give money from their annual income, the wealthy minority give from their assets. Studies looking at who is generous relative to their ability sometimes only compare income; others look at net worth. These can yield different results. For example, a family could have a low income but be quite wealthy because of assets, or have a low income and be poor.

Studies that calculate in which region of the country people are the most generous usually fail to take into account cost of living. For example, compare two states where the median income is $40,000 but in one state the median cost of housing is twice as expensive as in the other. The people living in the first state might well give less money away than those in the other state, but proportionate to their disposable income, they might be equally generous.

Almost all studies try to focus on formal philanthropic giving, but if we were to count the amount of money donated to homeless people on the street, or sent as remittances to family members in other countries, or given to help a friend pay for college or to help a poor family pay rent for a few months, not only would our studies show much more giving, they would probably reveal even more demographic differences among givers.

Looking at what charities report as their income would seem to give the most accurate data on how much people give to charity, but there are two factors that make this, too, a less reliable source. First, as mentioned, a lot of money donated by individuals doesn't necessarily go to established charities. Second, religious organizations are not required to file 990s (some do voluntarily), so we don't really have an accurate picture of how much income or what the sources of income are for religious institutions. Similarly, organizations with budgets of less than $25,000 are also not required to file a 990. For these many organizations, then, we are operating in the realm of guesswork about their total incomes and sources of income.

So you can see the problem of trying to learn who gives away money, how much they give, and where it goes: the majority of people do not declare their giving on their tax forms, and a large number of nonprofits are not reporting their income sources.

A final compounding factor is that who gives how much away has been changing as the U.S. economy has changed over the past ten years. For many years the bulk of money given away in the United States came from middle-class and working-class people. In 1998, Independent Sector's research showed that about 82 percent of all giving came from households with incomes of $65,000 or less, which was the majority of people. By 2000, the increasing disparity between rich and poor began to show up in giving. The most recent *Giving USA* notes that households with a gross income of $100,000 or less, which describes 92 percent of all households according to the IRS, contributed only about 52 percent of all giving, whereas households with a net worth of $5 million or more (1 percent of all households) contributed 28 percent of all gifts. Of course, this group also earns more than 40 percent of all income and owns more than 85 percent of all publicly traded stock, so as a group they are not particularly generous. Regardless of how the figures are analyzed, people with smaller household incomes now account for less total giving than they did eight years ago.

Giving USA notes, "The trend toward increasing inequality in income in the past two decades paired with different giving patterns to charitable organizations by income level will affect the overall distribution of contributions among non-profit organizations in the coming years." Further, as United for a Fair Economy—an independent organization that studies and reports on wealth and power in the United States—points out, the wealthy are growing wealthier as the middle-class loses ground. One indicator is the difference in pay between those at the top and those below them. As of 2004, the ratio of what the average CEO is paid (now $11.8 million) to what the average worker is paid (now $27,460) is 431-to-1. (If the minimum wage had risen as fast as CEO pay since 1990, the lowest-paid workers in the United States would be earning $23.03 an hour today instead of their current $5.15 an hour.) The disparities between what lowest-paid and highest-paid workers earn in the United States is the greatest in the world. This situation not only speaks to a need for a more just tax system, it also means that the majority of people do not have much money to contribute. As the gap grows and the middle class becomes smaller, giving by the majority of individuals may go down in actual dollars, even if it doesn't go down as a percentage of income.

THE TRUTH ABOUT GIVING

Despite the difficulties of learning exactly who gives and to what, the following facts are found in a number of studies, they have been found year after year, and they are borne out by the experience of development professionals all over the world.

About seven of every ten adults in the United States and Canada give away money. Where these numbers have been studied more locally, we have some interesting variation. For example, in Hawai'i nine out of ten adults give away money; in Alaska, six out of ten do. In Boulder, Colorado, where I grew up, a smaller percentage of the population gives away money than in nearby Denver. More people give away money in Nova Scotia than in British Columbia. (Here's a fun sampling from around the world: in Holland, almost 90 percent of the population gives away money, despite paying very high taxes. In Korea, 64 percent give; in the Philippines, 80 percent.)

Middle- and lower-income donors are responsible for a significant percentage of the money given—from 50 to 80 percent—and are the majority of givers.

Most people who give to nonprofits give to at least five and as many as fifteen groups.

About 20 percent of people on welfare give away money (with the average gift being $74), and about 97 percent of millionaires give away money (Center on Philanthropy data).

Volunteers are more likely to be donors than people who don't volunteer.

More people give away money than vote.

The majority of people who give away money describe themselves as religious or spiritual, whether or not they are involved in a formal religious or spiritual community.

And finally, a theme I will return to a thousand times in this book, people give when they are asked.

In the United States, the lion's share of private-sector giving, according to all studies, goes to religion. Religious organizations also make up the majority of nonprofits in the United States. Religion has lost market share over the years. When I entered the field of fundraising in 1976, religious giving was 50 percent of all giving; now it is just over 30 percent. Generation X seems to be giving less to religion than previous generations, but that may change as that generation ages.

Nonetheless, regardless of the methodology used or the variables considered, study after study give us a picture of a generous country, with most people making donations and feeling good about doing so. They also give us a picture of middle- and lower-income donors making up a significant percentage of all money given away and of a constantly increasing amount of money given every year.

Foundations and corporations, which have the false reputation of keeping charity alive, are overrated as a source of funds and the help they can provide is often misunderstood. While foundation and corporate giving will always play a vital role in the nonprofit sector, the limitations of that role must be clearly understood.

FOUNDATIONS

Foundations have relatively little money, and that money is in very great demand. Many of the larger foundations report receiving one hundred proposals for every two they are able to fund. As information about foundations becomes more easily available via the Internet, the demand is increasing. Online databases help potential grantees identify more and more sources. Many foundations now post their guidelines and annual reports on the World Wide Web. Some progressive foundations have adopted a standard grant application form, allowing grantees to submit exactly the same proposal to many different foundations. The very things that thus make foundations more accessible also make them inundated with requests.

Although many nonprofits, especially new or small organizations, think foundation funding would be the answer to their money problems, in fact foundation funding is designed to be used only for short-term projects. These include the start up of a new organization and its first few years of operation; capital improvements; new programs; one-time projects, such as studies or conferences; capacity building; or for help through a particularly rough period in the life of an organization for which it has a good excuse and a realistic recovery plan. More recently, foundations have been creating "initiatives," where they focus most or all of their grant-making on one area of their choosing, such as preschools, youth organizing, or immigrants rights. These initiatives are often helpful for bringing together a number of organizations working on the same issue, allowing them to share ideas and create joint strategies. Sometimes several foundations join an initiative. However, the foundation funding invariably dries up before the problems identified by the initiatives have been solved, leaving groups that have relied heavily on this funding in a bad way. Many foundations, recognizing the limits of their funding, have provided capacity-building grants, which are largely efforts to help organizations move away from the foundation to a more diverse set of income streams.

If an organization has come to rely on foundation funding, decreasing reliance should be an important part of its financial planning. If an organization has never become reliant on foundation funding, it should plan not to, and it should not make the mistake common to many small organizations of seeking more foundation funding as the years pass rather than less.

CORPORATIONS

Corporations are different from foundations in a key way: unlike foundations, whose job is to give money away, corporations exist to make money. Giving money away is primarily an activity that a corporation hopes will directly or indirectly help it to make more money. Even so, only 11 percent of corporations give away any money at all. Moreover, although they are allowed to give away up to 10 percent of their pretax profits, in fact the average amount these companies give away is a mere 1 percent of pretax profits. Corporations that do give money generally give it to the following types of organizations or activities:

- Organizations that improve the life of the community where their employees live (symphonies, parks, museums, libraries)

- Groups that help their employees be more productive by addressing common employee problems (alcohol and drug rehabilitation, domestic violence)

- Organizations that provide volunteer opportunities for employees, or to which employees make donations

- Research activities that will help the company invent products or market existing products (various departments in universities get much of their funding for such research from corporations)

- Education programs for young people to ensure an adequate future workforce for the company (literacy programs, innovative schools, scholarships)

More frequent and generous is corporate giving to match employee donations. Although many corporations have had matching gift programs for some time, the scale of today's matching programs have come to be called "employee-driven philanthropy." For this reason it is important to know where your donors work and whether their corporation will match their gift.

Aside from money, corporations make other valuable donations, such as contributions of expertise (loaning a worker to help a nonprofit with accounting, marketing, or personnel), space (free use of conference or meeting rooms), printing, discarded furniture and office equipment (computers, fax machines, copy machines), building materials, and so on.

The past couple of decades have seen many corporations joining with charities in what is called "cause-related marketing" efforts, in which a corporation donates a certain percentage of its profits from a particular item or a certain amount of each sale to its partner charity. The nonprofit group and the corporation advertise the arrangement and encourage people who may be choosing among similar products to choose the one that also benefits the charity. Variations on this theme include corporations that offer to give a percentage of profits to a certain kind of organization (environmental, progressive, feminist) or who allow customers to nominate groups that should receive corporate funding. Cause-related marketing has benefited many organizations by allowing shoppers to feel that their spending can also serve a charitable purpose. The drawback is that these donors do not become part of an organization's donor base, about which much more will be said in the course of this book.

Some organizations are not able to get corporate funding because their work is too controversial, others are not located near any corporate headquarters, and others will not seek corporate funding because they wish to avoid appearing to endorse a corporate product or a particular corporation's way of doing business. However, if your group does wish to seek corporate funding, keep in mind that the key element is knowing someone in the corporation. Having "a friend at the bank"—literally and figuratively—is important, and the many ways a corporation can help you should not be overlooked. Just like foundation giving, however, income from corporate giving should not be relied on.

THE POWER OF INDIVIDUAL GIVING

I hope it is clear by now that a broad base of individual donors provides the only reliable source of funding for a nonprofit year in and year out, and the growth of individual donations to an organization is critical to its growth and self-sufficiency. Further, relying on a broad base of individuals for support increases an organization's ability to be self-determining: it does not need to base program priorities on what foundations, corporations, or government agencies will fund.

Recipients of Charitable Giving

To really understand private-sector giving, it is important to look not only at who gives this money, but also at who receives it. Again, with only a few percentage points of variation from year to year, *Giving USA* has reported a consistent pattern of where gifts go. A little more than one-third of all the money given away in America goes to religious organizations, with education a distant second, followed by health, human services, the arts, and four other categories that receive small percentages of giving.

Uses of Contributions, 2005		
Contributions To	**Amount in Billions**	**Percentage of Total**
Religion	$93.18	35.8
Education	$38.56	14.8
Health	$22.54	8.7
Human services	$25.36	9.7
Arts, culture, humanities	$13.51	5.2
Public-Society benefit	$14.03	5.4
Environment and animals	$8.86	3.4
International affairs	$6.39	2.5
Gifts to foundations	$21.70	8.3
Unallocated giving	$16.15	6.2

Source: Giving USA, 2006.

Giving categorized as "public-society benefit" includes gifts to organizations concerned with community organizing, civil rights, and civil liberties, as well as gifts to United Way, Jewish Federation, and combined funds, such as the Combined Federal Campaign.

The category of "gifts to foundations" includes giving to community and private foundations and tends to vary from year to year. Giving to foundations was particularly high in 2005 because of several $1 billion gifts given in the last several years, including $3 billion given by Bill and Melinda Gates to their foundation, and $2.6 billion from the estate of Susan Buffett, both in 2004, and $51 million given for disaster relief.

The category called "unallocated giving" includes deductions carried over, that is, amounts claimed in one year for a gift made up to five years earlier. This situation occurs when charitable contributions exceed 50 percent of a taxpayer's gross adjusted income, when foundations make grants to organizations outside the United States, and most interesting to anyone concerned about privatization, some gifts to government entities. Since they are funded by taxes, government entities that receive private donations, such as public schools, public libraries, public health departments, and the like, are not required to report these gifts.

Giving to Religion

Religion as a category receives one-third of every charitable dollar, yet only a small percentage of giving to religion is from foundations and virtually none of it is from corporations. Until recently, because of the constitutional separation of church and state, religious activity received little government funding either, except for providing a specific social service. Under a controversial program of President George W. Bush's administration, religious organizations have been able to receive more government funding than in the past. Many religious groups opt not to apply for this money, however, because they do not believe religion should do the work of government; groups that have received such government funding often report that the amounts given are not as much as the controversy would have led the public to believe. Even with this money, it remains true that the vast majority of funding that religious organizations receive is from their own members.

We can learn a lot by examining what makes fundraising for religious institutions so successful. At first glance, many people think that religious institutions receive so much money because of their theology: the reward of heaven, the blessing of giving, the threat of eternal damnation for those who do not give. While these enticements may play a role in some people's giving, it is clear that in the wide variety of religious expression, these motives are not enough. Some religious traditions do not believe in any form of eternal life; others don't even believe in God. Even in traditions that encompass some of these beliefs, mature adults can be given more credit than to think that their behavior is based simply on a desire for rewards or a fear of punishment.

So why do religious organizations receive almost one-third of all private-sector dollars? Although religious institutions offer ideas and commitments that are of great value, the reason they get money—and this is key to understanding successful fundraising—is that they ask for it.

Let's take as an example a Protestant or Catholic church. (If you are of a different religious tradition, compare your own tradition to what follows.) Here is how they raise money:

They ask every time worshippers are assembled, which is at least once a week.

They make it easy to give: a basket is passed to each person in the service and all gifts are acceptable, from loose change to large checks. Everyone—whether out-of-town visitor, occasional church goer, or loyal and generous congregant—is given the same opportunity to give. The ushers are not concerned about offending someone by asking. They would never say, "Don't pass the basket to Phyllis Frontpew—she just bought the new carpet," or "Skip over Joe because he just lost his job."

They make it easy to give, even if you are not a regular congregant. Once a year, most houses of worship will have some kind of stewardship drive or all-member canvass; in many churches, someone will come to your house and ask you how much you will be pledging this year. You can pay your pledge by the week, month, or quarter, or give a one-time gift. The option of pledging and paying over time allows people to give a great deal more over the course of a year than most could in a single lump sum.

They provide a variety of programs to which you can give as you desire. If you are particularly interested in the youth program you can give to that, you can buy flowers for the altar, support the music program, or help fund overseas missions. Many churches have scholarships, homeless shelters, food banks, or other social programs. And of course, if you are a "bricks-and-mortar" person, you can contribute to any number of capital improvements—new hymnals, a new window, a better organ, or a whole new sanctuary.

Finally, religious institutions approach fundraising with the attitude that they are doing you as much of a favor to ask as you will be doing them to give. In other words, they recognize that fundraising allows an exchange to happen between a person who wants to see a certain kind of work get done and an institution that can do that work. If one of your values and beliefs is that a house of worship is important, then in order for that institution to exist you will need to help pay for it. Giving money allows you to express your desire and commitment to be part of a faith community and allows your commitment to be realized.

All organizations should institute the diversity of fundraising methods that characterizes most religious institutions. In the chapters that follow, I will show you how.

Principles of Fundraising

Let's start with a question: "What is the purpose of fundraising?" Here is the wrong answer: "To raise money." The only way you can raise money year after year is by developing a broad base of individual donors who feel loyal to your organization. The purpose of fundraising, then, is to build those relationships, or more simply put, the purpose of fundraising is not to raise money, but to raise donors. You don't want gifts, you want givers. You want people to make donations and feel so good about how they were treated and what you did with the money that they want to give again and again. They may even tell their friends about your organization, so you not only get money from them but from new donors as well.

Focusing on building a donor base rather than on simply raising money means that sometimes you will undertake a fundraising strategy that does not raise money in the first year, such as direct mail, or for several years, such as legacy giving. It means that you will relate to your donors as individual human beings rather than as ATMs that you engage when you want money but whom you otherwise ignore. It means you will plan for both the short term and the long term and look at the results of any fundraising strategy not only for the next month but also for the next few years.

DIVERSIFYING SOURCES

Focusing on raising donors means that an organization systematically diversifies its sources of funding, increases the number of people helping raise money, and diversifies the skills of those doing fundraising. The need for diversity is not a new lesson. People with only one skill have a more difficult time finding employment than those with a variety of skills. Investors put their money in a variety of financial instruments rather than in just one kind of stock. Since the 1980s thousands of nonprofits have been forced to curtail their services severely or to close their doors because the government funding they relied on so heavily ceased to be available.

Yet many organizations continue to look for the ideal special event that will fund their entire budget, or they search for one person, foundation, or corporation who will give most of the money they need, or they try to hire the perfect fundraiser who will bring in all their income without anyone's help. These groups reason that if they could use one fundraising strategy that was absolutely certain, tried and true, their money worries would be over. Unfortunately, no fundraising strategy or person fits that description. In fact, only if it maintains a diversity of sources will an organization survive for the long term.

What's the largest percentage of their income that an organization should rely on from one source? Think of it this way: an organization could lose 30 percent of its funding and probably survive, though it would be difficult, but the loss of more than 30 percent of funding would be catastrophic for all but the biggest organizations. That's why organizations should not receive more than 30 percent of their funding from any one source for more than one or two years. This guideline means that although you could have more than 30 percent of income coming from membership (and many groups do), you cannot have one member providing 30 percent of this money. (The IRS recognizes this principle with its "one-third rule," which states that an organization with one-third or more of its total income from one person, foundation, or corporation for more than three years does not meet the test of a public charity; if this condition persists for several years, an organization risks losing its 501(c)(3) status. Public charities are to be supported by a cross section of the public.)

There is no set number of sources that constitutes healthy diversity. Much will depend on the size of your budget, your location, and your work. However, the more people who give you money and the more ways you have of raising money, the better off you are.

WHY PEOPLE GIVE

Approximately seven out of ten adults regularly make donations to nonprofits. Of those, most support between five and eleven organizations, giving away a little more than 2 percent of their personal income. All fundraising efforts should go toward trying to become one of the groups that these givers give to, rather than trying to become the recipient of the first charitable donation of a previous nongiver. People who give money are not denying themselves food or withholding shoes for their children; these people are dedicated givers, and your organization's job is to become one of those they give to. To do that you must carefully examine what makes a person a giver.

Self-Interest

There are many reasons that people give to nonprofit organizations. The most common reasons vary from consumerism to tradition to deeply held belief. Some people give because they like the newsletter an organization provides or because they receive a free tote bag, bumper sticker, or some other tangible item. Some give to a certain group because everyone in their social circle gives to that group or because it is a family tradition. Some give because it is the only way to get something the organization offers (classes, theater seats, access to a swimming pool).

At a more altruistic level, there are more reasons for giving. People give because they care about the issue, they believe in the group, and they think the group's analysis of a problem and vision of a solution are correct. Often people give because they or someone they know were once in the position of the people the group serves (alcoholics, abused women or children, unemployed, homeless) or because they are thankful that neither they nor anyone they know is in that position.

People give because the group expresses their own ideals and enables them to reinforce their image of themselves as a principled person—for example, a feminist, environmentalist, pacifist, equal rights advocate, good parent, concerned citizen, or whatever image is important to them. Through their giving, they can say in truth, "I am a caring person," "I have deep feelings for others," "I am helping others."

Sometimes people give because they feel guilty about how much they have or what they have done in their own life, or they give in order to feel more assured of salvation and eternal life.

Above all, however, people give because they are asked, and being asked reminds them what they care about. When they are asked personally by a friend or someone they admire, in addition to feeling good about giving to the organization, they get to show themselves as a principled and generous person to someone whose opinion they value.

Although these motivations for giving are what impel most people to give, most nonprofit organizations appeal to two other potential motives that are not very persuasive. These are, "We need the money," and "Your gift is tax deductible."

Neither of these reasons distinguishes your organization from all the others. All nonprofit organizations claim to need money, and most of them do. The fact that the gift is tax deductible is a nice touch, but gifts to several hundred thousand other nonprofits are tax deductible too. Further, as I mentioned in Chapter One, the majority of Americans file a short form (that is, they do not itemize deductions to charities on their income tax returns), so they receive no tax benefits for their giving. Neither need nor tax advantage makes your organization special.

Giving as Fee for Service

The 70 percent of Americans who give away money pay nonprofits to do work that can only be accomplished by group effort. There is very little one person can do about racism or pollution or world hunger. Only as part of an organization can an individual make a difference in these or any other pressing social problems. Certainly, one person cannot be a theater or a museum or an alternative school. Donors need the organization as much as the organization needs them, and the money is given in exchange for work performed. In a way, donations are really fees for service.

ANYONE CAN DO FUNDRAISING

Most important for small organizations, it is critical to understand that fundraising is easy to learn. In the past thirty years there has been an increasing emphasis on fundraising as a "discipline." Colleges and universities now offer courses on various aspects of fundraising, sometimes as part of degree programs in nonprofit management, and professional organizations offer certification programs in fundraising. There are more and more people who are professional fundraisers. All of these developments contribute to the health and well-being of the nonprofit sector. But a course, a degree, or certification is not required for a person to be good at fundraising, and they will never take the place of the only three things you really need in order to be a fundraiser: simple common sense, a commitment to a cause, and a basic affection for people.

No one says at the age of twelve, "When I grow up, I want to be in fundraising." Instead, a person is drawn to an idea or cause and to an organization working on that issue. The organization needs money in order to pursue the cause, so the person decides to help with fundraising, even though it is not their first choice of how to be involved and even though they have at first found the idea of raising money slightly distasteful or a little frightening. With time and experience, many people find that fundraising is not as difficult as they had imagined; they may even begin to like it. They realize that people feel good about themselves when they give money to a cause they believe in and that to ask someone for money actually means to give that person an opportunity to express traditions or beliefs that are important to them.

People asked to raise money often confuse the process of giving money and the process of asking for it. In fact, there is a significant difference between the two. People feel good about giving money, but rarely do people feel good when they ask for money until they get used to it. People asking for money for their cause tend to project their own feelings of discomfort in asking onto the potential donor and then describe the donor in words such as these: "I really embarrassed that person when I asked him," or "I could tell she wanted to leave the room when I asked her," or "They were so upset that they just looked at each other and finally said yes but I know they wanted to say no." These descriptions of how the donor supposedly felt (embarrassed, humiliated, upset) are more likely to be descriptions of how the asker was feeling. The potential donor was more than likely flattered, pleased to be included, thinking about what amount he or she could give, or wondering if the asker was feeling all right.

The feelings of discomfort in asking for money are normal, and in Chapter Six I talk about them and how to deal with them. For now, be clear that asking and giving are two very different experiences, even when they happen in the same conversation. When people are recruited to ask for money, they must reflect on what they like about giving, not on what they hate about asking.

When an organization has a diversity of ways to raise money, it can use the talents and abilities of all the people in the group to help with fundraising. As volunteers and board members learn more about fundraising and experience success doing it, they will be willing to learn new strategies and they will begin to like asking for money. Further, an organization that has only one or two people raising its money is not much better off than an organization that has only one or two sources of money. Many small organizations have suffered more from having too few people doing the fundraising than from having too few sources of funds. In the chapters that follow, I discuss how to identify appropriate fundraising strategies and how to build a team of volunteer fundraisers.

Matching Fundraising Strategies with Financial Needs

Organizations have three financial needs: the money they need to operate every year, not surprisingly called *annual* needs; the money they need to improve their building or upgrade their capacity to do their work, called *capital* needs; and a permanent income stream to ensure financial stability and assist long-term planning, the source of which is either an *endowment* or a *reserve fund*.

ANNUAL NEEDS

Most organizations spend most of their time raising money for the program needs of the current year. This kind of fundraising is often referred to as the "annual fund" or the "annual drive," or to cover all tracks, the "annual fund drive." The annual fund uses several strategies, such as Internet, direct mail, special events, phoning, and personal visits. The purpose of the annual fund is to acquire new donors and to get current donors to give again and if possible, to give bigger gifts.

Because the overall purpose of fundraising is to build a base of donors who give you money every year, it is helpful to analyze how a person becomes a donor to an organization and how, ideally, that person increases their loyalty to the group and expresses that increased loyalty with a steady increase in giving.

In moving from having never given to a particular group to giving regularly year after year and sometimes several times a year, a person goes through three phases. The first phase starts when a person is asked to give to an organization she hears or reads about and likes the sound of and decides on the spur of the moment to make a donation. That first gift is called an "impulse" gift. Even if an impulse gift is fairly large, it will rarely reflect what the donor could really afford and it is generally based on little knowledge or commitment to the organization. This is the moment at which the organization seeks to move this donor to the second phase. The donor is thanked as soon as possible, then several times during the course of the year the donor is asked for additional gifts to different aspects of the organization's work. Ideally, the donor is asked in a few different ways, such as by phone, at an event, or with a personal letter.

If the donor continues to give for three or more years, she is called a "habitual" donor. Habitual donors see themselves as part of the organization and identify with the work and the victories of the organization. Some habitual donors have a bigger commitment to the organization than their gift reflects and have the capacity to make a bigger gift. Identifying and asking these people to increase their gift forms the basis of a major donor program.

Once donors are giving larger gifts than they give to most other groups, they have entered the third phase, called "thoughtful" giving. Instead of just giving what they are in the habit of giving, they now think about what they can afford and how making a large gift to one group will affect their other giving.

The process of moving people from nondonor to donor, then to habitual donor and from there to thoughtful donor is the main focus in planning the annual fund. To maintain its annual income, an organization has to recruit a certain number of new donors every year, upgrade a certain number of regular donors into major donors, and give all their donors three or four chances to give extra gifts.

A note on asking several times a year: Some people say they dislike receiving several appeals a year from a group. But because one donor doesn't like to be asked more than once a year, it doesn't mean that most people are like that. Many people don't even notice how often they are asked, particularly if you are using a few different strategies. Some donors give every time they are asked, and many donors find being asked a few times a year a good way to keep up with the work of the organization. However, since fundraising is a process of building relationships, if a donor says to you, "I only give once a year, so please only ask me once a year," then you will go into your database and suppress their name for any extra appeals. If a donor says, "Don't ever call me on the phone," you similarly note in their file not to call that person.

An organization can expect to retain about two-thirds of its individual donors every year, with the greatest proportion of their one-third loss being people who give once and not again. In planning fundraising strategies, then, you need to have a few strategies for the sole purpose of replacing lost donors. Organizations that lose a lot fewer than one-third of their donor base most likely do not have enough donors—almost any group can keep a small group of donors renewing year in and year out. You want to grow big enough that you are bringing in a lot of new donors, knowing that up to one-third of them will not stay. Organizations that lose more than one-third of their donors are not doing enough to keep them, and in the case of most grassroots organizations, this situation usually means they are not asking donors for money often enough. Remember, every organization the donor belongs to is asking several times a year, and the donor is also being solicited by other groups. If you only ask once a year, you become an minuscule percentage of the solicitations the donor receives. In fact, many lapsed donors will report that they never remember receiving any requests from the group and that it was not their intent for their membership to lapse. To retain your donors, you need to have a few strategies designed just for them. Section Two discusses these strategies in more detail.

Finally, you need to have some strategies to get current donors to give more money—these are called upgrading strategies. Sections Two and Three discuss a wide variety of these strategies and their uses.

CAPITAL NEEDS

In addition to the money your organization needs each year and what strategies will be used to raise that money, organizations occasionally need to raise extra money for capital improvements. Capital needs can range from new computers to the cost of buying and refurbishing an entire building. A capital expense is something too large for the annual budget to hold and something that is not an annual need. Most donors who give capital gifts have given thoughtfully to an annual fund. They know your organization, they believe in your cause, and they have the resources to help you with a special gift. These resources could be stocks, bonds, real estate, or any very large source of income. These gifts are given only a few times in a donor's lifetime, and they are almost always requested in person (for more on capital campaigns, see Chapter Twenty-Four, Understanding Capital Campaigns).

ENDOWMENT AND RESERVE FUNDS

An endowment or a reserve fund is a glorified savings account in which an organization invests money. It then uses the interest from that investment to augment its annual budget. The invested amount, or principal, is not spent. Endowment funds are raised in many ways, but the most common source is legacy gifts, such as bequests. A gift from a person's estate is in some ways the most thoughtful gift of all and usually reflects a deep and abiding commitment to an organization. It also reflects the donor's belief that the organization will continue to exist and do important work long after the donor is dead. The idea of making an endowment gift can be introduced to donors in a variety of ways, but usually a person making such a gift has a personal relationship with the organization. An endowment is much more permanent than a reserve fund, and organizations that hope that someday their work will no longer be needed (which is what most social change groups are working toward) will want to think carefully about having an endowment. A reserve fund allows you to put money aside, use the interest, and occasionally use the principal. How to set up an endowment is discussed in Chapter Twenty-Two.

THE STORY OF GINA GENEROUS

To understand how a person might move from not giving at all to becoming a thoughtful donor and then to leaving the organization a bequest, imagine the following scenario

Gina Generous comes home from work tired and frustrated. It's been a long day. She feeds her cats, kicks her shoes off, and sits down to leaf through her mail. Most of it she characterizes as junk and throws away, but one piece of direct mail catches her eye. It's not fancy or even very well designed, but it is from a local shelter for homeless women and their children, and Gina generally supports women's causes. She opens the letter, reads it quickly, and decides to send a small gift. As she waits for her dinner to cook, she writes out a check for $35 and puts it in the return envelope that came with the appeal. She mails it the next day then soon forgets about the group.

This impulse gift does not represent Gina's true giving ability or say very much about her commitment to that particular group. Now the homeless shelter must try to move Gina to the next level, that of a habitual donor, and they do. In a few days Gina again comes home tired and again feeds her cats and reads her mail. In it she has received a short, personal thank you note from the shelter. "Wow. How nice," she thinks. She again feels good about her gift, and the name of the organization is more firmly planted in her mind.

Over the next few months, Gina receives a copy of the shelter's newsletter. One day she happens to be in the neighborhood of the shelter and drives by. About three months later, Gina receives another letter from the shelter. This letter thanks her again for her previous gift and asks if she can make a special, extra gift to help buy some playground equipment for the children at the shelter. Gina is touched by the request and sends $50. Again, she is thanked promptly. Three months later, she is asked again for a special extra gift, this one to help defray the costs of a job training program that will partially be funded by the city. While Gina thinks this is an important program, she has also had to replace two tires on her car, so she does not give in response to this appeal. Three months after this—now nine months since her first gift—Gina is invited to an open house and tour of the shelter. She attends, and after the tour she meets the director and some board members. Everyone who attends the open house is asked to leave a check in a jar by the door if possible. Gina gives another $25. Over the next two years, this pattern is repeated. Gina comes to a few events. One year she packs up all the shampoo, conditioner, and soap she has brought home from hotels over the years and gives it to the shelter's holiday drive. When she is asked to help with the phone-a-thon, she spends an evening making calls to other donors.

By now, Gina has moved from being an impulse donor to being a habitual donor to the shelter. Whenever she receives a request for funds, she gives unless she really can't afford to. She now sees herself as a part of this organization and may even mention it to friends from time to time.

After two years of giving small gifts two or three times a year, either by mail or at a special event, Gina receives a personal letter signed by a board member asking her to consider upgrading her annual gift to $250. The letter thanks her for her past support, reminds her of how important the shelter is, and asks her not to make a decision until the board member calls her. Gina now has to think about the organization: How important is it to her? Can she afford it? Does she care enough to send $250 to this group? What will she want to find out from the board member to help make her decision?

Whatever her decision, Gina has moved to the next level, that of a thoughtful donor. She may decide to give $250, or she may decide to give $100, or she may continue to give small gifts a few times a year, but she has had to think about her giving to the shelter. After talking with the board member, she decides to give $250.

Over the course of about three years, Gina's relationship to the shelter went from impersonal (giving by mail) to a little more personal (attending events and volunteering for short-term projects) to very personal (being solicited by a member of the board).

Over the next few years, Gina is asked to give both time and money. After five years of being a regular donor to the shelter, she is giving $1,000 a year. That year, the shelter decides to buy a new building. The building will cost $1.5 million and enable the shelter to become a model, allowing them to conduct many programs on site. The shelter applies for and receives some state and federal funding to help purchase the building, along with $250,000 from two foundations and $50,000 from some corporate donors. They must raise the remaining $250,000 from individuals. They launch a campaign to ask each of their donors for a gift in addition to their annual gift. Gina is asked to serve on the capital campaign committee because she is both a reliable volunteer and a steady major donor. She now knows several board members and the executive director and development director. Gina not only agrees to serve on the committee, but she also decides to give $10,000 that she inherited unexpectedly from an aunt. She is happy to find a meaningful way to use this money.

After the campaign is completed, Gina is invited onto the organization's board. The next year, when the shelter institutes a legacy giving program, Gina changes her will so that the shelter is the beneficiary of the bulk of her estate.

The progression to this stage of highly committed donor is natural, and Gina feels good about it, but it is the result of careful planning on the part of the shelter and reflects its commitment to develop relationships with donors.

THREE GOALS FOR EVERY DONOR

An organization has three goals for every donor. The first is for that person to get to the point of being a thoughtful donor—to give the biggest gift he or she can afford on a yearly basis. (Such a gift usually comes from the donor's annual income.) The second goal is for as many donors as possible to give gifts to a capital or other special campaign. These do not have to be connected to capital improvements, but they are gifts that are unusual in some way and are only given a few times, or possibly only once, during the donor's lifetime. Capital gifts are usually given from the donors' assets, such as savings, inheritance, or property. A donor cannot afford to give assets every year, so will only give such a gift for a special purpose. The third goal is for every donor to remember the organization in their will or to make some kind of arrangement benefiting the organization from their estate. An estate gift is arranged during the donor's lifetime but wholly received by the organization on the donor's death. Obviously, these gifts are made only once.

Most small organizations will do well if they can plan a broad range of strategies to acquire, maintain, and upgrade annual gifts, but over time organizations need to think about capital and endowment gifts and learn to use fundraising strategies that will encourage such gifts. Grassroots organizations do receive bequests and gifts of property, art, appreciated stock, and the like. Only by asking will you find out what your donors might be willing and able to do for your group.

Matching Organizational Needs to Donor Giving	
Organization Needs	**Donor Helps Using**
Annual	Yearly income
Capital	Assets (savings, property, stocks)
Endowment	Estate

THREE TYPES OF STRATEGIES

Because all strategies are directed toward building relationships with funding sources—whether these sources are individuals, as this book stresses, or foundations, corporations, or government—it is important to understand the types of strategies that create or improve relationships with donors. There are three broad categories of strategies—acquisition, retention, and upgrade—and they directly relate to the cycles that donors follow: giving impulsively, giving habitually, and giving thoughtfully.

Acquisition Strategies.   The main purpose of these strategies is to get people who have not given to your group before to give for the first time. Direct mail appeals, Web site asks, or certain special events are the most common acquisition strategies. Acquisition strategies seek impulse donors, and the income from them is generally used for the organization's annual fund.

Retention Strategies.   These strategies seek to get donors to give a second time, a third time, and so on, until they are donors of habit. The income from retention strategies is also used for annual needs.

Upgrading Strategies.   These strategies aim to get donors to give more than they have given previously—to give a bigger gift regularly and later to give gifts of assets and a gift of their estate. Upgrading is done almost entirely through personal solicitation, although it can be augmented by mail or phone contact or through certain special events. Upgrading strategies seek to move habitual donors to being thoughtful donors. The income from thoughtful donors is used for annual, capital, and endowment needs, depending on the nature of the gift or the campaign for which the gift was sought.

As you create a fundraising plan, note beside each strategy you intend to use whether you are using it for acquiring, retaining, or upgrading donors, and make sure it is the best strategy for that purpose.

HOW ONE ORGANIZATION LEARNED TO USE A STRATEGY CORRECTLY

Eastside Senior Advocacy decides to hold some house parties to raise money. Seven board members will invite friends to their home and ask them for money for the group. The remaining five board members who don't want to have a party at their house will help with invitations, food, clean-up, and so on.

No thought is given to the purpose of these parties beyond the goal of raising money. No one thinks about whether these parties should be used for acquiring, keeping, or upgrading donors. Consequently, each board member has a hodgepodge of people they have invited to the event—some are donors, some never heard of the group but came because a friend asked them, and some came because they are neighbors and it seemed there would be free food. Because there is no attempt to sort lists ahead of time and because many of the board members travel in the same circles, several people are invited to more than one house party.

The parties make a total of about $6,000, so they are not a waste of time or energy, but some donors complain about being invited to so many events, and many people come to the parties but do not make a gift.

The following year, the organization decides to use the same strategy but to be more thoughtful in their fundraising approach. First, they compile a master list of everyone who is going to be invited to ensure that no one is invited to more than one party. Then they designate some parties as being only for people who have not given before, with a sprinkling of current donors to encourage those who aren't donors to give.

They also vary the way they ask for money at the parties. One board member charges people $35 to come to his party so that every person who is there will have made a donation, and he does not do another pitch at the party. Another feels that her friends will give more if she gives a pitch at the party, and she aims for first gifts of $50 to $250 from most of the guests. One board member with a particularly fancy house has an elegant party for current donors; this party is used specifically as an upgrade strategy. The donors who are invited are capable of giving more than they currently do. They are introduced to members of the board and given an opportunity to discuss a political issue related to this group's work and to make recommendations for action. The party is limited to fifteen people; in a follow-up solicitation after the party, each person is asked for $500.

By determining which parties are for which purpose, the organization now increases its earnings from these parties by more than 400 percent, to $25,000, acquires forty new donors, upgrades fifteen donors, and does not receive any complaints. As an unexpected side benefit, three donors offer to give their own house parties.

YOU CAN'T SAVE TIME

For small organizations, the ultimate reason to be thoughtful about fundraising strategies is to work smarter, not harder. The group in the house party example raised 400 percent more money in their second year of house parties by spending a little more time to think about the strategy more thoroughly. Small organizations with tight budgets have little room for errors that result from carelessness and lack of thought.

It is clear to me from years of working with nonprofit organizations that you can never save time. You can put time in on the front end, planning, thinking things through, and doing things right, or you can "save time" on the front end only to have to put it in later clearing up the mess, handling disgruntled donors, and having to do more fundraising because what you have done did not raise the money you need. This book will help you be a front-end time user!

Creating a Case Statement

The previous two chapters discussed the framework for fundraising, the logic of the fundraising process, and the fact that an organization will ultimately be supported not so much by money itself, but by relationships with individuals who give money because of their increasing commitment to the group. This chapter presents the first step in successful fundraising—creating a case statement.

Before you can begin to raise money, your organization must state clearly why it exists and what it does. This statement is presented in a written document that describes in some detail the need the organization was set up to meet, the way the organization will meet that need, and the capacity of the organization to do so. This is an internal document for use by staff, board, and key volunteers. This document is called your "internal case," and although it is not a secret document, it will not be that interesting to anyone at any distance from the organization. Language and ideas in this internal case will be used in documents making your "external case," such as on your Web site, in brochures, proposals, reports, and speeches—any time you are making a case for supporting your organization to an external source. Everyone close to the organization should agree with the information presented in the internal case statement, and nothing produced by the organization for external use should contradict it.

THE CONTENTS OF THE CASE STATEMENT

The easiest way to understand a case statement is to imagine the questions a person truly interested in your organization would ask you. The first question, "Why do you exist?" is answered by the *mission statement*. The second question, "What do you do?" is answered by your *goals*. "How do you accomplish those goals?" is answered by your *objectives*. These are a list of specific, measurable, and time-limited outcomes that tell how the goals will be met.

35

The next two questions get at credibility: How long have you been doing this work? What have you accomplished or what is your track record? The answers to these questions are your *history.* A similar set of questions, "Who is involved in this group? What kind of people do you have in leadership, how are they chosen, and what power do they have?" is answered in a section detailing your *structure.*

The final two questions relate to the organization's finances: How much does it cost for your organization to function, and where do you get your money? In other words, what is your *budget* and your *fundraising plan?*

Your internal case statement will have clear, concise explanations for each of these elements: mission, goals, objectives, history, structure, budget, and funding. Some organizations also like to have a statement of vision, which describes what the world would look like if your organization completely succeeded in its work. Such a vision statement is often the first element of a case statement.

Having this information in one document, with key people in the organization all having copies of it, saves a great deal of time and helps guarantee that information and philosophies that are presented by board members, staff, or volunteers in their personal fundraising letters, in speeches, or in conversations with funders or donors are consistent. Further, it reminds people of why they are raising money—to do the important work of the organization. A good case statement rallies people to the cause and reinvigorates staff and volunteers. Much of the case statement—objectives, history, budget, funding plans—need to be updated every year, and the entire document should be reviewed at least annually to ensure that everyone is still in agreement with its premises and that the words used still accurately describe what the organization is doing. Many organizations open each board meetings with a recitation of the mission statement and goals, a practice that they find helps keep the meeting on track and focused.

The following sections present an explanation of each of the components of the case statement.

The Mission Statement

The statement of mission, sometimes called the statement of purpose, answers the question, "Why does your organization exist?" This statement is your basic premise and should describe the one thing that unites everything you do. People in an organization will often claim, "We know why we exist," and then describe their programs, but it may not be clear to a listener that the programs meet any particular need or that there is a problem to be solved. For example, an organization that buys run-down or abandoned apartment buildings and then fixes up and rents each unit well below market rates to elderly poor people has this mission statement: "We believe decent, affordable housing is a right and not a privilege, yet thousands of seniors have inadequate or substandard housing and an increasing number have no homes at all. Housing for Seniors seeks to rectify this problem." At this time, their goal is to buy buildings and convert them to affordable apartments. However, their mission statement allows them to have a wide variety of goals, such as advocating with the city to provide housing, helping seniors stay in their homes, educating the public about the housing shortage, or providing loans to seniors for housing. They intend to pursue all these goals as they grow, and they will not need to change their mission statement as the reach of their work expands.

An educational organization that primarily teaches economic literacy has this lofty mission: "Authentic human freedom begins with every person living free of economic compulsion. Understanding how economic forces work and how they can be changed is fundamental to this freedom." Their goals include teaching people that practices that are unhealthy for people, such as unsafe workplaces, wage discrimination, toxic dumping, substandard housing, and poverty itself, are not necessary for an economy to be healthy and how society could be restructured to eliminate these injustices.

A mission statement should be only one or two sentences long. Its purpose is to interest a person by giving an easy-to-understand, short yet passionate description of why the organization exists. Keep in mind that when you talk or write to people about your organization, they, like you, have a lot on their mind. Your group and its needs are not foremost, at least at the beginning of a conversation. Further, we live in a world of constant messages—advertising, warnings, directions, prompts, signals. Study after study in publications such as *American Demographics* and *Advertising Age* show that people living in urban areas who drive to work, listen to the radio, and watch TV will be exposed to upwards of two thousand messages in a day. We are constantly screening and filtering, and our conscious mind doesn't even take most of them in. Your mission statement is one of those messages. In order to be noticed, it has to be brief, compelling, and intriguing. It has to make a person with a lot on their mind stop thinking about all their other cares and focus on your group.

In fact, a good mission statement does only two things: it is a summary of the basic belief of the organization and the people in the organization, and it makes the person hearing or reading it want to ask for more information: "Well, that's very nice, but how are you going to accomplish that mission?" This question allows the organization to describe its goals.

A hint about writing a mission statement: missions often start with "Because" or "Whereas" or with a noun, such as "People," "Rights," "The future." Avoid using infinitive verbs such as to do, to provide, to help. Infinitive language is goal language.

Goals

Goal statements tell what your organization is going to do about the problem and indicate the organization's philosophy, which may be expanded in the section on history. The goals are what really distinguish one organization from another, since organizations may have similar missions but very different agendas. For example, two organizations whose missions concern the health of children have opposite goals. Nonetheless, their mission statements are remarkably similar: "We believe that whatever promotes children's health and well being is the best public policy," says one, and "We believe the health of our children should be the highest priority," reads the other.

The first mission statement belongs to a group that documents the large number of children in their county who are not immunized, particularly poor children and children of undocumented workers. Despite the fact that immunization is free in their county, some parents are afraid to take their children for inoculations because one of the clinics has been raided by the INS; other parents do not understand the immunization process. This group believes that immigration status should not be questioned in the context of immunizing children, and it works to have inoculations administered to all children by providing them in schools, houses of worship, and in a mobile van that travels to migrant communities.

The other group believes that some vaccines used to immunize infants are the cause of the rising rate of autism. This group is opposed to all immunization because they believe that the risk of becoming ill from immunization is higher than the risk of contracting diseases such as diphtheria, typhoid, or polio that are now rare in the United States and Canada. Two organizations with the same concern about children's health, with very similar mission statements, governed and staffed by thoughtful people, but with very different goals.

Goal statements almost always start with infinitives: to provide, to ensure, to monitor, to educate. For example, "To ensure that old-growth forests are protected forever," or "To teach conflict resolution skills to all elementary school children," or "To find a cure for breast cancer."

Objectives

Objectives are statements describing how the group intends to accomplish its goals. Good objectives can be easily created and identified by using the acronym SMART: Specific, Measurable, Achievable, Realistic, and Time-limited. Goals last as long as they need to, but objectives are generally written as what an organization wants to accomplish in one year at the most, then they are evaluated and rewritten for the next period of time. For example, here is an objective from the economic literacy group: "We will teach ten weekend courses for teenagers during the months of September and October. Two courses will be in Spanish, one in Cantonese, and seven in English. Each course will have a minimum attendance of fifteen students and maximum of twenty-five. A pretest and posttest will be given to document learning, and the curriculum will be modified as indicated by the evaluations for use in the next round."

History

The history section summarizes when the group was formed and by whom and relates the group's major program accomplishments, including any major program changes. In describing your accomplished objectives, you have the chance to provide further documentation of the need your group was set up to meet. The more specific your objectives are, the more dramatic your history will be.

Here's an example: "Homes for Seniors originally focused on providing living accommodations for homeless seniors until we discovered that hundreds of seniors who have housing live in homes that are substandard, with poor insulation, dangerous wiring, and sometimes without running water. Every year since our founding in 1990, we have refurbished or upgraded between twenty and thirty of these housing units that were already inhabited, and we are continually expanding our programs to upgrade substandard housing." The group can then go on to describe their work in more detail.

There are no set rules for the length of the historical piece, but generally a summary of high points will do, with information on who to ask or where to go to get more details for people who want them.

The Structure

The structure shows that the way a group is organized is consistent with its overall mission. This section discusses staffing and board size, composition, and governance. Here are some examples: "We have four staff who work collectively," or "Our board of eleven members is composed of three current clients, five former clients, and three former staff people, so that all decisions about the organization are made by people most interested and knowledgeable about the effects of our work."

This section should be long enough to explain a complicated or nontraditional structure, but brief if the organizational structure is fairly straightforward. The way an organization is structured is a key to its accountability. For example, an organization that claims it is committed to full participation of all members of a multiracial community but with only white people on the board could be questioned about their understanding of community. An organization that claims to organize in low-income communities but whose board members are all well-paid professionals, none of whom are from the communities the organization serves, raises questions about the organization's philosophy of power.

More and more, donors request information on structural issues to help determine if the group understands the implications of its mission and goals. This section can also include brief biographical sketches of board members, resumes of staff, and statistics on numbers of members, volunteers, and chapters, if applicable.

A Fundraising Plan

The fundraising plan shows whether the organization has a diversity of funding sources and an understanding of the fundraising process. The fundraising plan shows all the organization's prospective sources of income and describes in a narrative fashion how this income will be raised or how these financial goals will be reached. Like the section on structure, the fundraising plan will show whether the organization's practices are consistent with its mission. For example, an environmental organization primarily supported by oil or timber corporations, or an organization working in the poverty pockets of an inner city with only major donor fundraising strategies both raise questions about how their financing can be consistent with their mission.

A Financial Statement and a Budget

A financial statement provides proof that the organization spends money wisely and monitors its spending—both in total amount and by category. The financial statement, consisting of an audited financial report, if available, or a balance sheet, is usually part of an annual report on the work of the organization.

The budget is an estimate of expenses and income for the current fiscal year and should include a description of how finances are monitored, such as "The finance committee of the board reviews financial reports monthly, and the full board reviews such reports quarterly."

DEVELOPING THE CASE STATEMENT

A case statement is usually developed by a small committee, but the board, staff, and key volunteers must all agree on its contents, particularly the statement of mission and the group's future plans. If the people who must carry out the plans don't like them or don't believe they are possible, they will not do good work for the group. Therefore, it is worth spending a good amount of time on developing the case statement. Hurrying a statement of mission or a set of goals through the board approval process in order to save time or get on with the job will come back to haunt you in the form of commitments not kept and half-hearted fundraising efforts.

Elements of the Case Statement

Section on	Establishes
Mission	**Why the organization exists**
Goals	**What it will do about why it exists**
Objectives	**How it will accomplish the goals**
History or track record	**Credibility, showing which objectives have been accomplished already**
Structure	**Who is involved, showing consistency of personnel with the goals**
Fundraising plan	**That the organization has a number of well-managed and appropriate income streams that will enable it to fulfill its mission over the long term**
Budget	**That salaries, benefits, rent, and other costs are consistent with the mission, and that the organization knows how much it will cost to do the job they have set out to do**

The Board of Directors

All over the world, nongovernmental organizations (NGOs) play increasingly critical roles in the development and maintenance of the quality of life of the people who live there. In countries like the United States, NGOs (usually called nonprofits) provide much of the available social services, arts and culture, shelter, research, education, advocacy, religion, pro bono legal services, free health care, and so on. In addition, nonprofits are leading the charge and in many cases are the only organizations working on saving the environment, ending racism, protecting and expanding our understanding of civil rights and civil liberties, creating art, preserving history, and advocating, educating, and organizing on any number of issues. In fact, in the United States almost everything that is creative and humane and that promotes justice is brought to us by a nonprofit organization. In many other countries, the government plays a much more important role in the life of the society and works with or through NGOs in doing so. This chapter focuses particularly on the role of nonprofits in the United States. Organizations from other countries are encouraged to research laws and structures that pertain to them.

The U.S. government recognizes that a nonprofit cannot exist in a for-profit, capitalist economy without a lot of help, and the help the government gives nonprofits is tax relief. Over the past several decades, a body of law has developed creating various forms of tax relief for organizations and tax avoidance for donors that help nonprofits survive financially. This body of law is under the Internal Revenue Service's code 501. The most advantageous status for an organization to have is a 501(c)(3) designation, which is the one that most organizations using this book will either have or aspire to. Organizations with 501(c)(3) status are exempt from many corporate taxes, can offer donors tax deductibility for their gifts, have access to foundation and corporate funding that individuals and small businesses do not, receive lower rates for sending bulk mail with the U.S. Postal Service, and enjoy a host of other exemptions from tax at both the federal and state levels. Because these exemptions from paying taxes and the subsidies such organizations receive are provided by tax revenue that costs all taxpayers money, the government has also created a structure to hold nonprofits accountable for these tax advantages. An organization's board of directors is the group of people that is responsible to the government for the actions of the nonprofit.

The broad purpose of a board of directors is to run the organization effectively. To qualify for tax-exempt status, an organization must file a list of the names of people who have agreed to fulfill the legal requirements of board membership. The board members are bound to ensure that the organization meets the following obligations:

- Earns its money honestly and spends it responsibly
- Adopts programs and procedures most conducive to carrying out its mission

The best summary of a board member's responsibility is contained in the state of New York's Not-for-Profit Corporation Law, the language of which has since been adopted by many other states. According to this law, board members must act "in good faith and with a degree of diligence, care, and skill which ordinarily prudent people would exercise under similar circumstances and in like positions."

Board members, in effect, own the organization. They are chosen because of their commitment to the organization and long-term vision for it. As the Council of Better Business Bureaus points out, "Being part of the official governing body of a nonprofit, soliciting organization is a serious responsibility and should never be undertaken with the thought that this is an easy way to perform a public service."

The responsibilities of board members fall into several broad categories. How any specific organization chooses to have board members carry out these responsibilities will depend on the number of board members, the number of paid staff, the sources of the organization's funding, and the history of the organization. There are few right or wrong ways to manage an organization, but there are ways that work better in some groups than in others.

With that in mind, let's look at board member responsibilities.

RESPONSIBILITIES OF THE BOARD

Board members are responsible for six areas of the organization's functioning.

Ensuring Organizational Continuity.   The board develops leadership within both board and staff to maintain a mix of old and new people in both spheres.

Setting Organizational Policy, Reviewing and Evaluating Organizational Plans.   The board ensures that the organization's programs are always in keeping with its statement of mission and that the statement of mission continues to reflect a true need.

Doing Strategic Planning.   The board forms long-range plans with reference to the case statement, focusing on the following types of questions:

- Where does the organization want to be in six months, two years, five years?
- How big does the organization want to become? If it is a local organization, does it want to become regional or national?
- What are the implications of world events for the organization's work, and what is its response?
- How can the group become more proactive, rather than reactive?

These and other questions are usually answered using a strategic planning process. Some organizations find it helpful to have a board-level strategic planning committee that raises and researches appropriate questions and brings recommendations to a strategic planning retreat for discussion and decisions.

Maintaining Fiscal Accountability.   The board approves and closely monitors the organization's expenses and income. The board makes certain that all the organization's resources (including the time of volunteers and staff) are used wisely and that the organization has enough money to operate.

Personnel.   The board sets and reviews personnel policies, hires, evaluates, and when necessary, fires staff. For staff positions other than the executive director, these tasks are often delegated to the executive director. She or he then takes the place of the board in personnel matters. The board hires the executive director and evaluates her or his performance regularly. The board is also the final arbiter of internal staff disputes and grievances and is ultimately responsible for maintaining good staff-board relationships.

Funding the Organization.   The board is responsible for the continued funding and financial health of the organization. With regard to fundraising, board members have two responsibilities: give money and raise money.

BOARD STRUCTURE AND SIZE

There is no evidence that any particular board structure works better than another. Each structure will have its strengths and weaknesses. The structure your organization chooses will probably stem from past history and the experience and desires of the present board members. Some groups work best with a collective structure, including open meetings, informal discussion, and decision by consensus. Other groups do better with a hierarchical structure, a parliamentarian who will help the group follow *Robert's Rules of Order,* and a formal method of discussion and decision making. The only rule is that everyone has to understand the structure you have. If one person thinks that she should raise her hand and wait to be called on before speaking while another person simply shouts out what he thinks, the board will have communication problems.

The size of the board also depends on the group, but there is evidence that the ideal size is between eleven and twenty-one members. A board of fewer than eleven members will probably have too much work, and one of more than twenty-one members is likely to be unwieldy, with work divided unevenly. If you already have a large board, work can be most effectively accomplished through small committees and few full board meetings. A small board can also be divided into committees, which can be fleshed out with nonboard representatives recruited to participate.

STATEMENT OF AGREEMENT

For a board to operate successfully, each member must understand and respect the organization's structure and decision-making process as well as the mission of the organization and must feel that she or he can participate fully in it. One technique that many groups have found helpful to achieve this understanding is to develop a statement of agreement for board members. This statement serves as a job description and clarifies board responsibilities and authority.

Here is a generic example of such a statement.

Statement of Agreement

As a board member of _____, I believe in the mission of the group, which is_____. I understand that my duties and responsibilities include the following:

1. I am fiscally responsible, with the other board members, for this organization. It is my duty to know what our budget is and to take an active part in planning the budget and the fundraising to meet it.

2. I am legally responsible, along with the other board members, for this organization. I am responsible to know and approve all policies and programs and to oversee their implementation.

3. I am morally responsible for the health and well-being of this organization. As a member of the board, I have pledged myself to carry out the goals of the organization, which are as follows: (summarize goals here). I am fully committed and dedicated to the mission and goals of this group.

4. I will give what is for me a significant financial donation. I may give this as a one-time donation each year or I may pledge to give a certain amount several times during the year.

5. I will actively engage in fundraising for this organization in whatever ways are best suited to me. These may include individual solicitation, undertaking special events, writing mail appeals, and the like. There is no set amount of money that I must raise because I am making a good-faith agreement to do my best to bring in as much money as I can.

6. I will attend _____(#) board meetings every year and be available for committee work, where appropriate, and phone consultation. I understand that commitment to this board will involve a good deal of time and will probably require a minimum of _____ hours per month.

---

7. I understand that no quotas have been set, that no rigid standards of measurement and achievement have been formed. Every board member is making a statement of faith about every other board member. We are trusting each other to carry out the above agreements to the best of our ability, each in our own way, with knowledge, approval, and support of all. I know that if I fail to act in good faith I must resign, or someone from the board may ask me to resign.

In its turn, this organization is responsible to me in a number of ways:

1. The organization will send me, without request, quarterly financial reports that allow me to act in good faith and with a degree of diligence, care, and skill that ordinarily prudent people would exercise under similar circumstances and in like positions.
2. Paid staff will make themselves available to me to discuss programs, policies, goals, and objectives.
3. Board members and staff will respond in a straightforward and thorough fashion to any questions I have that I feel are necessary to carry out my fiscal, legal, and moral responsibilities to this organization.

This kind of agreement defines understandings that may never before have been articulated. In doing so, it helps channel board members' motivation to serve the organization. It also improves relations between board and staff by making clear to staff the limits of board members' responsibilities and letting board members know when they can say, "No, this is not my responsibility."

Once developed, this type of contract can be read at regular intervals to remind people of their commitments. It can also be used for internal evaluation and to recruit new board members.

THE BOARD AND FUNDRAISING

The reluctance of board members to take responsibility for fundraising can usually be traced to two sources: board members don't understand the importance of taking a leadership role in fundraising, and they are afraid of asking for money.

Board members cannot give themselves wholeheartedly to the process of fundraising unless these two problems are resolved.

The reason that board members must take a leadership role in fundraising is simple: they own the organization. They have to show that they think the group is worth supporting by setting an example. They are responsible for the well-being of the organization and for its successes. Furthermore, an organization's supporters and potential supporters see board members as the people most committed and dedicated to the organization. If they, who care the most about the group, will not take a lead role in fundraising, why should anyone else? When the board does take the lead, its members and the staff can go to individuals, corporations, and foundations and say, "We have 100 percent commitment from our board. All board members give money and raise money." This position strengthens their fundraising case a great deal. Both individual donors and foundations often ask organizations about the role of the board in fundraising and look more positively on groups whose board plays an active part.

Board members are often reluctant to participate in fundraising activities because they fear they will be required to ask people for money. It's true that many fundraising strategies require board members to make face-to-face solicitations. This is a skill and thus can be learned, and all board members should have the opportunity to attend a training session on asking for money (see Chapter Six, Getting Comfortable with Asking for Money).

In a diversified fundraising plan, however, some board members can participate in fundraising strategies that do not require asking for money directly. While some can solicit large gifts, others can plan special events, write mail appeals, approach small businesses, send e-newsletters, market products for sale, write thank you notes, stuff envelopes, enter information into a data base, and so on. Everyone's interests and skills can be used. Board members inexperienced in fundraising can start with an easy task ("Sell these twenty raffle tickets") and then move on to more difficult fundraising tasks ("Ask this person for $1,000"). Some fundraising strategies will use all the board members (selling tickets to the dance), whereas others will require the work of only one or two people (speaking to service clubs or writing mail appeals).

People often bring to their board service two mistaken beliefs that hamper their participation in fundraising. First, they feel that since they give time they should not be called on to give money. "Time is money," they will argue. Second, if an organization has paid development staff, board members may feel that it is the staff's job to do the fundraising. Let us quickly dispel both of these myths.

Time and Money

Time is not money. We all have exactly the same amount of time—twenty-four hours every day. But we have vastly unequal amounts of money. Time is a nonrenewable resource—when a day is gone, you cannot get it back. Money is a renewable resource. You earn it, spend it, and earn more. Further, you cannot go to the telephone company and ask to volunteer your time in order to pay your phone bill. You cannot pay your staff or buy your office supplies with your time. Finally, people are rarely anxious about asking someone for their time, but most people are quite reluctant to ask someone for their money, even though for many people time is their most precious resource.

In trainings, I often use this example: "If a board member is assigned to call three people and tell them about a meeting on Wednesday night, he or she will do it. If two people can come to the meeting and one can't, the board member does not take this personally and feel like a failure. However, if this same board member is assigned to ask these same three people for $100, he or she will probably have to go to a training in how to ask for money before being comfortable carrying out that assignment." I have conducted thousands of trainings in how to ask for money but I have never been asked to lead a training in how to ask for time.

Comparing time and money is like comparing apples and asphalt. We waste the time of our creative volunteers when we don't have enough money, and we waste the money of our donors when we don't use volunteers appropriately. Board members must understand that contributions of time and money are very different, although equally important, parts of their role. People who want to give either one or the other are valuable to an organization, but are not suitable to be board members.

The Role of Paid Staff

Paid staff have specific roles in fundraising. These are to help plan fundraising strategies, coordinate fundraising activities, keep records, take care of routine fundraising tasks, such as renewal appeals, and assist board members by writing letters for them, forming fundraising plans with them, accompanying them to solicitation meetings, and so on. Generally, fundraising staff handle most or all of the process of approaching foundations or government entities for funding. Fundraising staff provide all the backup needed for effective fundraising. It is clearly impossible, however, for one person or even several people to do all the work necessary to maintain a diversified fundraising plan. Just as it is foolish for an organization to depend on one or two sources of funding, it is equally unwise for it to depend on one or two people to do fundraising.

Sharing the Work

The final reason for all board members to participate in fundraising is to ensure that the work is evenly shared. Fundraising is rarely anyone's favorite task, so it is important that each board member knows that the other members are doing their share. If some members do all the fundraising while others only make policy, resentments are bound to arise. The same resentments will surface if some board members give money and others don't. Those who give may feel that their donation buys them out of some work or that their money entitles them to more power. Those who do not give money may feel that they do all the work or that those who give money have more power.

When board members know that everyone is giving their best effort to fundraising according to their abilities, including making their own gift, the board will function most smoothly and members will be more willing to take on fundraising tasks.

COMMON BOARD PROBLEMS AND SUGGESTED SOLUTIONS

Although each board of directors will have its own problems and tensions to be resolved, many boards have a number of problems in common. They are discussed here, along with some solutions.

Board Members Are Overworked—Too Much Is Expected of Them. Nonprofit organizations use all of their volunteers to augment paid staff. The smaller the organization, the more responsibility volunteers will have, becoming more and more like paid staff. To a certain point this is fine. But there comes a time when board members are taking on much more work than they had agreed to. When board members find themselves attending three or four meetings each month and spending hours on the telephone, they begin to dread calls and meetings and to count the days until their term is up.

This dynamic can be changed or averted altogether by adhering to the following principles:

Board members should understand that they can say no to tasks that go beyond their original commitment.

Staff and board members should ensure that tasks given to the board have a clear beginning and end. Thus, when additional work is essential, board members should be assured that extra meetings will last no more than a month or two and that once that task is accomplished they will not be asked to do more than the minimum for a few months.

A careful eye should be kept on what the whole board does with its time. Board members (particularly the executive or steering committee) should ask, "Are all these meetings necessary? Can one person do what two have been assigned to do or two people what four have committed to do?" Consider having some meetings by conference call and doing routine business by e-mail.

Boards should not be asked to make decisions for which they are unqualified. Sometimes consultants need to be brought in to make recommendations or the board needs to be trained to handle tasks related to management and fundraising.

Individual Board Members Feel Overworked. This problem can arise either because those board members were given the wrong impression of the amount of work involved beyond attending regular board meetings or because they are already overcommitted in the rest of their lives. In the latter case they cannot completely fulfill the expectations of any part of their lives, so they feel overworked even while not doing very much for the organization.

A clear and precise statement of agreement, as discussed earlier in this chapter, will help with this problem. The statement can be used to screen out people who are overextended and to call current board members into accountability. A tip: Don't try to talk anyone into being on the board. When you ask people to serve on the board, tell them why they would be a good addition to the board and what you would expect from them. If their response is less than enthusiastic, let them go. We would not offer a job to someone who said, "I don't know if I have the time." A board role is a job, and it needs to be approached as such.

The Board Avoids Making Decisions. In this instance board members never seem to have enough information to commit themselves to a course of action and constantly refer items back to committees or to staff for further discussion and research. This problem is generally the result of inadequate board leadership. The board chair or president must set an example of decisiveness. He or she needs to point out that the board can never know all the factors surrounding a decision and yet must act despite factors changing on a daily or weekly basis.

The person facilitating a meeting should always establish time limits for each item on the agenda. This can be done at the beginning of the meeting. Close to the end of the time allotted for an item, the chair should say, "We are almost at the end of time for discussion on this item. What are the suggestions for a decision?" If the chair or facilitator of the meeting does not take this role, individual board members should take it on themselves to call for a time limit on discussion and a deadline for a decision. Very few decisions are irrevocable. Decisions can be modified, expanded, or scrapped altogether once they are made and put into action.

Decisions Are Made, Then Forgotten.   When this shortcoming is at work, the board both fails to implement its decisions and ends up deciding the same issue again in a few months or years. Further, board members feel that they are not taking themselves seriously and that their work is for nothing. Three methods can be used to avoid this problem. One method is to appoint a member to keep track of decisions and remind the board of them. The secretary of the board can serve this function or someone designated as board historian. This person should be familiar with the minutes going back three years and remind people of discussions and decisions already made.

A second, complementary, method is for decisions from board meetings (as distinct from minutes of board meetings) to be kept in a binder, tabbed by category, available at every board meeting. Such categories—not more than a dozen—would probably include fundraising, finance, nominating, policy, evaluation, and so on, with subcategories under some of these. Finance, for example, would include budgets, quarterly reports, and the audit. These decisions should also kept as computer files that can be e-mailed to committees pondering related issues to remind them of what has already been discussed or decided on this issue. The notebook can be indexed so that decisions can be easily found. The chair and executive committee should stay familiar with this book.

Finally, each board member should read and keep a copy of the minutes of every meeting. Then, each member can help remind the whole board of decisions already made. The minutes should be easy to read and available within forty-eight hours of every meeting.

A Few Board Members Do All or Most of the Work.   When this happens, those who do the work resent those who are not carrying their share. Those who don't work resent those who do because they imagine them to have all the power. Inevitably, some people will work harder than others, and some will work better. Nonetheless, the board should plan for work to be evenly shared and for everyone to take an active role, assuming that all members will work equally hard and equally effectively. People rise to the standards set for them. Mediocre work should not be accepted. Above all, board members must value everyone's contribution. The person who stuffs envelopes is as valuable as the person whose friend gives $5,000.

Staff or Board Members Don't Want to Share Power Evenly.   Sometimes people take and keep power because they enjoy having power and building empires. More often, though, they take power because they are afraid to let go—afraid that others will not do as well as they have. This is particularly true when some board members have served for many years or when a person on staff has seen a lot of turnover on the board. Whoever perceives that someone is hoarding power or refusing to delegate tasks (either staff or board) should address their concerns to the appropriate committee or the board chair. That person should use examples so that people can have a clear sense of what they are doing wrong and change their behavior accordingly. Generally, people will share power in an organization as others prove reliable.

MOVING PAST BOARD PROBLEMS

All of the dynamics described above, as well as others such as personality conflicts, deep political disagreements, or staff-board conflicts, can be serious enough to immobilize an organization. The board and staff may not be able to resolve the problem themselves. Sometimes they can't even figure out what the problem is. Board or staff members should not hesitate to seek help in that case. A consultant in organizational development or a mediator can help the group articulate and solve its problems. Although for a board to find itself in such an extreme situation is unfortunate, it is usually no one person's fault. Not to ask for help in getting out of the situation, however, constitutes a failure of board or staff members to be fully responsible.

Some conflict can be creative, and board members and staff should not shun difficult discussions or disagreements. There is built-in tension between program and finance committees, new and old board members, and staff and board personnel. As Karl Mathiasen, a veteran board member and consultant to organizations for social change, states in *Confessions of a Board Member*, "My own feeling is that if you go to a board meeting and never during that meeting have a time during which you are tense and your heart beats faster and you know that something is at stake—if you lack that feeling two or three meetings in a row, there is something wrong with the organization."

RECRUITING AND INVOLVING NEW BOARD MEMBERS

Once an organization has a clear sense of the board's roles and responsibilities, has defined the type of structure it wants (collective, hierarchy, or other), and has developed a statement of understanding or similar agreement, it can begin the formal process of recruiting additional board members. There are two key tenets of board composition: board members need to represent a diversity of opinion and skill while sharing a sense of commitment to the organization's mission and goals, and ideally, the combination of all the people on the board will provide all the skills required to run the organization.

To recruit board members, the current board should appoint two or three people to form a nominating committee. (In some organizations this becomes a standing committee of the board.) This small group will assess the present board's strengths and decide what skills or qualities are needed to overcome the board's weaknesses. The following chart is an example of a way to evaluate the current board and quickly spot the gaps. Each group should fill it in with the board membership criteria it has established. Note that for the first category, demographic, many groups think through how many people representing any particular demographic criteria they want. Of course, it is important to keep in mind that one or two people will not represent a whole constituency.

Current Board Evaluation

| | Name of Board Member | | | |
Board Needs	Montoya	Murphy	Hong	Burger
Demographic:				
Women		X	X	
Men	X			X
GLBT			X	
Latino	X			
African American				X
White		X		
Asian			X	
Other				
Budgeting			X	
Financial management				X
Personnel		X		
Fundraising:				
Personal asking	X	X		
Events				
Planned giving				
Marketing				
Web design				
Evaluation			X	
Public policy				
Organizing				X
Other:				

There is a common belief that a board should have "movers and shakers" on it. Bank presidents, successful business people, politicians, corporate executives, and the like are thought to be people with power and connections to money, making them ideal board members. However, an organization needs to define who the movers and shakers are for its work. Many of the people perceived to be most powerful in a community would be terrible board members, even if they would agree to serve. There are hundreds of successful organizations whose board members are neither rich nor famous and who have no access to the traditional elite but whose connections are exactly what the organization needs. Belief in the mission of the organization and willingness to do the work required are of far greater importance than being successful or wealthy.

First and foremost, board members and new recruits must understand, appreciate, and desire to further the goals and objectives of the organization. Enthusiasm, commitment, and a willingness to work are the primary qualifications. Everything else required of a board member can be learned, and the skills needed can be brought to the board by a wide variety of people and taught to others on the board.

In assessing what skills and qualifications your board lacks, then, don't just go for the obvious recruits. For example, suppose that no one on your board understands budgeting. An obvious solution would be to recruit an accountant or a corporate executive to meet this need. If you know someone in one of these areas who shares the commitments and ideals of your group, then certainly invite her or him to be a board member. But if you don't know anyone whose profession involves budgeting, use your imagination to see what other kind of person might have those skills. In one organization, a self-described housewife does all the budgeting and evaluation of financial reports. Her experience of managing a large family has taught her all the basics of financial management; she is completely self-taught. Anyone who has had to keep within a budget may have excellent budgeting skills: ministers, directors of other nonprofit organizations, people who own small businesses, and seniors living on fixed incomes.

Another example: If the gap on your board is in getting publicity, an obvious choice would be someone who works in the media or has a job in public relations. However, as many groups know, anyone willing to tell the story of his or her personal experience with a group or who is articulate about the issues can get media attention if a staff person lays the groundwork. A staff member can arrange an interview, send a press release, and put together a press packet. A volunteer can then do the follow-up required to get the media coverage.

The Recruitment

Prospective board members are found among friends and acquaintances of current board members, staff members, former board and staff members, and current donors and clients. Ideally, a prospective board member is someone who already gives time and money to the organization.

The chair of the board should send a letter to each prospective board member asking the person if she or he is interested in serving on the board and giving a few details of what that would mean. The letter should state that someone will call in a few days to make an appointment to discuss the invitation in detail. Even if the prospect is a friend of a board or staff member or is themselves a long-time volunteer, a formal invitation will convey that being on this board is an important responsibility and a serious commitment, and that it is a privilege to be invited. Whoever knows the board prospect can follow up on the letter by talking to the person about being on the board. If no one knows the prospect, two people from the board should see the person. If the prospective board member does not have time to meet and discuss the board commitment, this is a clue that he or she will not have time to serve and should be removed from the list of prospects.

Whoever meets with the prospective board member should go over the board's statement of agreement point by point. The current members should share their experiences in fulfilling their commitment and discuss what others have done to fulfill theirs. It is particularly important to discuss the amount of time board participation requires as well as expectations of board members in the area of fundraising. Do not make the board commitment sound easier than it is. It is better for a person to join the board and discover that it is not as much work as they originally thought than to find that it is much more work and resent having had the commitment misrepresented.

The contact person should feel free to ask the prospective board member how he or she feels about the group or what experience he or she has had in working with people of other classes, races, sexual orientations, and so on, depending on the composition of your board. Considering someone to join the board is as serious as selecting a partner in a business, finding a new roommate, or interviewing staff. Pay careful attention to whether it seems this person would take the job seriously and bring needed qualities to it.

Tell the person why you are asking her or him to join the board. Let them know that the nominating committee has given a great deal of thought to this choice. Give the person a few days to think it over, and encourage them to call for more information or with further questions. Let this be an informed and considered choice. It is better for ten people to turn you down than to get ten half-hearted new board members.

The Orientation

After a person has accepted nomination to the board and been elected, a current board member should be assigned to act as the new person's "buddy." The current board member should bring the new board member to the first meeting, meet with him or her (perhaps for lunch or dinner) once a month for the first two or three months, and be available to answer questions or discuss any issues regarding board functioning or responsibilities and the organization's work. New board members have many questions that they are often too embarrassed or shy to raise at a full board meeting. They will be incorporated into the life of the organization much faster if they can easily get the answers they need.

Before their first meeting, new board members should receive a packet of information, including a copy of the statement of understanding, the organization's bylaws, the case statement, and anything else that would be helpful to their understanding of the organization, such as an organizational chart, the current annual budget, brochures and other promotional information, and the names, addresses, phone numbers, and profiles of the other board members and of staff members.

Board members work best when they feel both needed and accountable. They will be more likely to keep their commitments when they know doing so is expected and that others are doing so also. When this tone is established at the beginning, the board will function smoothly.

ADVISORY BOARDS

In addition to a board of directors, small organizations often find it helpful to form advisory boards made up of people who can help with various parts of the organization's program, including fundraising. Although it involves a good deal of work and does not take the place of a board of directors, having an advisory board can be a helpful strategy for getting advice from a particular cross section of people (i.e. doctors, researchers, journalists, clergy) or in expanding your fundraising team (bringing on nonboard members to do a special event or to help solicit major gifts), or to serve as an editorial board for your publications. In some ways an advisory board is an administrative fiction. Unlike a board of directors, an advisory board has no legal requirements, no length of time to exist, and no purposes that must be fulfilled. Such a board can consist of one person or two hundred.

Advisory boards are variously named depending on their functions. An advisory board may be called a community board, auxiliary, task force, committee, or advisory council. Some advisory boards meet frequently; others never. Sometimes advisory board members serve the group by lending their names to the organization's letterhead. In at least one case an organization's advisory board was called together, met for the first time, then disbanded all in the same day, having accomplished what they had been asked to do.

You can form an advisory board for the sole purpose of fundraising. Since this board has no final responsibility for the overall management of the organization, its members do not have to meet the recruitment requirements of the board of directors. Furthermore, the advisory board can be completely homogeneous—something a group tries to avoid in its board of directors.

People like to be on advisory boards. It gives them a role in an organization without taking on the full legal and fiscal responsibilities of a member of the board of directors.

When to Form an Advisory Board

Organizations sometimes see an advisory board as a quick fix to their fundraising problems. They may reason, "Next year our group has to raise three times as much money as it did this year. Our board can't do it alone and we don't want to add new board members. So we'll just ask ten rich people to be on a fundraising advisory board and they'll raise the extra money we need."

There are two main problems here. First, finding "ten rich people" is not that simple. If it were, the group would already have a successful major gifts program. Second, a wealthy person doesn't necessarily have an easier time asking for and getting money than someone who is not wealthy. Nor will he or she necessarily be more willing to give your group money than would a "not rich" person.

There are, however, several conditions under which an advisory board is a solution to a fundraising need:

- Although the board of directors is already doing as much fundraising as it can, it is not enough. An advisory board works best when it is augmenting the work of an active and involved board of directors.

- An organization has a specific and time-limited project that needs its own additional funding. Such a project could be a capital campaign, an endowment project, or a time-limited program requiring extra staff and other expenses. The advisory board commits to raise a certain amount of money overall or a certain amount every year, usually for no more than three years.

- An organization needs help to run a small business or put on a large special event every year. The type of advisory board that runs a small business is usually called an auxiliary, as it does not have a time-limited function.

- An organization wants help in raising money from a particular part of the private sector, such as corporations, businesses, service clubs, or houses of worship. The advisory board, composed of representatives from these particular sectors, plans the campaign and the members solicit their own colleagues.

Forming the Advisory Board

If you decide that an advisory board is a good tool for your group, be sure to write out clearly your expectations of this group. Use the same specificity and thoroughness here as in drawing up a statement of agreement for your board of directors. In terms of fundraising, set an amount that you want the group to raise as a goal, the number of hours you expect them to work (per month, per event), and the number of meetings they will need to attend. Also suggest ways for them to raise money. (If you are forming this board because you don't know how to raise the money needed, let them know this at the outset.)

Be straightforward with prospects for your advisory board. Tell them your goals and choose people who can work to meet those goals. Use the same priorities in choosing members as when forming a board of directors. Of primary importance is the members' commitment to your organization and their willingness to express that commitment by fundraising.

Once you have formed an advisory board, the staff of the organization must provide back-up support as needed and guide the board as much as necessary. The chair of the board of directors or another designated representative should receive reports from the advisory board and frequently call or write the advisory board's chair to express the organization's appreciation for the advisory board's work. Advisory board members should receive minutes of every advisory board meeting, be phoned frequently, and generally treated like major donors to the organization (which they are).

Allow the advisory board to develop a direction. The first few months may be slow, but once an advisory board begins to work well and carry out its commitments, its members can raise a substantial amount of money every year.

USING OTHER VOLUNTEERS FOR FUNDRAISING

In addition to, or instead of, forming an advisory committee, many organizations have gone to a structure with a smaller board (between five and eleven members) and then used volunteers who are not board members to augment committees as needed. In this structure, there are no standing committees; instead, each committee is put together for a specific time and task. For example, two board members take on a major gifts campaign. They recruit five other people to help them for six weeks to meet a goal of raising $50,000 from major gifts. These five people care a lot about the organization but can't or don't want to take on full board responsibility. They are willing to work hard for a short period of time. In these organizations, most or all future board members have all first served on one of these ad hoc committees. Coming on the board becomes a reward for work well done.

 **PART TWO** # Strategies for Acquiring and Keeping Donors

The work of asking people who have not given to an organization to give a first time, and then if they give, asking them to give again and again forms the bulk of what fundraising is about. As I noted in Chapter One, most people who give one gift will not give a second time. About two-thirds of those who give a second time will give a third time. Each year that a person gives increases the chances that he or she will give the next year, so a higher percentage of donors will give for a fifth consecutive year than donors giving for a third consecutive year. Many organizations report donors giving to them for twenty-five or thirty years. Some of those donors become major donors, some provide capital gifts, and some include the organization in their will.

Building a donor base is labor intensive and requires persistence and minute attention to detail along with a healthy sense of risk and willingness to spend money in order to make money. Not all strategies suit all organizations, and every organization will need to figure out which strategies work best for them. At the same time, organizations need to resist the temptation to fly from strategy to strategy looking for the magic one that will solve all their financial problems. Strategies that work well have usually been honed over many years, with lots of evaluation and planning each year.

The strategies I discuss in the next twelve chapters are the most commonly used strategies for acquisition and retention—personal solicitation, direct mail, Internet, special events, phone banking, and a number of variations on those themes.

Although it requires the most nerve, asking someone in person for a donation is the most effective way to raise money, so the section begins with that strategy. The concluding chapter of this section is on writing thank you notes. I devote an entire chapter to it because thank you notes can also be varied and interesting and because thanking people for what they give to your organization is the best way, besides running your organization soundly and honestly, to get them to give again.

Getting Comfortable with Asking for Money

Asking someone you know for money in person is the most effective way to raise funds. If you ask everyone who you know gives away money to give a gift they could afford to a cause they like, half of them will give something. (People who fit this description are called *prospects.* Of course, not everyone you know will meet all three criteria.) Of the 50 percent that say yes to your request, half of those people will give you the amount you asked for; the other half will give you less. This is a much higher response rate than you can get from any other kind of fundraising. (For example, you can expect 1 percent of people to respond to a direct mail solicitation and 5 percent to give when asked by phone.) Moreover, the amounts you can ask for in person are much larger. It is rare, and usually silly, to ask for a $5,000 or $10,000 gift by direct mail or during a phone-a-thon, but it is appropriate to ask for such a sum in person if you know the prospect is someone who gives away money, could make such a gift, and has an interest in your cause. People need more personal attention for large gifts because they have to give them more thought.

In studies in which people are asked why they gave the last donation they made, about 80 percent say, "Because someone asked me." Of course, millions of smaller fundraising requests are done in person—canvassing, Girl Scout cookie sales, raffle ticket sales, Salvation Army buckets, panhandling, and so on all have a strong element of personal asking. These forms of personal solicitation will not have the 50 percent rate of success unless the solicitor is known to each potential donor, but they will have a higher rate of success than methods that don't use a face-to-face approach. Strategies to raise more substantial gifts for nonprofits, including major gifts programs, capital campaigns, and endowment drives, rely for success on personal solicitation.

Despite these facts, personal solicitation is one of the most difficult strategies to implement. It requires that people engage in an activity—asking for money—that most of us have been taught is rude or just not done. However, for organizations that are serious about fundraising, and particularly for organizations that would like to increase the number of people in their donor base who give at least $500 annually, learning how to ask for money in person is imperative.

WHY WE'RE AFRAID TO ASK FOR MONEY

If the idea of asking for money fills you with anxiety, disgust, dread, or some combination of these feelings, you are among the majority of people. If asking for money does not cause you any distress, you have either let go of your fear about it, you grew up in an household of unusually liberated attitudes toward money, or you may have come from a country that does not consider talking about money as taboo.

To identify the sources of our fears, we must look at both the role of money in American society and the attitudes about asking for anything that are the legacy of the strong Puritan ethic that is our American heritage.

Most of us were taught that money, sex, religion, death, and politics are all taboo topics for discussion with anyone other than perhaps one's most intimate friends or family. Mental illness, age, race, and related topics are often added to this list of inappropriate topics. Discomfort in talking about any of them will be stronger in some parts of the country or among some generations.

The taboo on talking about money, however, is far stronger than any of the others. Many of us were taught to believe that inquiring about a person's salary or asking how much he or she paid for a house or a car is rude. Even today it is not unusual for one spouse not to know how much the other spouse earns, for children not to know how much their parents earn, or for close friends not to know each other's income. Further, few people really understand how the economy works. They don't know the meaning of things they hear and read about every day—the stock market, for example, including the difference between a bear and a bull market, or what the rising or falling of the various stock market indices mean. In the past thirty years, more and more social justice groups have recognized that economic literacy is a key component in community organizing, but it will take decades to reverse the general ignorance about how the economy works and more important, how it could work.

Many people, misquoting the Christian New Testament, say, "Money is the root of all evil." In fact, Paul's letter to Timothy says, "For the love of money is the root of all evil. Some people, in their passion for it, have strayed from the faith and have come to grief amid great pain." In truth, money in itself has no good or evil qualities. It is a substance made of paper or metal. It has no constant value, and it has no morality. It can be used well or badly. It can buy guns or flowers. Good people need it just as much as evil ones. It is simply a means of exchange.

People will also say, "Money doesn't buy happiness" as a way of minimizing the power of money; they often go on to describe unhappy rich people they have known or read about, though most people secretly think that they would be happier if they had more money. Our attitudes about money are changing, giving us more mixed messages than ever. For example, in the 1990s many young people in the computer industry felt they were failures if they hadn't made a million dollars by the time they were thirty. (I'm often amazed at the lack of perspective in this aspiration: most people have no idea what percentage of the world's population lives in poverty or how many children starve to death every day.) More recently, a general rule widely publicized is that one must have at least a million dollars saved in order to retire with any degree of comfort, even though reaching that sum is completely unrealistic for most American workers. In another example of financial blindness, large corporations are often considered successful despite operating at a loss and are simply kept afloat by investor optimism. Sadly, our attitudes toward money change but do not get healthier.

Money is shrouded in mystery and tinged with fascination. Most people are curious about the salary levels of their friends, how much money their neighbors have inherited, how the super-rich live. How much money you have and how long you have had it denotes class distinctions and helps each of us place ourselves in relation to others—even while we maintain the myth that our country is a classless meritocracy. Consequently, people speculate a great deal about the place of money in others' lives. Money is like sex and sexuality in this regard: kept in secrecy and therefore alluring. But just as much of what we learned as children and teenagers about sex turned out to be untrue, so it is with money. The comedian Kate Clinton says she was raised to think about sex like this: "Sex is dirty. Save it for someone you love." Most of us can relate to that and can see much of what we learned about money in that same light: "Money is evil. Get a lot of it."

One major effect of money being a taboo topic is that only those willing to learn about it can control it. In the United States, an elite and fairly secret class controls most of the nation's wealth, either by earning it, having inherited it, or both. It serves the interest of this ruling class for the rest of us not to know who controls money and how to gain control of it ourselves. As long as we cannot ask about other people's salaries, we will not be able to find out that someone is being paid more because he is white or less because she is a woman. As long as we do not understand basic economics, we will not be able to advocate for or even know what the most progressive tax structure is, finance our nonprofits adequately, or create a society in which wealth is more fairly and equally distributed, which is, after all, the main underlying goal of social justice movements.

Political activists and participants in social change must learn how to raise money effectively and ethically, how to manage it carefully, and how to spend it wisely. In fact, activists who refuse to learn about money, including how to ask for it, wind up collaborating with the very system that the rest of their work is designed to change.

The idea of asking for money raises another set of hindering attitudes, which are largely the inheritance of a predominately Protestant culture infused with a Puritan ethic that affects most Americans, including those who are not Protestants. This set of values conveys a number of messages that influence our feelings and actions. For example, a Puritan ethic implies that if you are a good person and you work hard you will get what you deserve. It further implies that if you have to ask for something you are a weak person, because strong people are self-sufficient. Further, the mythology continues, if you have to ask for help, most likely you have not worked hard enough and you probably don't deserve it. Rounding out this series of beliefs is our deep distrust in the ability of government to solve social problems and a general conviction that the government wastes our money.

All of these beliefs can be found among people on both the left and the right sides of the political spectrum as well as across age and race lines and all religious orientations. Where these beliefs will not be found is in two places:

Other countries. Although many countries have various taboos related to money, none have as many self-canceling and contradictory ones as the United States. Our taboos about money are not universal.

Children. Children have no trouble asking for money. They do not subscribe to the idea that self-sufficiency means not asking or that polite people don't ask. They ask, and they ask again and again. Our taboos about money are not natural—we are not born with them.

Our beliefs about money are learned, and therefore they can be unlearned. The wonderful writer Ursula LeGuin once said in a lecture, "I never learned much from my teachers, but I learned a great deal from my un-teachers: the people who said to me, 'You shouldn't have learned that and you don't need to think it anymore.'"

Fundraising for social change is in part about raising the money we need, but over a longer period of time it is also about creating healthy attitudes toward money, and many people find that aspect of fundraising to be most fascinating.

To get over your own anxieties about money, it is helpful to reflect on how you were raised to think about money and about how you want to relate to money now that you are an adult. It takes time and work, but you can adopt new and healthier attitudes toward money.

SPECIFIC FEARS

With these very strong taboos operating against asking for money, it is a wonder that anyone ever does it! Understanding the source of our discomfort is the first step toward overcoming it. The next step is to examine our fears of what will happen to us when we do ask for money. When people look at their fears rationally they often find that most of them disappear or at least become manageable.

Fears about asking for money fall into three categories:

- Those that will almost never happen ("The person will hit me." "I'll die of a heart attack during the solicitation.")

- Those that could be avoided with training and preparation ("I won't know what to say." "I won't know my facts, the person will think I am an idiot.")

- Those that definitely will happen sometimes, maybe as much as half the time ("The person will say no.")

In the last category—things that will happen—most people not only fear the possible outcome that the person will say no; many also fear that asking will have a negative effect on a friendship and that a gift from a friend will obligate them to give to the friend's cause in turn. Let's look at each of these more closely.

"The Person Will Say No."   Rejection is the number-one fear. Unfortunately, being told no will happen at least as often as being told yes. Therefore, it is important to get to the point where you don't feel upset when someone says no. You do this by realizing that when you ask someone for a gift, you are seeing them at a single moment in their lives. A thousand things have happened to the person prior to your request, none of which has anything to do with you but many of which will affect the person's receptiveness to your request. For example, the person may have recently found out that one of their children needs braces, that their car needs new tires, or that a client is not able to pay a bill on time. This news may affect the prospect's perception of what size donation he or she can make. The person may wish your organization success but may have already given away all the money they can at this time or may have determined other priorities for their giving this year. Events unrelated to money can also cause the prospect to say no: a divorce proceeding, a death in the family, a headache. As the solicitor, none of these things is your fault. Many of them you could not have known ahead of time and you may never learn them because the prospect keeps them private. By feeling personally rejected you misinterpret the prospect's response and flatter yourself that you had something to do with it.

As the asker, you have to remember that, above all, the person being asked has the right to say no to a request without offering a reason. Most of the time you will not know exactly why your request was turned down. Your job is not to worry about why this prospect said no but to go on, undaunted, to the next prospect.

"Asking a Friend for Money Will Have a Negative Effect on Our Friendship."   Many people feel that friendship is outside the realm of money. They feel that to bring money into a friendship is to complicate it and perhaps to ruin it. Friends are usually the best prospects, however, because they share our commitments and values. They are interested in our lives and wish us success and happiness. To many people's surprise, friends are more likely to be offended or hurt when they are not asked. They can't understand why you don't want to include them in your work.

Further, if it is truly acceptable to you for a person to say no to your request, your friend will never feel put on the spot. Your friend will not feel pressured by your request, as if your whole friendship hung on the answer. When asking friends, make clear that yes is the answer you are hoping for, but no is also acceptable. Say something like, "I don't know what your other commitments are, but I wanted to invite you to be part of this if you can."

"If the Person Says Yes to My Request I Will Be Obligated to Give to Their Cause Whether I Want to or Not." This quid pro quo situation ("this for that") does happen from time to time, and it happens frequently with some people. Giving money to a cause at the request of a friend so that you can ask them later for your own cause, or feeling you must give because your friend gave to your cause is not fundraising. It is simply trading money; it would be cheaper and easier to just give to your cause and let your friend give to theirs. Also, a person who gives out of obligation to a friend will not become a habitual donor. They will cease to give as soon as their friend is no longer involved.

If someone you ask for money gives to your organization, you are not obligated to that person except to make sure that the organization uses the money wisely and for the purpose you solicited. The obligation is fulfilled if the organization is honest and does its work. The solicitor does not materially benefit from a solicitation. They present the cause and if the prospect is sympathetic, he or she agrees to help support it. The cause was furthered. Beyond a thank you note and a gracious attitude, the solicitor owes the donor nothing. If the donor then asks you to support his or her cause, you consider the request without reference to your previous request or its result. You may wish to support the person or the cause, but you are not obligated to do so. If you think that someone is going to attach strings to a gift, don't ask that prospect. There are hundreds of prospects who will give freely.

Far from being a horrible thing to do, asking someone for money actually does them a favor. People who agree with your goals and respect the work of your group will want to be a part of it. Giving money is a simple and effective way to be involved, to be part of a cause larger than oneself.

Many volunteers find that it takes practice to overcome their fears about asking for money. To begin soliciting donations does not require being free of fear; it only requires having your fear under control. Ask yourself if what you believe in is bigger than what you are afraid of. An old fundraising saying is that if you are afraid to ask someone for a gift, "Kick yourself out of the way and let your cause do the talking." The point is this: if you are committed to an organization, you will do what is required to keep that organization going, which includes asking for money.

The Logistics of Personal Solicitation

I t takes time to work through all your anxieties about asking, and some people never do feel completely comfortable with the process. That's OK—you can ask even if you feel nervous about it. In this chapter, we look at the process you use to identify whom to ask and how you go about asking.

ASK A PROSPECT

Because personal solicitation is, by definition, done on a person-by-person basis, it takes more time than most strategies. For example, a direct mail appeal can reach hundreds or thousands of people with one letter, duplicated and stuffed into envelopes. A Web site can be reached by millions of people without wearing it out. Volume is the key to those strategies. The opposite is true in personal solicitation. It is done strictly person by person. Therefore, we are looking for people who are worth that much time.

In traditional fundraising, personal solicitation is generally used to ask for gifts of $1,000 or more. For smaller organizations, however, donors who could give a gift of $250 or more are worth the time a personal solicitation takes, and defining a major gift as $250 or more opens the possibility of becoming a major donor to more people. The question that determines whether a person is a prospect could be phrased this way: "What evidence do I have that if I asked this person for thirty to sixty minutes of their time to meet with me, thus also investing thirty to sixty minutes of my time (plus preparation), this person would be likely to make a gift that is significantly bigger than one they might have made if approached through a less time-consuming strategy?"

Three broad qualifications determine if someone is a prospect and therefore worth your time:

- **A**bility to make a gift of the size you are looking for
- **B**elief in the cause or something similar
- **C**ontact with someone in the group who is either willing to ask this person or willing to allow their name to be used in the asking

When you have positive, verifiable evidence of A, B, and C, you have a prospect. If one or two of the criteria is missing you have a potential prospect, usually called a *suspect*. Let's look at each of these criteria in depth, beginning with the most important.

Contact

Contact is the most important of the three criteria and also the most overlooked. Do you know the prospect? Does anyone you know know the prospect? Without contact, you cannot proceed with a personal solicitation because there is no link between your organization and this person.

There are three ways for a person to have contact with your organization:

- A board member, staff person, or volunteer knows the person.
- A board member, staff person, or volunteer knows someone who knows this person. The person with contact is either willing to let you use their name in the approach ("Mary Jones suggested I call") or better yet, is willing to call on your behalf ("Joe, this is Mary. I'm giving money to a really amazing group and was hoping you would be willing to see a couple of their representatives, let them tell you about the group and ask you to join.").
- The person is currently a donor to your group, but no one close the group knows the person. In that case, when you call you will say, "We don't know each other, but we share a commitment to_____, and I want to talk with you about an exciting project we are about to undertake."

Belief

In thinking through why someone who is not already a donor might believe in your organization, return to your case statement (discussed in Chapter Four). What values does your group espouse? What organizations have similar values, even if their goals are different? Be broad minded and creative in assessing potential linkage. For example, people who give to children's organizations are often interested in environmental issues because they are concerned about the kind of world the children are growing up in and will inherit as adults. People giving to environmental groups are likely to be interested in health issues. People who give to libraries will often support literacy programs or creative educational projects that help people appreciate the value of reading. In addition to reviewing the case statement, ask staff, volunteers, and board members to write down all the values they hold dear and what beliefs of theirs tie in with your group. This should provide a broad list that you can use to help screen potential prospects.

In addition to looking for similar values, look for other things that might link a person to your group. Do you serve a neighborhood that the person's family comes from? If you have clients, do your clients patronize the prospect's business?

Try not to draw conclusions from facts about people that could lead you to assume they won't be sympathetic to your group. For example, many Jews are critical of Israel. Many Catholics are prochoice. Many donors to the arts are concerned about censorship, so they are also likely to give to organizations working to protect civil liberties. People live in a context; knowing one fact about them can lead you to wrong conclusions if you are not careful.

Ability

Although first in the A-B-C order, ability is actually the least important factor in identifying prospects. We can safely assume that if a volunteer or staff person in an organization has friends or colleagues who give away money and believe in the cause, those same people have the ability to make some kind of gift even if it is very small. The question is, how much should they be asked for?

One of the biggest mistakes fundraisers make is assuming that how much a person can give will be related to how much money they have. Obviously, how much money a person has influences how much they can give at one time, but sometimes people will give more than they could have given in one gift by giving over time through pledges or credit cards. Many wealthy people could afford to give much more than they do, while many poor people give a high proportion of what little they have. Stockbrokers, bankers, and financial planners are interested in how much people have because they are selling the idea that they can help them have more. Fundraisers are interested in how much people give, so giving is the behavior to focus on, not having.

In terms of identifying how much a person can give, first you need to figure out if that person gives away money. To do so, ask the contact what other groups the prospect supports and look at lists of donors printed in other organizations' newsletters, annual reports, and programs. Listen closely to what people say. Do they complain about getting a lot of direct mail? ("I seem to be on everyone's list.") This is probably a person who gives by mail. Do they complain about how many phone calls they receive? ("Just when we're sitting down to dinner, the phone rings, and it's the disabled, or the whales, or the rainforest.") These calls are rarely random—they are made to people who give by phone. Is the person very busy? With what? Board meetings at the legal aid society? Organizing a special event for International Women's Day? Volunteering with the PTA? Being a docent at the art museum? Working for a political candidate? These involvements all signal someone who participates actively in nonprofit causes.

Next, to determine the size of a possible gift, the following guidelines are useful. All of them assume some evidence that the person is interested in your cause.

To determine whether someone could give $100 to $499, you need to know little more about them than that they are employed in a job that pays a living wage, that they are not supporting very many other people (children, partner, elderly relative), and that they have given in that range to some other group.

To determine if someone could give in the $500 to $1,000 range will require knowing that the person has a well-paying job or some inheritance or a healthy retirement income, or that the person is married to or living with someone who has any of these advantages. People who give in this range usually are not the sole support of their household or the household is not very large.

To determine if someone could give more than $1,000 will require a little more knowledge, particularly that the person has given in this range to other groups, but most important as you get to these larger gifts, the person is usually a donor of some size to your organization. No matter how wealthy and generous someone is, that person will rarely start giving to a small organization with such a large gift unless there is an immediate and compelling reason to make a big gift as the first gift. (I discuss these larger gifts in Part Three, Strategies for Upgrading Donors.)

Ultimately, you will not know with any certainty how much any person can give because you can't know all their circumstances and because their perception of what they can afford can change from day to day. You make your best guess and you ask. People are rarely insulted to be asked for more money than they can afford; it's flattering to have people think you are that successful financially.

STEPS IN CREATING A PROSPECT LIST

Now that you know how to define a prospect, your group can begin to create a list of people who qualify as prospects you will ask for gifts. The first step is for the people who are going to be involved in the personal solicitation strategy meet and create a master prospect list. Having all the names in one place ensures that no one gets asked by more than one person and that the right person does the asking in each case. Also, in a group setting people get more excited about the process and come up with more names and more enthusiasm for asking than they would on their own. Moreover, when more than one person knows a prospect, more information can be collected and verified.

The easiest way to create a master prospect list was developed by fundraising consultant Stephanie Roth and works as follows. Each person at the meeting first creates her or his own personal list, set up as in the illustration below, of all the people they know or who would recognize them if they were to call. No one should censor themselves by saying, "He hates me," or "She's a tightwad," or "I can't ask them!" Each person just makes the list of their contacts, remembering that being the contact is not necessarily the same as being the solicitor. Who will solicit the gift will be decided once the prospects are identified.

Prospect Identification List

Contact Name:_____

Person I Know	Believes in Cause	Gives Away Money	Amount to Ask For
			$
			$
			$
			$
			$
			$
			$
			$
			$

Beside each name the contact notes whether or not the potential prospect believes in the cause. If they don't know what the person believes in, they put a question mark. Next, they cross off all the people whom they know don't believe in the cause. Next to the names of the people who believe in the cause they make a note of whether they know for a fact that this person gives away money. If they don't know, they put a question mark. They cross off anyone they know for a fact does not give away money. Next to all the people who remain—that is, people they know, who they know believe in the cause, and who they know give away money—they note the amount they think the prospect could give. This can be any amount, but this exercise is generally used to find people who can give between $250 and $2,500. If they don't have any idea how much the prospect could give, they put a question mark. Now, everyone reads his or her list of firm prospects—that is, those people about whom they were able to answer affirmatively in all categories—to the group. One person compiles the master list, either by writing these names on a piece of easel paper or entering them into a handwritten or computer-based spreadsheet. If anyone else knows the prospects, they can confirm the information or add other information. The master prospect list will look like the example below.

Master Prospect List

Name of Prospect	Contact	Solicitor	Amount to Be Solicited	Other Info

Next, each person reads the names of people on their list that have question marks concerning belief or whether they give money to see if anyone else can fill in this information. If no one else knows the person, he or she is not a prospect. If someone does know them, they are either moved to the master prospect list or crossed off based on the additional information.

The final master list, then, contains the names of people whom someone knows, who believe in the cause, and who could make this size of gift. The final step is to decide who is going to ask each person. The decision about who asks is based on who has the best relationship with the prospect, who is willing to ask, and who the prospect would feel most comfortable being solicited by. For example, let's say the choice of solicitor is between a close friend of the prospect and a business colleague that the prospect likes and admires. On first thought, you would say the friend should ask, but you may do better to go with the business colleague who can present this in a businesslike way. Another option is for them to go together. Ultimately, the person most likely to do a good job is the best solicitor.

From the master prospect list, a prospect record will be developed for each prospect containing more detailed information about that person. This is the job of development staff. If your organization does not have staff, one or two people from the board should take on this task. Keep in mind that you need to know less about someone you are asking for $500 than about someone you will approach for $2,500. This information is kept in a database and added to or corrected as you learn more. Eventually, as at least half of the prospects become donors, it will be helpful to have information recorded about them already. The following types of information should be discovered and recorded for each prospect.

It is imperative for one or two people to take on the task of collecting this information and recording it systematically. The information must be accurate and confidential. Nothing should appear that is only known from gossip or that is not helpful in seeking a gift ("Had an affair with the Methodist minister" may be interesting, but is not prospect information). Some kinds of information will be more useful to some groups than to others. A group working with prisoners may wish to know if the prospect or anyone in the prospect's family has spent time in prison. Otherwise, that would probably not be appropriate information. People working in historic preservation may want to know how long someone has lived in a community, whereas people working on animal welfare issues will be more interested in knowing whether the person has pets or livestock or likes animals.

```
┌─────────────────────────────────────────────────────────────┐
│                      Prospect Record                           │
│                                                                 │
│  Date: _____         │
│  Name: _____         │
│  Address: (work)_____         │
│  Address: (home) _____         │
│  Phone: (work) _____ (home) _____ (cell)_____     │
│  Fax: (work) _____ (home) _____                │
│  E-mail: _____         │
│  Contact(s): _____         │
│  Interest or involvement in nonprofits (be specific): _____   │
│  Donations to nonprofits: _____         │
│  Evidence of belief in our group: _____         │
│  Occupation: _____         │
│  Employer: _____ Matching gift possible? _____   │
│  Household composition: _____         │
│  Other interests/hobbies: _____         │
│  Suggested gift range: _____         │
│  Anything else we should know (such as, hates to be called at home, more  │
│  likely to respond to e-mail than regular mail, makes all decisions with  │
│  partner): _____         │
│  Suggested solicitor: _____         │
│  Relationship to solicitor: _____         │
│  Result: _____         │
│                                                                 │
└─────────────────────────────────────────────────────────────┘
```

The most helpful tip for putting together lists of prospects is to put yourself at the top of the list. In fundraising we say that the first time you ask someone for money in person, you should always get a yes, because the first person you ask should be yourself. Once you test the proposition that the group is worth supporting against your own bank account, you will have a much clearer sense of who else you know who might give and what amount they might consider.

After all the solicitors have made their own donations and appropriate and adequate information has been gathered about the prospects, the solicitors should each have a list of people they are going to approach. They should plan to approach the people most likely to say yes first. These do not have to be your potentially biggest donors—what is important is to have two or three good experiences before you encounter anyone saying no. In our "Brussels sprouts before dessert" culture, solicitors sometimes start with the hardest people "to get them over with." Don't do that. You need the experience of hearing someone respond positively early on to carry you through some of the harder requests.

HOW TO APPROACH THE PROSPECT

The solicitors are now ready to approach their prospects. The most formal approach involves three steps:

1. A letter describing the organization or the specific need, including a sentence or two indicating that you wish to ask the prospect for a gift and requesting a meeting to discuss it further, followed by
2. A phone call to set up a meeting, and then
3. The meeting itself, in which the gift is actually solicited

Obviously, if you are approaching your spouse or your best friend, you can skip the letter and perhaps even the phone call. In other cases, particularly for smaller gifts the letter may be enough, and there will be no need for a phone call. In others, the letter and a phone call will be enough, and there will be no need for a meeting. Deciding whether a meeting or follow-up phone call is necessary will depend on your knowledge of the prospect and how much money you are requesting. Some people are very comfortable giving $250, $500, or even $1,000 in response to a phone call from someone they know. If the prospect lives far away from the organization or the solicitor, they may be more willing to have a long phone call than to expect the solicitor to visit them.

Regardless of how generous, easygoing, or committed your prospects are, they will be more likely to give if you follow up your letter with a phone call, and they will almost always give more in a meeting than when asked over the phone. Remember, you are requesting a thoughtful gift—a gift that is big enough that a person needs to think about whether they can afford it and whether they wish to give your organization a gift that big. You want sufficient time with prospects to answer all their questions and concerns. It takes about thirty minutes to have the conversation you need to have, and a thirty-minute meeting seems a lot shorter than a thirty-minute phone call.

The Letter

The letter should raise the prospect's interest, giving some information but not enough for a truly informed decision. The letter should be brief, not more than one page. Its purpose is to get the prospect to be open to the phone call in which the solicitor requests a meeting. In other words, the letter introduces the facts that you will be asking for a large gift for your organization and that you want the prospect to be willing to give a short amount of time to hear why you want this gift and why you think this prospect will be interested. No commitment to give or to be involved in any way is asked for in the letter—only a request for the prospect to discuss the proposition of a gift with the solicitor. Here is a sample letter.

Ms. Concerned Activist with Good-Paying Job
Professional Office Building
City, State, ZIP

Dear Connie,

For several years you have heard me talk about Downtown Free Clinic. As you know, I have recently been elected to serve on the board, which I am really excited about! At a recent meeting, we made a decision to launch a major gifts campaign, the main purpose of which is to help the clinic become financially self-sufficient. In the future, we want to depend on a broad base of donors rather than on foundations and government grants, which have proven most unreliable.

The goal of the campaign is $50,000 the first year. All of us on the board have made our own commitments, which total $15,000. We are now turning to people like yourself to raise the rest. We need some lead gifts in the range of $1,000 to $2,000 from people of standing in the community whose word and example carry weight. I am hoping you will consider being one of the leaders in the campaign because of your long-time activism in community health care.

(Include one more brief paragraph on the current programs of the organization.)

I know this is a big request, and I don't expect you to decide based on my letter alone, so I am hoping we can meet and talk. I am very excited about the direction Downtown Free Clinic is taking and I can't really do it justice in this letter.

I'll call you next week to set up a time. Hope you are well. Enjoyed seeing you and your family at the baseball game last week.

Best always,
Annie
Another Concerned
Activist

The letter is straightforward. Connie knows what the request will be, including the amount. She knows what the money is for. If giving to this organization at all is out of the question, she can decide that now. If giving a lead gift is out of the question, it is implicit from the letter that a smaller gift is an option. Her importance to the campaign has been stated, which is flattering, yet there is nothing she needs to do at this point except wait for the phone call. No action has been requested—in fact, she has specifically only been asked not to decide.

The Phone Call

If you are the solicitor and you say you are going to call, you must call. Rehearse the phone call beforehand to anticipate questions or objections the prospect may have. Be sure you know exactly what you are going to say from the very first hello. Many people find it useful to write down what they will say, in the same way that one writes a script for a phone-a-thon (see Chapter Twelve, Fundraising by Telephone).

The phone call is the most difficult part of the solicitation. It is essential to arranging a meeting, and if you are not going to ask for a meeting, it will make a difference as to whether the person gives at all. There is a lot of pressure on this call. Also, you have no body language to help you infer what the prospect is thinking and feeling. You can't tell if he or she is frowning, smiling, in a hurry, or busy. You can't rely on how people sound on the phone. People who are easygoing may sound brusque or harried on the phone. If you reach someone on a cell phone, they may be hard to hear and your conversation may break up before you are finished. Some people simply do not like to talk on the phone, and their dislike of being on the phone may come across to you as a dislike of talking to you or a reluctance to discuss a gift. Finally, a phone call is always an interruption, even if the prospect really likes you.

All of these things can make a solicitor anxious; anxiety, unfortunately, makes for poor phone calls. Anxious people have a hard time listening to others because they are too absorbed in thinking about what they are going to say next. Practicing the phone call a few times with other people in your organization will help you be less anxious.

There are two things that can happen when you make this phone call: either you won't reach the prospect, or you will.

You Don't Reach the Prospect.   In fact, 90 percent of the time you phone someone you will get some kind of gatekeeper—an answering machine, voice mail, a secretary, someone else in the household. When this happens, leave a brief message that includes a good time to call you back and say that you will try again. Leave at least three such messages before you give up on this prospect. Messages are not reliable. Voice mail gets erased accidentally, messages written on pieces of paper get lost, numbers get transposed, names are spelled so wrong that the prospect cannot recognize who called, prospects try to call you back and get a busy signal or carry your message around with them meaning to call but never finding the time, and so on. Many people are finding that leaving their e-mail address in addition to their phone number will at least result in some response from the person, as people use e-mail at all hours of the day and night. Again, don't assume that because you can't reach the prospect the answer is no. However, your time is valuable also, and leaving more than three messages for one person is not as useful as moving on to the next prospect.

If you have made a serious effort to reach a prospect and have not succeeded, you may want to ask the contact for more information about the prospect. You may find out that the prospect is out of the country, or is tending to a sick relative, or that you can make an appointment with the prospect through her secretary, or even that the secretary is authorized to handle these kinds of requests.

You Do Reach the Prospect.   To ensure that you have not caught the prospect at a bad time, first ask if this is a good time to talk. Once that is established, get right to the purpose of the call. If you have sent the prospect a letter, inquire about whether the prospect received it and had a chance to review it. Be clear about the purpose of the phone call, which is to ask for some time to discuss the possibility of the prospect making a gift—not to ask for the gift. The prospect does not need to decide about his or her gift until the meeting.

Be sure not to read meaning into statements the prospect may make at this point that can be taken at face value. For example, do not hear, "I don't want to give" in a statement such as "I'm very busy this month," or "I have to talk to my spouse before making any decision." Instead, in the first instance say, "I can understand that. How about if I call you next month, when things might have slowed down for you?" In the second instance say, "Would it be possible for me to see you both in that case?" Hear everything the prospect says as being literally true. If she says, "I've already given away all the money I am going to give this year," then ask if you can meet so that your group can be considered next year. If she says, "I need more information before I can meet," ask what information would be most helpful, tell her you will send it today, and then suggest pencilling in a meeting for a later time after the prospect has had time to review the information.

If the prospect tries to put you off, do not assume that he or she is saying no. In fact, people who make a lot of big gifts will often use put-offs to determine whether you are serious about the organization and whether the organization can really do its work. This is particularly true for community organizing projects. It is hard to believe that a group will really face down corporate intimidation or stand up to political power if its members fold at the first sign of resistance from some-one they have identified as a person who believes in their cause!

There's one more logistical item to consider before you pick up the phone: where to try to reach the prospect. In the older and simpler days, fundraisers chose between calling the person at home or at work. This was sometimes a hard deci-sion, and none of us imagined it would get more complicated with cell phones. Now the person could be anywhere. A general rule is to call people where you know them. Where would you call them if the topic weren't money? You will probably call your neighbors at home. Friends you can often call anywhere, including on their cell phone. Colleagues are generally approached through work. Increasingly though, people don't have land lines at home and calling a number other than their work number means getting a cell phone. Thus, the first question you will always ask in any call becomes even more critical now: "Is this a good time to talk ?" Or "Do you have a couple of minutes right now?"

The Meeting

Once you have set up an appointment, you are ready to prepare for the face-to-face solicitation. This is not so frightening as it seems. First of all, the prospect knows from your letter or your phone call that you will be talking about making a contribution. Since he or she has agreed to see you, the answer to your request is not an outright no. The prospect is considering saying yes. Your job is to move the prospect from consideration to commitment.

The purpose of the meeting is to get the gift. As the solicitor, you must appear poised, enthusiastic, and confident. If you are well prepared for the interview, this will not be too difficult. Board members and volunteers can go with each other or bring a staff person to such a meeting to provide any information the solicitor doesn't have. If you do go in pairs, be sure you know who is going to begin the meeting and who is going to actually ask for the gift.

The solicitor's job is to ask for the gift. The prospect's job is to decide whether he or she is going to give a gift and of what amount, ask for more time to think about it, or say no. It is important that the solicitor does not get personally caught up in the prospect's response. You are not a good fundraiser if someone says yes nor a poor fundraiser if someone says no. If you are asking enough people, a certain per-centage of them will say no. In fact, a sign that you are not asking enough people is when you go for a long time without anyone saying no.

Meeting Etiquette. Regardless of how well you know this prospect, the subject of this meeting is business. You should begin the meeting with pleasantries, catch up on family and friends briefly, but avoid the temptation to have a long chat before getting down to the subject at hand. It is often helpful to say early in the meeting, "Well, you know why we are here, which is to ask you to consider making a gift to Important Group. Before we get to that, however, we want to tell you some of the exciting things we are doing." This moves everyone into the conversation about the group and its fundraising goals.

Next, keep in mind that the more the prospect is encouraged to talk, the more likely he or she is to give. No one likes to be talked at or lectured. Ask the prospect what they know about your group, how they keep up with the issues your group works on, and other open-ended questions. Share your own experience with the group and tell stories that illustrate facts rather than just giving a dry exposition of what the group does. Sentences that begin, "I am most excited by" or "I got involved with Important Group because of my own situation (or commitment or long-standing interest in)" are much more likely to be listened to than "We started in 1997 with funding from the Havelots Foundation."

In addition to asking questions, pause for a few seconds between every few sentences. Wait to see if the prospect wants to add anything or has any questions or objections. If the prospect says something you don't understand, ask for clarification or say, "Tell me more about that." If the prospect says something that offends you or that you don't agree with, don't pretend to agree. Don't sacrifice your integrity for this gift, but see if you can find a way to counter what the prospect said without getting into an argument. You can use phrases like, "I can see why you say that because that is the impression that the media gives, but in fact . . ." or "We have discovered that fact-fact-fact, which is why we have designed the program the way we have." Said without rancor or defensiveness, statements like these can allow the prospect to change his mind without looking stupid.

Toward the end of the half-hour interview or when the prospect seems satisfied with what you have said, you are ready to close—that is, to ask for the gift. Repeat the goal of the campaign and the importance of the work of the group in one or two sentences. Then, looking directly at the prospect, ask for a specific gift: "Will you help with $2,000?" or "I'm hoping you can give a gift in the range of $500 to $1,500," or "Do you think you could consider a gift of $2,500?" There are no magic words for the close—what is important is that you figure out a phrase that suits your personality and includes the range or the specific gift you want. Then be quiet. At this moment, you give up control of the interaction. At last, you are asking the prospect to make a decision. Wait for the prospect to speak, even if you have to wait what seems like several minutes. If you are anxious, time will seem to pass very slowly. Keep looking at the prospect without staring. You can breathe easy now because you have said everything you need to say and you have put your best foot forward. Take a deep breath in and release it slowly. Smile a little and don't frown. You want to look relaxed and confident.

The Prospect's Response.   At this point the prospect will say one of six things, or some variation on these themes:

1. "Yes, I'll help." Thank the prospect. Be grateful and pleased, but don't be overly effusive or you will give the impression you didn't think the prospect was really a generous person. Arrange for how the gift will be made (by check, by pledge, by stock transfer; now, later). The easiest way to do that is to ask, "How would you like to pay that?" Once those arrangements are made, thank the prospect again and leave.

2. "I'd like to help, but the figure you name is too high." This is a yes answer but for a smaller gift. You can say, "Would you like to pledge that amount and contribute it in quarterly installments over a year's time?" Or you can say, "What would you feel comfortable giving?" or "What would you like to give?" Avoid the temptation to bargain with the prospect. Once the prospect has decided on an amount, follow the procedure in #1.

3. "That's a lot of money." This statement is generally a stall. The prospect feels he can give what you have asked, which is a big gift for him. He wants to be sure that your organization agrees that the gift is large. Your answer: "It is a lot of money. There are not many people we could ask for that amount." Or "It is a lot of money. That's why I wanted to talk to you about it in person." Or "It is a lot of money. It would be a big help." Then be quiet again and let the prospect decide.

4. "I need to think about it." Some people truly cannot make up their mind on the spot and if pushed for an answer will say no. Ask the prospect, "What else can I tell you that will help you in your thinking?" and answer any remaining questions. Then say, "May I call you in a few days to see what your decision is?"

Set a time when the prospect will be finished thinking and will give you an answer.

5. "I need to talk to my spouse (or partner or other party)." This probably does mean the person needs to talk to someone else; however, it is surprising that the prospect didn't say that when you set up the meeting, so it probably also means the person needs more time. Often it means that the person has another question or objection but is embarrassed to say it. This is called the "shadow question," and you need to surface what it is. You will do that by saying, "That makes sense. Is there anything your partner will want to know that I can tell you now?" The prospect may then tell you what's bothering him. "My partner will want to know why you spend so much on office space," or "My partner will want to know why you take money from Possibly Bad Corporation and will wonder if that affects your work." You can then answer these objections. You will end this solicitation by getting some agreement as to when the prospect can talk to the person they need to consult and when you should get back to them.

6. "No, I can't help you." Although this is an unlikely response at this point, it should be treated with respect. Nod your head and wait silently for a longer explanation. Generally the prospect will expand to provide a reason. "You know, I just don't really agree with your approach. I thought when I heard more about it I might understand and agree, but I don't." Or "I just can't get past the fact that Person I Hate is the chair of your board." Don't join in trashing this person, but don't spend a lot of time defending them either unless your defense is confined to discussing their work for your group. "He has done really good work for us, but I know he is controversial."

In the highly unlikely situation that you have remained silent for at least a full minute and the prospect hasn't volunteered any explanation for saying no, you can ask for one. "Would you say a little bit about why you are saying no?" Or "I am going to be asking other people as well. Are there any ways I can improve?" If asked nondefensively, you will probably receive an answer. If the answer is a misunderstanding, clear it up and you may get a yes or at least, "I'll think about it." Don't spend much time trying to change the prospect's mind or you will seem disrespectful. Often, people who say no to a request like this later say yes as they learn more or have time to think more about what you have said. Try to end the meeting with a question the prospect can say yes to. "Would you like to stay on our mailing list?" Or "When Person You Hate leaves the board, can I call you?" Or just, "What is best way to get downtown from here?" Thank the prospect for their time and leave. Remember that you have an unspoken but very important agreement with all the people you ask for money: if they agree to be asked, you will respect their right to say no.

Immediately after the interview send a thank you note regardless of the response you got at the meeting. Another thank you note should come from the organization when the gift is received.

Although it can be anxiety-producing to ask someone for a large gift, it is also thrilling when a prospect says yes, and it is not a big deal when someone says no. Most of the time people say no for understandable reasons that have nothing to do with you. With practice, asking for money becomes easier and easier. And most people are encouraged by being able to set aside their own discomfort about asking for money for the greater purpose of meeting the needs of the organization.

Understanding Special Events

Special events, also often called "fundraising benefits," are social gatherings of many sorts that expand the reputation of the organization; give those attending an amusing, interesting, or moving time; and possibly make money for the organization sponsoring the event. The variety of special events is practically limitless, as are the possibilities for money earned or lost, amount of work put in, number of people participating, and so on. Special events are arguably the oldest fundraising strategy and certainly the most common around the world. In every country where I have taught fundraising or read about fundraising, special events have played a big role. Because of their variety and flexibility, special events are excellent strategies for acquiring, retaining, or upgrading donors, and organizations that are serious about building a broad base of individual donors need to have at least one or two special events every year.

Events are often misunderstood and misused. What they do well—increase visibility—is often not the goal, and what they do badly—raise lots of money—is too often the only thing people are seeking when they plan them. Keep in mind, then, that special events should have three goals:

- To generate publicity for the organization
- To raise the visibility of the organization
- To bring in (new) money

Generating Publicity.   Generating publicity means getting a particular audience to pay attention to the organization for a limited time by means of advertising the event and by the quality of the event itself.

Enhancing Visibility.   An event raises the overall profile of the organization in the community. Visibility is the cumulative effect of publicity. With each successive event, and in combination with other fundraising and organizing efforts, the organization becomes known to more and more of the people who should know about it. The visibility of your group can be assessed by asking this question: Of the people who should know about you, what percentage do? This percentage is called your *visibility quotient.* Assessing a visibility quotient requires thinking through what types of people should know about your organization and what mechanisms reach those potential donors. For example, if you are regularly featured in the local newspaper, you may be well known to those who read the paper, but you also need to reach people who don't read any newspapers, which is now a majority of young people and larger and larger numbers of all people. In that case, getting more print publicity will not help you; you may need to move to radio, speaking engagements at houses of worship, or a door-to-door canvass in order to reach new constituencies. Events are excellent publicity-generating tools because they give the media a hook around which to focus attention on the group. A newspaper or radio station may be interested in discussing the event or even doing a profile of it—an auction, self-defense class, or concert—and will mention the sponsoring group's name, thus raising visibility.

Raising Money.   Raising money is a secondary goal for a special event because there are many faster and easier ways to raise money than this one. An organization that simply needs money (perhaps from being in a cash flow bind or having an unexpected expense) will find that the slowest ways to raise that money are seeking government funding or having an event. On the other hand, an organization that wants to raise its profile, bring in new people, and possibly make money will find a special event an ideal strategy. In many cases special events can lose money or barely break even and still be successful because of the publicity and visibility they produced.

TYPES OF PEOPLE WHO ATTEND SPECIAL EVENTS

There are two categories of people who attend events: those who come because of the event itself and those who come both for the event and to support your group. In the first category are people who would come to a particular event no matter who sponsored it. These people attend flea markets, dances, movie benefits, decorator showcases, auctions, and the like. Many times these people will not even know the name of the group sponsoring the event. In a similar vein are small businesses or corporations that will buy ads in an adbook, donate raffle prizes, buy tables at luncheons, or even underwrite an event but would not give an organization money under other circumstances. They want the advertising and resulting goodwill the event gives them, along with the chance to target a specific audience inexpensively. Raising money from a person or a business that would not give you money otherwise does not constitute donor "acquisition," but it is a smart use of an event and provides another income stream. Of course, the event should also be designed to draw people who are interested in your group. However, for organizations in rural communities or serving a very small constituency and unable to build a large base of donors, events that draw people to the event rather than the cause will be important for raising money.

The second type of people who attend events are those who are both interested in the event and believe in your group's work. They may not have heard of your organization before learning of this event, or they may already know of your organization and want to support it while getting something important to them. For example, women wanting to take a self-defense class may choose one sponsored by the local rape crisis program rather than a commercial gym in order to support the rape crisis program. After the classes, some of the participants may want to join the program as volunteers and paying members. People who buy all their holiday presents at a crafts fair put on by a public radio station or who enter marathons sponsored by groups they believe in are good prospects to follow up with direct mail or e-mail appeals.

Among the second type are people who appreciate your organization's work but can't afford or don't want to donate more than a small sum. For them, buying a $1 raffle ticket or attending a $6 movie benefit is a perfect way to show their support.

CHOOSING A FUNDRAISING EVENT

Several criteria should be considered in choosing a fundraising event: the appropriateness of the event, the image of the organization created by the event, the amount of volunteer energy required, the amount of front money needed, the repeatability and the timing of the event, and how the event fits into the organization's overall fundraising plan.

Appropriateness of the Event

To decide if an event is appropriate, ask yourself, "If people knew nothing about our organization except that it had sponsored this event, what would they think of our group?" If you think their thoughts would be neutral or good, then the event is appropriate. If you think that you would want them to know more about the group than just what the event implies about it, you should think again. Examples of inappropriate events abound. In the extreme, if you are the symphony you don't sponsor a pie-eating contest; if you run an alcohol recovery program you don't have a wine tasting. Often, however, the question of appropriateness is subtler than in those examples, as shown in the following two case studies.

A QUESTION OF CONSISTENCY

An organization working to end sweatshop conditions in garment factories around the world plans a luncheon to which they will invite one thousand people in the hope that three hundred will attend. The development director asks a large print shop employing more than seventy-five people to print their invitations and adbook as an in-kind donation. He then finds out from a worker at the print shop that the working conditions at this business are not good: the workers are exposed to toxic fumes, they are paid minimum wage and receive no benefits, and they are laid off during slow periods, then rehired when business picks up. A union has been trying to organize the workers at the print shop. A member of the union calls the development director of the antisweatshop organization and asks him not to use this shop. She explains the terrible working conditions and points out the lack of consistency for an organization whose mission is to stand up for workers everywhere to take their business to such a shop. However, the lure of free printing for 1,000 invitations and 750 copies of an adbook, saving the organization as much as $2,500, is too much to pass up. The development director thanks the union organizer for her comments, but says that his using this print shop will not worsen conditions there and that not using it will not improve conditions.

The union knows that this organization's events get a lot of publicity and often attract powerful people. They decide to organize an information line outside the event. The line is not a picket line, and they don't ask people to boycott the event, but union members and volunteers hand out information about the print shop outside the hotel where the event is held. The workers at the hotel, members of a different union, spontaneously decide to join the information line. As a result, the event becomes a public relations nightmare from which the organization does not recover quickly. They learned the hard way the importance of political consistency.

A QUESTION OF JUDGMENT

A women's health organization in a large West Coast city offered as a top raffle prize a case of fine, expensive wine. During their promotion, a number of studies were released showing the high rate of alcoholism among women. An internal debate ensued over whether it was appropriate for a group working to prevent dangerous drugs and devices from being given to women to offer alcohol—a potentially dangerous drug—as a raffle prize. Proponents argued that only 10 percent of the population are alcoholics and that alcohol does not harm most people who use it. The chance of an alcoholic winning that prize was slim compared to how many people would be attracted to the raffle because of this prize. However, opponents swayed the group by reasoning that they would not approve of a contraceptive that hurt 10 percent of its users. The group withdrew the prize, not wanting to promote a drug with any potential for harm.

Image of the Organization

In addition to being appropriate, the event as much as possible should be in keeping with the image of the organization or should promote the image the organization wishes to have. Although considerations of appropriateness sometimes include those of image, image is also a distinct issue. Many events that are appropriate for a group do not promote a memorable image of it. For example, a library would choose a book sale over a garage sale, even though both are appropriate. An environmental organization would use a whitewater rafting trip over season tickets to the ballet as a door prize, even though both are nice prizes. An organization promoting awareness of the problem of high blood pressure might choose a health fair over a dance. The idea is to attract people to your event who might become regular donors to your organization by linking the event to your mission.

Energy of Volunteers

Looking at the volunteer energy required to plan and mount an event involves several considerations. How many people are required to put on this event? What would these volunteers be doing if they were not working on this event? Do you have enough volunteers who have the time required to produce this event—not only to manage the event on the day of its occurrence but to take care of all the details that must be done beforehand?

Volunteer time is a resource to be cultivated, guided, and used appropriately. For example, don't use someone with connections to major donor prospects to sell T-shirts at a shopping mall on Saturday afternoon. Similarly, a friendly, outgoing person who loves to talk on the phone should be the phone-a-thon coordinator or the solicitor of auction items and not be asked to bake brownies for the food booth at the county fair. Obviously, what the volunteer wants to do should be of primary concern. People generally like to do what they are good at and be involved where they can be most useful.

Front Money

Most special events require that some money be spent before there is assurance that any money will be raised. The front money needed for an event should be an amount your organization could afford to lose if the event had to be canceled. This money should already be available—you should not, for example, use funds from advance ticket sales to rent the place where the event will be held. If the event is canceled some people will want their money back, but you may not get your whole rent deposit back. Events that require a lot of front money can create a cash flow problem in the organization if the need for this money is not taken into account.

Repeatability

The best event is one that becomes a tradition in your community, so that every year people look forward to the event that your group sponsors. Using this criterion can save you from discarding an event simply because the turnout was small the first time you did it. Perhaps you got too little publicity and only a handful of people came. If each of those people had a great time and you heard them saying, "I wish I had brought Juan," or "I wish Tiffany had known about this," then it may be worth having the event again next year. To decide if an event is repeatable, evaluate whether the same number of people working the same number of hours would raise more money producing this event again.

Timing

You need to find out what else is happening in your community at the time you want to hold your event. You don't want to conflict with the major fundraising event of a similar organization, nor do you want to be the tenth dance or auction in a row. If you are appealing to a particular constituency, you need to think of their timing. Farmers are mostly unavailable during planting and harvest seasons; Jews will not appreciate being invited to a buffet on Yom Kippur; gay men and lesbians may not come to a silent meditation scheduled during the Gay and Lesbian Pride Parade, and so on.

The Big Picture

The final consideration is the place of the event in the overall fundraising picture. If you find that the same people attend all your organization's events as well as give money by mail, you are "eating your own tail" and need to rethink how you are using events. If you cannot seem to get publicity for your events or you are unable to find an event to reach new constituencies, then maybe special events is not the right approach. If after analyzing your donor base you decide that your organization needs to increase its number of thoughtful donors, then you won't do as many events whose main purpose is acquisition. In other words, the results of special events (new names, publicity, new volunteers) must be fed into the overall effort to build a donor base or the effort of the event will have mostly been wasted.

HOW TO PLAN A SPECIAL EVENT

Special events require more planning time than one would imagine. Because so much can go wrong, and because many things often hinge on one thing so that one mistake can throw off weeks of work, events must be planned with more attention to minute detail than almost any other fundraising strategy.

The Committee for Special Events

There must be a small committee of volunteers overseeing the work for the event. If an event is so complicated that it is unrealistic for volunteers to be able to manage (a conference, a giant gala, a multiday fair), then hire an event planner. Using your own paid staff to plan and carry out a special event is not a good use of their time. Presumably, this is not what they were hired to do, it is not their expertise, and if you factor in the cost of their time on the event and the opportunity cost of what they are not doing while they are working on the event, you will see that your event is costing a much larger amount of money than the budget for it indicates.

The job of the committee is to plan and coordinate the event, not to do every task. After planning the event, most of the committee's work is delegating as many tasks as possible. Keep the committee to between five and seven people. Larger committees are unwieldy and can be counterproductive. With a larger committee planning the event, it is likely that the planning process will take longer, that the committee meetings will be like special events themselves, and the committee members will burn out and not want to help with this or any other event again. It is also likely that a large committee will have only five real workers.

Each special event should have its own committee, although there can be overlap from one event to another. Special events are labor intensive, however, and people need to have a rest period between events and a chance not to participate in every one. The committee must have staff and board support, and everyone must agree that the chosen event is a good idea.

Tasks of the Committee

There are three simple steps a special events committee should take to ensure the success of the event: detail a master task list, prepare a budget, and create a timeline.

Detail a Master Task List.   On a piece of paper or a spreadsheet, create columns with the following labels: What, When, Who, and Done. Under "What" list all the tasks that must be accomplished. Include everything—even those things you are sure no one would ever forget, such as "Pick up tickets at printer" or "Send invitations to the board." Every minute detail should be on this list. Under the column "When" note beside each task when it must be finished. Now put the list into chronological order so that you have a list of things that must be done and the order in which to do them. Next, complete the "Who" column—to whom the task is assigned, and note the date the task is to be completed under "Done."

Putting this information on a computer-based spreadsheet means that each year you can easily change it and that updates or parts of the master task list can be e-mailed to anyone who needs to see them. However, people have planned events for centuries without computers, so don't feel that this step is essential.

Master Task List			
What	**When**	**Who**	**Done**

Prepare a Budget.   On a piece of paper or in a spreadsheet program, make two sets of three columns as shown on the following page:

Event Budget		
Expenses	**Estimated**	**Actual**
Item	$	$
Item	$	$
Item	$	$
Total expenses	$	$
Income	**Estimate**	**Actual**
Item	$	$
Item	$	$
Item	$	$
Total income	$	$
Net	$	$

Look at the master task list. Put anything that will cost money in the column marked "Expenses" and anything that will raise money in the column marked "Income." When you have listed everything, subtract expenses from income to find the projected "net income," or financial goal, of the event. The budget should be simple but thorough, so that all costs are accounted for and planned on.

As you budget, remember that an estimate is not a guess. If someone says, "The estimate for food is . . ." or "The estimate for printing is . . .," it means he or she has called several vendors for prices, bargained, and is satisfied that the estimate will be the price or very close to the price you will actually pay. As costs are incurred they can be noted in the column "Actual" for each item. As much as possible, put off paying for anything until after the event is over and be sure you work in cancellation clauses for rentals or other contracts. For example, if a hall rents for $600, with $300 required as a deposit, try to reserve the right to cancel as close to the date of the event as possible and still get all or part of that $300 back.

Ideally, of course, you will aim to get as many things as possible given as in-kind donations, but don't budget to get anything for free. Always put down a price in the budget. Estimating its cost will protect you in case you do have to pay for something you had planned to get donated, and it will also give you a cushion in case you have an unexpected expense.

Create a Timeline. To ensure that you have thought of everything that should be done and that you have allowed enough time to do everything, think backwards from the target date of your event. If you want to have a dance the evening of August 10, what would you have to do the morning of August 10? How about on August 9? To do those things, what would you have to do in early August? What would have to be in place by July 15? Work back in this way to the day you are starting from. By this backward planning, the committee may find out that it is impossible to put on the event in the time allowed. In that case they must either modify the event or change the date. Thinking through each week's tasks for the timeline may also surface expenses you hadn't thought of or make clear some additional tasks. Add these to your task list and budget.

As you plan, remember to take into account that, although there may be ninety days between now and the event, there may be only sixty working days because of schedule conflicts, weekends, and so on. For example, if a number of your volunteers have children, you should check a school calendar to make sure you don't need anything done on the first or last day of school, during a vacation, or on commencement day. Few organizations can have a New Year's party as a fundraiser simply because they cannot get anyone to work during the two weeks preceding New Year's Day.

Establish "go or no go" dates. On your timeline, you will notice that there are periods of intense activity as well as lulls throughout the time leading up to the event. The periods of intense activity, where several tasks must be accomplished and each is related to the other (for example, design, layout, proofread, print, and mail invitations) are called "task clusters." These groups of tasks must be accomplished as projected on your timeline. The date by which each cluster must be accomplished is a "go or no-go" date. At those dates, evaluate your progress and decide if you are going to proceed with the event or if you are too hopelessly behind or too many things have gone wrong and you would be better off to cancel or modify the event. Go or no-go dates are also set for when expenses will be incurred. The night before you send your invitations to the printer is a go or no-go date because you will owe the printer the money whether you do the event or not.

Once the committee has prepared the task list, the budget, and the timeline, they are ready to assign tasks to other volunteers. When you ask volunteers or vendors to do things, give them a due date that is sooner than the one in the "When" column of your task list. That way, in the best case you will always be ahead of your schedule; in the worst case—if the task is not completed—you will have some time to get it done.

What Not to Forget

Here is a checklist of commonly forgotten items in planning an event:

- Liquor license.
- Insurance (on the hall, for the speaker, for participants). Contracts vary on this. It often happens that a hall or auditorium is inexpensive because insurance is not included but is required of the renting organization. A one-night insurance policy or a rider on an existing policy can cost as much as $2,000.
- Logistics of transporting food, drink, speakers, performers, sound equipment, and the like to and from the event.
- Lodging for performers or speaker.
- Parking: either in a well-lit lot or available on well-lit streets.
- If there is going to be food: platters, plates, utensils, and napkins. Don't forget things like salt and pepper, hot and cold cups, cream and sugar.
- Heat or air conditioning: Is it available, does it cost extra, will you need to bring your own fans or space heaters?
- Receipt books for people who pay at the door or who buy anything sold at the event.

Here are some questions you need to ask before the event:

- Is the venue wheelchair accessible? Make sure that all rooms are accessible, especially the men and women's bathroom doors, stalls, toilet paper dispensers, and sinks. Sometimes a building will be labeled "wheelchair accessible" when only the front door and one area of seating is actually accessible.
- Where and how to dispose of trash. Are there clearly marked recycling bins and trash cans?

- Will you allow smoking? If so, where, and is that clearly marked?
- Does the invitation's reply card fit into the return envelope?
- Has everything been proofread at least five times?
- Is the organization's address, Web site, and phone number on the reply card, flier, poster, invitation, everything else?
- Is the event advertised on the Web site, can people buy tickets online, and is there an announcement of it on your voice mail? Who should add the event's name and date as part of their e-mail signature?
- Are the price, date, time, place, directions, and RSVP instructions for the event on all advertising and on your Web site?
- Have you considered the necessity of child care or language translation?
- How safe is the neighborhood? Will women feel safe coming to the event alone?
- Can you see and hear from every seat? (Sit in a number of seats to make sure.)
- Who will open the room or building for you? Do you need a key?
- Where are the fire exits?
- Do you know how all the lights work?
- What has to be done for cleanup?

The Evaluation

The final step in planning a special event is evaluation. Within a few days after the event, the planning committee should fill out an evaluation form like the one illustrated on the following page. Save this evaluation, along with copies of the advertising, the invitations, and any other information that would be useful for next year's planning committee.

The evaluation will allow you to decide whether or not to do the event again and will also ensure that the same number of people working the same amount of time will raise more and more money every year. It should not be necessary to create the planning documents described in this chapter more than once. Once you have created them, every year a new committee can modify and add to them, with each committee building on the knowledge and experience of previous committees.

Special Event Report (Evaluation Form)

Approximately how much time did the committee spend on this event? (In evaluating time spent, try to subtract time spent fooling around, but be sure to count time members spent driving on errands and speaking on the phone.) _____

Did this event bring in any new donors? _____

How many? _____

Can people who came to this event be invited to be donors? _____

Did this event bring in new money? _____

Does this event have the capacity to grow every year? _____

What would you do exactly the same next time? _____

_____

What would you do differently? _____

_____

List sources of free or low-cost items and who solicited them, and indicate whether you think these items will be available next year:

_____   _____

_____   _____

_____   _____

What kind of follow-up needs to be done? (such as thank you notes to people who went out of their way to help, bills to pay, prizes to be sent to those who weren't at the drawing, tablecloths or platters to be returned to those who loaned them)

_____   _____

_____   _____

_____   _____

Which committee members did what work?

_____ _____

_____ _____

_____ _____

Which committee members would be willing to work on this event next year?

_____ _____

_____ _____

_____ _____

Other comments:

_____

_____

_____

_____

Making the Most of Special Events

This chapter discusses two events: a house party and an annual dinner. It also covers two important components of many events: a raffle and an adbook. These four activities have been chosen because they are relatively easy to organize in the sense that they follow a formula and taken as a whole, they demonstrate all the principles of fundraising that are discussed in this book. An annotated glossary of special events—a quick look at twenty-two events, their possible net income, and the time it takes to organize them—can be found in Resource A.

HOW TO PUT ON A HOUSE PARTY

One of the easiest special events and sometimes one of the most lucrative is the common house party. It seems ludicrous to describe how to do a house party, since anyone who has ever put on a birthday party, school picnic, or anniversary celebration, let alone a small wedding or bat-mitzvah, already knows most of what there is to know about putting on a house party. However, because sometimes the most seemingly simple events are fraught with pitfalls, I describe here both the obvious and not-so-obvious details about giving a house party.

First, the basic definition of a house party: someone involved in a nonprofit group invites their friends to a party at their house. The purpose of the party is to educate the friends about the work of the nonprofit group and ask them to make a contribution. The party is also a place for those attending to meet new people, see old friends, and eat good food, so it sets up a cordial atmosphere for the request. Finally, a house party allows someone not familiar with the group to learn a lot about it, ask questions, and get some personal attention without being obligated to give a donation. People can either give a very small gift or not give at all without feeling embarrassed, and they can usually attend the house party without having to pay to get in.

House parties are a useful venue for an organization to explain a complicated issue to many people at once, allowing the audience to ask questions and get more information. A house party can be used to see what questions friendly people may have about an issue or strategy and thus help prepare the group for more hostile audiences. It can also be a safe gathering for people to discuss an issue in a way that a more public event would not be. House parties have been widely used over the past many years to raise money for unions, peace and justice work, and gay and lesbian organizing, as well as for hundreds of political initiatives and candidates.

In addition to providing an opportunity for explaining an issue, a house party can be the venue for a group of people to meet someone famous or important or who brings interesting information about the issue your group is working on. Recently released political prisoners, journalists who have witnessed atrocities, academics discussing their research, or activists of various kinds can tell their story to an audience that is then moved to help. The host describes what people can do to respond (vote, give money, boycott, give money, demonstrate, give money).

No matter what else you ask people to do at a house party, ask them to give money. It is the only thing they can do right on the spot, and it is usually the most passive action, requiring the least amount of work. The final use of a house party, which underlies all the other uses, is to expand the organization's donor base.

There are five steps to putting on a house party:

1. Finding people willing to host a party at their house and take on other responsibilities related to the event

2. Preparing the list of people to be invited

3. Designing and sending the invitation

4. Choreographing the event, particularly the pitch

5. Following up and evaluating

Finding the Host

The host of a house party has several responsibilities, the least of which is providing the house and the food. The host invites anyone he or she thinks might be interested in the organization or the topic being discussed. At the party, the host or another person gives an appropriate description of the organization and the issues. Then the host makes a pitch for money. Because the host is asking her or his guests to join them in making a significant gift, she or he (or they) must have already made a donation that is significant to them. Even if the host does not want to be the person making the pitch (in which case the host introduces the person making the pitch, such as a staff person or another board member), she or he must have the conviction of having made a meaningful donation in order to be a credible host.

The ideal host is someone close enough to the organization to understand the importance of the organization and to be willing to conquer their fear of asking friends for money but not so close that all their friends are donors already. A major flaw of house parties is that the same people attend several house parties for the same organization. Those people may enjoy each party, but wind up feeling "nickel and dimed to death," and the donor base of the group is not expanded.

Who to Invite

Once someone has volunteered to host the party, the organization's staff can help that person decide who should be invited. A house party can have any number of people, but it generally works best when there are at least twelve guests and not more than fifty. Figure out how many people the house or apartment can comfortably accommodate. If you are planning a presentation, you will need to make sure most of the people can sit down at that time. If the pitch is to be short, then having enough seats will not be so important.

As a rule of thumb, you need to invite three times as many people as you want to attend the party. There should be one person from the organization, such as a board member, volunteer, or staff person, for every five to ten guests, so include them in the numbers.

Obviously, start with the host's friends. Don't forget neighbors. Sometimes a house party is also a way to meet neighbors. For example, a member of an organization working to end the death penalty had a house party at his apartment. Knowing how emotional some people can be about this issue, he was nervous to invite people he didn't know well. Nevertheless, he decided to take a risk and invite his entire apartment building. A neighbor from another floor, whom he had never met, gave $2,500 that night!

Suggest that the host think about inviting people from their religious or spiritual center, social clubs, work, and their relatives. Except for those people specifically invited to mingle and represent the organization, don't include very many people who are already donors. The exception is donors whose gifts you want to upgrade; in that case, focus on those who could be asked to give more money than they currently do.

The Invitation

The invitation does not have to be fancy, and it can be printed at an instant-print copy shop, so expense shouldn't be an issue. Desktop publishing programs mean that good-looking invitations can be turned out inexpensively. Many people are comfortable using virtual invitations, such as e-vites, and know that their friends and acquaintances are steady e-mail users. The only problem with e-vites is getting people who are not able to come to send money anyway. With printed invitations, an option is given for the person invited to send back a donation even if they do not plan to attend. With virtual invitations, it is helpful if you can direct decliners to a Web page that encourages making a donation.

Whether virtual or paper, the invitation should reflect something about the host and the crowd being invited. This will make people want to attend. Whether your invitation is serious or light, educational or assuming knowledge on the part of the invitee, always include the following elements:

- An indication that people will be asked for money. "Bring your checkbook" is the most direct way to make this known. You might also say, "Bring your questions and your checkbook," or "Find out how your contribution can be instrumental in starting (or stopping, ending, creating, propelling, saving X)." One lighthearted invitation said, "Of course, you'll be asked for money. Come anyway. The worst thing that will happen is you'll have to listen to something you don't agree with, but you'll get free food!"

- A way for people to give without coming to the party. On the invitation's return card include the option, "I can't come, but I want to help. Enclosed is my donation."

- Encourage people to bring friends. Require an RSVP so you will know how many people are coming.

- Give people clear directions to the house. If finding the place is at all confusing, draw a map. Include the phone number and e-mail of the host.

Send the invitation at least three weeks before the party so you have plenty of time to hear from people and to make follow-up calls.

Choreographing the Event

Where most parties fail is in not having thought through exactly how the event will go. To avoid this danger, imagine yourself a guest at the event and play over in your mind what will happen.

You walk or drive up to the house. Is it obvious where to park? This can be important if the host shares a driveway with people not attending the party, if there is a hidden ditch near the house, or if the neighbors are the kind that are likely to call the police about a guest parked too near the crosswalk. Is the house obvious? Is there a porch light? Is there a sign saying, "Marvin's house party here"? This is especially important in rural communities, where homes can be hard to see, and in big apartment complexes where it may be confusing to find the right unit.

You come into the house or apartment. Is it obvious where to put your coat? If not, someone needs to be stationed at the door to provide that information. Ditto for the bathroom. Is there a place where people will sign in and pick up literature about the group? There should be a guest book for everyone to sign their name, postal and e-mail addresses, and phone numbers.

You look around for people you know and make your way to the food. Is there a traffic jam at the food table? Pull the table out from the wall so people can serve themselves from all sides of it. Put the drinks on a separate table removed from the food table to force people to move on from the food or from the drinks. If possible, have several small platters of food rather than two or three large platters. Are the plates big enough? You don't want people to have to come back for five helpings to feel satisfied or to stay hungry because they are too embarrassed to keep going back for more food. People returning to the food table creates a traffic jam; people feeling hungry or frustrated creates a non-money-giving atmosphere. If the house allows it, there can be several food tables in different rooms serving different kinds of food. Serve things that are easy to eat while standing up—finger food rather than items that need a fork and knife. Don't serve anything that would be a disaster if spilled (such as red wine on light-colored carpeting, chili on the beige couch).

Once you get your food, you look for a place to sit. Are there enough chairs? Make sure no chair is sitting alone or obstructing people coming in and out of the entrance or the bathroom or kitchen. When you are done with your food, where will you put your empty dish? Make sure there are several trash cans around for disposable dishes and utensils, an obvious table or plastic tub for dishes needing to be washed, and a container for recyclable beverage bottles and cans.

TWO HOUSE PARTIES FOR ONE GROUP

An organization of Catholics advocating the ordination of women had two house parties. Each party was geared to a different audience; everything from the invitations to the pitch reflected that difference.

One party was given by three Catholic nuns who live in a group house. They invited other sisters as well as people from their local parish who they thought would share their belief that women should be able to be priests. These women are well known in the community for being outspoken and courageous. Most of the people they invited were Catholic. Their invitation was on a standard sheet of paper, on the top of which was the slogan, "If you won't ordain women, don't baptize them." Further down was a description of the group, the list of the party's hosts, and the date, time, and place of the event. The page concluded with, "Eat, drink, and bring your checkbook." It was simple, direct, and appealed to a group of people who were familiar with the issues.

At the party there was no formal presentation aside from the pitch. The party attracted about fifty people, raised a little over $1,500, and signed on twenty new members. Almost everyone attending made a donation.

The second house party was given by a married couple who are members of the parish and active in the organization. They invited people from their workplaces (the husband works in a shelter for homeless people, the wife for a public interest law firm handling mostly sex-discrimination cases), from other churches, and neighbors. Most of those invited were not Catholic and some were probably not religious. Many have been active in women's organizations. Their invitation was done in a card format, with a quote from one of Paul's letters in the New Testament on the front: "In Christ there is neither male nor female, Jew nor Greek . . . all are one." The inside described the organization and invited people to hear a talk about the history of women in the Catholic church and the importance to the women's movement of the push to ordain women. The speaker was one of the nuns who gave the first party.

More than forty people came to this party. Many asked difficult questions about the priority of this effort in light of the many needs of women, the point of being ordained into a patriarchal and hierarchical church, why the women didn't seek ordination in a different denomination, and so on. The discussion was lively and sometimes heated. At the end, the wife of the couple explained her commitment to this cause and asked everyone to join her and her husband in giving $100 or more. Twenty people gave $100 or more, including one new donor who gave $1,000; another ten people gave less than $100. The total raised was $3,100. Of the thirty people who gave, twenty-five had never given to this organization before. About a dozen people did not give at all, but the hosts reported that several of them gave later and that the party had been important in raising consciousness on the issue.

The Special Moment: The Pitch

Everything at the house party should be built around the pitch. Make arrangements ahead of time with at a couple of people so that when the host says, "I hope you will make a donation," they pull out checkbooks or hand over checks to members of the organization. They don't have to be ostentatious about it, but a few people have to break the ice and show that this is the time to give money.

Some people object to this practice, claiming that it is both manipulative and imposes too much pressure. However, a little more thought will show that it is the considerate thing to do. Few people have the self-confidence to be the first to do anything. When the host asks for money, many people are prepared to give, but everyone has a brief attack of anxiety, "Perhaps this isn't when you give the money," or "Perhaps I am the only person in the room who believes in this cause," or "Perhaps everyone else already turned in their money and I will look odd if I give my money now." Having some people go first gives permission for everyone else who wants to give to do it now. Much like ushers at plays who show you to your seat without being asked or clerks in clothing stores who hand you the appropriate accessory (without you having to reveal that you wouldn't have known what to put on with that outfit), the people who make the first donation show that giving is the right thing to do at this time.

Time the pitch so that the most people will be present when it is made. This is usually forty-five minutes to an hour into the party. The host calls for people's attention. The members of the organization discreetly get envelopes ready and the "plants" space themselves around the room. The host introduces himself or herself and welcomes everyone. If there is a presentation, the host introduces the presenter. (If there is more than one host, such as a couple or a group, they should take turns talking so it is clear that both or all are involved.)

After the presentation, the host should be the one who gives the pitch. If the presenter is a famous person or somehow special to the work of the group, that person can sometimes make a formal request for money, followed by the host saying, "I hope you will join me in helping this important cause." It doesn't matter if the host is nervous or doesn't like asking for money. Your proceeds will be reduced by at least half without a pitch—or at least a strong indication of support—from the party sponsor.

Sometimes people argue that doing the party—loaning the house, arranging for the food, giving the time—should indicate the host's interest. Indeed it does. It shows that the host helped save the group the cost of renting a conference room at a hotel. But in order for the guests to give money, the host must also say that he or she gives money and wants anyone who agrees with him or her to do the same.

How the pitch is made determines how the money will be collected. This is also decided ahead of time. The best way to get the most money at the party is to pass around envelopes immediately after the host speaks. If you would prefer, the host can say, "Please put your donation in the basket over there," and point to a place. Or the host can say, "You can hand me your check or give it to any of the people wearing a Youth Now T-shirt." In any case, tell people how and when to give the money.

After the pitch is made, the host should remain standing in front of the group and give people a few moments to write their checks. A very effective method is to say, "Let's just have a moment of silence right now so that everyone can write a check or make a pledge. For those who have already given, just sit quietly for a moment while everyone else has a chance to catch up with you." Then wait a minute and say, "When you have finished writing your check and putting it in the envelope, pass it to . . ." and then tell people whom to give their envelope to. This method ensures that no one who wants to give will leave without making a gift but gives those who do not wish to give a way to sit quietly without being embarrassed.

House parties often fail at the moment right after the pitch. For example, at one house party the host said, "I hope you will all think about making a gift to this group, which is my favorite." Then, without missing a beat he said, "Now that the fundraising part is over, eat up and drink up! Let's have fun." People did exactly as they were told. For a few seconds they thought about giving a gift, then headed for the food. No envelopes were present, and no method of collection was obvious.

At another party, the hosts showed a videotape about the group, then took the tape out of the TV monitor and went into the kitchen. People sat around chatting about the tape, then got up to get drinks and food. After a while, the hosts re-emerged and went on with the party. People could be heard asking, "Are we supposed to give money?" or "What are you supposed to do with the money?" Perhaps out of fear of being rude, they did not ask the hosts.

In those cases, the parties raised almost no money and left people feeling that house parties are a waste of time. They are if not done properly.

Evaluation and Follow-Up

After each party, take some time to evaluate what went well and what could have been done better. Particularly if you have a regular presentation, think about the length, the relevance, how to get a discussion going, and so on.

Be sure to write thank you notes to everyone who gave money, and put those people on the organization's mailing list. If the host failed to make a pitch, then immediately send the guest list an appeal letter. If people gave, go over the list of donors with the host and if there are people missing from it who the host thinks would have given but didn't take the opportunity or forgot, he or she should call them. If the host does not want to make those calls, then send them an appeal letter as soon as possible.

Like all fundraising strategies, house parties only work if someone actually asks for the money. Otherwise a house party is just a party—fun but no funds.

THE ANNUAL DINNER

In Chapter Eight, I said that one of the criteria to consider in choosing an event is that the event is repeatable. Many organizations find that creating an event that is associated with them and occurs every year is the most lucrative way to use the strategy of special events. This annual event becomes their signature event. They may or may not do other events during the year, but they will always do this one. A relatively easy and malleable signature event is the annual dinner.

An annual dinner is a banquet generally held at a hotel or other venue that can accommodate a large number of guests. During the dinner, the organization presents a short program of some sort. The program often honors someone or presents a speaker, comedian, or singer, and certainly includes bragging briefly about the group's accomplishments. The dinner may include a silent auction or dancing afterward, but the main reason that people come is that they have come every year. Many of the people who come know each other. They bring new friends with them and have the most fun when the program is brief and the time for mingling and eating is long.

An annual dinner takes two or three years to really reach its stride, but it is worth the investment. The first year people close to the group come and have a good time. Perhaps there are only fifty people at the dinner. The next year, many of them bring friends and the ranks grow to one hundred, the following year to one hundred and fifty, then two hundred. When the event draws an audience of two hundred to three hundred people, it does not need to grow and does not need to rely on all of the same people coming back every year. There are dozens of grassroots organizations that have five hundred people come to their signature event: some come every year, some every two years, some have come once but continue to give to the event, some always bring friends, others always say they are going to come and don't show up, but in all cases the event is noticed.

A really well-organized annual dinner takes at least six months to plan. It is a lot of work, but the work is predictable and generally proceeds in the following pattern.

Form an Annual Dinner Committee

Identify four or five volunteers who will shepherd the event. They will set a date for the event and prepare the master task list, budget, and timeline detailed in Chapter Eight. The ideal members of the committee include at least one or two volunteers who have organized an event of comparable complexity in the past. It could have been a small wedding or commitment ceremony, the grand opening of a business, or something similar—it does not have to have been for a nonprofit, but it should have been a large event with a lot of details. People with this experience know the importance of keeping on schedule, and they expect that some things will not go according to plan so they are able to be flexible and solve problems quickly. In addition, people on this committee need to be able to spend weekday time on the event: making calls, visiting venues, interviewing caterers, and the like.

If the income stream for the event includes other mini-events, such as a raffle or adbook (described later in the chapter), silent or live auction, or reception ahead of time, the committee will need to form subcommittees to take care of each of these components. In other words, the dinner committee will serve as the master or oversight committee; then there will be an adbook committee, a raffle committee, and so on. These subcommittees operate fairly autonomously, but they must be included in the overall planning so that they don't step on each other's toes in arranging prizes, underwriting, or auction items, and they must coordinate their work with the designer and the printer for all the different components. The first year of an annual dinner there should be no more than one other component in addition to the dinner.

Recruit Volunteers

Once the master committee has completed the task list, budget, and timeline, and the board of directors or whoever has the authority to do so approves those items (a process that can take a full month), they are ready to begin recruiting the small army of volunteers that will ensure a successful event. If the event is well organized and the master committee has recruited enough volunteers, the process of working on the event will be fun, which will guarantee that at least some of the committee members will be willing to serve the following year.

This army of volunteers will be recruited to serve on one of the following five committees:

Honorary Committee. This is a group of people who actually do very little. They are well known in the community you want to attract to the event, and they lend their names to give interest and credibility to your event. You can use their names on your invitation and possibly in soliciting gifts. Honorary committee members also make a donation to the event (usually significant, such as buying a large ad or a table) and give the event committee names of people or businesses who should be invited to buy tickets, tables, or underwrite the event in some way. Often, members of the honorary committee don't come to the event, and that should not be a requirement.

Publicity Committee. This small committee of two or three people is in charge of publicizing the event in all media. Media obviously include your Web site, radio, newspapers, and possibly TV, but this committee also needs to think about where your constituency gets information about what is going on in their community.

Church bulletins, posters at every Laundromat and supermarket, and announcements at service clubs or union meetings can often attract more people to the event than newspaper coverage.

Arrangements Committee.   This committee is in charge of the many details that make or break an event: food, drink, flowers, valet parking, sound systems, child care, translation, and the like. They work with the master committee to identify what arrangements they are in charge of, and they should not be seen as a catch-all committee to do whatever other people don't want to do.

Materials Committee.   This committee is in charge of writing and designing the invitation and any other materials required for the event, such as a program, posters, fliers, and so on. Having one committee take care of all materials ensures a uniform look and message.

Invitation Committee.   This committee is responsible for getting all the lists for the invitation and getting it mailed in a timely way. They generally are not in charge of designing the invitation.

Sponsorship or Underwriting Committee.   This committee is in charge of soliciting businesses, corporations, or even major donors to buy a table or pay a chunk of the event's cost in return for having their name prominently displayed at the event.

Clean-Up Committee.   This committee is responsible for bringing or locating garbage bags and trash and recycling receptacles after the event is over and knowing where the cleaning tools—brooms, mops, cloths—are kept or providing them. They are responsible to put chairs and tables away, return platters, vases, and the like to their rightful owners and to know what the rules of the venue are for adequate clean-up. Because there is generally a cleaning and security deposit involved, someone from the master committee will want to be on this committee.

In addition to all these tasks, the master committee may want another small group to handle all the logistics for the night of the event—decorations, registration, seating, problems.

Balancing having enough committees to get the work done with not having so many that they are impossible to keep tabs on is a constant struggle. Building in regular reporting times and deadlines helps a great deal, as does having the committees be as small as possible while still able to get the work done.

As your event grows, you will want to consider hiring an event planner to take the place of some of the volunteers and to coordinate others. A good event planner is well worth their fee, and it is a much better use of money to hire such a person than to rely on your already overworked staff to pick up any pieces the volunteers weren't able or just did not do. Using staff on these kinds of events is a hidden cost but a real one.

Get the Money Ahead of Time

The ideal event is paid for and the cash is in hand well before the night of the event. Sponsors have sent in checks, attendees have sent in money for tickets, adbook ads are paid for, and so on. Any money that is raised the night of the event is extra. That way, if something goes wrong the night of the event, such as an earthquake, hurricane, or chemical spill, you may be able to negotiate keeping most of the money you have raised even if you have to cancel or postpone the event. If something goes wrong at the event—the master of ceremonies is ill, the speaker can't be heard because the sound system is bad—you can apologize and continue with the event without worrying that people aren't going to pay.

The most important thing is to have a lot of decent-quality food and drink. If people have enough good food to eat, they will generally be satisfied.

The Day of the Night of the Event

On the day of the event, the master committee and a representative from each subcommittee meet together and review the master task list, which has now become the master checklist. These lists should be almost grimy because of how often they have been reviewed, added on to, and modified. The purpose of this meeting is to walk through the event one last time to make sure every detail has been thought of. From the point of view of someone attending, what does the event look like?

The person arrives at the venue. Parking is clearly marked or easy to find. When she enters the venue, there are signs pointing her to the event. She checks in at a table where four or five people keep the process brief and the lines to get in short. The check-in sheet shows that she has paid and that she has asked to sit at the Morgan table. The check-in person welcomes her warmly, tells her where the Morgan table is, and invites her to go to the drink table and enjoy some hors d'oeuvres.

Once she has her drink, she can stop by a literature table nearby, where she can chat with a person staffing the table about what good work the group does and buy a T-shirt or a raffle ticket, if a raffle is part of the event. Once she and most people are seated, but before the dinner begins, board members circulate and greet people. They introduce themselves to people they don't know and thank them for coming. They point out the program books (which are really adbooks) at each place.

The master of ceremonies (MC) introduces himself or herself, welcomes people, gives a brief overview of the program, and tells people how they will get their food. Either people are served at their table or—more often and less expensive—they serve themselves from a buffet. The MC points out the buffet lines (of which there are at least four) and where to get drinks. With a really big crowd, it is best to call people up table by table.

The food is served efficiently and the Morgan table is impressed. As they are finishing and their plates are being cleared, the program begins. Everyone who needs to use the microphone knows how to work with it, as they have been shown ahead of time. The program is entertaining, moving, and concise. There are no long gaps between the time someone's name is mentioned and when they arrive at the stage because a stage manager is constantly cueing people. A discreetly placed timekeeper sits in a front table and cues speakers with signs that say, "Five Minutes," "Two Minutes," and "Stop Now." None of the guests know that there is a Stop Now sign because no one has had to use it.

At the end of the program, the MC or other designated person gives a pitch for more money. Envelopes are on each table along with the adbooks, and people are encouraged to make an extra donation right then and there and turn it in to the people circulating with baskets. (Depending on the nature of the event and how much people have paid to get in, the pitch can raise an additional sum of a few hundred to a few thousand dollars.) At the end of the program, people are encouraged to get dessert from the buffet table and to stay and have fun. If there is a raffle drawing, that happens after dessert; if there is a silent auction, successful bidders are announced at the end of the program. Many people leave shortly after the program, but a critical mass stay for quite a while longer, talking and having fun. Finally, as all plates, food, tablecloths, and so on are cleared away, the last of the crowd leaves. The clean-up committee does whatever needs to be done and the event is over.

If the walk-through looked like that, you have thought of everything that can be thought of. If as you walked through you realized you had not built in a time for dessert to be served or did not have a designated timekeeper, you have time to take care of those details.

The committee in charge of the event evening arrives at the site at least two hours early. They help with putting up decorations, placing adbooks and contribution envelopes on each table, and taking care of any other details that can only be taken care of right before the event.

If the group is as prepared as I have recommended, even if something happens at the event that you have not prepared for, there are enough of you to figure out a plan. If you are running out of food, you will notice ahead of time and race out and buy some more. If you have a shortage of chairs, you will go around asking all board members and staff to give up their chairs and you will try to borrow more chairs from a nearby place. You have close to two dozen people who have put a lot of time and effort into this event. They will help, as will people attending.

After the Event
Shortly after the event, write up a final report as recommended in Chapter Eight. Count your income and pay your bills. Write thank you notes to everyone who did anything to help and take yourselves out for a nice meal to celebrate a job well done.

HOW TO DO A RAFFLE
A common, easy, and fun way to raise almost any amount of money is a raffle. Almost everyone is familiar with raffles, having bought tickets for them, perhaps even won a prize in one.

Because raffles are so common, most people don't realize that they can be complicated; when you are organizing a raffle, you can make your life more difficult by not paying attention to the myriad details that a raffle involves.

The first fact to keep in mind is that raffles have to be organized carefully so that they don't violate gambling laws. Although laws against raffles are rarely enforced, it is important to organize your raffle so that you are within the bounds of the law. In addition to federal and state laws, you need to find out the laws in your own community. Don't think that because you are a nonprofit you are exempt.

Sometimes you will need to register with the sheriff's department; in some towns, laws against raffles are strictly enforced and you simply will not be able to do one. In this section I discuss how to set up your raffle so that you will be within the laws of most states. Ironically, but perhaps not surprisingly, states with their own lottery tend to be more likely to stop a raffle from taking place than states without a lottery.

Raffles basically appeal to people's desire to get something for less than it is worth. Your organization gets some gifts donated, which are used as the prizes. These gifts can vary from straight cash to services such as childcare for an evening or having your windows washed, to adventures such as trips or products such as microwaves, VCRs, and so forth. Generally, there are five to ten prizes, one of which is a grand prize. Tickets are sold for somewhere between $1 and $10 each. Many more tickets are sold than prizes available, so a person's chances of winning are small. At an appointed day and time, all the tickets are put into a barrel or other container, stirred up, and a neutral person (such as a small child) draws out the winning tickets. The organization makes money from the number of tickets sold. There is no other source of income in a raffle. The costs can be kept low; ideally, the only costs are printing the tickets and getting the prizes to the winners. As a result, most of the income is profit.

There are three parts to a successful raffle, each requiring three steps.

Organizing the Raffle

Step 1: Get the Prizes. Bring together a small committee of two or three people to decide when the raffle will be held and what the prizes are going to be. It is helpful if the prizes have a theme, such as vacations, services, household, or restaurants. Make a list of all the vendors who might give you a prize and list specifically what you want from them, such as dinner for two, a weekend at a vacation cabin, and so on. Remember that people who own small businesses, particularly those in storefronts, get asked to donate raffle prizes a lot. They may have policies against doing it; they may donate to five charities and are not taking on any more; they may be having a hard time in their business and not be inclined to give you anything. Have three times as many places to seek prizes as the number of prizes needed.

The small committee then goes out and solicits the prizes. Be sure to stress to each merchant how many people will see the tickets, how much other publicity you are going to do, that you will not ask for another item this year, or whatever is true for you. Merchants must think about how giving your organization an item is good for their business, and you must help them in that thinking.

Once the prizes have been obtained, the small committee goes on to manage the rest of the details of the raffle.

Step 2: Get the Workers.   While you are soliciting prizes, start calling your volunteers to ask how many tickets they are willing to handle. Some people hate raffles—don't push them into taking tickets; they will resent it, and probably won't sell their tickets. Recruit people who work in large office buildings or unions, or who have large families or large circles of friends. Offer a prize for the person who brings in the most money for the raffle.

Keep track of who said they would distribute tickets. Raffles are a good opportunity to get some peripheral people involved, so don't just go to your reliable volunteers who already do everything else. Ask each person if they know someone who would be good at selling tickets. People's spouses or lovers, neighbors, business partners, and other acquaintances can be recruited for this effort.

Step 3: Get the Tickets.   Once they have the prizes, the committee decides which prizes will be the grand prize, the second prize, and so on. They decide on the date of the raffle drawing. Raffles should go on for at least one month and can go on for up to six months without losing momentum. The ideal time for a raffle is two to three months.

Printing the tickets requires attention to detail. (See illustration for the points discussed.) First of all, it is with the tickets that groups usually run afoul with the law. This is because raffle tickets cannot actually be sold. We speak of "selling" tickets, but technically, what we should say is that the ticket is free but a donation of $1 (or whatever the amount) is requested. In principle, someone can ask for a free ticket and not give you any money. If you were to turn down that request, it would be clear that you are selling the ticket, and that is against the law. In this chapter I refer to selling the tickets because that is the common shorthand; however, keep in mind that we are not truly selling anything.

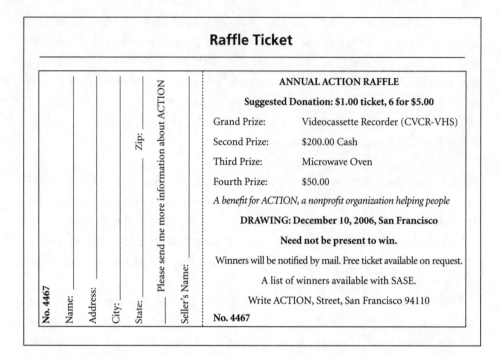

Raffle Ticket

No. 4467

Name:

Address:

City:

State:

Zip:

Please send me more information about ACTION

Seller's Name:

ANNUAL ACTION RAFFLE

Suggested Donation: $1.00 ticket, 6 for $5.00

Grand Prize: Videocassette Recorder (CVCR-VHS)

Second Prize: $200.00 Cash

Third Prize: Microwave Oven

Fourth Prize: $50.00

A benefit for ACTION, a nonprofit organization helping people

DRAWING: December 10, 2006, San Francisco

Need not be present to win.

Winners will be notified by mail. Free ticket available on request.

A list of winners available with SASE.

Write ACTION, Street, San Francisco 94110

No. 4467

You must print on the ticket how a person can get a free ticket and that a list of winners will be available, which helps ensure that the prizes are actually awarded. To increase sales, indicate that the donor doesn't have to be present to win.

The tickets must be numbered so that they are easy to keep track of. Although it costs more to have the printer number the tickets, it is worth it. Many organizations try to save money by not having numbered tickets or by numbering the tickets themselves. This is a foolish use of time. It is also critical that the ticket stub be perforated so it can be easily separated from the body of the ticket. Don't save money by printing cheap raffle tickets. Your volunteers will not distribute them as easily, and donors will be reluctant to give their money when the ticket does not appear properly done.

Not all printers can print raffle tickets. Find a printer who can, even if you cannot use your regular printer. Needless to say, seek to have the printing donated, but don't scrimp on print costs. They should be your only cost.

Notice in the illustration that the seller is asked to sign his or her name on the ticket stub. This is another incentive that you can build into your raffle: giving a prize to any person who sold winning tickets. You are obviously more likely to win such a prize if you have sold a lot of tickets.

To promote the organization, offer people a box to check to get more information about the group's work. If you do make such an offer, be sure you go through every ticket as they are turned in or after the drawing and send information to those who checked the box.

To know how many tickets to print, add up how many tickets the volunteer workers are willing to take and note what your goal is for the raffle. You may have to recruit more volunteers, which usually isn't hard to do once the raffle is under way. Always print at least two hundred more tickets than your financial goal, because some tickets are bound to be lost or mutilated.

One final word concerning the law: many groups send raffle tickets to possible donors through the mail. This is against postal law and, if caught, your letters will be sent back. If you send the tickets by bulk mail, you risk having your bulk mail permit revoked. In any case, raffles are not mail appeals. If you want to use the mail to raise money, do so, but do not combine raffle sales and mail appeals.

"Selling" Tickets

Step 4: Distribute and Keep Track of the Tickets.   Make a list of everyone selling tickets and the numbers of the tickets they take. Keep track of the tickets as they are returned. Have a date by which the tickets and the donations are to be turned in.

Step 5: Encourage the Workers.   E-mail or call your volunteers at least once a week to see how they are doing with their tickets. Remind them of the deadline and to send in their stubs and donations (rather than sending cash through the mail, they might want to substitute their own check and keep the cash). To encourage competition, tell them who is winning the "most tickets sold" prize so far. The job of the small committee is not to sell tickets but to keep other people selling them.

A raffle works best when organized like a pyramid, with the most tickets being sold by a large number of workers and the smaller number of workers distributing the tickets to others. Raffles fail when there are not enough people out selling tickets or when the people who take tickets don't sell them. Be sure to have a lot of people selling tickets and keep reminding them of due dates, praising those who are doing their job, and encouraging those who aren't. Every volunteer ought to be able to sell a minimum of twenty-five tickets. Most people who live in a town or city can sell fifty tickets in two or three weeks with no difficulty. Some people will be able to sell one hundred or more in one or two months. If you have a prize for the person who sells the most tickets, you may find some of your competitive volunteers really sell a lot of tickets. For example, a rural community in Northern California has a huge event once a year called "Western Weekend." The teenage girl who sells the most tickets becomes the Queen of the event, leading teens to sell hundreds of tickets in a community of less than 2,000 people plus tourists.

Step 6: Set Up the Drawing.   Some organizations hold the raffle drawing as part of another event, such as a dance or auction. You don't need to have another event—it is fine to have a small party for all those who worked on the raffle and who sold tickets and do the drawing there. The drawing is held on the date printed on the ticket. If you have good food and drink, the drawing is a celebration and a reward for a job well done as well as a way to ensure that all the sold tickets are turned in on time.

Wrapping Up the Raffle

Step 7: Round Up the Tickets.   Surprisingly, most people find the most difficult task in a raffle lies not in getting the prizes and not in getting the workers, but in getting the tickets and the cash back.

Some volunteers will be careless with their ticket stubs, or they will return stubs and promise cash later or claim to have sold tickets when they really haven't. If you have encouraged people to turn in money and stubs as they go along, you will have less difficulty than if you wait until just before the drawing. Final submission of stubs and cash—as well as unsold tickets—should be due at least three days, and preferably five days, before the drawing. That way, you can ensure that you have all the tickets accounted for well ahead of time.

Getting stubs and cash in during the course of ticket sales helps deal with the problem of all the transactions being in small amounts of cash. Someone sells three tickets to a coworker, puts the stubs and dollar bills into their wallet, then goes to lunch and uses that cash for lunch without thinking. Later, they turn in more stubs than cash; without a careful record keeping system, this error might not be caught.

Another advantage of getting ticket stubs in well ahead of time is that some donors try to make their stub into the winning one by bending down a corner, sticking something on the back, or tearing it nearly in half and then taping it together. Workers will sometimes fold ticket stubs or spill stuff on them. These stubs cannot be used, and new stubs must be written. This is one of the uses of the two hundred extra tickets. For the drawing to be fair, the stubs must be as uniform as possible.

Step 8: Hold the Drawing. When the time has come to hold the drawing, get a big box or barrel for the ticket stubs. To guarantee neutrality, have a small child or blindfolded adult do the actual drawing. Be sure to mix and remix the stubs thoroughly after each prize is drawn. Start with the least-valuable prize and work up to the grand prize.

After the prizes are drawn, announce the prizes for top salespeople and award these. Many organizations give several prizes to their salespeople. In addition to the person who sold the most tickets, they award a prize to the person who got the most prizes donated, the person who got the most other people to sell tickets, the person who sold the most tickets in a week or to a single person, and so on. Having a lot of prizes for salespeople is a good motivator for those who are competitive during the selling process and a nice reward at the end.

After the drawing, sort through the tickets for people who checked that they were interested in getting more information about your organization, if you haven't identified them as the tickets came in. It can be labor intensive to sort through the ticket stubs to identify just the people who checked that box. However, this is an easy way to get hot list and is worth the effort.

Step 9: Send Out the Prizes and Thank You Notes, and Evaluate. Arrange for the winners to get their prizes, either by picking them up at your office or receiving them in the mail. Send thank you notes to each person who sold tickets and to all the merchants and others who donated prizes.

Make a final count of your money. Note how many tickets were unsold, where the problems were with the workers, the merchants, the tickets themselves, and so on. Create a file with all the information about the raffle, including lists of winners, people and businesses donating items, and volunteers. Add notes about timing and other issues. Next year, it will be much simpler to do the raffle if a committee can pull up this file and benefit from the previous year's experience.

ADBOOKS

An adbook provides a way for your organization to raise money from businesses and corporations by selling them advertising space in a booklet, program, menu, or other printed item that will be distributed to people who are coming to an event. Businesses whose owners may not care about the issues you represent may still buy an ad because they know your constituents will be likely to patronize the businesses that advertise in the adbook. Further, businesses are more likely to take out ads in an adbook than to make an outright donation to an organization because the cost of an ad can be taken as a business expense, which offers a higher tax deduction than a charitable gift.

Adbooks are a superb fundraising strategy if they are done well and on a regular basis. Some organizations use sales of ads as a way to underwrite conventions, luncheons, concerts, or any special event where a program or printed agenda would be appropriate. Adbooks are lucrative because the business buying the ad is paying anywhere from 200 to 1,000 percent more for the space than its actual design and printing cost.

An adbook can be as simple as a folded sheet of paper with ads on both sides or as complex as a full-scale paperback booklet printed in color. An adbook can also include coupons.

One advantage of adbooks as a fundraising strategy is that the process of soliciting ads helps train volunteers to ask for money face-to-face while giving the donors a concrete value for their money. Some volunteers who are reluctant to ask for outright monetary donations are willing to approach businesspeople to buy ads. They know that businesspeople want and need to advertise and that they are always looking for creative ways to reach more people. The advantage to the advertiser is that the cost of space in your adbook is always less than the cost of an ad of comparable size in a newspaper. Even though a newspaper reaches more people, if the advertiser's goods and services are particularly useful to your audience, your adbook reaches more targeted prospects. Further, increased public awareness about corporate responsibility has created a large group of consumers who prefer to buy from businesses and corporations that are perceived to be involved in the community. Numerous studies show that a customer will choose a product made by a company that supports nonprofits over a similar product from a company for which that information is not known. To appear in an adbook is good business, particularly if that adbook will be seen by a large number of people.

There is one caution with adbooks: sometimes the IRS counts adbook income to a nonprofit as unrelated-business income and charges tax on that income, known as unrelated-business income tax or UBIT. Unless your adbook is very lucrative and you do an adbook frequently, you are unlikely to run afoul of the IRS for income from an adbook. Unrelated-business income tax is much more commonly levied on ads that appear regularly in nonprofit groups' newsletters.

Like all fundraising strategies, an adbook requires careful advance planning. The first step is to plan the distribution of the adbook, what the book will look like, and the cost of the ads.

Distribution and Design

If you are planning an adbook for a special event, the distribution will be simple: all those attending the event will receive one. However, if the adbook is to be distributed more widely, you need to decide how you will get it out: will you send one to all your donors, put stacks of them in stores, hand them out in your neighborhood to people on the street, or use some other distribution strategy? Your distribution plan may influence businesses in their decision of whether to buy an ad.

In order to sell ads, you need to know what shape and size the adbook will be so you can determine the size of the ads and their price. The final number of pages will depend on the number of ads you sell.

Pricing Ads

There are no set formulas for determining how much to charge for ads. Check with other groups in your area that have done successful adbooks and see what they have charged. The price of the ads will depend in large part on how widely your adbook will be distributed and how elaborate it will be. If it is being given out to two hundred people, ads will be less expensive than if three thousand people will get one. If it is printed on glossy paper or in color, the ads will cost more than if it is simply printed in black and white on regular paper. There should be some variation in price between ads on the inside cover of the adbook and those on inside pages. Cover-page ads (including those on the back cover and the two inside covers) are usually at least twice the price of ads within the book because the exposure is so much better. Some groups charge more for ads in the centerfold as well, since they too will have more exposure.

The ads are sold either by dimension in inches (display ad) or by the number of words (classified ad). A display ad is prepared by the advertiser and sent to you either in hard copy or as a digital file; in either format, it should be camera ready—that is, ready to go to the printer. (If you give people the option of sending you copy that you design for a display ad, you can charge a design fee that covers your cost and gives you a small added profit.) For a classified ad, the advertiser sends the ad copy and you have the message designed for inclusion in the book. Display ads can be sold in full-page, half-page, one-third page, one-quarter-page, and sometimes one-eighth-page sizes (depending on how big one-eighth of a page would be). Some groups choose only to have display ads so that they will not have to design classified sections. People pay proportionately more for smaller ads than bigger ones because it is much less work for you to solicit and produce two dozen big ads than fifty small ones.

It is a good idea to give businesses and individuals the option of buying a single line in your book and listing those advertisers as friends or sponsors. These listings are less expensive—between about $25 and $50. They do not advertise a person or business beyond listing their name, but they do show that the person or business is supportive of your organization. The price of any ad can include one or two free tickets to the event or some other type of recognition at the event, such as a large poster on which all advertisers are listed.

Once you have the dimensions of your adbook and have set prices for the ads, prepare sample pages to be given to volunteers selling the ads. A sample layout for a two-page spread in an adbook whose final dimensions are 8.5-by-11 inches is shown, along with suggested prices for each portion of a page.

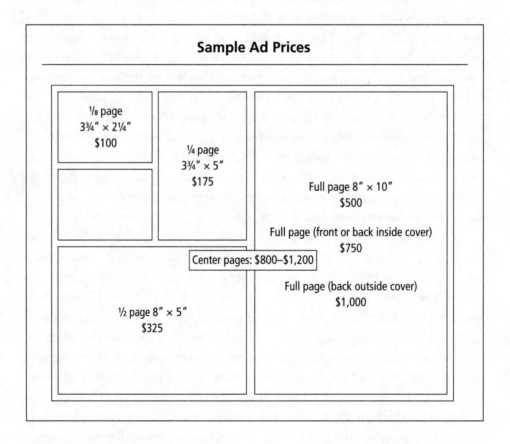

Sample Ad Prices

⅛ page
3¾" × 2¼"
$100

¼ page
3¾" × 5"
$175

Full page 8" × 10"
$500

Full page (front or back inside cover)
$750

Center pages: $800–$1,200

Full page (back outside cover)
$1,000

½ page 8" × 5"
$325

Timeline

The next step is to set a timeline for ad sales. If the adbook is for an event, the deadline for final sales must be at least one month before the event to allow for design, layout, proofreading, and printing of the book.

Prepare the timeline in the same way as for a special event, with a master task list and a budget, as described in Chapter Eight. A large adbook will require about an eight-week sales period. Planning and preparation of materials and training the sales force will all need to be done two weeks before sales begin. Four weeks at the end of the sales period will be needed for layout, proofreading, and printing. Thus, the total timeline will cover fourteen weeks.

Getting Ready to Sell

Make a list of businesses and individuals who might want to purchase ads. Ask volunteers, board members, and staff to list all the businesses they patronize, companies they work for, companies their spouses and friends work for, and businesses that would serve a large cross section of your donors. (For example, a women's organization would be sure to include women's clothing stores, beauty salons, and women's magazines.) To help people recall all the possible businesses they patronize, give them a list of suggestions, including banks, restaurants, fruit and vegetable stores, supermarkets, butchers, clothing stores, bakeries, liquor stores, and such people as doctor, dentist, lawyer, mechanic, therapist, hairdresser, chiropractor, accountant, and plumber. Include in the final list all of the vendors your organization uses as well as other nonprofits with whom you have worked over the years, unions, friends and family of staff or board, politicians, and even major donors.

Set up a database with the name, address, phone numbers, and a contact person for each potential advertiser. Include the name of the person who uses the business and any other information that will be helpful to the salesperson. (For example, Joe's Auto Supply, Joe Jones, owner, 512 Main St., 835-4692. He is board president's brother-in-law; also, Sally buys everything for her motorcycle there.)

Print out a master list of prospects and have volunteers sign up for as many prospects as they feel comfortable taking. Don't skip this step, because you want to make sure that one business isn't approached by two people and that the best person makes the request for the ad. Most important, you need a master list to keep track of how the volunteers are doing. Ideally, you will be able to enter the name of the volunteer who will be asking into the database record of each business, then print out a list for each volunteer of their prospects. If you are a neighborhood or community group, you may also wish to have some volunteers simply approach every store on a square block of the neighborhood in addition to any other businesses you may be approaching.

In addition to their prospect lists, the volunteers each need a number of other items:

- A supply of brochures describing the work of your organization
- Sample ad sheets with order forms to give each business
- Instructions for how camera-ready ads are to be sent
- Return envelopes in case the business owner wishes to mail in their ad or payment
- Receipt books to record payments received at the time of sale

Prepare the volunteers for difficult questions they may encounter, and provide possible answers, including convincing arguments. Each volunteer should stress how many good customers the adbook will reach, how inexpensive the ad is, and how much members of your organization enjoy the prospect's business, store, or service.

Selling the Ads

Depending on the type of business you are soliciting and the general style of your community, volunteers may first want to call the business owner or manager and make an appointment. In soliciting ads from corporations or large firms, sending a letter or e-mail, then following up with a phone call and visit, will be imperative.

Two or three volunteers should act as team leaders for the rest of the sales force. The team leaders play the same role as the planning committee for a special event. While they should sell ads, their main function is to encourage people on their team and to make sure that volunteers are making their calls. Volunteers must understand that they will be turned down more often than not. It will take from five to eight solicitations for every sale. Team leaders should stress that, as is the case when soliciting major gifts, the salesperson will rarely know exactly why they were turned down. They shouldn't spend a great deal of time thinking about it; simply go on to the next prospect.

Thank businesses immediately after they send in their ads and their money. Some businesses will not send payment until the adbook is published. Careful records will show which bills remain outstanding, and those businesses can be billed again after they receive a copy of the adbook. Because they have filled out and signed an agreement specifying the size and wording of the ad, it is extremely rare for businesspeople not to pay.

As sales are made, a progress chart should be posted at the office, and progress reports should be given to salespeople to encourage them. Once a week every salesperson should be given (or e-mailed) a list of the businesses that have already bought ads. They can take this list with them on solicitations; business owners may be persuaded to buy an ad when they see the names of colleagues who have done so.

When the adbook is produced, send each business a copy. Encourage your members to support the businesses they see in your adbook and to thank them for supporting your organization.

Producing the Adbook

After all the ads are in and the sales period is over, the book must be produced. Once the sales force has done their task, a second set of volunteers handles the production and distribution. A graphic designer or person with layout skills should be asked (or paid) to help ensure that the ads are laid out straight, that all the ads fit properly on each page, and that all the ads fit in the book. Layout can be done by hand or using a graphics program on a computer. Attention should be paid to putting ads that look nice together on the same page and to having some white space on each page so that the ads don't look crowded. Great care should be taken to proofread all copy and to keep the display ads and all the copy clean.

Aside from the ads, several pages should be devoted to the group and the event, either throughout the adbook or in a specific section of it. These pages include the conference agenda or program notes of the event, information about your group, and a membership form. Many organizations also include a brief history of their organization, a page listing and thanking all their donors, and short biographies of board and staff. If the event associated with the adbook is a tribute or awards dinner, then include a profile of the persons, ideas, or groups being honored. High-quality, good-contrast pictures are nice inclusions in an adbook.

When the book is ready for printing, someone who knows about paper stock and the printing process should help select the paper and ink color and specify the printing process. Print enough copies to give one to everyone who comes to the event (or for whatever distribution system you have chosen), everyone who made a donation to the event but did not come, and all advertisers and foundation funders. In addition, print enough so that there is a supply to hand out over the course of the year and enough for next year's sales force to show when they go to solicit ads.

The first year you produce an adbook is the most difficult. Businesses are taking a chance that you will do what you say in terms of quality and distribution of the book. If your adbook is successful and people patronize the businesses they have read about there, repeat sales will be easy to get. New businesses will be able to see exactly what they will get for their money. If they like what they see, they will be more inclined to buy.

Adbooks can be lucrative not only because the ads bring in much more money than the cost of printing them but also because they are a repeatable commodity. They not only help train volunteers in fundraising techniques, they are also good for building community relations with businesses. They should only be done, however, when the group has the lead time, an adequate number of volunteers who can devote time to the adbook and are not also organizing the rest of the event, and access to the design and printing expertise required.

Using Direct Mail

Direct mail is a strategy of sending a form letter that asks for money to hundreds, thousands, or even millions of people by bulk mail. It is a strategy widely used in the United States, Canada, Australia, and England, but not used at all in countries where people don't send money (in the form of checks, money orders, or credit card authorizations) through the mail.

Direct mail is greatly augmented by the Internet; in some places and with some causes online giving has overtaken using postal mail in popularity. You may be tempted to skip this chapter if you think that your organization will focus on raising money through the Internet or other strategies; however, the psychology of direct mail is important to understand and is useful in almost any communication you have with donors. Further, direct mail remains the only strategy that allows you to get something tangible (an envelope containing a request) into the hands of anyone served by the U.S. Postal Service for about $1 per address. Used carefully, the return is not only gaining numbers of new donors and eventually a solid income stream, but identifying donors to whom you had no other access. Stories abound of donors recruited through direct mail whom no one in the organization had ever met sending $500 and $1,000 in response to a first appeal, or donors whom no one knew leaving an organization money through a bequest after giving $35 a year for years and years.

I emphasize throughout this book that all strategies must be used in conjunction with each other. Direct mail, as you will see, is the most obvious example of this tenet.

A direct mail appeal is very simple: it contains a letter describing the organization and its needs and a self-addressed envelope, making it easy for the donor to return a gift. Even with the Internet, direct mail is still the most common fundraising strategy in use today. Letters that are addressed to an individual—"Dear Mrs. Smith"—or letters sent by first-class mail are not technically considered direct mail pieces, although these more personalized letters may borrow from direct mail principles in their look or style of writing, and identical text may be going to dozens—or thousands—of recipients. In the United States, direct mail letters are sent in minimum quantities of two hundred, presorted by ZIP code for the post office; at the post office they receive bottom priority for processing in return for a deep discount in the postage.

Direct mail solicitation (often derisively called "junk mail") has been in wide use since World War II. In the 1970s and 1980s, direct mail fundraising was so popular that many organizations derived the bulk of their income from it. Over time, as the market has become saturated with it, its effectiveness has decreased. People have become accustomed to receiving direct mail, making letters from groups one never heard of no longer as interesting to open.

To get a sense of the volume of direct mail, consider that 40 percent of the total mail in the world is generated in the United States and that 40 percent of that mail is direct mail, both from commercial and nonprofit sources. This means that about one out of every six pieces of mail worldwide is direct mail. For many Americans, far more than one out of six pieces coming through their mail slots is an unsolicited fundraising letter.

Some fundraising professionals (and probably thousands of consumers) have questioned whether direct mail continues to be an effective fundraising strategy. Despite all the bad publicity it gets, however, direct mail remains the least expensive way to reach the most people with a message that they can hold in their hands and examine at their leisure. A well-designed and well-written direct mail piece sent to a good list can still yield a response that makes it worthwhile: 0.75 to 1 percent on a first-time response, and 10 percent and often more from donors who have given before. Many groups also use direct mail letters to communicate with current donors and to ask for additional gifts. Used properly, direct mail is one of the most powerful strategies a small nonprofit can have. I am going to describe how direct mail works in a larger organization and then how a grassroots organization can adapt it to their circumstances.

THREE FUNCTIONS OF DIRECT MAIL

Direct mail soliciting has three functions; along with special events, it is one of the most versatile methods for developing closer relationships with donors. The three functions overlap with the strategies discussed in Chapter Three: acquisition, retention, and upgrading of donors.

Get Someone to Give for the First Time.   Donor acquisition is the main reason many organizations use direct mail. To see how it works, consider the experience of People for Good. People for Good trades five thousand* names of their donors for an equal number of names of donors to another group, Friends of Progress. People for Good compares the names they got from Friends of Progress with their own donor list and pulls out anyone who already gives to both groups. To the rest of Friends of Progress, People for Good sends a direct mail appeal asking for a donation to their work. They get a 1 percent response, which is fifty gifts. Their cost was $1 for each piece of mail (including postage, printing, paper, and the use of a mail house), for a total cost of $5,000. Most of the fifty donors give $40, which is the suggested donation, but three give $25, ten give $50, three give $100, one gives $250, and one gives $500. They also experience an increase in traffic to their Web site and a few donations are made online, but they can't attribute that directly to this appeal, so they don't count it in their analysis. (It is common in fundraising to report the "average" gift, but this number can be misleading. In this example, the average gift was $58 because a few bigger gifts came in. Use "mode"—the gift received most often—and "median"—the midpoint, at which there is the same number of gifts above this point as below it—for meaningful analysis. In this example, knowing that most people gave the amount that was asked for—the mode gift—indicates that the amount suggested was reasonable.)

---

*Five thousand names is considered by most experts to be an appropriate test-sample size. The idea is that if you get a 0.75 percent or better response on five thousand names, you should send the appeal to the whole list that these names came from. If the response is less than 0.75 percent, you can change the appeal or abandon the list. To take advantage of direct mail's discounted postal rates, you only need two hundred names, but two hundred is not considered statistically significant for predicting future response on that or a similar list.

People for Good brings in $2,905 on the mailing, giving them a net cost of $2,095—that is, the income subtracted from their $5,000 cost, or about $42 for each of the fifty donors they acquired. These donors will now be moved to the next stage. From this accounting, you can see right from the start that there is no point in starting a direct mail program unless you are willing to go all the way with it, because the first mailing usually loses money and sometimes a lot of money. Read on to see how that money will not only be recouped, but grow.

Get Donors to Repeat Their Gift.   Once a person becomes a donor, the organization tries to get that person to give routinely. The best way to do that is to thank the donor within seventy-two hours of receiving their gift and then to ask the donors for money more than once a year. Small organizations should ask their current donors for money at least two or three times a year, either through the mail or with a combination of mail, phone solicitations, and special events. These requests are interspersed with newsletters (paper or e-newsletters or both). This frequency of asking will not offend people and keeps the name of your group in the donor's consciousness. It also enables you to take advantage of the ups and downs of each donor's cash flow situation. Every time you ask your donors for an extra gift by mail, you can expect that about 10 percent of them will respond. In this phase you make back the money you spent acquiring these people. Keep in mind that most people making a first gift will not make a second gift, but more people who make a second gift will make a third, and most people who make a third gift will make a fourth, and so on, assuming the organization continues to do good work and treats their donors properly.

Get Donors to Renew Their Gift.   To be considered active (as opposed to lapsed), donors must make a contribution at least once a year, thus renewing their commitment to the organization. Most organizations have a renewal rate of about 66 percent—which is enough to generate a profit, including making back all the money you have invested in acquisition. Donors acquired through direct mail who show their commitment to the organization by renewing their gift are donors the organization might not have found otherwise who can be asked to volunteer, to give more money, to help with fundraising, to show up at demonstrations, and so on.

Direct Mail Plan: One Organization's Results

Income

Acquisition Mailings

    10,000 pieces of mail × 1% response = 100 donors;

    mode gift of $40, plus a number of other gifts received:

Income	$6,000

    Three more mailings to those who gave asking for

    extra gifts:

    10% response per mailing from 100 donors =

    30 extra gifts

Income	$1,500

    Three renewal mailings to these 100 donors;

    66 renew at $50–$500

Income	$4,000
Total revenue	$11,500

Expenses

Acquisition Mailings   (**Renting or exchanging lists, printing, postage, and other expenses**)

    10,000 pieces at $.85

    (higher volume will give you lower costs) $8,500

    Further mailings to 100 donors

    3 × 100 × $1 $300

    Renewal mailings (one to all 100 donors, a second

    to those who did not respond to the first, a third to

    those not responding to the first two)

200 letters × $1	$200
Total expenses	$9,000
Net gain: 66 donors	$2,500
Net income per donor	$38

Large organizations that frequently send direct mail appeals often have a fund of $5,000 to $50,000 that they constantly reinvest in these appeals. Money coming in from one appeal is invested in the next until the fund is depleted. Organizations spending that kind of money often hire direct mail consultants to design their appeals and to handle all the details of writing, printing, and mailing them. It probably goes without saying that a mail appeal is a gamble—you might get 0.05 percent response or even no donors at all. By carefully looking at lists and by paying attention to what you send the donors and constantly fine-tuning the appeal package, you decrease—but do not eliminate—your risk. (Chapter Eleven describes the appeal package in detail.)

USING DIRECT MAIL ON A SMALLER SCALE

By now, you are probably thinking, "Well, that counts my group out. We don't have the money, we don't have the lists, and we can't wait a year or two for the repeat gifts and renewals to start making money."

Don't despair. There is a way for even small groups to use mail appeals effectively. They must decrease the risk by decreasing the amount of money spent on each mailing. At the same time, they must try to increase the response rate so that they at least break even on first-time mailings to a list and with luck, make money.

These goals can be achieved in two ways: by mailing to more carefully selected lists and by mailing to fewer people at one time. In the example above, we used the conventional estimate of a 1 percent response from a new list; this estimate is useful for planning costs. However, direct mail expert Mal Warwick cautions, "There is so much variation in response from one organization to another and from one appeal to another that using this 1 percent figure as success can steer organizations onto the wrong path." Factors such as attracting bigger donors, finding a whole new constituency of donors, testing messages, and so on are often as important as the percentage of response. Attracting a smaller response on the first mailing but a higher percentage of donors who renew year in and year out would make the mailing worth its costs. Despite this optimism, small organizations need some measurable gauge, and percentage of response will give you a way to budget money spent for money earned.

Let's look at a direct mail scenario again but on a much smaller scale and with much more targeted lists.

Direct Mail Plan: A Much Smaller Scale

Income

Acquisition Mailings

500 pieces of mail × 2% response = 10 donors;
mode gift of $40, plus a number of other gifts received:

Income	$600

Three requests for extra gifts to the 10 new donors:

10% response per mailing = 3 extra gifts

Income	$250

Renewal letter with follow-up call to 10 people;
7 renewals

Income	$350
Total revenue	$1,150

Expenses

500 pieces of mail × $1	$500
30 letters asking for extra gifts × $1	$30
Renewal letter with phone follow-up to 10 people	$10
Total expenses	$542
Net gain: 6 donors	$608
Net income per donor	$101

As you can see, the average net income per donor from smaller mailings is much higher and the risk much lower than with larger mailings. However, neither set of income figures is particularly impressive given all the work involved. The costs examined here don't count the costs of staff time to acquire the mailing lists, produce the direct mail package, write thank you notes, and complete other fulfillment (such as newsletters). Again, one wouldn't enter a direct mail program if this were the only kind of income you could expect.

An organization must be prepared to take the donors it has acquired, identify those who can give much more, and then ask them to do so. The organization must ask some people to volunteer and others to bring in other donors. Over the long term, some donors will include the organization in their will.

Direct mail illustrates more than any other strategy the fundraising principle of building relationships: if you are not willing to keep track of your success so that you know which lists work which don't, if you are not willing to ask donors over and over, and if you are not willing to ask some donors for very large gifts, then you might as well not acquire them at all.

DEVELOPING LISTS FOR MAIL APPEALS

The cornerstone for the success of any mail appeal is the list of people who receive it. Compile or choose lists carefully. Make sure that each person's name is spelled correctly and that the address and ZIP code are correct. People tend to be miffed when their name is misspelled, and a wrong ZIP code will mean the letter won't be delivered.

Lists are divided into three categories of expectation, which describe the likelihood of people on that list making a donation. These categories are hot, warm, and cold.

Hot Lists. A hot list consists of people who have already made some kind of commitment to your organization. In order of decreasing heat, these people are your current donors, from whom can you expect a 10 percent response to any one mail appeal and of whom you can expect 66 percent to give a second time; lapsed donors from the past two years (expect a 3 to 7 percent response rate); volunteers and board members who are not yet donors (various response rates depending on the group; however, the response rate should not be lower than 5 percent and could be as high as 95 percent with good follow-up); and the close friends and associates of all of the above people who are not yet donors (2 to 5 percent response rate).

Warm Lists. A warm list consists of people who have either used or heard of your services, people who are donors to organizations similar to yours but have not heard of your group, or people who have come to your special events. These lists should yield a 1 percent response rate but also give you donors you may not have other access to.

Cold Lists. A cold list is any list that is more than a year old or any list of people about whom you know little or nothing. The phone book is an example of a cold list.

Hot Lists

The hottest list of people for any organization is its list of current donors. The second-hottest list includes friends of current donors, because most people's friends share their values and commitments. Therefore, to find new hot names to send appeals to, send current donors an annual mailing with a form on which to send the names and addresses of friends they think would be interested in your organization, as in the illustration.

Names of Friends Reply Form

Name and address: _____

__ You may use my name __ Do not use my name

1. _____

2. _____

3. _____

4. _____

__ I would rather not send in names, but I will distribute fundraising requests myself. Please send me ____ letters to send or give to friends.

__ I am willing to help with fundraising in other ways. Please call me _____ or e-mail me_____.

Some people will send only one or two names, and most people will not send any, but others will send in dozens of names. With a mailing list of one thousand donors, you can be assured of getting at least two hundred names from this type of appeal. Many organizations regularly remind their current donors to send in names of potential contributors by including a coupon in their newsletter and a request for names in other appeals.

Another source of hot prospects is your board members, volunteers, and staff. On a yearly basis these people should also be asked to provide a list of names, which can be compared to the current mailing list; anyone who is not already a donor can be solicited. Of course, any board member, staff person, or volunteer who isn't already a donor is a hot prospect as well.

Some statisticians claim that every person knows 250 people—relatives, school friends, colleagues, neighbors, and so on. Of this number, perhaps only ten or twenty will be suitable prospects. Nevertheless, with each volunteer or member contributing some names, you will soon have the two hundred needed for a bulk mailing. For rural organizations or groups just starting out, don't wait until you have two hundred names—go ahead and send the letter by first-class mail.

Warm Lists

People who buy any of your organization's products, such as booklets, educational materials, and T-shirts, are excellent prospects for a mail appeal because they are known buyers. Certainly, their names should be kept so you can advertise any new items you produce to them, and some of them will become members of your organization. The same is true of people who attend conferences, seminars, or public meetings that you sponsor. To keep mailing costs down, you can also ask people who buy products or attend seminars you have sponsored for their e-mail address and advertise to them that way (see also Chapter Thirteen for more about e-newsletters).

People who attend special events who are not donors should receive an appeal soon after the event. Pass out a sign-up sheet or conduct a door prize drawing to get names and addresses. People who previously gave your organization money but no longer do also constitute a warm list if you have correct addresses for them.

If your organization gives people advice, referrals, or other service over the phone or through the mail, create a system to gather the names of people served, unless that information is confidential. This list is the least warm because not all the people calling you are donors to anything, you don't know if they were satisfied with what they got from you, and they may feel they deserve to get the information you are giving out for free. However, some will be grateful and want to help, and some will prefer to pay for the information rather than accept it for free.

Keep a log of these types of contacts in a database on your computer and merge these every so often to eliminate duplicates and to pull out anyone who is already a donor to create a list of prospects. (If your organization only has one computer or has volunteers who are not used to using a database, use the old-fashioned method of writing down names and addresses either on a list or directly onto envelopes.) When people call, respond to their request and then ask if you can send them more information about your organization. Make sure you tell people your

Web site address, and make sure your site also encourages giving. People who don't want an appeal will decline to give their address. Some of these people will go to your Web site later and become donors. Names from information requests that come through the mail can be transferred directly onto carrier envelopes; every time you have compiled two hundred envelopes you can send an appeal by bulk mail. Some groups prefer to send appeals by first-class mail as the names come in. This ensures a hotter prospect, as people are more likely to open first-class mail, and they are receiving the mailing much closer to the time they have been in touch with you, but mailing first class is obviously more expensive than sending by bulk mail.

Renting and Trading Lists

The other type of warm lists are lists of people who belong to organizations that are similar to yours. To get these names requires renting or trading mailing lists. No one actually buys a mailing list outright. By renting it, they acquire the right to use the list one time. Many organizations with large or specialized mailing lists rent their lists as an income stream. You may have noticed that if you give to one organization you will receive appeals from several similar organizations within a few weeks. Your name has been rented because you are a proven "buyer" through direct mail.

You rent mailing lists either from a mailing list broker or from another organization. Professional mailing list brokers have a wide variety of lists available, which are used by both nonprofit organizations and businesses. Most brokers will send you a free catalogue of the categories of names available and the number of names in each category. The variety is astounding. A quick glance through one catalogue shows these possible offerings: sports medicine doctors, corporate secretaries in corporations with budgets greater than $250,000, earthquake research engineers, season ticket-holders to dance performances, donors to animal shelters, women in the press, or even the fascinating category, super-wealthy women (a list of 236,000 names nationally).

These lists come to you in ZIP-code order. The lists generally cost $75 to $125 per thousand names, with a minimum rental of two thousand to five thousand names. For a small additional fee, you can have lists crossed with each other, yielding the names, for example, of all the super-wealthy women who are donors to animal shelters or of earthquake engineers who are donors to historic preservation projects. A caution here: grassroots groups often assume that people in lucrative occupations (doctors, lawyers, stockbrokers) will be generous donors. This is not the case—there has to be some evidence that the people on list of doctors you have rented are also interested in your issue. Also, just because someone is in a lucrative profession and gives to other charities, they are not necessarily worth your direct mail investment. Be judicious in using rented lists.

To find mailing list brokers, look in the Yellow Pages under Mailing Houses, Mailing List Brokers, or Fundraising Services and Consultants. Also, ask organizations that use direct mail services for their recommendations.

Many low-budget organizations trade mailing lists with other organizations for a one-time use. Usually, lists are traded on a name-for-name basis: two hundred names for two hundred names and on up. A group can also trade names for as many names as they have and rent the rest. If your organization has five hundred donors and you want another group's list of two thousand donors, trade your five hundred and pay for the remaining fifteen hundred. Depending on your relationship with the other organization, it may rent the list to you simply for the cost of producing the list on labels or the cost of the labels plus handling, or it may seek to make some profit.

If you almost never rent your list, each of your names may be worth between two and five names of an organization that rents their list more often. If you have a mailing list of two hundred donor names that you have never rented out before, you may be able to trade for a list of one thousand.

Dos and Don'ts of Sharing Lists

Organizations often feel reluctant to share their donor lists with other organizations. One fear is that their donors will prefer the other groups and stop giving or give less to their group. Studies of donors show that this is not true. In fact, donor loyalty to the first group they give to in a series of organizations with related goals is increased as they learn of similar organizations. In other words, if a person gives to an environmental organization and then is solicited by several others, he or she may think, "I already support a group that does good work on the environment," or "I've been concerned about environmental degradation for a long time, and it's good that a lot of groups are working on it." Furthermore, most people who give to charity give to a number of them—usually between five and eleven. Often, most of the charities are similar: they may all be arts organizations or environmental groups, or they may be civil rights and civil liberties causes, but there will be some similar theme in all the charities. People change one or two charities each year, dropping one and taking on a new one. You are going to lose some donors every year (about one-third), but you will not lose donors simply by sharing your list.

To ensure that the names of donors who might take offense at being solicited by organizations other than yours are excluded from your rented lists, simply include a line in your newsletter or on your reply device that says, "From time to time we make our mailing list available to other organizations that we feel would be of interest to our members. If you would rather we did not include your name, please drop us a line (or check here on the form) and we will make sure that you do not receive any of these mailings." You can publish this announcement in every issue of the newsletter and put it in the subscription form on your Web site to be sure that every donor sees it. Very few people will actually write in with this request, but it is worth it to keep those that do happy. Most people like to get mail, and although they grouse about how much direct mail they get, they also feel important and needed because of the volume of mail that comes to them, and they have too much going on their lives to spend a lot of time and energy being mad about a mail appeal.

Do not steal mailing lists or use mailing lists that are marked "members only" or "do not use for solicitation." Because mailing lists are fairly easy to compile and acquire, once you have the systems in place there is no need to be underhanded with others' lists. Further, your organization's reputation may suffer. Almost all mailing lists, particularly those rented from commercial firms, have a certain number of dummy names: names that are placed to identify the use of that list. The letter addressed to a dummy name goes to the source of the list. Suppose you have liberated the list of members of a service club that has given your organization a donation. John Q. Jones is on that list, put there by the service club itself. ("Q" ensures that this is likely an unduplicated name.) When a letter arrives addressed to John Q. Jones, the service club knows it came from their list and will check out whether someone gave your organization permission to use the list. The situation can then become unpleasant and counterproductive to your fundraising efforts. A final rule about list acquisition and development: Do not save mailing lists. On a list that is more than three months old, 7 percent of the addresses will already be inaccurate. After you have used a list twice (if you have permission to do so), you have gotten 90 percent of the response you are going to get from that list. Concentrate your efforts on getting new names and refine your systems so that the names are as hot as possible. The quality of the list is pivotal to your direct mail success.

Although Chapter Thirteen covers acquisition using e-mail, I will point out here that these cautions apply as well to e-mail solicitation. Do not add someone to your e-newsletter list without their permission or request, do not send solicitations by e-mail unless you know the list very well, and be very careful in sharing e-mail lists. Spam is an enormous problem, and you don't want to add to it or be accused of doing so.

The Logistics of Direct Mail

A direct mail appeal needs to be conceived of as a package rather than as simply a letter in an envelope. The work of your organization is only one variable in determining the success of your appeal. The appeal is "wrapped" in a certain way to entice the donor to open the letter, then to read the letter, then to fill out a check and put it in the return envelope. This is a lot of pressure on a few pieces of paper with no power of their own.

This chapter discusses all the elements of putting together a direct mail package as well as a number of ways to use direct mail in seeking first-time, additional, and renewal gifts, what to do with the responses, and how to evaluate your direct mail programs.

THE DIRECT MAIL APPEAL PACKAGE

The standard package has four parts: the carrier or outside envelope, the letter itself, the reply device, and the return envelope.

Each part of the package is complementary to the others, and all the elements work as a unit to have the maximum effect on the person receiving the appeal. We will examine each element separately and then discuss putting the elements together.

The Carrier (Outside) Envelope

Many mail appeals fail because, although much attention has been spent writing an effective letter, it is enclosed in an envelope that no one opens.

First-class personal and business mail can be sent in an envelope simply with the recipients' address and a return address, and the sender can be reasonably certain that someone will open the letter. In the case of first-class mail, the envelope is simply a convenient way to deliver the letter. In a fundraising appeal sent by bulk mail, however, the outside envelope has an entirely different purpose. It must grab a prospect's attention and then intrigue them enough that they want to open it and see what's inside. The envelope in this case is like gift wrapping. Everyone wants to know what's inside a present. In fact, gift wrapping works so well that even when you may know what the gift is, there is still the thrill of discovery in removing the wrapping.

That thrill and that curiosity is what you should strive for with mail appeals. Make the prospect want to know what is inside the envelope.

Getting Personal.   Think about how most of us leaf through our mail. We may have bills that we set aside and fliers and newsletters that we glance at and either discard or put in a pile to read later. But if we find an envelope with our name handwritten on it, we will often put down the rest of the mail to open that envelope. If there are no such envelopes, we may open envelopes that promise interesting content in either words or pictures, or envelopes from organizations that we know and respect or from places we can't recognize just from the address. Maybe we see mailing labels inside, so we open that envelope. If an envelope offers us a way to save money, we open that one. If we are in a hurry, we throw away mail more quickly than if we are not. If we are procrastinating about doing something else, we may read something that on any other day we would discard immediately. Some marketing experts estimate that up to 70 percent of mail is thrown away unopened. So in designing your carrier envelope, use your own experience as to what you open first and what you are unlikely to ever open. However, don't rely on your experience alone. A fun conversation is to ask colleagues, neighbors, and friends to look at five appeal letters and tell you which one they would open first or which one they would throw away immediately. You will generate several different opinions, which is why you will never find one style of envelope that always works, with the exception of those that are hand addressed, which almost everyone will agree they will open.

If possible, then, write the addresses by hand. If you have a large volunteer pool or fewer than one thousand addresses, this is not too arduous a task if divided over several people. In addition to or instead of writing the addresses, you can make your letter look as though it was sent first class by using a precanceled bulk-mail stamp in place of the more common postal indicia. These stamps may be purchased at the post office where you send your bulk mail. The rules for sorting and handling the mail are the same as for any other bulk mailing.

Other Ways to Draw Attention.   Consider the rest of the envelope. If you are in a major metropolitan area where a lot of mail appeals originate, don't put your name and return address in the upper left-hand corner of the front of the envelope. Either use only your address without your organization's name in that spot or put your return address on the back flap of the envelope. In either case, the prospect asks, "Who is this from?" and opens the envelope to find out.

USE COMMON SENSE

Mission drives fundraising, and the truth of this tenet can be seen even in the design of carrier envelopes. Here are two examples:

A national organization advocating for the rights of GLBT (gay, lesbian, bisexual, and transgender) people is always careful to use its initials or an innocuous logo with their return address on mail appeals. They do not wish to endanger anyone who receives the appeal, even if this practice cuts into their response because some people throw away the appeal without recognizing who they are.

An animal rights organization has compelling and disturbing photos of animals used in research. Although putting one of these photos on an envelope would certainly grab attention, they are conscious that children may see this letter, so use no graphic photos in that way.

Timing and world events also play a role in designing carrier envelopes. Shortly after the attacks on the Pentagon and World Trade Center on September 11, 2001, a handful of envelopes were sent to Washington, D.C., containing military-grade anthrax. Some postal employees were sickened and a few died. The envelopes containing the anthrax had handwritten addresses and were made to look like something schoolchildren would send. For months afterward, everyone was on the alert for handwritten envelopes from an unknown sender. During that time, direct mail had a better chance of being opened if it looked impersonal.

If you are in a rural area, it is likely that the people receiving your appeal will open all letters that originate in their county or small town. In that case, you want your name and return address to be fairly prominent on the front of the envelope.

Most mail appeals are sent in standard business-size envelopes (called No. 10). Your appeal will stand out if it arrives in a smaller or an odd-size envelope. Personal letters are not generally sent in business-size envelopes, so to make your appeal look more personal, send it in a No. 6 ¾ or No. 7 ¾, or in an invitation-style envelope. If you use smaller envelopes, make sure your return card and return envelope are smaller yet so that they will fit into the carrier envelope without needing to be folded. One caution: odd-size envelopes and letters can run up your printing costs, sometimes significantly, so check with your printer before making a final decision.

The least effective strategy is placing what's known as "teaser copy" on an envelope; however, it should not be totally disregarded. Teaser copy is a text, drawing, or photograph on the envelope that intrigues the reader or causes some emotional response meant to make them open the envelope.

Envelope color is another variable to experiment with, but in choosing colors, make sure that the type is still readable against the color of the envelope. Bright colors can grab attention, but readability is key.

You may wish to experiment with various styles of outside envelopes to find which methods work best for your organization. Save mail appeals that you receive and are moved to open, and figure out what about the envelope caused you to want to look inside. The more creative you can be in designing the outside envelope, the greater chance you will have of the prospect reading your appeal.

The Letter

Because of the cost and volume of direct mail, it has been studied very carefully for close to forty years. A few simple principles about writing a direct mail letter have emerged. In thinking about these principles, keep in mind that a direct mail appeal is not literature. Many otherwise good writers are not good writers of direct mail letters. The direct mail letter is not designed to be lasting or to be filed away or to be read several times with new insights emerging from each reading. It is disposable, part of a culture acclimated to disposable goods of all kinds—from diapers and cameras to contact lenses. The function of the fundraising letter is simply to catch the reader's attention and hold it long enough for the person to decide to give. The recipients of fundraising letters most often read these letters on their own time. It is not their job to read the letter, and if the letter has its intended result, they will wind up paying money for having read it.

Also keep in mind how adults respond to input: when reading, watching TV or a movie, listening to a lecture, or even, to a lesser extent, listening to someone they care about, they subconsciously go back and forth between two questions. The first question is, "So what?" If this question is answered satisfactorily, they move to the next question, which is, "Now what?" This seesaw is a strong screening device for filtering out trivia, boring details, and rhetoric. To be sure, what is trivial and boring to one person may be profound or lifesaving to another, so the answers to these questions will vary from person to person. However, details about when your organization was founded or the permutations of your organizational structure will not pass the "So what?" test, and the myriad problems that led to your current budget deficit will only bring on a fit of "Now what?" questioning.

As you write your letter, then, imagine the reader asking at the end of each sentence, "So what? What does this have to do with me, people I care about, or things I believe in?" If the sentence stands up under that scrutiny, then read the next sentence while asking, "Now what?" Does this sentence offer a solution, provide more information, inspire confidence in the group?

Using the "So what—Now what?" spectrum as the foundation, build your letter on the following principles:

People Have Short Attention Spans. A person should be able to read each sentence in your letter in six to fifteen seconds. Each sentence must be informative or provocative enough to merit devoting the next six to fifteen seconds to reading the next sentence.

People Love to Read About Themselves. The reader of the letter wonders, "Do you know or care anything about me?" "Will giving your group money make me happier, give me status, or relieve my guilt?" "Did you notice that I helped before?" Therefore, the letter should refer to the reader at least twice as often and up to four times as often as it refers to the organization sending it. To do this requires drawing the reader into the cause with such phrases as, "You may have read . . .," "I'm sure you join me in feeling . . .," "If you are like me, you care deeply about . . ."

When writing to solicit another gift or a renewal from someone who is already a donor, use even more references to what they have done: "You have helped us in the past," "Your gift of $50 meant a great deal last year," "I want you to know that we rely on people like you—you are the backbone of our organization." Using the word "You" makes your letter speak *to* the reader rather than *at* them.

People Must Find the Letter Easy to Look At. The page should contain a lot of white space, including wide margins, and be in a font that is clear and simple. Break up paragraphs so that each is no more than two or three sentences long, even if such breaks are not absolutely dictated by the content. Use contractions (won't, you're, can't, we're) to add to the informal style. This is a letter, not a term paper. Do not use jargon or long, complex words. Go on to a second or even third page in order to ensure that the letter is easy to understand.

People Read the Letter in a Certain Order, and They Rarely Read the Whole Letter.   People often read the PS first. Then they read the salutation and the opening paragraph and no matter how long the letter is, they read the closing paragraph. If they did not read the PS first, they read it now. Up to 60 percent of readers decide whether or not to give based on these three paragraphs and will not read the rest of the letter. The other 40 percent will read selective parts of the rest of the letter, usually parts that are easy to look at, such as facts set off in bullets or phrases that are underlined. Only a small number of people will read the entire letter.

The Postscript.   This is often the first—and sometimes the only—sentence people read. The PS is most commonly used to suggest action: "Don't put this letter aside. Every day new cases come our way and we need your help." Sometimes it offers an additional incentive for acting immediately: "Every gift we receive before April 15 will be matched by Nofreelunch Foundation," or "We have a limited supply of *Excellent Book* by Important Author. Send your gift of $50 or more as soon as possible to be sure that you get one." The PS can be used to tell a story:

> PS An independent study showed that the quality of our schools has improved because of Community Concern. It also showed that we have a long way to go. For the sake of the children, please make your donation today.

Or it can make the reader part of the story:

> PS You cared enough to come to our community meeting last week. We hope you will join us in our critical work by making a donation now.

The Opening Paragraph.   Use the opening paragraph to tell a story, either about someone your group has helped, some situation your group has helped to rectify, or about the reader of the letter. There is a saying in fundraising: "People buy with their hearts first and then their heads." Programs and outcomes need to be described in people terms (or animals, if that is your constituency). Remember that people have read a lot of stories in direct mail appeals and newspapers and have seen even more on TV. They are used to being entertained by stories at the same time as they are skeptical of their authenticity, so make sure that your story is true (even if facts have been changed to protect someone) and that it is credible and typical. (You don't want someone saying, "What a sad story, but that could only happen once, so I'm not going to give.") Finally, have the story resolve positively because of the work of your organization. Here are some examples.

Someone the Group Has Helped

> Toni has been homeless for two years, moving in and out of shelters. Like half of the homeless people in our community, Toni works full time, but she has not been able to save the money she needs for the security deposit on an apartment. This week, because Homes Now has paid Toni's security deposit, she will be able to move into an apartment of her own.

The paragraph ends here. The body of the letter goes on to explain how many working people are homeless and how this group helps homeless people with housing, job training, and child care. If this letter were being used with current or former donors to Homes Now, the opening paragraph would use this sentence in place of the third sentence: "However, this week, because of the help of donors like you, Homes Now paid Toni's security deposit for her and she has moved into an apartment of her own."

A Situation the Group Helped to Change

> To some people it looked like a vacant lot, full of weeds, old tires, and paper trash. So when Dreck Development proposed paving it over for a parking lot, few people objected. After all, it is in a poor neighborhood and a parking lot would be useful to commuters who work in the industrial park a few blocks away. To Joe Camereno, the lot looked like a park. He called Inner City Greenspace and asked us how to go about protecting this vacant lot. Today it is Camereno Park. How did this come about?

The opening ends here. The rest of the letter lets people know how Inner City Greenspace helps neighborhoods transform vacant lots, treeless streets, and abandoned buildings into more livable community spaces.

Where the Reader Is Part of the Story

> As a resident of Rio del Vista, you were probably as shocked as I was to learn of the toxic waste dump proposed for Del Vista Lake last year. Working together, we were able to save the lake, but now a dump is proposed for Del Vista Canyon. We've got another fight on our hands.

The letter goes on to explain why Rio Del Vista is often targeted for these projects and what can be done about it.

Any of these styles of opening can be effective. The one you use will depend on your list and the stories available or the role of the reader in the situation described.

The Length.   There is has been much debate about the length of a direct mail letter. Many people claim that they never read a long letter and object to groups wasting trees to print them. Some direct mail consultants, on the other hand, advise their clients to send letters that are four to six pages. In fact, the evidence is overwhelming that longer letters are more successful: a two-page letter will get a better response than a one-page one and three to four pages will often get a better response than two pages. It is also true that consumers don't read these long letters—in fact, most of them only read the opening, the closing, and the postscript.

So why do longer letters work when people don't read them? Because a longer letter makes it look as though your organization has more to say and therefore has more substance to its work. It says to the reader, "We know you are not some slouch that will give to just anything, so we will explain ourselves." And it allows the organization to take the space it needs to make a case for itself without jamming words onto the page. For most small-budget organizations, two or three pages are effective. Remember that a letter can be printed on both sides of the paper.

The Closing Paragraph.   The other paragraph people read, the last paragraph of the letter, suggests the action you want the reader to take. It is specific and straightforward:

> Send your gift of $35, $50, $75, or whatever you can afford. Use the enclosed envelope and do it today.

> For your gift of $35, you will receive our quarterly newsletter, Chew On This. Above all, you will know that your gift has provided free dental services to people who cannot afford to see a dentist.

If your group has several different membership levels, give only the simplest description in the letter. This last paragraph is a short paragraph. Explain the full details of benefits on the reply device.

The Rest of the Text

The rest of the letter tells more of your history, discusses your plans, tells more stories, gives statistics, and lists accomplishments. To break up the text, use devices other than straight paragraphs. These devices might include bulleted text, such as this:

Because of us:

- In 2003, a city ordinance banning the distribution of birth control to teenagers was repealed as unconstitutional
- All teenagers in this community receive sex education as part of their biology courses
- We remain the only independent clinic providing referrals and birth control to anyone who needs it, regardless of their ability to pay

Or underlining:

When it got up to *ten drive-by shootings* in one month, with *half of the victims children,* the neighborhood association had enough!

Or adding a brief note that looks handwritten:

You can help!

Or:

Every gift makes a difference. Send yours today.

Who signs the letter is not critically important. If a famous person can be found to sign the letter, then the letter should be from that person. "I am happy to take time out of my busy movie schedule to tell you about Feisty Group." Otherwise, the chair of the board or the executive director can sign. The letter should be signed, however, and it should not be signed by more than two people or it begins to look like a petition. The person who signs the letter should have a readable, straightforward signature.

The Reply Device

Many years ago, when fundraising was in its infancy, the reply device was called "The little card that people send in with their check." This little card is now known as "the reply device."

The Psychology of the Reply Device.   In the letter, the organization refers to the reader using the word "You." The reader reads about herself or himself. In the reply device, the reader responds to the organization while continuing to read about himself or herself. The reader is asked to respond by saying, "Count me in" or "I agree" or "I'm with you."

More and more, when people open mail from groups they have heard of or causes they believe in, they move right to the bottom line—how much will it cost to join? For this, they look to the reply device. If the reply device holds their attention, they may return to the letter or they may just give without referring to the letter at all.

The reply device may be the one piece of paper the donor keeps from the mail appeal, as happens when someone reads an appeal letter, decides to give, then puts the return envelope and reply device into their "Bills to be paid" pile and throws the letter away. Two weeks later, the reply device must rekindle the excitement that the letter originally sparked, using a fraction of the space. For this reason, the design of the reply device is very important.

The reply device is usually printed on paper or card stock that fits easily with a check into the return envelope. Making the bottom portion of a letter the reply device or using a separate card or slip of paper allows you to change the reply device with every letter without incurring a great deal of cost.

Another option is the wallet style of envelope; in that style the reply device is the back flap of the envelope itself. In general, these are more expensive to print so groups usually print them in quantity; once printed, no further customizing can be done, so their use is discouraged. Further, a reply device that is separate from its envelope allows for one or the other to get lost without the person losing the address of your group, and you can use the return envelopes for other things you may want people to return.

The Design.   If possible, the reply device should display the logo of the group and have a catch phrase to remind prospects of what the group stands for or its mission. Some organizations put a brief description of their group or their project on the back of the device. Be sure your organization's return postal address and its Web site address are somewhere on the card.

Probably the trickiest part is wording the donor categories and benefits briefly. Many organizations use a simple series of boxes with differing amounts of money being suggested as donations, with the benefits the same for any amount of money. (You'll find a discussion of benefits at the end of this chapter.) If you have more elaborate benefits of membership or incentives for giving, put the amount first, then describe the incentive. Here's an example:

$35: Includes newsletter

$50: Includes newsletter plus free T-shirt (specify color and size below)

Pledge ($10 per month minimum): Includes newsletter plus *Very Good Book* by our own Roberta P. Activist.

Unless you have really clever names or particularly good incentives, naming your membership categories is not worth that much. "Patron," "Benefactor," "Friend," all have little or no meaning and inevitably reflect a hierarchy of giving that is just as well avoided.

The rest of the card must have room for the name, address, and phone number of the donor, or a place for a label, and a statement about how to make out the check or charge a credit card. Make sure the response you want is obvious and easy to comply with: note on your reply device to whom to make the check payable and whether or not the contribution is tax-deductible. (For more on using credit cards to accept donations, see Chapter Nineteen.)

People will read the suggested amounts until they find a number they are comfortable with or the amount that the letter has most emphasized. The following type of arrangement is fairly standard:

❑ $25   ❑ $35   ❑ $50   ❑ $100   ❑ other _____

You may wonder whether to start with the highest suggested gifts or put a large number in that second slot. These strategies are not effective because people will not pay more than they can afford and you don't want to scare them off. A group with the following sequence may wind up giving a message that small gifts are not encouraged:

❑ $100   ❑ $50   ❑ $35   ❑ $500   ❑ other _____

On the other hand, do not suggest an amount you would rather not receive, such as $5. If someone wants to or needs to send only that much, they can check "Other." By suggesting it, you will get that amount from people who could have given a lot more.

When it comes time to evaluate your appeal, you will want to be able to distinguish one appeal's response from another's. You do this by coding the reply device for each appeal in some way. If you have access to inexpensive printing, you could print each reply device in a different color, add a number or date to a bottom corner, or change the device that goes with each mailing in some other way. If you don't have a way to have the reply devices printed differently, a cheap and easy method is to put a dot with a colored marker on each reply card and note which color you are using for which mailing.

The Return Envelope

Aside from the wallet-style envelope discussed earlier, there are two styles of return envelopes: business reply envelopes (called BREs) and plain, self-addressed envelopes. With a BRE, the organization pays the cost of the return postage; this amounts to about twice as much as a first-class stamp but is only paid on those envelopes that are returned. With a plain, self-addressed envelope, the donor affixes a stamp.

For small organizations, BREs are not necessary, and organizations have ceased using them as consumers have become aware of the cost. Unless you are working with a sizzling hot list of current donors, do not put a first-class stamp on the return envelope. Your response rate will be too small to justify this expense. On the other hand, do not try to save money by omitting an envelope altogether. Your percentage of response will decline significantly if you do not use a self-addressed envelope of some kind.

Other Enclosures

The letter, reply device, and return envelope are all that is necessary to make an excellent mail appeal. There are some additions you can use if you wish. Whether they will increase your response rate depends on many other variables, but they might.

The Lift Note. A lift note is a small note equivalent to the notes in commercial direct mail packages that say, "Read this only if you have decided not to buy our tires." The note usually appears to be handwritten or at least printed in a different font from the text of the letter. It is from someone other than the signer of the letter and provides another compelling reason to give. For example, a letter signed by Judy Blacetti, director of an organization that helps seniors learn to use computers, had this lift note:

> I didn't want to learn to use a computer, but to please my son, I took a course at the Senior Center. This old dog has learned a lot of new tricks! I now teach other seniors how to use computers. It's fun, but also has a serious side, as people do research on medicine they have been prescribed or on their civil liberties or credit offers to see if they are legitimate. People can e-mail their kids and grandkids, and sometimes information found on the Internet saves money and may save lives. The courses are cheap because the teachers are all volunteers. Won't you help?—Lois Smith, age 82.

Of course, most people will read the lift note first, even though it reads as though you would read it after the letter. People's curiosity is aroused and they now read about Lois Smith in the letter.

A Newspaper Article.   If your organization has received positive press, reprint the article. If possible, reprint it on newspaper-quality paper so that it looks as though you cut the article out of the paper. People tend to think that if something was in the newspaper it is more true than if you say it yourself.

An Internal Memorandum.   Similar in theory to a lift note, these documents give readers the impression that they are learning something that they would not normally be privy to. For example, an organization working to feed starving people in the Sudan used this internal memo:

> TO: Joe *(the director, who signed the letter)*
>
> FR: Fred Smythe, Comptroller
>
> RE: Recent food shipment
>
> Joe, we can't continue to send this much food without a lot more money. I'm way over budget already and getting more and more requests from the field. There is no way we can send medical supplies as well. You have got to cut back.

Joe then scrawls the following note on the memo:

I received this memo just as I was about to send you this letter. Please help with as much as you can as soon as you can. Lives hang in the balance.

Fact Sheet.   A well-designed, easy-to-read fact sheet highlighting exciting facts about your organization can take the place of one page of your letter. Many organizations now use a fact sheet with a two-page letter and their results are as good as when they used a longer letter. Even though the number of pages is the same, a fact sheet is handy because the same one can be used with several different letters. A fact sheet should be on your organization's stationary. Among the "facts" should be that you depend on donations from individuals and what the minimum donation is for a person to become a member of your organization. This information reinforces the message of the letter, reaches those people who only read the fact sheet and not the letter, and allows you to use the fact sheet in other kinds of mailings or give it away by itself at rallies, house parties, or other events.

Brochure.   Surprisingly, using a brochure in a direct mail appeal will almost always decrease your response. Brochures are more complicated to look at than fact sheets or newspaper articles and require more of the reader's attention. Because a brochure does not generally emphasize giving, it can wind up holding attention but not achieving the purpose of the mailing. Brochures are designed to be given away at special events or to people wanting more information, and to be sent with personal letters asking for money.

Putting the Package Together

Be sure that your letter and enclosures are free of typographical errors. One typo can change the meaning of a sentence or more often, render it meaningless; moreover, typos give a bad impression of your group's work. Make sure that your return address and your Web site address are on everything: the reply device, the letter, and the return envelope. That way if someone loses the return envelope, she or he can still find you. Although the letter itself should be in a clean, readable font, the carrier envelope, reply device, and return envelope generally should be in a larger, bold font. Remember, the only impression that donors recruited by mail will have of your group will be from what they get in the mail.

Be sure that the envelope color and the paper stock for your letter do not clash. Avoid strong colors, such as bright yellows or reds, and any dark-colored paper. People with vision problems have a difficult time reading type on dark-colored paper, and you don't want to lose a prospect because he or she couldn't read the letter. Use sharp contrast in your type and paper color so that the words are easy to read. Use recycled or tree-free paper and soy ink in the printing whenever possible; if you do, put the recycle graphic on your letter so that people will know you have paid attention to this detail. Similarly, if possible use a union printer and put their union "bug" on the letter and envelope. Although response is not necessarily higher, those donors who do notice are pleased that you have not left your values behind to promote your cause by mail.

Do a spot check of all the printed materials before they are mailed. Sometimes a printer's mistake may leave the middle twenty-five letters smeared or blank. Although you can't look at every piece individually, you may be able to stop a mistake from being sent out.

Fold the letter so that the writing appears on the outside rather than on the inside, as with a normal letter. A person pulling the letter out from the envelope should be able to begin reading it without having to unfold it or turn it around.

Some states have laws that require that you to send a copy of each appeal to a government agency for approval before sending it out or to list your federal identification number on everything you send. Be sure to investigate and comply with these laws.

When to Send an Appeal

There is a saying among direct mail consultants that the best time of year to send an appeal is when it is ready. There is much truth in this saying, because there are no really bad times of year and no really excellent ones; the best time will always be when the appeal is fresh and exciting. One thing to keep in mind is that appeals to current donors may do better at the end of the year than acquisition mailings to potentially new donors. Moreover, your mailing can be derailed by major natural disasters (tsunamis, hurricanes, earthquakes) at any time of year.

Every organization needs to adjust the timing of its direct mail appeals according to its constituency. Farmers have different schedules than schoolteachers. Your constituency's religion and how fervently they practice it will affect some timing. Elections will affect timing. Even the activities of other organizations your constituents belong to may have an impact. As such, you will want to mail over many months and keep track of what works best for your group.

BENEFITS AND PREMIUMS

An organization that intends to have a large base of donors who repeatedly give small gifts must establish a workable benefits program. The purpose of a benefits program is to give donors something tangible for their donation. Benefits are important for the simple reason that Americans are consumers. We are accustomed to getting things for our money, and even nonprofit organizations compete for the consumer dollar on this level.

The psychology of a benefit is this: the donor sends a gift and your organization, in gratitude for the gift, sends a free benefit. The donor is not buying the benefit, which costs much less than his or her donation.

Although supporting the work of the organization gives the donor a feeling of goodwill, this feeling lasts only a little while; the donor needs a reminder of their gift and of the work of the group. A thank you note is the first reminder. As mentioned before, it should go out within seventy-two hours of receipt of the gift. The second reminder is the item or items that the organization will send the donor regularly.

In setting up a benefits program, the organization must define what relationship their donors will have to the organization. If you want your donors to have a feeling of ownership and involvement in your organization, you should consider establishing a membership program. Each donor is then called a member. If your bylaws already specify the rights of members, and if you do not wish to give donors voting or other rights specified by your bylaws, amend your bylaws to include a class of nonvoting members, number unlimited. If you do not wish to have members, you might establish giving categories such as "Friend," "Supporter," "Benefactor," and the like. Or you can create giving categories that do not convey any sense of relative importance by calling them A, B, C.

After you decide what to call your donors, you must decide what you are going to give them and whether donors who give more money will get more attention. Most organizations find it useful to have three donor categories to reflect greater contribution amounts. Each category has incentives to join at that rate. The categories might be as follows:

- Basic: $1–$99—includes basic benefits package

- Midrange: $99–$999—includes basic package plus a book, T-shirt, or other incentive

- Major Donor: $1,000 and up—includes the rewards of basic and midrange giving along with regular reports on the progress of the organization and individual attention

The Basic Benefits Package

The most common benefit is a newsletter. Appropriately, this benefit regularly reminds donors of your work, encourages them to feel proud of their part in your accomplishments, and provides information not available elsewhere or a point of view not generally expressed in the mass media. Other possible basic benefits include a T-shirt, bumper sticker, bookmark, membership card (which doesn't have to entitle the member to anything), discounts to special events, or other educational materials.

There are two guidelines for choosing benefits for donors. First, the fulfillment costs (that is, how much money it costs your organization to produce and send the item you promised) should never be more than one-fifth of the lowest membership category. Second, while you can always add benefits, it is far more difficult to take them away.

In deciding on a benefits package, then, start with small benefits that you know your organization can continue to afford and that you have the staff or volunteers to provide. The difference between a bimonthly newsletter and a quarterly one will not be nearly as important to the donor as it will be to your budget, staff, and volunteer time.

If you decide to have incentives for larger donations, try to find something that promotes your organization. A book about the work you do or that is related to a topic you address is good. Books can usually be purchased directly from the publisher in quantities of ten or more for 40 percent off the cover price. Paperback volumes are fine. Paperweights, tote bags, bookmarks, bumper stickers, T-shirts, and the like are all acceptable as well. Specialty merchandising firms can send you catalogs of available items on which they can print your logo or message at low cost.

The problem with books or any other benefit, however, is that it may not be easy to find a new one every year, which is why many groups offer premiums to encourage people to give but do not offer them as rewards for renewing or up-grading their gifts.

Premiums

Premiums are additional thank you gifts for donating within a specified time period. Announcement of a premium is often included in the mail appeal letter at the postscript, whose main purpose is to move the donor to act:

> PS Send your gift by December 1 and we will send you a special edition of a calendar created by a local artist for our group.

Or:

> PS We have a limited number of signed lithographs that we will send to the first fifty donors. Join today.

You don't want the renewing donor to put your appeal in the pile of bills to be paid later or to lose the appeal, so you offer a premium to encourage the donor to act promptly.

Premiums are particularly useful in securing upgraded gifts. The majority of these donors are probably going to give anyway; the premium simply encourages them to give sooner and more. For example, letters to people who gave $25 could entice a higher gift with a statement such as, "Gifts of $40 or more receive two free tickets to the spring concert."

The best premiums from your organization's point of view are ones that you already have. For example, suppose you are doing a concert and ticket sales are slow. Offer renewing donors a free ticket for renewing by a certain date. Or suppose you have had too many calendars printed and cannot possibly sell them all before the beginning of the new year. Offer them as a premium.

In using premiums for acquiring new donors, remember to add the cost of the premium when figuring the cost of the mail appeal. The cost of the premium will lower your net income, but if you gain even one or two percentage points in response, the cost will be offset.

You can also use premiums when you don't wish to commit yourself to a regular benefit—just send the premium item when you have it.

It is imperative to remember that benefits and premiums do not take the place of personal attention and that many donors do not want more tote bags, refrigerator magnets, and the like. In *Donor-Centered Fundraising,* Penelope Burke cites research showing that many donors no longer want any "stuff." They would prefer personal notes on a thank you letter and occasional reports on your work, including reports given in person at special events or delivered personally through phone calls or letters.

USING DIRECT MAIL TO SEEK RENEWAL GIFTS

The final use of direct mail is to renew gifts on an annual basis. There are many ways to set up renewal programs, but a simple, tiered renewal program based on size of gift works well. First, sort your donors according to their giving as small, midrange, and major donors. Small donors are people whose total giving is less than $100 in one year. Midrange donors are people giving between $100 and $249 annually, and major donors are people who annually give $250 or more. (You can adjust these numbers to fit your constituency—the point is to create three categories of donors who are treated in somewhat different ways.)

You could use direct mail to renew all your donors, with slightly different letters for each tier. However, it is better to use this system: at renewal time, all donors of small gifts receive a form letter asking them to renew their gift, all donors of midrange gifts receive a personalized letter, and all major donors receive a personal letter followed by a phone call and sometimes a visit. Although it is more work to segment your donor list in this way, your renewal rate will be higher and your chance of upgrading your donors is better. If you have a smaller donor base (fewer than five hundred donors), you should personalize as many renewal letters as you can. (For more on segmenting donor lists, see Chapter Twenty.)

The list of small donors is further divided into four categories according to when the person gave—spring, summer, autumn, winter. Once each quarter, the names of donors needing to renew in that quarter are generated from the database and they are sent a renewal letter with a reply device and return envelope. This is a much easier system than trying to write to people on the anniversary date of their gift, and it is much more effective in terms of renewal rates and cash flow than writing to everyone once a year regardless of when they gave.

The renewal letter follows the format of direct mail appeals. It starts with a sentence or two about the donor, affirming the importance of individual donors to the health and work of the organization. The letter goes on to list a few of the organization's accomplishments during the previous year and asks for a renewal gift, requesting that the donor increase their gift if possible. Although a renewal letter need be no longer than one page, do not jam the letter onto the page. Do not try to save space by saying so little that you wind up being cryptic or giving the impression that not much actually happened during the year. If you have more to say about your work than will fit nicely on one page, go on to a second page or the back of the page. Remember, for these donors especially, what they get from you in the mail is most or all of what they know about your work.

The reply device should be designed specifically for renewals, so the donor feels that he or she is a part of a group being asked to give again, rather than a new person being asked to give for the first time. In addition to the renewal, you can use the renewal reply device to ask the donor for other things, such as in this example:

❏ Here are the names of three people I think would be interested in (Name of Group):

_____

_____

_____

❏ You may use my name when writing to them.

❏ I would like membership information to send to (#)___ friends. Please send me membership packets.

❏ I would like information about legacy giving.

❏ I would like to volunteer. Please get in touch with me at the following phone number/e-mail address: _____

_____

Don't put more than one or two of these other options on the reply device, and vary them over time. After six to eight weeks, generate a list of any donors who haven't renewed yet and send them a shorter and firmer letter:

In your busy day, you may have forgotten to renew your commitment to Good Group. Please don't put this letter aside. Renew today.

Most organizations find it effective to send three renewal notices over a six- to eight-month period. They may then call the donors they have not heard from and ask them to renew. Donors who haven't responded after three renewal notices and a renewal call and who haven't given for the past fourteen months or more should be suppressed from getting a newsletter. Let them miss one or two newsletters before another notice is sent that says something like this:

> We miss you. We need you. I'd like to send you our next newsletter so you can keep up with all the important work people like you are making possible. Please use the enclosed form to send in a gift or let us know why you are not contributing at this time. Thanks.

A word of caution: there are many donors on your list who will respond to requests for extra funds and not to your renewal appeals. In their minds, they have given already this year. Any gift a person makes during a twelve-month period makes them a "current" donor. Sometimes organizations that have memberships get snippy with donors who have given but who haven't renewed their membership. Unless membership entitles you to something that your other gifts don't, this is silly and actually can alienate the donor. When you finally take someone off your list, make sure they really have not given for at least fourteen months.

Most social change organizations allow people to receive the newsletter or stay on the mailing list without paying if the person is interested in the group but can't afford to join or to subscribe. This practice is certainly appropriate; however, you don't want to keep people on your list whom you never hear from. Many times these people do not read your newsletter or your appeals and don't even remember how they got on your list. Because I teach fundraising to hundreds of groups a year, I get a lot of newsletters and mailings. One organization, to which I have never and will never donate, has been sending me their newsletter since 1981! I have moved to three different states and had nine different addresses during this time. I have written asking to be taken off the list, I have called, I have sent the newsletter back marked "Return to sender." Keeping me on their list is a waste of resources; unfortunately, I know from speaking with other people that this kind of waste is not unusual.

We hear stories every so often of someone who was on a group's list for ten years without giving a gift and then gave $100,000 or left the organization $20,000 in their estate. I am sure this happens from time to time, and it is true you will miss these people. However, the cost of keeping all the people on your list who don't give on the off chance that one will give is not sensible. Think of it this way: imagine one of your poorer donors who works at a low-wage job and sends $35, which may represent half a day's pay after taxes. He thinks you are going to do good work with the money he sends and probably would not be happy to know that some of his hard-earned money is being used to send newsletters to people you have not heard from in years.

Make this your general rule: to be considered an active donor and stay on your mailing list, a person must show their interest in a tangible way every twelve to sixteen months. They need to make a donation, indicate that they want to stay on the list even if they cannot donate, or volunteer. A quarterly renewal system for small donors will help you keep your mailing list clean and up to date and ensure that you are not spending money, paper, printing, and staff energy on people who are not going to respond.

In Chapter Ten I noted that a normal renewal rate is 66 percent—that is, 66 percent of people giving you a gift in one year can be expected to give you a gift the following year. The remaining 34 percent will not renew. No matter how often you appeal to people and how wonderful your organization is, many people will only give once and not again, or some will give two or three times and not again. Whether they renew probably has little to do with you and more to do with them changing jobs, marrying, divorcing, moving, getting sick, or changing their giving priorities because of one of these events. Therefore you must attract enough new donors every year to replace 34 percent of your donor base.

If your renewal rate is less than 66 percent, you are probably not doing enough to keep your donors. Examine your program to ensure that you are keeping up the following practices:

- Writing to donors more than once a year asking for money
- Thanking donors promptly with a personal note
- Sending at least three renewal notices
- Keeping records that are accurate and up to date

If your renewal rate is more than 66 percent, your organization does not have enough donors. Any organization can have an 80 percent to 90 percent renewal rate if they are only working with a handful of donors. A 66 percent renewal rate is a sign of health. It means you are bringing enough people into your system to ensure that you can develop a decent number of major donors if you work with the other strategies in this book. The donor pyramid gets smaller as your donors move up from first time to habitual to major donors. There are fewer and fewer at each stage. In order to have an adequate number at the top, there must be an adequate number at the bottom.

APPEALING TO CURRENT DONORS

Once your organization has acquired donors, it should appeal to them several times a year. Too often, appeals to current donors are overlooked. Years of testing have proven that some donors will respond every time they are asked and others will give less automatically but more than once a year, and that donor renewal rates are higher for all donors (even those who do not respond to extra appeals) when they receive several appeals a year.

Many organizations have discovered that they can raise enough money from their current donors with repeated appeals to enable them to scale down their recruitment of new donors. Many large organizations appeal to their donors eight to twelve times a year, which tends to have a saturating, and in the case of many donors, alienating effect. Experience with hundreds of grassroots social change organizations shows that two to four appeals a year will raise significantly more money and increase renewal rates without irritating your donors. Since most people who give or buy by mail may get as many as twelve hundred pieces of bulk mail a year, two to four appeals a year from your group will barely make a ripple in the volume of mail most of your donors are receiving.

Repeated appeals are successful for a number of reasons. First, a person's cash flow can vary greatly from month to month. A person receiving an appeal from a group he or she supports may have just paid car insurance, so the appeal gets thrown away. If the organization were to ask again after two more months, the person might have more money available and make a donation.

Second, different people respond to different types of appeals. Sending only one or two appeals a year does not allow for the variety of choices donors want. Organizations often discover that donors who regularly give $25 a year will give $50, $100, or more when appealed to for a special project. People who respond to specific project appeals are often called bricks-and-mortar people. They "buy" things for an organization: media spots, food for someone for a week, a job training program, a new building.

We rarely know why people don't respond to appeals. Despite this lack of knowledge many people are willing to make the assumption that the donor doesn't want to give, when any of the following circumstances might be true:

- The donor has been on vacation and mail has piled up, so anything that is not a bill or a personal letter, including your appeal, gets tossed.

- The donor is having personal problems and cannot think of anything else right now, even though he or she might be quite committed to your group.

- The appeal is lost in the mail.

- The donor meant to give but the appeal got lost or accidentally thrown away before it could be acted on.

Donors do not feel "dunned to death" by two to four appeals a year. On the contrary, they get a sense that a lot is happening in the organization. Their loyalty is developed when they know that their continuing donations are needed. Most important, they have an opportunity to express their own interests when a particular appeal matches their concerns.

WHAT TO APPEAL FOR

Once an organization has accepted the idea of sending appeals throughout the year, they often wonder what they are going to say in each one. Here are twelve ideas to help you choose some approaches. Some of these appeals are taken from or modeled on specific groups' letters. Some will suit one organization better than another, but almost any organization should be able to find one or two ideas that they could modify and use for their group. (See Resource B, Variations on the Mail Appeal Package, for more ideas.)

Seasonal Appeals

End of Year.   "As you close your books for this year, please remember *(organization)*. We have many more clients this time of year, and your additional support can ensure uninterrupted service."

Beginning of Year.   "One of my New Year's resolutions was to give more money this year to *(organization)*. I realized that, like many of my resolutions, this one could fade if I didn't act now. So I sent an extra $25 on January 5. I imagine that many of our members made a similar resolution. Perhaps you did. If you are like me, time may pass without action. So join me, and send that extra donation now."

Holiday Appeals

Lincoln's Birthday.   "President Lincoln was only one of the more famous people to be killed with a handgun. I know you want to end this senseless violence. An extra donation from you, sent today, will give us the extra funds we need to work on *(special program)* against handguns (*or* crime in the street *or* to strengthen our community organization activities *or* to escort people who are alone across campus)."

Valentine's Day.   "Do you often think of important people on Valentine's Day? Do you remember them with flowers, candy, or cards? I know I do. This year, I thought of other important people in my life—the people at *(organization)*. They really depend on us, their members, for the financial support they need. Will you join me in sending an extra donation? You can send flowers or candy as well. Simply use the enclosed card."

Labor Day.   "A time to take the day off. But what about all the people who want to work—people who are unemployed? For them Labor Day is another reminder of their joblessness. Our organization is providing training to thousands of people so that they can get good jobs in areas needing workers. Remember the unemployed this Labor Day with a gift to *(name of organization)*."

Columbus Day.   "Columbus discovered America. This is one part of American history almost everyone knows. The problem is that this is only a half-truth: Columbus discovered America for white people. There were already people here—our people. We are Americans. Yet our history since Columbus has been one of genocide, displacements, and oppression. At the Indigenous People's Organizing Project, we are determined to reclaim Columbus Day. You have helped us in the past. Will you help us, on this holiday, to continue our vital work?"

Thanksgiving Day.   "We would like to make Thanksgiving Day a little brighter for hundreds of people in our city who cannot afford to buy food. With your donation of $14.50, we will provide a family with a turkey and all the trimmings. Please give whatever you can."

Winter Holiday (Christmas, Hanukkah, Winter Solstice).   "We are just $2,000 short of our goal to buy a new furnace for our runaway house (*or* send our staff person to the state capitol to press for the bill we have been working so hard on *or* distribute thousands of leaflets telling seniors how to get their homes insulated for free). Can you help us meet our goal with a special end-of-year donation?"

Old Standbys

Anniversary. "Our organization is now entering its third (fifth, fiftieth) anniversary of service to the community. Celebrate with us by sending $1 (*or* $10 *or* $100) for each year of the important work we have done. For your gift, we will be pleased to send you a special anniversary parchment, suitable for framing. In addition, if you donate $1,000 or more, there will be a special reception honoring Famous Person, who has been so helpful to our cause."

Famous Person. "I'm Very Famous TV Star. You may have seen me on television. In my personal life, I am very concerned about birth control (*or* tenants' rights *or* public education). I believe that Good Organization defends our rights in this area. Please join me in supporting them." (Famous person can be truly famous, such as a movie star, or someone well known only in your community and widely respected there.)

Another Member. "My name is _____ . I have been a member of Good Organization for five years. In that time, I have witnessed the continuing erosion of our rights and the seemingly malicious efforts of our leaders to take what little we have left. All that stands between them and us is Good Organization. In the past five years, our organization has succeeded in (*name program successes*). That's why I am giving a little extra this year. Thirty dollars is not a lot, but it really helps, and if everyone gave just $30, $50, or even $100, it would really add up. Will you join me?"

Urgent Need. "We have an urgent need to raise $2,000 to alert the public to the hazards of chemical dumping being proposed for the east side of town. This little-known bill, which has the support of our supervisors, will bring unwarranted health hazards to more than one thousand people. The town council is trying to slide this bill through without our knowledge. We must protest. Help us stop this outrage now with an extra donation of $25, $35, or whatever you can send."

HANDLING RESPONSES TO YOUR DIRECT MAIL APPEALS

There are few things as thrilling as receiving gifts from a successful mail appeal. When you go to your mail box and pull out all the return envelopes that you know have gifts made by check or credit card, it is tempting to just deposit the money and go home early. But receiving the gifts brings on a whole new set of tasks.

All donors must be thanked, preferably within seventy-two hours of their gift arriving and certainly within seven days. Sometimes you will not be able to meet this time frame, so remember that a late thank you is always better than no thank you. (See also Chapter Seventeen, Writing Thank You Notes.)

The gift must also be recorded (for additional detail, see Chapter Thirty, Keeping Records). Use the following steps:

- Photocopy checks before cashing them. This step is a bookkeeping basic, but it also helps with fundraising, as a lot of information is on a check.

- Note in the database the day the gift arrived, what appeal it was responding to, and when the thank you note was sent out. Also note new information that should be entered into the database, such as a new address.

- Cash the check or run the credit card as soon as possible. People wonder if an organization really needs money when their check is not deposited quickly or if their gift does not show up on their next credit card statement.

EVALUATING YOUR APPEAL

In order to know if your appeal has been effective and which of your appeals are the most effective and why, you must track and evaluate them. Without evaluation, all fundraising is simply shooting in the dark. To get maximum benefit from a mail appeal program, evaluation is essential. The process of tracking is simple: you want to note how many people responded to a particular appeal and how much money each appeal brought in.

Tally the responses as they come in from each appeal. (You can do this on a spreadsheet program on a computer, but it is really easier to do on a piece of scratch paper by hand.) The heaviest response will come during the first four weeks after you could reasonably expect most people to have received the mailing (always send one to your organization in order to get a sense of how long it takes to arrive). Ninety-five percent of the responses will be in by the end of two months. Your tally might look like this:

Mail Appeal #1 Response

Week	Number of Responses	Total Received That Week
1	42	$1,680
2	85	$4,675
3	122	$5,002
4	67	$2,345
5	40	$1,600
6	25	$1,000
7	18	$630
8	7	$280

At the end of each week, also track and record the data below. Keeping track week by week will make the final evaluation much easier. After two months, add up the responses and the money earned and evaluate the appeal in these categories:

- Total number of gifts received and amount given
- Number of donors by category (less than $25, $25–$49, $50–$99, and so on)
- Percentage of response (divide the number of responses by the number of pieces mailed)
- The gift received most often (the mode gift, as described in Chapter Ten, not the average gift)
- Cost of mailing
- Ratio of income to expense (divide the amount of money you received by the amount you spent)
- Any narrative comments, such as "Send earlier next time," or "Joe's Printing said he would do free printing next time."

The percentage of response and the mode gift are the most important aspects of the evaluation. The percentage of response tells you much more important information than the amount you earned from the mailing. For example, one organization's appeal to one thousand names generated only two responses (0.002 percent); one response was for $10 but the other was for $1,500! The board was told that the mail appeal had generated $1,510 but not the percentage of response, so they decided to do more mailings to similar lists. They quickly spent all their profit because the lists were virtually worthless and their original response (which was extremely poor) only appeared successful because of the chance response of one major gift.

After you finish your evaluation, place the mail appeal with all of its components and the evaluation in a file folder. If you decide to repeat the mailing, you will have all the information you need in one place.

After several mailings, pull out all the evaluation forms and see what they have in common. Do some types of lists seem to respond better than others? Did the mailing offering a special benefit do better than the one without? Does one set of facts or one particular story seem to stir more people to give?

Remember to test only one variable at a time. You cannot find out if more people respond to one benefit or another in a mailing that is also testing a lift-out note with a letter against a letter alone. Also, you must use portions of the same list to test responses to different variables. You cannot test one variable on a list to a service club and another on a list to a group of health activists.

If you have mailed fewer than two thousand pieces, the results of your evaluation will not be statistically significant. However, using your instinct and what information you are able to garner, you should be able to make some educated guesses about what is working well with your direct mail program and why.

Fundraising by Telephone

With the predictability of gravity, I always know that when I get to the part of a training or consultation where I recommend using the phone, I am going to get more pushback than from almost any other strategy. People invariably say, "I hate being phoned." "I always hang up right away." "I would never give to an organization that phoned me." But usually after four or five expostulations on the evils of phoning, someone (often someone under thirty-five) will say, "I gave over the phone just the other night when the library called." "So did I," says someone else. At that point usually one of the people who never gives by phone says, "Well, that's different—that's the library. I gave to them also." We laugh and move on to explore the wide world of dialing for dollars.

For many years, telemarketing grew and grew, and although it was very unpopular, it did work with a large cross section of the population. In 2003, Congress passed one of the most popular pieces of legislation ever, the "Do Not Call Act." You can now opt out of receiving telemarketing calls just by registering your phone number with a master "Do Not Call" list. Nonprofits are exempt from the Do Not Call list. Do Not Call has decreased the volume of calls phenomenally, actually making the environment more friendly to callers from nonprofits.

Phoning works. Phone-a-thons continue to result in a greater percentage of response than direct mail, and they are an excellent way of reaching a large number of people with a (somewhat) personal message.

Like direct mail, phone-a-thons can be modified for small organizations in a way that allows them both to raise money and not offend donors. The two modifications small organizations make are to use very warm lists (such as lapsed and current donors, friends of board members, staff, and current donors, or lists of donors to similar organizations) and to use volunteers to do the calling. Even if a person is annoyed to be phoned during dinner, they will be less annoyed by a volunteer who is giving their time and doesn't sound as smooth as a professional telemarketer.

A basic fundraising axiom is that the closer you can get to the prospect, the more likely you are to get the gift. Phoning, as a telephone company ad used to say, is "the next best thing to being there."

BASIC TECHNIQUE OF THE PHONE-A-THON

In its simplest terms, a phone-a-thon involves a group of volunteers calling people to ask them to support your organization with a donation. A phone-a-thon is an excellent way to involve volunteers in fundraising because it teaches them how to ask for money in a way that they may find less intimidating than soliciting donations in face-to-face situations.

Phone-a-thons can be good moneymakers. They are usually inexpensive to produce and have a high rate of return. Between 5 and 10 percent of the people reached will contribute, possibly more when calling lapsed donors to renew their gifts and definitely more when calling current donors about a specific campaign. The costs involved include printing and postage, any toll-call charges, and food and drinks for volunteers doing the calling. If you haven't already, arrange for your organization to be able to accept credit card donations. You will get larger gifts and have a smaller loss of pledges using credit cards. (See Chapter Nineteen for more on accepting gifts by credit card.)

A phone-a-thon can be organized by one or two people. It takes several hours of preparation followed by a five-hour block of time for the event. Several people are needed to make all the calls (for how to determine how many people, see the formula below).

Preparation

To prepare for a phone-a-thon, the organizers take the following eight steps:

Step 1. Prepare the List. Make a list of people who will be called. These potential donors are people who have either expressed an interest in your organization, have benefited by something you have done for them, or are past or current supporters of your organization. People attending community meetings you have organized, alumnae, and members of and donors to similar organizations are all prospects. Get their names and look up their phone numbers. (Organizations in small towns or rural communities or organizations that serve a specific neighborhood or geographic constituency may be able to use the phone book as their source of names, but generally this is too cold a list.)

Create a master list of prospects to be called, either by using a computer-based spreadsheet or a handwritten list with columns for names, phone numbers, codes indicating the person's relationship to the organization (L = lapsed, FB = former board member, CL = client, and so on), and any information it would be helpful for the telephone volunteer to have, as in the following illustration. The list will also have a column for recording whether the prospect made a donation and for how much, which will be filled in after the calling is completed.

January Phone-A-Thon: People to Be Called

Name	Phone	Code	Notes	Donation?	Amount

If the only phone number you have for a person is known to be for a cell phone, it's best not to call, especially when calling for acquisition. When you have a choice of a home phone or cell phone, use the home phone. If you know that a former donor, board member, or alumnus does not have a land line, you can call their cell phone. When reaching someone on a cell phone, it is particularly imperative to ask whether this is a good time to talk and to be willing to call back or be called back when the person is at a better point (for example not driving) to talk.

Step 2. Create a File Record or Card for Each Prospect. The volunteers will use these cards (see illustration) to record the result of the phone call. After the calls have been made and these cards are filled in, you can use them to check off the names on the master list and record whether a donation was made and the amount.

```
┌─────────────────────────────────────────────────────────────────┐
│              Phone Prospect Record Card                           │
│  ───────────────────────────────────────────────────────────     │
│                                                                   │
│  Name _____ Phone _____ Code _____        │
│                                                                   │
│  Address _____         │
│                                                                   │
│  Donation made?   ❑ Yes: $ _____    ❑ No                          │
│                                                                   │
│  Credit card type and number _____        │
│                                                                   │
│  Address verified?   ❑ Yes   ❑ No                                 │
│                                                                   │
│  Want more info?   ❑ Yes   ❑ No (note whether sent)               │
│                                                                   │
│  ❑ Not home. Message left?   ❑ Yes   ❑ No                         │
│                                                                   │
│  Thank you sent?   ❑ Yes   ❑ No                                   │
│                                                                   │
│  Other _____          │
│                                                                   │
└─────────────────────────────────────────────────────────────────┘
```

Step 3. Set a Date for the Phone-A-Thon.   When looking for a date, pay attention to other events in your community. Don't call, for example, on an evening when everyone will be at an anniversary party or benefit auction for another group. Most people find that calling on a Tuesday, Wednesday, or Thursday night between 6 P.M. and 9 P.M. at the beginning of the month (near payday) works best.

Some groups call on weekends with success, but calling on a sunny weekend afternoon may bring people racing in from their yard or interrupt them while entertaining and may irritate more people than necessary. No one is sitting in the sun on a Wednesday evening at 8:00 P.M. Pay attention as well to what's on television: don't call during the Superbowl, on an election night, or during the Academy Awards.

Step 4. Write a Script.   Generally, volunteers can ad lib after the second or third call, but initially a script of what to say gives them a feeling of security. The script should be brief and to the point, as in the following sample.

SAMPLE PHONE-A-THON SCRIPT

"Hello, my name is Jill Activist, and I am a volunteer with Good Organization. May I speak with you for a minute?" *(Pause for answer.)*

"Thank you. I am calling tonight as a part of a phone-a-thon. Are you familiar with our work?" *Or* "Did you read about us in the Daily Blab?" *Or* "Did you receive our recent appeal?" *(Pause for answer.)*

If the person is a current of former donor, use this sentence instead of "Are you familiar with our work?": "You have helped us in the past (or recently), and first I want to thank you for that."

If the response indicates little familiarity with the organization's work, say "We are a group of concerned people working on . . ." *and give a two-sentence or fifteen-second summary of your work. (Pause.)*

If a current donor, then remind the person of your work, "As you know, we are engaged in . . ."

If there is no reaction or a positive reaction from the person being called, continue: "Our goal tonight is to raise $_____ . We are asking people to help us with a gift of $35 or more. So far, ___ *(number of)* people have pledged and we have $____ toward our goal. Would you care to make a donation?" *(Pause for answer.)*

If the answer is positive, continue: "We are trying to keep track of how much we have raised. What amount may I put you down for?" *(Pause for answer.)* "Thank you so much. Will you be able to pay by credit card?" *If yes, then get the credit card number and whatever other information you have been instructed to get for credit cards. If the prospect is hesitant to give you a credit card number, say,* "If you prefer, I can send you an envelope for you to use. Let me just verify your address." *(Read the address.)* "Thank you again. Good night."

In addition to the script, write up a list of questions that volunteers may be asked, with suggested answers. Include questions and statements such as, "Why haven't I heard of you before?" or "I sent you guys money and never got anything."

Step 5. Prepare Three Letters and Appropriate Enclosures.   Samples of each letter are given below.

A. A Letter for People Who Say Yes

Dear _____,

Thank you so much for joining Good Organization with your gift of $_____ this evening.

As you probably know, Good Organization is primarily supported by donations from people like you. Your gift will help us continue our work of _____

_____ . (Describe in two or three sentences.)

Please fill out and return the enclosed card with your check or your credit card information in the envelope provided. You will begin receiving our newsletter in two weeks.

Sincerely,
Name of volunteer

Return Card Format

Name _____

Address _____

❏ Enclosed is my pledge of $ _____. I look forward to receiving the newsletter and other benefits of membership.

❏ Please charge my VISA/MC $ _____

Card # _____

Expiration date _____

Name as it appears on card _____

Signature _____

Sign me up for the e-newsletter. E-mail address: _____

Make checks payable to: Good Organization.

Mail to: Our address

Web site: www.goodorganization.org

(Include a return envelope with a first-class stamp affixed.)

B. "Sorry We Missed You" Letter to People Who Weren't Home

Dear _____,

Sorry we missed you this evening. We tried to call you because we wanted to ask you to join (or renew or tell you more about) Good Organization.

Good Organization is . . . *(brief summary of not more than three to five short sentences).* Our main program goal for this year is . . . *(The exact language of this paragraph will depend on whether you are asking for a renewal or a new gift.)*

I hope you will want to join us in our important work. For a gift of $_____, we will be pleased to send you our quarterly newsletter, *The Right-On Times.* For a gift of $100 or more we will include a beautiful *(or important)* book *(or calendar or picture).*

Please take a moment to read the enclosed fact sheet, then fill out the membership form and send it with your check or credit card information today.

Sincerely,
Name of volunteer

PS For more information and to sign up for our free e-newsletter, check out our Web site at www.goodorganization.com.

If you have the capacity to take donations online, you will want to note that in your letter also.

C. Letter to People with Questions about the Organization

Dear _____,

Thanks for talking with me this evening.

I am enclosing the information we discussed, which I hope will answer your questions. Please feel free to contact our office to discuss our organization further if you wish, and check out our Web site at www.goodorganization.com.

I hope that after reading this information you will decide to make a donation. I am sure that once you read about us you will agree that our work is very important. Please support us in whatever way you can.

An envelope and membership form are enclosed for your convenience, or you can give online at www.goodorganization.com. I look
forward to hearing from you.

Sincerely,
Name of volunteer

Enclose with both the second and third types of letter a reply card or form that
the donor will fill out (as discussed in Chapter Eleven, The Logistics of Direct
Mail), a fact sheet or brochure about your organization, and a return envelope. It
is not necessary to put a postage stamp on any of these envelopes.

To decide the quantity of each letter to have printed, count the number of people you will be calling and assume that you will reach one-third of them on the
night of the phone-a-thon. Of this number, depending on how hot your list is, up
to one-third of those people will say yes and need Letter A; another one-third of
those reached will say, "Send me more information," and need Letter C; the rest
will say no. The other two-thirds or more of people phoned—those not reached—
will be sent Letter B. Much depends on how good your list is, but this formula
should give you enough letters without having lots of them left over. (You could
also photocopy the letters as you go along, if you have access to a high-quality
copier. If you are working with a small list, you could print each letter off your
computer.) If you do not date the letters and avoid using any reference to a month
or day, you can use the same letters at other phone-a-thons throughout the year.

If you are working with large lists and might have two hundred or more people who will receive either Letter B or Letter C, you can send those by bulk mail if
each one is exactly the same. In that case, use the salutation "Dear Friend."

Step 6. Determine the Number of Phones and Volunteers You Will Need.
To figure out the number of phones you will need, estimate that one person
can make about forty phone calls in an hour (although they will talk to no more
than fifteen people), and that people will call for no more than three hours. Therefore, one person can make about 120 calls in an evening (including calls to people
who aren't home) and fill out the appropriate follow-up letters and mailing
envelopes.

To get by with fewer phones, people can work in teams of two to a phone. In this
arrangement, as soon as one person has made a call and is filling in the appropriate

letter, the other person begins a call. This way the phone is always in use. Sometimes a phone team agrees that one person will do all the talking and the other will do all the writing. Phone teams can make about thirty calls an hour or fifteen per volunteer per hour. Since most people will not call for three hours straight, you will need one or two extra volunteers to make maximum use of the phones available.

Suppose you have six hundred names to call. If one person made all the calls it would take fifteen hours (six hundred calls at forty calls per hour). If each person has his or her own phone, five volunteers using four or five phones, along with one or two extra volunteers to spell people, will be able to get through the calls in one evening. In addition to the calling, allow two to three hours (or one or two extra volunteers) for stuffing envelopes, making sure all the needed information is recorded, and cleaning up.

You may wish to conduct the phone-a-thon over two nights. This has two advantages: You can call more people or use fewer volunteers, and you can call people on the second night who weren't home on the first night.

Step 7. Find a Place.   You will need one room or a suite of connected rooms with one or more telephones in each one. Depending on the number of telephones in your organization's office and the number of volunteers you have, you may have enough lines there. Real estate offices, travel agencies, law firms, large social service organizations, mail order businesses, and the like are good candidates to let you borrow their telephones for the evening. You will be trusted not to disrupt or take anything, to clean up before you leave, and in most cases to pay for any long distance calls.

Sometimes small organizations decide to conduct a phone-a-thon with volunteers working from their homes. Although there is nothing wrong with this method and just as many calls can be made, it is more fun and generates more momentum to have everyone in the same office. In addition, you will not be able to keep tabs on the volunteers and make sure that they are being assertive enough in their asking. In a group setting, successful calls or rude responses can elicit immediate praise or sympathy as appropriate. A group effort is also helpful in keeping track during the evening of how much is being pledged. (If you have to use individual homes, have at least two people at each home.)

Step 8. Recruit Volunteers.   Use the phone-a-thon as an opportunity to bring in some new volunteers. People who have limited time or who cannot volunteer during the day can often be recruited to work one evening on a phone-a-thon. It is a straightforward commitment for a short time period and does not require preparation outside of a training session during the hour before phoning begins.

THE NIGHT OF THE PHONE-A-THON

The person or committee planning the phone-a-thon should arrive at the place where the phoning will take place thirty minutes before everyone else. Be sure that desktops or tabletops where volunteers are to sit are cleared off so that your papers do not get mixed up with the papers of the person who uses that desk during the day. On each desk, put a stack of the three different letters, their enclosures, the return envelopes, the mailing envelopes, and a couple of pens. Put a list of names to be called, a stack of cards on which to record the calls, and a script by each phone.

Bring in juice, coffee, and snacks. Pizza, sandwiches, or other simple dinner food should be provided if volunteers are arriving at dinner time. The food should be kept in one part of the office, and volunteers should be discouraged from having food by their phones. Pay attention to details like bringing in napkins, plates, and eating utensils. In a borrowed space take out your own trash. Do not serve alcohol.

After all volunteers have arrived, been introduced to each other, and had a chance to eat, go through the phoning process step by step. Review the script and make sure people understand and feel comfortable with it. Review difficult questions they might receive and simulate a few phone calls (one from each of the response categories: yes, maybe, no). Be sure people understand the different letters, know what to write on each, what enclosures go with them, and what information needs to be noted on the cards.

Make people practice at least two times. Have them sit so they can't see each other (back-to-back works well) and go through the script, including ad libbing to questions their mock prospect asks. For a really good practice session, have people move to different rooms and call each other on their cell phones. This warming up is very important. It builds cohesion in the group and allows you, the coordinator, to make sure people are really going to ask. Take a few moments to get feedback on the exercise, which will probably have raised some additional questions beyond those you have already prepared people for.

You will need to decide whether volunteers are to leave a message on an answering machine or simply hang up. If you're going to send out a "Sorry we missed you" letter, you can instruct people to leave a brief message such as the following: "I wanted to talk with you about our work, but I'll send you some information instead. I hope you'll be able to help us." Be sure the message you leave is brief, since people only like to listen to long messages from new lovers or old friends.

After the orientation, each volunteer or phone team goes to a desk. The committee that has planned the phone-a-thon begins making calls immediately to set the tone and the pace. When a few people are on the phone, shy volunteers will feel better about beginning to call. Try to avoid a situation where everyone in the room is listening to one person's phone call unless that person feels comfortable with that role.

A staff person or a phone-a-thon committee member acts as a "floater." He or she answers questions and fields difficult phone calls. The floater also continually tallies how much money has been pledged and records the changing total on a large board visible to the group. (If people are calling from different locations, updated information can be sent frequently by e-mail or instant message.) The volunteers then change their scripts to reflect new totals.

Each individual should be encouraged to take breaks as they need to, but the group as a whole does not take any breaks.

At 9:00 P.M. stop the phoning and begin wrapping up. The first step in wrapping up is to finish addressing all envelopes and to gather up the cards of people phoned. Gather up any leftover forms, envelopes, letters, and return cards. Tally the final amount pledged and let the volunteers know how successful the evening has been. If the amount pledged is below your goal, explain that you set your goal too high. Do not let the volunteers leave feeling discouraged.

The callers should be able to leave by 9:30 P.M., leaving the planning committee to do any final cleanup.

AFTER THE PHONE-A-THON

Within two or three days, send all the volunteers a thank you note for their participation. If you borrowed a space to conduct the phone-a-thon, write the owner or manager a thank you note as well. Thank everyone for whatever they did to make the event a success.

During the next two weeks you should collect about 90 percent of the pledges made. As each one comes in, a thank you note should go out. At the end of two weeks, go through your list and identify anyone who said they would give but has not yet sent in their money. Send them a gentle reminder, like the one below, accompanied by a return envelope and a reply form. Most organizations do not find it worth the time and cost to remind people of their pledge more than once.

Reminder Letter

Dear _____,

This is just a note to remind you of your pledge to Good Organization made on the night of _____. In case you misplaced our letter and return envelope we enclose another. Thanks again for your pledge of $ _____.

Sincerely,
Name of volunteer

Generally, about 7 percent of people who pledge do not send money. (Some people's way of saying no is to say yes and not follow through.) If you have a higher loss than 7 percent, it may be that your volunteers noted someone as yes who only said she would think about it. Make sure volunteers understand how important it is to be accurate and that they need to hear what the prospect said, which may be different from what the caller wants to hear.

Tally up the final amounts received and write an evaluation of the event. The evaluation should note how many people were called, how many pledged, how many pledges were received, how many volunteers participated, where the phone-a-thon was held, who arranged for the space (if donated), and include copies of all the letters and return forms used. File all this away so that the next time you do a phone-a-thon you won't have to start from scratch.

GETTING PUBLICITY FOR YOUR PHONE-A-THON

A phone-a-thon may be a good time to generate some publicity for your group. Publicity can make the community more aware of your group's work and can alert listeners or readers to the fact that many of them will be receiving phone calls from your organization on a specific day or evening. The organization's address, phone number, and Web site address can be included in all publicity so that people can make their donation ahead of the phone-a-thon and avoid being called.

Unless you are on very good terms with press people, the phone-a-thon alone will not be a newsworthy event. Although radio stations or local newspapers may run a short press release or a public service announcement (PSA) describing the phone-a-thon, an article or an interview is unlikely to come out of the phone-a-thon alone. It would be best, therefore, to use the occasion of the phone-a-thon to emphasize a new program, tell a human interest story, or have some other newsworthy reason to get press attention in which you mention the phone-a-thon.

All of your publicity should emphasize the need for community support. Stress that your organization relies on the community for the bulk of its support—or wants to rely on the community if you don't now. Talk about what a gift of $35, $50, or $100 will do for the group so that people have a sense that a small gift can make a difference.

Use a Public Figure

One way groups have interested the press is by having one or two famous people participating in their phone-a-thon. "Famous people" include not only national celebrities but also people only well known in your community, such as the mayor, city council members, a well-respected community activist, the president of the community college, or a major corporate executive. The novelty that someone famous would help your organization lends credibility to your group. Also, almost everyone is flattered to be called by someone famous. If you decide to ask public figures to participate, be sure that they are well liked by your constituency.

Public figures can simply come for the first half-hour of your phone-a-thon and make a few calls without making an enormous time commitment to the event. It is an easy way for both you and them to gain goodwill while they show their support of nonprofit organizations and of the work of your organization in particular.

Court the Media

If you can't get any publicity through your press contacts, simply send a letter to the editor of the local paper. Be sure to send it in time for publication (particularly if you are dealing with a weekly paper). Many groups have found that letters to the editor are an effective way to get publicity for many issues. Again, give the address, Web site, and phone number of your organization and the date of the phone-a-thon.

If you do get any publicity (even a simple press mention or public service announcement aired), write or call press contacts with the results of the phone-a-thon and emphasize what a difference their publicity made. Include with your letter a press release or PSA announcing the success of the phone-a-thon and a statement of thanks to the community for being supportive. A letter to the editor is also a good way to follow up publicity. It is important to sound successful even if your phone-a-thon was not as successful as you had hoped.

There are drawbacks to extensive publicity that should be taken into account before seeking it. Publicity for a direct service organization may generate more clients than donors. One organization, whose purpose was to help people with work-related injuries get the benefits they deserve, got a full-page interview about their work and their upcoming phone-a-thon in the local paper. The night of the phone-a-thon, which was held at their office, volunteers were swamped with incoming calls from people needing the organization's help. The phone-a-thon was a financial failure, but the experience certainly demonstrated the need for this group's work.

A second disadvantage of publicity is that phone calls may keep coming in long after the phone-a-thon is over. If you gave your office number, your staff or daytime volunteers will need to respond to those calls in addition to doing their regular work. While handling the calls is not too time-consuming, making sure the right information goes out and keeping track of pledges and so forth can be.

If you have taken all these contingencies into account, publicity may turn a good phone-a-thon into a giant fundraising success.

OTHER USES OF THE PHONE-A-THON

There are three more common uses of the phone-a-thon technique: using the phone only to get prospects, following a mail appeal with a phone-a-thon, and using a phone-a-thon to renew lapsed donors.

Phoning for Prospects

This takeoff on a sales technique means phoning a large number of people, giving basic information about your organization, and asking if the person would like to know more. If the person says yes, he or she turns into a prospect. There is no attempt to solicit a gift at the time of the phone call. The purpose of the call is to create a hot list for later fundraising mail appeals.

During the telephone conversation the caller determines the degree of interest by asking the prospect some open-ended questions about what they know of the organization and whether they support its work. When interest is present, the prospect will be sent more information about the organization and a list of ways that they can help, including giving money. Some organizations use this opportunity to seek new volunteers, get support for or against a piece of legislation, or ask for items that the program needs (for example, a shelter might ask for food or clothing). A return envelope is included in the mailing.

This strategy does not raise money per se. Instead it acquires donors. The costs of phoning and of any mail and follow-up may well be only slightly less than the total amount received as gifts. Nevertheless, the organization now has a group of new donors, many of whom will renew the following year and may give in response to appeals during the current year.

This strategy is best for new groups that do not have an established constituency or for groups that have little name recognition even if they have existed for some time. It also works well for political organizations seeking to familiarize people with their candidate or their election issue.

The script and the training of volunteers for calling are different for this method than with an ordinary phone-a-thon. The purpose of the call is only to determine interest and to get permission to send more information. Therefore, the script would be something like the following example:

SCRIPT TO DETERMINE INTEREST

"Hello, I am Jane Smith, a volunteer with Shelter for the Homeless. I would like to talk to you for a minute, and I will not be asking you for money. Is this a good time?" *(Pause.)* "Thank you. I'll be brief. Have you heard of our program?" *(Pause.)*

If the answer is "No" or I don't know very much," continue: "Shelter for the Homeless is a thirty-bed facility for homeless single people and families. It also provides job counseling and referral, meals, and child care so that parents can look for work. Did you know that there are more than two thousand homeless people in our community and more arriving every day?" *(Pause.)* "We know that some people disagree with our approach or feel that some of the people using our services are freeloading, while many other people believe our program provides an important community service. What do you think?"

Generally, the answers fall into three categories:

- People who are basically in favor of your work

- People who like your program generally but have a specific objection to something about it

- People who feel that everyone should help themselves and that your program is undermining the moral fabric of the country

For answers in the first category, the caller in this example might say:

"I'm glad you feel that way. The shelter relies on community support for more than three-fourths of its budget, and it is good to know that members of the community like what we are doing. I wonder if I could send you a brochure and some other information about our services and about different ways that citizens can help us. There is no obligation and no one will call you afterwards, but you may find the information interesting." *(Pause for answer.)*

If the answer is yes, then verify the name and address, thank the person for his or her time, and say good night.

If the answer falls in the second category, the specific objection in this case might be something along this line: "I support the ideals of your program, but the problem is that more people move to our community because you are here. We can't continue to absorb people this fast."

The caller needs to agree with the prospect in some way in order to acknowledge that the prospect's objection is valid. In this case, the caller could say:

"It does seem that the more services that are provided the more people there are who need them and that it's an endless cycle." *(Pause.)* "But in our case it is interesting to know that no more people are moving here now than before we opened the shelter." *Or* "Communities with no services for homeless people are also finding their homeless population is growing. In fact, sometimes people who are out of work call us from other states and we are able to discourage them from moving here because our economy is so tight right now. Then they don't have to come and learn the hard way."

When a person's objection is acknowledged as valid and then corrected or new information is supplied, he or she usually becomes more receptive. If the person says something like, "I didn't know that," or "I am glad to hear that," ask if you can send him or her more information just as for prospects in category one.

In case of answers in the last category, simply say (and mean it), "I appreciate your candidness. It helps us to know why people don't like our program. Thanks for your time. Good night."

Training volunteers for this type of phone work is much more detailed. Volunteers must be able to listen, deal with difficult questions, and know when to give up. Each call will take longer than calls in a fundraising phone-a-thon. Callers must be clear that they are only calling to determine interest, not to convert people.

Callers should practice handling difficult questions and responding in depth, and they should familiarize themselves with many facts about the organization and the issues.

No list is needed for this phone-a-thon. The phone book can be used or you can do a random calling of any list of people. You can also use this strategy to determine the interest of people who give to an organization doing work in an entirely different arena from yours, but where there could be a connection. For example an AIDS-related service organization traded their list for a list of donors from several arts organizations and called them to determine their interest in the service organization. Because the arts community has been hard hit by the AIDS epidemic, there was a high level of interest and the arts group gained many new donors.

You may want to consider using professional telemarketers for this type of phoning. Although you will pay them, they are used to dealing with objections and can be counted on not to take people's comments personally. There are many reputable telemarketing firms, some of which specialize in phoning for nonprofits. Your organization may be too small for them to consider taking you on as a client, but they may have freelance people you could hire. You may also want to consider asking someone from such a firm to provide the training to your volunteers.

Phoning After a Mail Appeal

This method is quite straightforward. A mail appeal is sent to a list of prospects. After two weeks, all the prospects who have not sent money are called. The purpose of this method is to increase the return from the mail appeal.

The script is the only part that is slightly different from a regular fundraising phone-a-thon, in that a sentence is added such as, "I am Joe Reilly from the Greenbelt Project. We recently sent you a letter about our work. Did you have a chance to read it?" Depending on the answer, the rest of the script is the same as that described in the first section of this chapter. If the person has read the letter and seems in favor of your goals, skip right to the question, "Will you be able to help us with a gift of $____?"

You will not indicate in the original letter that the prospects will be called. You want as many people as possible to send in their gift without being called. Some organizations have successfully tried a variation on this method by telling prospects in a letter that they will be called unless the organization hears from them by a certain date prior to the phone-a-thon.

Phoning for Renewals

As discussed earlier, in average organizations about one-third of all members do not renew their donations from one year to the next. As a result, organizations spend most of their renewal budget trying to woo these recalcitrant members back into the fold. Usually, an organization will send the member two or three renewal letters one month apart, each notice firmer or more pleading than the one before.

The phone-a-thon can be used in place of either the second or third renewal notice. In addition to saving the cost of printing and postage, it provides a way to have much more personal contact with donors than is generally possible. Over time you will notice a cross section of your donors who respond more to being phoned than to mail. For those people, you may not send any renewal letter, but instead call them each year. (See also Chapter Twenty, Segmenting Donor Lists to Build Loyalty.)

Many organizations have renewal phone-a-thons twice a year. They find that although the response to a second or third renewal letter is 2 to 5 percent and sometimes less, the response to phoning is at least 10 percent and can be as high as 30 percent. These organizations are cutting their member losses by 5 percent or more. This guarantees that the organization will have at least a 66 percent renewal rate, and they may be able to add another 5 percent onto that.

A renewal phone-a-thon is almost exactly like a regular fundraising phone-a-thon. First, identify from your mailing list all the people whose memberships have expired within the last six months, or if your organization doesn't have members, those donors who have not given in thirteen or more months, not including those who have had less than a month to renew. (Unless your organization is in a terrible financial bind and you really need the money, a person will feel harassed if you call too soon after your first renewal notice is sent.)

Next, prepare the letters to thank people for renewing and to contact people who weren't home when you called, as discussed in the first section of this chapter. Both of these letters are brief. The point is to remind the member of his or her commitment to give; there is no need to convince the person of the worthiness of your organization. Each letter is accompanied by a return envelope and a return form (pledge card).

When volunteers call the lapsed donors, they will generally hear the following reasons for not renewing: out of work, forgot about it, thought they had renewed, didn't receive the renewal letter, or they were just about to renew and are glad you called.

It is important to believe whatever the member might say. A person who claims to have renewed although you have no record of receiving their renewal could be asked to produce a canceled check, but it is easier and more productive simply to take their word for it and reinstate them on the mailing list. Follow the adage, "The customer is always right."

When someone says that they no longer agree with the course you are taking or that they have a disagreement about a particular issue, ask them to explain. It may shed light on how the public perceives something you have done or you may be able to clear up a misunderstanding.

At the end of the phone-a-thon, make sure you have carefully sorted all the names into those who have renewed, those who requested to be taken off the mailing list, and those who were not home. Deal with complaints that same evening with a letter such as this:

Dear Mr. Upset,

We are sorry you have not received your newsletter for the past two years. At your request, here are all the back copies you have missed. We will enter your name on our mailing list for the next year as a complimentary member. Your past support means a lot to us, and again, we apologize.

As you can see, grassroots organizations can take advantage of fundraising by telephone. In addition to raising money, finding prospects, increasing renewal rates, and allowing an organization to have more personal contact with it donors, fundraising by telephone has an added advantage of teaching volunteers how to ask for money. The skills volunteers learn through phone-a-thons can then be put to use in major donor campaigns.

Using the Internet

The fastest-growing area of fundraising in the world is on the Internet. Online giving, using e-mail to keep in touch with donors and even to solicit donations, and organizational blogs and e-newsletters are in wide use. However, the Internet has also proved to be disappointing to a large number of grassroots organizations that saw visions of sugar plums if they only built a fancy Web site or started an e-newsletter. Although some organizations raise $100,000 or more every year online, dozens more report getting only a handful of new donors using the same technology. So what should a small, probably never-going-to-be-famous organization do with regard to the Internet and fundraising? How much should such a group invest and what kind of returns should they look for?

Although references to using the Internet occur throughout this book, this chapter focuses more specifically on using a Web site for fundraising. I must confess at the outset that, either by generation or temperament or both, I find the kind of communication that other (often younger) people take for granted—text messages, instant messaging, e-vites—still feels new to me and not that interesting. I find e-mail to be in equal parts helpful and bothersome. I'd rather pick up the phone than send an e-mail, I dislike instant messaging, and I have never sent a text message. My personal virtual preferences may provide a clue to those of many others and a warning not to assume universal familiarity or ease with the technology on the part of your donors.

There are two other considerations as well: first, everything in this chapter runs the risk of being outdated almost before the book is published; and second, there is a clear digital divide between large or high-profile nonprofits and small, grassroots nonprofits. Figuring out how much time and energy an organization with one or two beleaguered staff and an already highly involved group of volunteers should put into expanding their Web presence is tricky and will vary from organization to organization.

All that notwithstanding, I do recognize that there are wonderful opportunities on the Internet for fundraising, and every organization, regardless of how tiny or rural, can and should take advantage of what the Internet has to offer. Of course, as with all fundraising, anything you do on the Internet needs to be part of a larger plan, coordinated with all other communication, and integrated with your programs. That there are no stand-alone strategies is quite obvious with the Internet.

The advantages of the Internet are clear. More than sixty million Americans use e-mail every week, and about half that many surf the Web. Of the 80 percent of private-sector funding donated by individuals, giving through the Internet accounts for an exponentially increasing number of donations, particularly gifts in the $35 to $250 range. Some organizations report that gifts given over the Internet are larger than those given by direct mail. Giving online is growing by leaps and bounds; many Internet experts predict that as much as 40 percent of small donations will be made online within the next five years. Knowing how to attract, and more important, keep donors online is a new science and we learn more about how to do this every day. I encourage you to go online and see all the information that is available. (See Resource E, For Further Information, for a number of helpful Web sites and books about fundraising on the Internet.)

For many nonprofits, organizing and fundraising via the World Wide Web is tailor-made for a culture that increasingly expects everything to be available all the time. The Web is a 24/7 proposition (available twenty-four hours a day, seven days a week) that allows your organization to be "open" across time zones and international boundaries even when your office is not.

The digital divide between rich and poor decreases daily as corporate and individual donors make sure that libraries and schools are outfitted with the latest technology. Internet access at senior centers, community centers, and Internet cafes makes access to the Internet possible across all class, race, and age lines and means Internet access is almost universal. In fact, one of the fastest-growing populations of Internet users is senior citizens. The divide is far from over, however, and organizations serving poor and rural communities have a different experience—even of the use of e-mail—than organizations in larger communities.

THE ABSOLUTE NECESSITIES

To take advantage of the fundraising capabilities of the Internet, there are some things you must have: e-mail and high-speed service, your own domain name, and your own Web site.

E-Mail and High-Speed Service

The vast majority of even tiny nonprofits now have e-mail; if you don't have it, you need to get it. Not having e-mail puts you at almost the same disadvantage as not having a telephone. Further, you need to have high-speed Internet access rather than dial-up, unless high-speed access—via satellite, cable, or DSL—is not available in your community. The time you waste waiting to get online with a dial-up service costs you far more than the monthly cost of a high-speed service.

Your Own Domain Name

You also need your own domain name—that is, the name by which you are recognized on the Internet. A domain name costs between $100 and $150 per year and allows you to build a consistent brand and to promote the name of your organization. If for some reason the name of your organization is not available as a domain name, then use a phrase that will remind people of your work. "Youthforchange" or "Homesforall" or something close to your organization's name and message will work for a domain name.

Your Own Web Site

A Web site is almost as imperative as e-mail, but it needs to be conceptualized as part of your communications plan. Just to take some obvious examples, the logo on your Web site needs to be the same as the logo on your letterhead. Just as you think about the audience you are writing to in a direct mail appeal or who will come to your special event, you need to think about who is going to use your Web site and tailor it to that audience. Look at the Web sites of organizations that are similar to yours and see what they have done.

Don't try to save money by building a site cheaply or using someone to build the site who understands only the technology and not the marketing of Web sites. Hiring a Web designer is a good investment. Designing a Web site can cost almost any amount of money, but be prepared to spend at least $500. As you budget for it, think about what you get with a Web site—anyone in the whole world who has access to the Internet can now find out about your organization. Many people will never visit you in person; this will be their only impression of you.

A Web presence and Web strategy can easily cost $5,000 even for a small organization, so this is a project you might want to approach your major donors to underwrite. Many sophisticated donors understand the need for a high-quality Internet presence and will help you with an extra gift. Dropping unprofitable fundraising strategies and freeing up the money to focus on your Web site is another way to pay for it. Many groups have found the money for their site simply by eliminating people from their mailing list who have never donated or haven't made a gift in several years. One organization with a mailing list of ten thousand and a donor base of two thousand dropped five thousand names from their list after they figured out that it was costing them $2 per person per year to keep those nondonors on the list. They invested the $10,000 they saved into creating and maintaining what is now a successful Web site.

Of course, having a Web site is not like having a refrigerator or having a painting, where the initial investment is almost all the money you are going to spend. A Web site is actually more like the laundry—you no sooner catch up with the laundry than you are behind again. The site needs new content at least monthly, and it will need to be redesigned every few years. These are expenses you must plan for. Most small organizations find that having a talented freelance webmaster is the best solution. Some organizations have an in-house webmaster whose job is to maintain the organization's Web presence as well as manage other communications and publications.

Most organizations that I work with have a Web site, and in many cases their sites are pretty good. However, they are often lacking one critical detail, which is a "donate now" icon on the home page and on as many other pages as possible. The "donate now" button can take a user to a page that they download, fill out, and send in with a check the old-fashioned way. However, if you accept credit cards—and doing so is something you should explore—figure out how to have people become donors online using their credit card. One way to be able to accept credit cards is through a service such as Network for Good or Groundspring, nonprofits that exist to collect donations for other nonprofits and that can handle credit card donations and even pledges. If you anticipate a high enough volume or you sell products and services on your site as well as accept donations, you will want to explore having your own system.

DRIVING TRAFFIC TO YOUR SITE

Part of the planning for your site is determining who it is for and how you are going to get these people to visit it. This is called "driving traffic" to the site; it is the difference between a merely well-designed site and a successful one. There are literally billions of Web sites in the world, and some of the nicest ones remain unknown and unvisited because no one thinks to look for them. There are some simple and low-cost ways to drive traffic to your site.

Make sure your Web address is on everything you publish—your business cards, your e-mail signature, your letterhead, your newsletter (in several places, often as a footer on the bottom of each page)—and that it is part of your voice mail message and on any information you give out about your organization.

Register with all the key search engines: Yahoo, Google, and the like (find a list of current search engines at www.searchenginewatch.com). Further, ask your webmaster to make sure that your "meta tag" and "title"—two items hidden at the top of the code for your site—have as many relevant words as possible so that search engines can index your site. Get help thinking through the two- or three-word title for your organization that will show up in a Web search as a description of your organization and that you want people to click on to come to your Web site. For example, if I type your issue and the town I live in into Google or another search engine, your site should come up in the results, preferably at or near the top of the list. The three words that will be used in the sentence that describes your group need to be accurate and interesting so that I will want to click on them and go to your homepage.

Make sure that any directories of nonprofits, service providers, chambers of commerce, and so on list your Web site along with your postal address.

Link to other organizations and make sure they link to you. Make a list of organizations you would see as allies or as offering complementary information to yours and make sure that people can go to their sites from yours and vice-versa. Every so often visit related sites and see what they say about you.

E-mail is one of the best ways to get people to visit your site. A simple and easy thing to do is to gather as many e-mail addresses of donors as you can and send them an e-mail newsletter or e-mail alert each month or quarter. You can use this communication to announce new content on your site or to suggest action, about which they learn more details by going to your site from a link in the e-mail message.

As with all fundraising strategies, never promise on the front end what you can't deliver on the back end. If you say your e-newsletter is quarterly, it has to come out quarterly and not twice a year! I have signed up for more than a dozen e-newsletters and never gotten them. On the other hand, I am on lists of e-newsletters that I never signed up for. It does not make sense to add someone to your list who hasn't asked to be on it, and it really doesn't make sense not to add people when they have used your Web site to sign up. Be sure that "fulfillment"—the cost in time and money to fulfill promises made—is built into to all your planning.

USES OF E-MAIL

E-mail can be used in a variety of ways to help build and maintain a donor base, including e-newsletters, correspondence with donors, and keeping board members and volunteers up to date.

E-Mail Newsletters

Some organizations simply post their paper newsletter on their Web site. Other organizations have done away with paper newsletters altogether and only send e-newsletters. Neither of these decisions is proving to be wise. E-newsletters and paper newsletters are actually quite different. An e-newsletter is much shorter, both overall and in each story, than a printed newsletter. In an e-newsletter, you tell a short version of the story, then provide a hyperlink that takes readers to your Web site for more information. An e-mail newsletter generally emphasizes different information than your paper newsletter, and you hope some cross section of donors will read both. For these reasons, e-newsletters and paper newsletters need to be conceptualized as different forms of communication. Having only an e-newsletter can decrease your visibility to donors, since that kind of newsletter is far too easily deleted from a long list of e-mail.

VIRTUAL OR PAPER?

The *Grassroots Fundraising Journal,* a magazine I co-founded in 1981, is constantly looking for ways to save money in order not to have to increase subscription rates. One of our largest costs is printing and postage, so we mentioned in a regular "Letter from the Publisher" column that we were exploring moving the *Journal* from paper to an e-format. We asked readers to send us their reactions if they had any. Interestingly, we got more response to this possibility than to anything else we had ever published! Dozens of readers e-mailed or wrote in with their opinions. Only one person spoke in favor of going virtual and one other said she was willing to see the *Journal* move to a virtual format. Everyone else, many of whom identified themselves as "under thirty," asked, begged, and pleaded for us to stay in paper. Some wrote about when they read the *Journal:* "I read the *Journal* on the subway on the way to work." "I read the *Journal* sitting in the car waiting for my kids to come out of school in the afternoon." "I always take the *Journal* with me and read it whenever I am waiting for a meeting to start." Many others wrote about their relationship with computers: "I am on my computer all day and I do not want to have to read the *Journal* online." "I already spend a lot of time downloading and printing other stuff—you would just be pushing the cost of printing on to me." "I get so sick of being on the computer, and the *Journal* is something I can take outside on my lunch hour." Some readers even offered to pay a higher subscription rate to keep the *Journal* in paper (the solution we actually successfully moved to). To me, this was a lesson in the value of asking your constituents what they think and also in the fact that communicating on paper is far from over, even in this high-tech age.

E-mail is especially effective for posting information alerts or calls to action—anything that requires an instant response. And unlike paper, to send one hundred thousand messages by e-mail costs no more than sending one or one hundred.

Corresponding with Donors

You can also use e-mail to correspond with donors (although do not use it as the only way you send thank you notes). When you leave a message for a donor on the phone, leave both your phone number and your e-mail address as a way to get back to you. There are more and more instances of an entire solicitation being done online, with a commitment to a gift given by e-mail. E-mail can be used in the place of an introductory postal letter—in fact it can be used most places where you might have used postal mail, with one caveat: it is still worth the personal touch to send handwritten (if possible) thank you notes through the postal mail (for more on thanking people, see Chapter Seventeen).

E-mail is a great way to send short notes to major donors during the year, keeping them posted on things you think they would find of interest. The savings in dollars and time of maintaining relationships by e-mail is one of its great benefits.

Working with the Board and Volunteers

E-mail is an excellent way to keep board members and volunteers posted on internal happenings that would be interesting to them but would not go in a general newsletter. Many groups use e-mail to encourage board member efforts in fundraising with notes like this: "Update on Major Donor Campaign. Eric Johnson just concluded a request for $1,000 and the donor is sending it today. He is following up with three other prospects. Martha was finally able to set up a meeting with the two donors who may give us $10,000 on Tuesday. Keep your fingers crossed. Earlyse is the leader in number of gifts so far—five at $250 and four at $100! Good work, everyone!"

Some organizations have created an internal listserv of board and staff members, enabling any of them to post information to the group. Some organizations have a member listserv, where any member can ask a question, give advice, or announce upcoming events. This feature is particularly useful in coalitions or associations of several organizations. In this situation, someone needs to moderate the listserv to make sure that one or two people don't dominate or that the content stays focused.

Some organizations are also taking advantage of blogging, a form of communication that was originally a personal posting of a diary or a journal (known as a Web log). Most of us are familiar with blogs that are sent by friends who are traveling to fun and interesting places or are having some other kinds of adventures they want to share with a number of people and are willing to have read by anyone who comes across the blog. Executive directors, board chairs, and sometimes program staff are now starting blogs reflecting on various aspects of their work and their personal feelings and thoughts about it. Blogs can come out as frequently or infrequently as the person wants, as they don't carry the expectation of regularity that a newsletter implies. Further, a blog can contain much more emotional content and often creates a different and sometimes deeper relationship with readers than a newsletter. People can respond to blogs, so they also can be a way of testing an idea.

RECEIVING DONATIONS AND PAYMENT ONLINE

There are two ways to receive donations online: by creating a secure area on your Web site where people can make donations or purchases, or by using a charity portal to handle payment transactions for you.

Creating a Secure Area

If your organization already has the capacity to accept donations via credit cards and electronic fund transfers, and you have items for sale or you can expect to receive a number of donations through your Web site, you will want to have a "secured area" on your site where people can key in their credit card number to donate or buy online with the assurance that their transaction is safe (by being encrypted before it is transmitted).

Many organizations have found receiving donations or making sales this way to be extremely lucrative, but it also adds a layer of work. Someone has to download the orders and fill them. The site has to be programmed to send an automated reply message acknowledging the order or donation. Credit card numbers have to be processed. All of this work will be worth it as the site gets more traffic and more donations come in, but there is an initial investment that may take a while to pay off.

Charity Portals

Another way to receive donations or fees for goods is by using what's known as a charity portal. These are Web sites run by both for-profit and nonprofit groups that list a variety of charities on a site, with a description of each charity and a way to donate to each one. The theory is that there are people wanting to give money who do not have a way to find groups that meet their values. These people would go to a charity portal, look under "children," or "environment," or whatever they care most about and find names and descriptions of groups they can give to. When they donate, the sponsor of the portal takes a small percentage of the donation and sends the rest to the specified charity. Some portals are designed to let people buy products, then donate a portion of the sale to a charity.

If you decide to register your group with a portal, try to choose one that is itself a nonprofit. A nonprofit portal is less likely to advertise to your donors or to sell information they have gleaned about your donors to other advertisers. Make sure you know what you get from being registered and what the costs are. Also, make sure you will be sent the names and addresses of the donors and not just the money the donors sent. Some donors have been disgruntled to learn that the charity they chose never knew who they were, but that their name was sold to other Internet companies or catalog companies wanting to expand their pool of potential customers.

Remember that above all, you want people coming to your Web site, where they can be invited to make a donation. Anything you do, including being listed on another site, needs to lead to that end.

NO MIRACLE, BUT ANOTHER STRATEGY TO EXPLORE

The Internet is neither a miracle cure to your fundraising problems nor something to be suspicious of. It is simply another strategy. It appeals to a younger, generally well-educated and possibly affluent group of people. It appeals to people who feel that they have little or no time. Through search engines, it allows people who may have never heard of your group to find out about it. The Internet can be used to build a certain kind of feeling of belonging on the part of people who may never make it to your office or to an event you put on.

Using the Internet effectively requires an ongoing investment of time and money. For organizations that make that investment and don't try to short-circuit the process, it can be worth the effort.

Establishing Voluntary Fees for Service

The director of a program serving seniors in a small industrial city in Michigan described his experience in starting a fee-for-service income stream. His organization provides a wide range of services to people sixty-five and older, including Meals on Wheels; transportation to medical appointments; help with doing taxes or dealing with Social Security, Medicare, and private insurance; leisure activities in a community center as well as field trips; and help with aging parents. All of these services had been free. The agency's $750,000 budget was mostly provided by United Way, grants from the city and county, and some foundation grants. The director was very good about writing proposals, submitting reports, and maintaining relationships with those funders. A small percentage of the budget—about $15,000—came from individuals, but there was no real system in place to acquire or renew these gifts.

Five years ago, the city entered into a state of decline, with high unemployment and a low priority on senior services. During that time, the city first cut and then completely withdrew its funding for the senior program. The United Way also cut their contributions by half, with further cuts expected. Reluctantly, the senior service program director created a free-will donation system to encourage those who used the service to contribute toward its cost. He posted a large sign in the community center:

The Cost of Providing Services

One delivery of a meal (Meals on Wheels)	$7.00
One trip to and from a medical appointment	$5.00
Support group counselor (per person)	$7.00
Private counseling (per hour)	$40.00
Lunch at the community center	$5.00
Field trips per person per day	$10.00
Magazine subscriptions (average)	$15.00
Books and DVDs for the library (average)	$12.00
Internet access (per day)	$5.00
New games for the game room (average)	$15.00

Any amount you can pay toward these services is gratefully accepted and will be put right to work.

Thank you.

This same announcement now appears in the program's newsletter, on its Web site, and on a sign in their van. No one actually asks for money. To donate, one has to be able to read the sign, then put money in a box, hand it to the person in charge, or give online.

Over the past three years, this director reports, there has been a 300 percent increase in the number of people using the various services the center provides. Puzzled, he has investigated. Has the town's senior population tripled? No. Are three times as many seniors falling into need for these services? No. Finally, he surveyed center users about what brought them to the center, how they found out about it, and what they liked about it. Among other things, he learned that people liked being able to pay for the service. Several people made comments to that effect:

"I never used this place before because I don't like taking things for free. I am not so poor to need free service. I can pay my own way."

"I can take care of myself pretty good and I don't need handouts. I've worked hard all my life. I like coming to the center and seeing people, and the prices are affordable. Sometimes I put in a little extra for someone who isn't as well off."

The experience of this organization is repeated over and over again as organizations, forced to start suggesting donations to their clients, discover that many of the clients prefer to pay. More and more organizations are realizing that giving services away to people perpetuates a patronizing and condescending system in which some people are seen as needy and others as those who meet needs. Further, when clients pay what they can, they feel empowered to demand better services or to ask questions of their service provider. These reactions strengthen the organization providing the service, as they begin to get accurate feedback on their work. From a fundraising viewpoint, fees can also provide an income stream that helps keep an organization afloat.

Many nonprofit organizations have mandatory fees. They charge below the "market rate" for their service, but in order to get the service, one has to pay a fixed price or a fee determined by some criteria, such as income or reimbursement from insurance. Health clubs, counseling services, job training and placement services, public swimming pools and recreation areas, national and state parks—many of these have mandatory fees.

This chapter discusses how organizations that have traditionally provided free services and wish to charge voluntary fees can determine those fees and collect them.

VOLUNTARY FEES

You can charge voluntary fees in one of two ways: you can still provide services for free but request money to help cover the cost, or you can ask that people pay an amount they choose for the service, with whatever they pay being acceptable.

Which system you use depends on the nature of your clients. Organizations serving the homeless will probably not require a contribution. Cultural organizations, groups serving the working poor, mental health providers, and so on may opt to require some payment.

You can also mix the two methods. For example, one homeless shelter provides shelter, showers, and clothing for free and does not attempt to charge. But they have a suggested voluntary donation of $0.50 for meals and a mandatory processing fee of $10 for job placement (collected after the person has received their first paycheck). This agency now receives donations from clients for almost 70 percent of their meals served, with many people giving $1, and a collection rate of 80 percent on their job fee.

Museums, theaters, and other cultural facilities will often have a mandatory fee, but their schedule will also include a day or evening when admission is free or they may waive the fee to a resident of the city or someone under sixteen years old or a senior. Corporations will sometimes underwrite a day at an art museum or the botanical garden in exchange for good publicity. The group then advertises that its facility is free to everyone on that day.

STAYING LEGAL

Charging fees is not illegal, but if you are asking for donations rather than fees, they must be perceived as voluntary by the client for you to be true to your nonprofit status. No coercive measures can be used to collect voluntary fees. A coercive action would be one that makes a person feel the service was not really free, that he or she was the only one asking for free service, or some other method of seeming to intimidate a person into paying something or more than they want to. Behavior that is coercive can be a matter of perception, but any obviously coercive actions need to be avoided.

Here's an example: one free-meal program separated those who had given a donation from those who had not, with those who contributed placed at tables with tablecloths and given dessert. In another instance, admission to a class on how to prepare for job interviews was free, but the person registering people loudly announced each donation that was given so that someone sitting across from her could record it. Although thoughtless and probably unintentional, this practice caused some who had intended to take the course for free or even for a low price to pay more than they had wanted to; others simply left before reaching the registration table.

People tend to be embarrassed by any practice that makes them feel as though they don't have enough money. Any system that can embarrass someone may cause them to feel pressured to pay more than they want to or can afford; at that point the voluntary fee is no longer truly voluntary. (Ironically, as the story that opened this chapter showed, this same embarrassment can arise from an agency insisting on providing service for free to those who want to pay something, which can also keep people from seeking services they need.)

The second legal obligation is that your fee, whether voluntary or mandatory, be well below what a for-profit business would charge for the same or a similar service.

SETTING THE FEES

There are several ways to set your fees. The least effective, judged by the amount of money raised, but least intrusive is to post a sign near a collection box that simply reads, "Donations," or "Donations welcome," or "Your gift ensures that we can continue to provide this service to others. Thank you." You will tend to get only people's spare change; however, you will never be accused of forcing someone to give, and this can be a good way to introduce the idea of giving to your clients.

If all your services cost about the same amount, you may want to suggest a range for the voluntary contribution. You could post a sign that said, "The cost of providing our services ranges from $10 to $25. Any amount you can pay will ensure that we can continue to provide these services to all who need them. Thank you." If you want, you can add an explanation, "The budget for the services you are receiving was previously provided by the government (or United Way or foundations), but these funds have been cut back. To make sure that we can continue to help people, we are asking all our clients to give what they can. Thank you."

The most effective system is one similar to that used by the senior center described in the beginning of this chapter. A wide range of costs was established, and people could donate toward only the service they had used. Just as when fundraising from individuals, asking for a specific amount rather than leaving the amount up to the prospect will result in more people giving something, so suggesting specific amounts for services rendered will bring more donations overall and will show that you are serious about raising money and know what you are doing.

Most service providers have someone who staffs a desk by the front door. This person should be trained to ask for money, particularly if any of your clients cannot read a posted sign. The front-desk person adds to whatever they would normally tell people, "The service is free, but if you want to make a donation, that helps us keep our doors open. The donation box is over there." Many clients will ask if there is a charge, which makes it easier to explain. For clients accustomed to getting the service for free, explain that you are still providing it for free but that you are asking people who can help to do so. If you hand out literature to your clients, include a card explaining your need and a return envelope. They can drop the envelope in the box provided or send it later. When introducing voluntary fees, err on the side of being too low key rather than too assertive. Over time, as people have a chance to think about it and talk to each other, they will start to give more money.

INTRODUCING THE PROCESS OF COLLECTING FEES

At first, volunteers and staff are often uncomfortable with the process of asking clients for money, regardless of what process you use. In discussing the move to asking for money, validate everybody's feelings: Yes, it is difficult to ask for money, and it may be more difficult to ask people who have very little. It would be a much better world if people did not have to pay for things to which they are entitled—housing, health care, education, or food—and did not have to feel embarrassed about receiving these necessities. Next, place the new policy in context: Your organization has to keep on providing services, and your costs are going up while your ability to get government (and possibly other) grants is probably going down. Your clients would much rather you exist than watch you go out of business. They will help if they can and will feel good about helping.

Once everyone has a few experiences of asking for money and seeing people feel good about giving, their initial discomfort will go away.

WHEN SERVICE IS PROVIDED BY PHONE

So far, we have concentrated on organizations that can collect fees at the door or at the time of service. But what if your way of providing service is by telephone or by mailing information? Your organization has a harder task. Certainly, you cannot ask someone calling a crisis hotline for a donation once they have calmed down. Voluntary contributions for service will not be possible in those cases. However, if your information is not crisis-related, after you are finished giving it ask if you can send more information about your organization and how it is supported. With the information include a letter asking for a donation and a return envelope. Refer all such callers to your Web site as well.

If your service includes mailing information to people, include a card and return envelope. The card should tell how your group is supported and ask the person to return the envelope with a donation as soon as possible. A card is more effective than a letter because the letter may get put aside while the person is looking at the other information you sent. However, they will be inclined to put the card with the return envelope and respond once they have determined that your information is useful. You may also wish to use a wallet-style envelope where the outside flap serves as the reply card (see Chapter Eleven for more on reply devices).

Make sure your Web site has several obvious icons that ask people to donate. People visiting your Web site may well not be people in need, and their capacity to give may be much higher than that of your clients.

Setting up a voluntary system for collecting money from clients will create a steady income for you, and the amount may be larger than you think. Further, the system may inspire people who are not clients to give. Many times volunteers are just as uninformed about how your organization is supported as are clients. Once educated, volunteers often give regularly. In the case of the senior program in Michigan, several seniors asked their grown children for help. This led to a number of major and corporate gifts and generated a lot of in-kind support in the form of computers, DVDs, and more volunteers. Finally, you may even get more clients, which will serve your broader mission.

Door-to-Door Canvassing

Canvassing is a technique that involves a team of people from your organization going door-to-door or standing on the street requesting contributions for your organization's work. The canvassing technique is used primarily by local groups and by local chapters of state or national organizations. Canvassing is primarily an organizing strategy; no organization should undertake a canvass simply to raise money. Canvasses work best when the organization is doing work that directly affects the people being canvassed. Canvassing is often used in relation to political campaigns to get out the vote or to drum up support for a candidate or issue. Used in the context of organizing, canvassing can be an excellent strategy for acquiring new donors; by returning to neighborhoods, it can also be used for retaining donors.

There are two kinds of canvass: a door-to-door canvass and the increasingly common street canvass. (Many of the techniques discussed in this chapter can be applied to a phone canvass, which can be conducted using the principles of a phone-a-thon described in Chapter Twelve.) Door-to-door canvasses and street canvasses are similar both in terms of advantages and disadvantages and in terms of organization. This chapter primarily focuses on door-to-door canvassing because it has the greater potential to acquire donors who can then be renewed and upgraded.

Although part-time or temporary canvasses can be run with volunteers, most canvassing is a full-time operation involving salaried or commissioned employees who work forty hours a week and solicit in commercial districts or residential neighborhoods on a regular, revolving basis. Well-run canvasses can bring in from $50,000 to $500,000 or more in gross income annually. However, they are labor-intensive and generate high overhead that absorbs between 60 percent and 80 percent of the gross earnings of most canvasses.

ADVANTAGES AND DISADVANTAGES

There are three main advantages to canvassing as a fundraising strategy. First, an established, well-run canvass can provide a reliable, and sometimes significant, source of income for your organization. Second, the volume of personal interaction from face-to-face contact with dozens of people each day can bring as many new members as any other high-volume strategy. Third, canvassers bring back to the organization the public's opinions and perceptions of what the organization is doing.

There are also disadvantages to a canvass. If it is done on a full-time basis, it requires separate staff and office space as well as extensive bookkeeping and supervision. As with a small business, canvass income can be unreliable if the top canvass staff is not well organized or not good at managing a staff or if too many canvasses are operating in an area. The canvassers themselves can give the organization a bad reputation if they are unkempt, rude, or unpleasant to the people being canvassed. A final disadvantage is that many donors do not like to give to organizations that use canvassing because they know that much of their donation is going to support the high overhead costs.

ELEMENTS NEEDED TO RUN A CANVASS

Four elements must be present for an organization to operate an effective canvass. First, and most important, the organization must work on local issues or issues that affect the people being canvassed. People give at the door or stop and visit with someone on the street when they perceive that an issue affects them. The work of your organization can have national impact and your organization might be a branch of a national group, but especially in door-to-door canvassing, you must explain how this issue affects the resident directly.

Second, people must feel that even a small donation will make a difference. Many people make a cash donation to a canvass, but even those who give with a check or credit card will rarely give more than $100. People must feel that their small donation is needed and will be well used.

Third, people must feel confident about your organization. Their confidence will be inspired by your organization's accomplishments, which must be clear and easy to discuss. Newspaper articles about your work are a major boon to canvassing. A specific plan of action that can be explained simply and quickly and that sounds effective is essential. Some organizations' work lends itself naturally to canvassing because it is on issues of general importance and interest to the majority of people, such as health care for all, lower utility rates, or fixing up public parks. Canvassing on behalf of litigation can work if the suit is easy to understand and if there is a clear "good guy" (your group) and "bad guy." Complex regulatory reform or issues requiring historical background, legal knowledge, or patience in listening to a long explanation do not lend themselves to canvassing.

Finally, you must be able to distinguish your organization from any other organization doing similar work without implying any disrespect for the other organization. In some communities where there are not only two or more organizations working on similar issues but also several organizations canvassing, potential donors get confused and then angry that they are being solicited so often for issues that seem interrelated. People will explain to your canvassers that they just gave to your group last week, that someone from your organization was just there. No amount of protest from you will change their minds. The only thing that will help is to distinguish your group clearly from any other.

All these requirements for a successful canvass, except the focus on local work, are also necessary for many other fundraising strategies, particularly mail appeals and phone-a-thons, where the object is to get the donor's attention quickly and hold it long enough to get the gift.

SETTING UP A CANVASS

First, check state and local laws and ordinances concerning canvassing. If canvassing is heavily regulated in your community, it may not be worth the time involved to comply with the regulations. Some communities have tried to stop canvassing operations altogether by enacting ordinances governing what you can say when soliciting door-to-door and establishing strict qualifications for canvassers, including expensive licensing. Being able to canvass on a busy street may be regulated differently from a door-to-door canvass. If your canvass violates even a minor subregulation, city or state authorities could force it to cease operation and the episode may bring bad press for your organization. Many of these ordinances have been challenged in court and found unconstitutional, but most organizations have too much work to do to take on costly and lengthy legal battles in this area.

You can find out about state laws governing canvassing from your state attorney general's office, which is usually the office that monitors all rules related to charitable solicitation. Many states publish handbooks on canvassing regulations.

Local ordinances are sometimes more difficult to discover, as several city departments may have jurisdiction over different parts of the canvassing operation. Contact the police department and ask for notification and application procedures for a canvass. Be sure to write down whatever the person tells you and get his or her name so that if you get a different story from another police official you can refer to the initial phone call.

Contact the city attorney's office for information regarding solicitation of money for charity. Sometimes the mayor's office has some jurisdiction over these matters. In general, informing as many people in official capacities as possible about your canvassing operation will ensure the least amount of interference later.

Study the Demographics

After making sure that you can comply with the law, you must determine if your community is a good candidate for a canvass. Gather demographic data on your area: for various neighborhoods, find out the population density, the property values, how many of the people are homeowners, what type of work most people do, what the income levels are, and so forth. This information is available from various sources, including the census, items in the newspaper, volunteers and board members who have lived in the area, the chamber of commerce, and from developing your own sense from driving around the neighborhoods.

Remember one important point in assessing demographic data: a canvass rarely does well in an affluent neighborhood, and canvassers sometimes conclude that "rich people" are unfeeling tightwads. It's true that affluent people generally do not make contributions at the door. Their charitable giving is usually done in response to major gift solicitation, personal mail appeals, or special events. Canvassing operations do best in middle- and lower-income neighborhoods, where giving at the door is more common.

Another demographic item you need to evaluate is whether the population is dense enough per square mile to make it worthwhile to canvass. Canvassers need to be able to reach eighty to one hundred homes per night (assuming a high number of people not home). This means that there must be enough people in the area and that the terrain must be flat enough to allow canvassers to walk quickly from house to house. It is much harder to run a successful canvass in a rural area simply because of the distance between houses and the lack of people.

Finally, you need to evaluate whether the area is safe for canvassers. A good canvasser may be carrying $500 or more by the end of the evening, much of that in cash. Canvasses in high-crime areas (which still can be successful) sometimes send their canvassers in pairs, but this doubles the labor cost. Others have a roving car to check in on canvassers and to pick up their cash.

Hire Staff

If you determine that your area can support a canvass, you are ready to hire canvass staff and prepare materials for them. The staff of a canvass varies from place to place but typically includes several individuals and the following roles.

Canvass Director. This person supervises the entire canvass operation, including hiring and firing canvassers, researching areas to be canvassed and mapping out the revolving canvass for the area over the course of a year, keeping the organization in compliance with the law, keeping up to date on new laws, and planning and updating materials.

Field Manager(s). Each of these staff people transports and supervises a team of five to seven canvassers. Each field manager assigns their team to various parts of the neighborhood, collects the money at the end of the evening, and trains new canvassers on the team. This person also participates as a canvasser at the site.

Support Person. The support person serves as secretary, receptionist, bookkeeper, and office manager. She or he keeps records of money earned by each canvasser, replaces canvass materials as needed, schedules interviews with prospective canvassers for the canvass director, answers the phone, and generally acts as backup person for the canvass operation. This person does not canvass.

Canvassers. These are the people actually carrying out the canvass. Canvassers work from 2 P.M. to 10 P.M. five days a week. They usually have a quota—that is, an amount of money they must raise every day or every week. Their pay is either a percentage of what they raise (commission), a straight salary, or most commonly, a base salary plus commission.

Canvassers must represent the organization accurately and be respectable ambassadors for it. The individual canvasser is often the only person from the organization whom donors will see and may well be the only face a donor will ever associate with your group.

Because the pay is low and the hours long and arduous, there is a high turnover in canvass staff. In the summer, college students help expand canvassing staff. In the winter months, recruiting canvassers is more difficult, and in places where there is low unemployment, recruiting canvass staff can be almost impossible.

Develop Materials

Canvassers must be equipped with various materials. These include any identification badges or licenses required by the city or state, clipboards to carry the materials to be given away—brochures about the organization, return envelopes, and newspaper clippings about the work of the group—and a receipt book.

Many canvassers use a petition to get the attention of the person being canvassed. The canvasser asks, "Would you sign a petition for . . ." and briefly explains the cause. While the person is signing, the canvasser asks for a donation as well.

Canvassers should try to get the gift right at the door. However, for people who need to think about whether to give or discuss it with a partner or spouse, the canvasser can leave a brochure and a return envelope. A brochure should also be given to people making a donation because some of them will send an additional donation after reading it. Canvassers should not assume when people say they need to think about your request that they mean they are not going to give. This is a common mistake. The canvasser should leave the materials and act as if they believe the person. Many people do not make decisions on the spur of the moment, and people who need to think about what their gift will be to your group may well become major donors.

All of the information is carried on a clipboard, which makes it easy to display and lends a degree of authority to the canvasser. People are more likely to open their doors to someone who looks like he or she has a good reason to be there.

The Canvasser's Work Day

At the beginning of the canvassers' work day, their field manager describes the neighborhood they will be canvassing and relates any new information or special emphasis on issues that they should present to this neighborhood. The crew has a late lunch or early dinner and the field manager drives them to the canvass site. They begin canvassing around 4 P.M. and end at 9 P.M., when they are picked up by their field manager and taken back to the office. They turn in their money, make their reports, and finish around 10 P.M.

Because canvassing is hard work, essentially involving daily face-to-face solicitation with a "cold" list, it is critical that the rest of the organization's staff and its board members see the canvass staff as colleagues and as integral to the total operation of the organization. To help build this support, many organizations require noncanvass staff to canvass for an evening every couple of months.

Second only to quality of canvass staff in ensuring the success of a canvass is an efficient record-keeping system. After each neighborhood is canvassed, an evaluation of the neighborhood should be filed along with the demographic data on that neighborhood that led to its being chosen as a canvass site. These data can then be reevaluated in light of the canvassers' experience. Any special considerations, such as "no street lights," can also be noted in the evaluation.

Many people worry that theft by the canvassers will be a problem. Theft occurs no more often by canvass workers than by any others. Careless bookkeeping, however, can cost money and can give the impression that money has disappeared. At the end of the evening, both the canvasser and the field manager should count each canvasser's money brought in. The field manager enters the amounts under each canvasser's name on a "Daily Summary Sheet." The money and the summary sheet are then placed in a locked safe, and the secretary or bookkeeper will count the total again in the morning and make a daily deposit to the bank. At the end of the week, the bookkeeper tallies the total receipt of each canvasser and prepares the payroll.

Canvassers who fail to bring in their quota for more than a week must be retrained or fired. Strict discipline is important in a successful canvass; keeping performance records will help to maintain a good canvass team.

Canvassing is an excellent strategy for some groups; if done properly it can be a good way to mobilize members and make money. However, there are many pitfalls, and it is neither a simple nor a low-cost strategy. Canvassing changes the nature of the organization. It doubles or triples staff size and requires office space and additional equipment. Only organizations that have thoroughly researched the pros and cons of canvassing should consider using this fundraising method.

Opportunistic Fundraising

I lived in Appalachia for a number of years, and an expression I would hear often in response to a question about when something was going to be done was, "I'm fixin' to do that." This could mean the person was just about to do the task in question, the person was going to get to it later, or the person had no intention of ever getting to it. The actual meaning had to be inferred from body language, knowledge of the person, and knowledge of the difficulty of the task. Many of the people I meet are "fixin' to" fundraise: some will get to it by this afternoon, some by next month, and some never.

One thing that will help you if you really want to raise more money is to do a thorough inventory of all the work you do now and see how fundraising could easily be built into it. This is called "opportunistic fundraising," which simply means taking advantage of a situation you are in anyway. This kind of fundraising doesn't take extra time and doesn't require a lot of planning ahead. But it does require an awareness and sensitivity to the opportunities that present themselves.

Let's look at a couple of weeks in the life of an advocacy organization working on reproductive rights.

Sunday.   Volunteers from the advocacy organization are stationed at various locations around a community: outside of five grocery stores, near the doors of three liberal Protestant churches, and near a coffee shop in the middle of a large shopping mall. Their intent is to inform people that the local school board has eliminated sex education in the schools, although the only mention of sex will be in the context of abstinence. Their literature contains information about the poor results of "abstinence-only" education elsewhere, with evidence of higher rates of teen pregnancy and sexually transmitted disease than before the policy was implemented. They ask people to sign up for an e-alert for more information and to come to school board meetings when the issue is being discussed. They also suggest that parents or teachers bring the issue up in their local PTA and they show people samples of a kit with fact sheets and suggested actions to get the school board to reverse this decision and give people a card with a Web site address where they can download a copy of the kit. They have placed themselves in zip codes where the vast majority of people will agree with them. They want to focus on education, not fundraising, so they don't ask people to become members of the advocacy organization and they don't have a jar out at any of their locations to collect money.

Here is what they find: Although many of the people coming out of the grocery store and churches either don't have children or have grown children and many of those at the mall are teenagers, the volunteers are able to recruit a number of parents and teachers to sign up for the e-alert. Most interesting, however, is that over and over they hear this refrain: "I'd be happy to contribute some money," or "How can I become a member of your organization?" or "Is there anything I can do if I don't have kids in the school system?" The teenagers have a different refrain, "This policy is so messed up" and "My mom says it's stupid." One suggests to her friends, "Maybe we could do a car wash or something to help raise money."

Monday.   Talking over the experience from Sunday's efforts, they conclude that although they met their goals for talking to parents and teachers, they missed a great opportunity to involve a lot of other people, particularly those whose involvement would mean making a donation. They decide to revise their tactics for the following weekend.

The Next Sunday.   Once again the organization's volunteers spread out around the community with the same literature, but today they also have membership forms, a jar for collecting donations, and business-size cards that give people their Web site address and information about membership. The mall volunteers, using the wireless capacity of the coffee shop, set up a laptop computer and a printer so that people can look at their Web site and if they want, print out the free, downloadable information or join online. The group has also prepared a special handout for teenagers.

This Sunday, they sign up thirty members at $35 each, are given two checks for $100 each, and later download the names of ten new people who joined online. In addition, their jars have collected nearly $200. With only slightly more work, they continued their educational and advocacy push, but this week they also raised more than $1,500.

Tuesday.   The executive director of the reproductive rights group attends a lunch meeting of the chamber of commerce. She has joined the chamber to take advantage of some of the educational opportunities they provide and to give her organization more visibility in the small-business community. At lunch, the owner of an office supply store comes over and wishes her luck in all the important work her organization is doing. He hands her his card and says, "If there is any way I can help you, let me know." She calls him later and asks for two things: "Can our volunteers set up their information station in front of your store this Wednesday, and would you consider donating or deeply discounting office supplies for us?" She adds the second half of the question based on her experience on Sunday. Yes to both, he says. A 50 percent discount on office supplies for a year saves the organization more than $2,000.

Thursday.   The public policy director of the reproductive rights group meets with staff from a number of other organizations concerned in one way or another with reproductive rights issues. Some work in social service agencies, others in education, and others are also involved in advocacy. The purpose of the meeting is to prepare a joint statement to the press on the school board issue and to compare notes on their other work.

All the organizations are feeling stressed about money. "Is there anything we can do together to help all our fundraising that won't take much time?" someone asks. Ideas are bandied about, but the simplest one is for each organization to make sure their Web site is linked to all the other organizations' sites. They also decide that each organization will add a link on its homepage to a description of each of the other organizations at the meeting, highlighting their work on reproductive rights. Each group contributes three sentences about themselves and one group's webmaster formats these for posting on each site. There is no clear income from this action, but each group now has heightened visibility for very little work.

(Months later, a foundation program officer sees this joint effort and thinks it is a great example of working collaboratively. He proposes that these groups apply for a small grant to fund a weekend retreat to explore more collaborative options.)

Friday Night. The development director meets friends for dinner and a movie. One friend says her mother saw the volunteers from this organization outside of her church but didn't have time to stop. Does the development director have anything with her she could give her mother? Of course she does: she has the business cards created for last Sunday's work and she hands one to each of her friends. By the following Tuesday she has a check from her friend's mother for $500.

Find Your Own Opportunities

It is true that organizations working on immediate and hot-button issues will be able to generate cash in the moment, but every organization has opportunities for fundraising every day that they fail to take advantage of. Doing an audit of your day will reveal these opportunities.

Review the opportunities that might arise for your group in each of the following typical daily events.

Communicating with People. Most organizations communicate with people on the phone, in person, or by e-mail every day. Certainly, most conversations cannot include a fundraising component, but many more could than presently do.

In Person. Anyone talking with people about your group (and that probably includes everyone who has any role in your group, including board and staff members, volunteers, even other members) could hand someone they're talking to a generic business card for your group that would contain a giving option on the back. (The front would have only the group's name address, phone, and Web site, but no person's name.) The back of the card would look like this:

I want to help. Here is my gift of

   ❏ $45   ❏ $100   ❏ other $ _____

Make checks payable to Good Group and send to the address on the front of this card, or donate online at www.worldpeacesoon.org.

Make sure everyone in your organization has some of these cards. Board members and volunteers can write their own name on the card. People should be encouraged to hand them out like candy.

E-Mail.   Most people have a "signature" on their e-mail. Where appropriate, add a line that says, "You can help—donate now at www.ourgroup.org."

Voice Mail.   If you have voice mail, be sure that one choice is "If you wish to make a donation, or speak with the development director . . .," or "For information about how to donate, visit our Web site, www.goodgroup.org, or leave your address at the tone and we will send you free information."

In other words, make fundraising part of your message—these soft asks will offend no one and will help raise money.

Publications.   Many organizations produce brochures, reports, booklets, and even books. All of these should contain information about how and why to give. This information should be placed where a person would be likely to see it, usually at the front or back of the publication. Where appropriate, include return envelopes.

Other Opportunities.   Let people know that money is one way they can help if they want to.

> When people e-mail with questions, answer the question and include a hyperlink to your Web site.
>
> When people write to you for a publication, include fundraising materials in your response.
>
> When you visit your major donors, ask them for names of people they think would be interested in giving.
>
> When giving a speech, tell people how they can help, and be sure to mention making a gift and telling others about giving.
>
> Use birthdays, weddings, Christmas or Hanukkah or other holiday times to suggest that people make a gift to your organization in lieu of a present. Many people feel that they have enough stuff and many are happy for a chance to give something meaningful.
>
> Make sure all program staff, organizers, administrators—all nonfundraising staff—are helped to figure out when and where adding a fundraising pitch

would be appropriate. Conduct an inventory of their days, and show them where fundraising might be included.

During staff meetings, ask people to report how they included fundraising in something they did or why they decided not to include it. Learning that there are far more opportunities to ask for money than we have realized also goes hand-in-hand with learning when a fundraising pitch would be out of line. By sharing information like this, you will also learn where fundraising pitches simply are not worth the time or the money, and where they really pay off.

Here are some more examples from a variety of organizations.

A theater sells sweets, coffee, tea, wine, and soda before every play and during intermission. Near the cash register, they put a jar with a notice that change dropped in will go to one of their programs. Every night, people drop in between $30 and $50 extra dollars.

A program serving homeless people has an art program. Some of the homeless people who participate create attractive works. From time to time, local galleries have displayed and sometimes sold the art. Several people have asked if the art pieces are available on note cards or T-shirts they could buy. In response, the organization creates a series of note cards using some of the images from these art works. Boxes of cards sell out quickly, so the program reprints them and offers them on their Web site. These cards become a small but reliable income stream and a further source of visibility, which leads to other donations.

A garden store donates most of the plants, seeds, and compost for a youth program's organic garden. The garden, which is located in a well-trafficked area, displays a small board thanking the store for its support and telling more about the garden. As a result of this notice, the store owner is often praised by his customers for his support of the garden. He decides to mobilize that praise by putting the youth program's brochures in his store, with return envelopes and by having the phrase, "Looking for a great cause? Go to www.youngsprouts.org" print on the bottom of his receipts. The envelopes used in his store are marked so the group knows the origin of the donation. The organization receives three or four donations a month in these envelopes, including an occasional large gift.

By doing an opportunity inventory, almost any organization can raise more money with only a small amount of extra effort.

Writing Thank You Notes

Early on in my fundraising career I learned a valuable lesson about thank you notes. I had gone to work for an advocacy group working on women's health issues. The organization was run collectively by two utterly overworked staff people and forty volunteers. The group had won recognition for their work to expose and eventually remove from the market a dangerous birth-control device and for championing reproductive rights issues. Several months before I began working there, a woman who had read about the group's victories in the newspaper sent $25. She did not receive a thank you note. She did, however, receive the group's newsletter and she heard about the group from time to time. A year after making her gift she received a form letter requesting a renewal. She threw it away.

Some time later, this woman learned that a friend of hers was a volunteer in the collective. "That group sounds good," she told her friend, "but they don't even have it together enough to send thank you notes for gifts. I can't imagine that they are really fiscally sound or that they use money properly."

Her friend defended the group: "We do really good work. We don't send thank you notes because we are too busy doing other stuff. It is not fair to conclude that we don't use your money properly just because you don't get an acknowledgment."

The one-time donor replied, "It is fair. It is my only contact with them. They claim to want a broad base of support, yet they show no regard for their supporters. But since you are in the group, I'll give them something." She sent $15.

I was hired during the year between this donor's $25 gift and her $15 one. I had been brought up in the school of thank you notes, from thanking my grandmother for birthday gifts when I could barely hold a pencil to writing thank you notes for every gift that came into the seminary where I had my first fundraising job. So without much thought, in response to this $15 gift, I sent this woman a scrawled three-line thank you note: "Thanks for your gift of $15. It's a help financially and also a great morale boost. We'll keep in touch."

Two weeks later, this woman sent $100. Again, I scrawled a thank you note, with an extra line about her generosity. A few months later, she sent $1,500. I wrote another thank you note and asked if I could come and see her. She turned out to be both quite wealthy and very supportive of women's rights. She told me that she usually gave relatively small initial donations to organizations to see how they would respond. She wanted to see how much regard they had for people giving small gifts. She said, "If I send $500 or $1,000, almost any organization will thank me. Many grassroots groups talk a good line about not making class distinctions and everyone being welcomed, but the only people they really care about are the program officers of foundations and wealthy donors." She had decided to give money only to groups that had proven that they valued all gifts. I was flabbergasted that a sign of proof could be a sloppy three-line thank you note, but for her it was better proof than a longer form letter with her name typed in and certainly far better than no acknowledgment at all.

Since then I have seen over and over that a simple, handwritten note or typed thank you letter with a personal note as a postscript can do more to build donor loyalty than almost any other form of recognition. Unfortunately, thank you notes tend to be one thing that organizations are sloppy or even thoughtless about. They either don't send them, send them weeks late, or send a preprinted card or note with no personal note added. These practices are unjustifiable. Sending thank you notes too easily falls far too low on people's work priority lists. They have to be placed at the top. In fact, there is a saying in fundraising that forces thank you notes to be a high priority: Thank before you bank.

PEOPLE LIKE THEM

It is not clear to me why people like thank you notes so much, particularly when there is usually very little content in the note. Probably reasons vary. Like our wealthy, testing donor, some see them as a sign that the group values all gifts. Others may just like to know that their gift has been received and appreciated. Whatever the reason, for fundraisers it is enough to know that donors value being thanked. Doing what donors like—as long as we stay inside the mission and goals of the organization—builds donor loyalty. A loyal donor is a giving donor, giving more and more every year.

DON'T DO AS I SAY

What about the donor who claims not to want a thank you note, or the one who even more strongly states that thank yous are a waste of time and money?

The donor who claims not to want a thank you note should get one anyway. These are usually people who are genuinely trying to save groups time. You will have greater loyalty if you send a thank you note anyway. When these donors say, "You shouldn't have done that," or "That's really not necessary," they often mean, "Thank you for taking the time. I can't believe someone would bother to notice me."

The second style of donor, the one who actually resents thank you notes, probably should get a call thanking them for their gift. Even a brief message left on a phone machine will be appreciated. Sometimes donors don't know that the Internal Revenue Service requires organizations to send receipts to donors for any gift greater than $250. A thank you note will double as a receipt if you name the specific amount of money the donor gave. You should also note at the bottom of your receipt or thank you note that "No goods or services were received in exchange for this gift."

If the person is very close to your group—perhaps a volunteer, board member, or someone who used to work for the organization—you can combine your thank you call with another function, such as to remind them of a meeting: "I called to thank you for your gift—we can really use it. By the way, don't forget about the meeting Wednesday at 7 P.M. at Marge's."

Overall, experience shows that, all else being equal, when you thank donors you are more likely to keep them and when you don't you are more likely to lose them. Of course, there will be exceptions to this rule, but it is almost impossible to figure out who is really an exception and who is just pretending to be, so thank everyone and save yourself worrying about it.

DO IT NOW

How can you most efficiently thank your donors, and who should do it? Perhaps the most important rule about thanking donors is that no matter who is doing it—from the board chair to an office volunteer—gifts should be acknowledged promptly—ideally within three days of receipt, and certainly within a week in any circumstance. If possible, the person who knows the donor should sign the thank you note.

If you are fundraising properly, you will have dozens of donations coming in from people you don't know. Volunteers and board members can send thank yous to these donors. Writing thank you notes is actually a good way to get board members who are resistant to fundraising to do some, because the thank you note is part of fundraising.

LOGISTICS AND CONTENT

Buy some nice note cards or have some made with your logo on the front. There is only a small amount of space to fill on a note card, so you can take up the whole space with a few short sentences. That is much better than a three-line thank you on a full sheet of stationary.

People should come to the office to write the notes, and only the most loyal, trustworthy people should ever be allowed to write notes at home. It is just too tempting to put them aside at home. Also, information about a person's gift, while not secret, is not something you want sitting around someone's living room.

The only requirement for handwritten thank yous is legible handwriting. The format is simple:

> Thank you for your gift of $_____. We will put it right to work on *(name your program or most recent issue).* Gifts like yours are critical to our success, and we thank you very much.
>
> Sincerely,
> *(Your name)*
> Board member

If the writer knows the person, they follow the same format but adds something more personal: "Hope your cat, Fluffy, has recovered from her spaying."

It may be that handwriting thank you notes or handwriting all of them is impossible, especially when you get a lot of contributions, such as at the end of the year when volunteers aren't as available or after a successful direct mail appeal when you are swamped for a few days with responses. Then you go to the next step, which is a word-processed letter. This letter should go on the organization's stationary and needs to be a little longer. Most databases can be programmed to generate a form letter to which you can add a personal note.

Start the text several lines down the page and use wide margins.

Dear Freda,

Thank you so much for your gift of $100. We have put it right to work at our shelter. As it turned out, your gift came at a particularly crucial moment, as the coffeemaker in our community room had just given its last gasp. We were able to buy a new, heavy-duty coffeemaker on sale, which wouldn't have been possible without your gift.

I am hoping you will be able to come to our art auction next month. We'll be showing the works of some well-known local artists and featuring paintings and sculptures by some of the residents of the shelter. I enclose two complimentary tickets.

Again, thank you so much! I look forward to staying in touch.

You will notice that the letter refers to a recent event (the coffeemaker giving out). This gives a sense of immediacy to the gift. If the organization had incurred a much greater cost, they could still have referred to the gift in this way:

Your gift came the same day our boiler broke for the last time. I would have been really discouraged, but your contribution cheered me up. Fortunately, we were able to get a refitted, good-as-new boiler for much less than a new one would have cost.

The letter also invited the donor to an event. You do not need to be having an event, nor do you need to provide free tickets. The point is to refer to things happening in your office every day. Give your donors some sense of your daily work. Even things that seem routine to you can be made to sound interesting. Here's an example:

Dear Ricardo,

We got a pile of mail today—bills, fliers, newsletters, and then, your gift of $50! Thank you! $50 really goes a long way in this organization, and we are grateful for your support.

I just finished talking with a woman who used our educational flier with her son. She said she had expected a miracle, and though of course that didn't happen, maybe something more lasting did. Her son called the HelpLine. It's a start, and that's what we provide for people.

I hope you will feel free to drop by sometime. Though we are usually busy, we can always take a few minutes to say hello and show you around. I'll keep you posted on our progress.

Or:

Dear Annie Mae,

I just came in from an eviction hearing for one of our clients. I feel really good because we won and we got some damages to boot! Then, going through the mail, I came to your gift of $25. Thanks! I feel like you are a part of this victory.

Or:

You wouldn't believe how many people came to our community meeting last night—more than fifty! People are hopping mad about this incinerator proposal, and I am feeling confident that we may be able to defeat it and finally get the recycling bill passed. Your gift of $50 will go a long way in helping with fliers and phone calls. Thanks for thinking of us at this time. You don't know what a great morale boost it is to receive gifts from supporters like you.

If you have a matching campaign or a goal for an annual campaign, then refer to that:

Your gift of $100 will be matched dollar for dollar. Your gift brought us to nearly $2,000 raised in just two months!

Or:

Your gift of $75 took us over the $1,000 mark in our goal of $3,000. Thanks!

If you are a volunteer, mention that in your thank you:

> Giving time to this organization is one of the high points of my week. I know we are making a difference, and I want you to know that your gift helps make that difference too.

THE FRIENDLY FORM LETTER

The least effective option for thank you notes, but one you sometimes have to resort to, is the form letter. If you use a form letter, acknowledge that is it impersonal, but give some sense of the excitement that would lead you to use such a method. Here's an example:

> Thank you for your recent gift. Please excuse the impersonal nature of this thank you—we are no less enthusiastic about your gift for not being able to write to each of our donors. The response to our call for help with sending medical supplies to Cuba was both gratifying and overwhelming. We will send you a full report about this effort in a few weeks. Right now, we are packing up boxes of supplies—supplies you helped pay for. Thanks again!

COMMON QUESTIONS

There are three common questions remaining about thank yous. The first is, How do you address people you don't know? The choices are by first name only, by first and last names (Dear John Smith), or by title (Dear Mr. Smith). There is no clear right or wrong answer on this point and no way to avoid possibly offending someone. You will probably offend the least number of people by using titles: "Dear Mr. Smith" or "Dear Ms. Jones." Certainly, you could write to the person according to how they write to you. A letter signed, "Mrs. Alphonse Primavera" should be answered in kind. If there is ambiguity about whether the donor is a man or woman, write "Dear Friend." If you live in a fairly casual community, you can use a first name, "Dear Terry," or "Dear Lynn."

Don't waste a lot of time worrying about the salutation. Having received many thank yous that say, "Dear Mr. Klein," I know how off-putting it can be, but it does not cause me to stop giving to the group. Anyone who will stop giving you money because you (or anyone else) cannot tell from their name whether they are male or female, or whether they prefer to be called by their first name, last name, Mr., Ms. or Mrs., doesn't have much loyalty to your group. Far more important is to make sure donors' names are spelled correctly. People are far more attached to their name than to their honorific.

The second question is, Do all donors get a thank you? The answer is always yes. You have no idea how much a gift of $25 or $5 or $500 means to someone. You need to act as though you would like to get that amount or more again. You also don't know whether people use getting a thank you note to judge whether to continue giving to your organization. Why take a chance?

The final question is, Do all donors get the same thank you? No, because the notes, if possible, are personalized. If you have thousands of donors, you will not be able to write to them all personally, so sort out the ones you know and write personal notes to them. Major donors should also get personalized thank you notes, even if no one in the organization knows them personally. Ditto for donors who give year after year regardless of the amount of their gift. The most important thing is to make sure each donor gets something.

Keep up with thank you notes as gifts come in. Each thank you is a link to the donor and you should see it as paving the way not only for the next gift, but also for all the ways donors can help you.

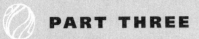

PART THREE # Strategies for Upgrading Donors

The goal of any organization that gains the support of a broad base of individual donors is to become the favorite organization of a cross section of its donors. The financial payoff in building a base of donors is twofold: first, having a large number of small donors will yield a profit, and those donors will bring in other donors, and second, a subset of donors will give larger and larger gifts. Undoubtedly, the most money in fundraising is from major donors and bequests. By building relationships with donors, your organization is in a position to ask people who are giving donations regularly to consider giving bigger gifts, and you are likely to receive a positive response from some of them. You want your donors to think, "That is the group to which I give the most money," or "That is an organization I would do a lot for." The strategies described in this section are used in that process.

The process of getting current donors to give more money is called *upgrading* and those donors who respond to these strategies have become the *thoughtful* donors described in Chapter Three, Matching Fundraising Strategies with Financial Needs.

It is highly unusual for people to start their giving to an organization with the largest gift they can afford, so almost all thoughtful donors will come out of the donor base that is built using the strategies described in Section Two. The only time someone's first gift might be the largest gift they can give is when they or someone close to them has been deeply affected by the issue the organization addresses or the service it provides.

Thoughtful gifts are most often gifts of more than $250; a thoughtful annual gift may be thousands of dollars, and a capital or endowment gift will be even higher. In this section, I use $250 to describe the minimum thoughtful gift and then discuss much larger gifts. It is important to note, though, that if your organization's donor base has a large number of low-income or poor people, there will be people giving less than $250 who are nevertheless giving your organization the biggest gift they can afford. For this reason, some organizations will set $100 or even $50 as the minimum major gift. On the other side are people giving $1,000 for whom that is not a particularly big gift and who easily could give more if you asked them.

When you identify donors who are giving what is a thoughtful or significant gift for them, even if it is a smaller amount of money, treat them with the same respect with which you treat thoughtful donors who give larger gifts.

In fundraising, we spend a lot of time working with the people who can give large amounts of money. All donors expect that bigger donors would get more attention and would think it odd and not a good use of resources for an organization to do otherwise. But we don't overlook other kinds of giving and the significance of gifts to any donor. First, that is the right thing to do. Second, there is a practical angle: someone who gives $10 each quarter through a pledge program may get a better job or a cheaper apartment and change their gift to $10 each month. When he or she gets promoted, the gift may increase to $50 each month. Or a person may give a small amount for years, then leave their estate to the organization. In fact, research shows that long-time, loyal donors making small gifts are most often the ones who leave an organization a gift through a bequest.

Through the process of identifying prospects, described in Chapter Seven, The Logistics of Personal Solicitation, and through careful and thorough record keeping, we can keep track of all our thoughtful donors, not just the ones who are able to give large amounts of money.

The strategies described in Section Two, which are primarily used to acquire and retain donors, can also be used to some extent to upgrade donors. Similarly, many of the strategies described in Section Three could be used for acquisition or retention. However, used to their best advantage, the strategies in this section are really about fund *raising,* and are the logical sequence to the strategies described before.

Building Major Gifts Programs

The financial payoff for all fundraising is receiving large gifts from some of your donors. To build a major donor program, no matter the size of the organization, a majority of staff, board, and volunteers must feel comfortable asking people for money in person. (See Chapter Six, Getting Comfortable with Asking for Money.) For many people, that comfort starts with being able to ask someone for $10 for a ticket to a benefit event such as a dance or for $35 to become a member.

Some people never move past that level of comfort, but if an organization is to grow and thrive, a critical mass of board, volunteers, and staff must be able to ask for much larger gifts—$500, $5,000, $50,000, and even more.

A person doesn't have to like asking for money to be able to do it. Some of the most successful fundraisers I have known have confessed that they always feel anxious when asking for money. But they do it anyway, and sometimes their nervousness makes them prepare more thoroughly for the solicitation and feel even better about themselves and their group after they complete it.

Once an organization is in the habit of asking for large gifts, it quickly moves to needing a more systematic plan for soliciting such gifts. That system is a major gifts program. Some groups prefer to do their major donor fundraising in the form of a campaign; major gifts campaigns are discussed in Chapter Twenty-Three.

Before beginning a major gifts program, your organization must make a number of decisions: how much money it wishes to raise from large gifts, the minimum amount that will constitute a major gift (in this book it is $250), how many gifts of what size are needed. In addition, you must decide what, if any, tangible benefits donors will receive for their gifts and what materials will be needed for the solicitors. Finally, a core group of volunteers must be trained to ask for the gifts.

SETTING A GOAL

The first step in seeking major gifts is to decide how much money you want to raise from major donors. This amount will be related to the overall amount you want to raise from all your individual donors and can be partly determined based on the following information. (For more on goal setting, see Chapter Thirty-Nine, Creating a Fundraising Plan.)

Over the years fundraisers have observed the following pattern of how gifts come into healthy organizations:

- 60 percent of the income comes from 10 percent of the donors
- 20 percent of the income comes from 20 percent of the donors
- 20 percent of the income comes from 70 percent of the donors

In other words, the majority of your gifts will be small, but the bulk of your income will come from large donations. Based on that pattern, it is possible to project for any fundraising goal how many gifts of each size you should seek and how many prospects you will need to ask to get each gift.

For example, if your organization must raise $50,000 from grassroots fundraising, you should plan to raise $30,000 (60 percent) from major gifts, mostly solicited personally; $10,000 (20 percent) from habitual donors, mostly solicited through phone, mail, and regular special events; and $10,000 from people giving for the first or second time, solicited from mail and online appeals, speaking engagements, special events, product sales, and the like.

If you have 500 donors, then, expect that about 50 of them will be major donors, about 100 of them will be habitual donors, and about 350 will be first- or second-time donors or donors who give small gifts every year, but for whom your organization is not a high priority.

The lowest major gift you request should be an amount that is higher than most of your donors give but one that most employed people can afford, especially if allowed to pledge. Even many low-income people can afford $25 a month or $250 a quarter, which brings being a major donor into the realm of possibility for all people close to your group.

Some organizations try to avoid setting goals. Their feeling is that they will raise as much as they can from as many people as they can. This doesn't work. Prospects are going to ask how much you need; if this answer is, "As much as we can get," your group will not sound very well run. If prospects think a group will simply spend whatever it has, they will give less than they can afford or nothing. Further, without a goal there is no way to measure how well the organization is doing compared to its plans. Just as you wouldn't instruct a builder to build a house that will be "as big as it needs to be," or "as big as we can afford," you can't build a donor base with vague or meaningless assertions.

APPORTIONMENT OF GIFTS

It would be great if you could say, "Well, we need $40,000 from 10 percent of our donors, so that will mean two hundred people giving $200 each." But two hundred people will not all behave the same way—some will give more, most will give less. Based on this reality, fundraisers have made a second observation: for the money needed annually from individual donors, you need one gift equal to 10 percent or more of the goal, two gifts equal to 10 percent (5 percent each) or more of the goal, and four to six gifts providing the next 10 percent of the goal. The remaining gifts needed are determined in decreasing size of gift with increasing numbers of gifts. Using this formula, you can create what is called a Gift Range Chart or a Gift Pyramid.

Let's imagine an organization that needs to raise $100,000 from a wide variety of individual donor strategies. Using the pattern outlined earlier, $60,000 will be raised from major gifts. Their gift range chart will look something like the following:

Major Donor Gift Range Chart			
Goal: $100,000			
	Number of Gifts	Size of Gifts	Total
Major Gifts	1	$10,000	$10,000
	2	$5,000	$10,000
	5	$2,500	$12,500
	10	$1,000	$10,000
	20	$500	$10,000
	30	$250	$7,500
Total	68 gifts	$250–$10,000	$60,000 (60 percent of total)
Other Gifts	100	$100	$10,000
	150	$50–$75	10,000
Total	250 gifts	$50–$100	$20,000 (20 percent of total)
Remaining Gifts	Many	$5–$99	$20,000 (20 percent of total)

The most important and useful part of the chart is the top part, which plots sizes and number of major gifts. It should not be seen as a blueprint. If an organization has one donor who can give 15 percent of the goal, then ask for that; in that case you will need fewer gifts at the lower end of the chart. An organization in a rural community may not be able to generate the number of gifts needed, so it will have to get fewer gifts at larger sizes.

The chart serves as a guideline and a reality check. For example, if your goal is to raise $100,000, but the biggest gift you can imagine getting is $500, then you will probably have to lower your goal. The chart is also helpful for board members and other volunteer solicitors who may have difficulty imagining raising $100,000 but can imagine thirty people giving $250 each.

HOW MANY PEOPLE TO ASK

Every fundraising strategy, presuming it is done properly, has an expected rate of response. For major gifts, the expected response rate is that 50 percent of prospects will say yes to making a gift when the gift is requested by someone who knows the potential donor, knows that that prospect believes in the cause, and knows that the prospect could give the amount of money being asked. However, if the prospect does say yes, there is a further 50 percent chance that he or she will give less than the amount requested.

Based on this understanding, for every gift you seek through personal solicitation, particularly at the upper reaches of the chart, you will need at least four prospects—two will say yes and two will say no. Of the two who say yes, one will give a lesser amount than requested. Because the prospects for higher gifts who say yes but give less than asked for help fill in the number of gifts needed in the middle and bottom ranges of the chart, you will need only two or three new prospects for every gift needed in those ranges. Overall, look for about three times as many prospects as gifts needed. For the $100,000 goal, then, the top portion of the chart would be expanded to include numbers of prospects:

Major Donor Gift Range Chart and Prospects

Goal: $100,000

	Number of Gifts	Size of Gifts	Total	Number of Prospects
Major Gifts	1	$10,000	$10,000	4
	2	$5,000	$10,000	(×4) 8
	5	$2,500	$12,500	(×4) 20
	10	$1,000	$10,000	(×4) 40
	20	$500	$10,000	(×3) 60
	30	$250	$7,500	(×3) 90

TOTAL 68 gifts = 222 individual prospects

In other words, when your group asks four qualified people for $10,000, two will say no, one will give $10,000, and one will give less than $10,000. As you go down the pyramid, you are filling in the next layer with the smaller gifts from the higher layer, so you don't need to identify quite as many prospects for the gifts you need in the lower layers of the chart. When all is said and done, it may turn out that you only needed twice as many prospects rather than three times, but it is always better to err on the side of too many than too few.

MATERIALS FOR MAJOR GIFT SOLICITATION

In addition to the gift range chart and a list of prospects, three more elements need to be in place before your organization can begin to solicit major gifts: a benefits program, materials that describe your work and how to make donations, and people to solicit the gifts.

Benefits

First, you need to decide what, if any, benefits people will receive for giving a major gift. While helping the organization is the main satisfaction for the donor, an added incentive, such as a mug, an invitation to a special reception, or a T-shirt, will show that you appreciate the extra effort the donor is making and will remind the donor of their gift to your group.

There is no evidence that one kind of benefit works better than another (see also the discussion of benefits in Chapter Ten). Certainly, the benefit should not be very expensive. Under IRS law, any value of a benefit that exceeds the vague criterion of "token" is not eligible for the same tax deduction as the rest of the gift. For example, if someone gives $500 to an organization and receives an etching worth $50, the donor can only claim $450 of this gift on their tax return because $50 is more than a token amount. If the same group gave a T-shirt or tote bag worth little or nothing on the open market, the donor could claim the whole $500 as a tax deduction. The IRS is increasingly questioning expensive benefits for donors.

The benefit should be easy to mail, which is why many groups use T-shirts or books as benefits. Because of the number of items people can commonly get for their gifts to public television, libraries, or major national organizations, a small organization should probably offer something that is related to its programs. For example, an organization working for stricter controls on and alternatives to the commercial use of pesticides sends its major donors a short booklet on alternatives to pesticides for home gardens and indoor plants. An after-school program for inner-city children aged eight to eleven asked the teachers to save drawings the children made that they didn't want to take home. The organization sent the best of those artworks along with their thank you notes to donors. This benefit is truly of token value, but it is very popular with donors. Now the organization has one day on which the children are asked to make "thank you" drawings.

A major donor program can be run successfully without giving any benefits beyond what are offered to all donors, such as the newsletter. This approach will only work if the donors are thanked personally and promptly and if the organization keeps in touch with them using the ways recommended in the section on renewing major gifts later in this chapter. Personal attention and information on what work the group was able to do as a result of their gift will always be more effective in maintaining donors than any nominal benefits.

Descriptive Materials

Materials that describe your program are the second element needed for soliciting major donations. An organization should have a well-designed, easy-to-understand brochure. It does not have to be elaborate or printed in several colors, but it should be professionally laid out, well written, and free of grammatical and typographical errors. Because this pamphlet will be used primarily in personal solicitation, it should focus on ways to make thoughtful gifts. For example, if you have an electronic funds transfer program or a pledge program, or if you accept credit cards or you are seeking gifts of stocks and bonds, you can explain all that in the brochure. The brochure is a published version of your case statement (see Chapter Four). It also helps volunteer solicitors by giving them something to leave with a donor and to refer to if they forget some information they meant to impart. Return envelopes and return cards must be included with the brochure. A version of this brochure should also appear on your Web site, with the option for people to donate online.

Solicitors

Finally, you need to have a core group of people willing to do the soliciting. Some of these people should be from the board of directors, but the board's work can be augmented by a group of volunteers. These people should be trained in the process of asking for money (see Chapters Six and Seven). They do not have to have previous experience in asking for major gifts, nor do they need to know many prospects personally. But they must be donors—ideally, major donors—themselves.

KEEPING IN TOUCH WITH MAJOR DONORS

One of the most frequent complaints from major donors is that organizations treat them like ATMs—they punch in the amount they want and then walk away until they need money again. To keep donors interested in your group requires showing some interest in the donor, particularly some interest in why the donor is interested in your group. To give major donors this extra attention takes work, but it is worth it for several reasons: first, courtesy; second, because it brings donors closer to the work of your group, making them potential activists or advocates; and third, because it will bring in more money.

You should be in contact with your major donors two or three times a year in addition to the time when you ask the donors to renew their gifts. You will want to be in touch with some donors more often than that, depending partly on the size of their gift and mostly on their personality and expressed level of interest. Remember that major donors are a good source of feedback, advice, and volunteer energy, as well as a source of other major donors.

There are several easy ways to keep in touch with major donors that make them feel personally appreciated and do not cost the organization much in time or money. You can choose from the suggestions here or develop your own system, but be sure to get a system in place.

Send a Holiday Card During December.   The card should wish the donor happy holidays and be signed by the chair of the board, a board member with a personal relationship to the donor, or a staff person. If possible, write a brief note on the card. The card goes alone—no return envelope, no appeal letter. (You may also send major donors a year-end appeal in a separate mailing.) Unless your organization is religiously identified, make sure the card has no religious overtones, including cultural Christian overtones such as Santa Claus, elves, or Christmas trees. The same applies to the postage stamp you choose.

Attach a Personal Note to Your Annual Report.   All donors should receive a copy of your annual report. Those going to major donors should have a personal note attached. The note can be on a Post-it and does not have to be long. It says something like, "Thought you'd be interested in seeing this since you have been so important to our success," or "I hope you are as proud of our work as we are—your gift helped make it possible." It doesn't matter if you don't know the donor—a personal note shows that they are appreciated. If you know that something in your report will be of particular interest, note that: "Paul, that program you asked about is featured on page five," or "Fran, check out the photo on the back inside cover." Staff usually write these notes, but again, board members with relationships to these donors can write them as well.

Report Successes During the Year.   If you have positive press coverage, if you win a victory in your organizing or litigation efforts, if you are commended by a community group, service club, or politician, take the opportunity to send a special letter to major donors telling them of the event. If possible, include a copy of the article or commendation. This letter does not have to be personalized.

Note a Donor's Accomplishments.   If you know a donor's birthday, send a card. If you learn that someone graduated from college, won an award, or had a baby, send a card. Don't spend a lot of time trying to learn this kind of information, but pay attention and respond when the information comes your way. If you have your donor's e-mail address (and you should) you can send e-cards to save postage.

Include Brief Personal Notes with All Mailings.   You can include a brief note with anything major donors will be getting anyway, such as invitations to special events or announcements of meetings.

Include Major Donors in Some General Mailings.   Although you will not send major donors all the requests for extra gifts that are sent to the rest of your donor base, when a mail appeal is particularly timely or concerns a specific issue that will be interesting to them, include major donors in the mailing.

Send a Quick E-Mail.   You will be in touch with many of your major donors by e-mail, particularly if you have an e-newsletter. From time to time, drop them a quick e-mail note or forward something that you think they will be interested in seeing.

By keeping in touch with your major donors, you will lay the groundwork necessary to approach them for a renewal of their gift in the second year they give and a request to increase the size of their gift the third year of their giving. Even if no one in your organization has ever met this major donor and their gift came unsolicited, through personal notes and letters you will begin to build a rapport that will make it easy to meet the person in the future.

RENEWING MAJOR DONOR GIFTS

The process for approaching major donors to renew their gifts will vary depending on the amount they have given. This section describes how to ask for renewals of various size gifts.

Gifts of $250 to $499

Near the anniversary of the donor's gift, send a letter asking them to give again. The letter should be personalized, with a handwritten note added as a postscript. In the letter, describe the highlights of the year just passed and attribute some of that success to the donor's gift. Wherever possible, use stories to illustrate your work rather than simply narrating one dry fact after another. One paragraph should be devoted to the needs of the coming year. The next paragraph asks the donor to renew their gift. The letter should ask for the same size gift as the donor gave the previous year, which both reminds the donor of the amount of their last gift and shows that your organization keeps careful records. Include a reply card and a stamped return envelope marked to the attention of the person signing the letter.

Gifts of $500 to $999

Use the format for gifts up to $500, but follow your letter with a phone call within ten days. In the letter, let the donor know you are going to call. The phone call will go something like this:

> "May, this is June calling to follow up on my letter."
>
> "Yes, June. It's lovely of you to call. I've already sent in my check—and congratulations on your good work."

June can then thank May for renewing her gift and ask if she has any other questions or tell her something that wasn't in the letter (but be brief!). The whole interaction will take five minutes unless May has some questions.

Gifts of $1,000 or More

Send a much briefer letter telling the donor you would like to visit with him or her and that you will phone to set up a time. If you are simply asking for a renewal, the telephone request for a meeting will often go like this:

> "Frank, this is Earnest. Did you get my letter?"
>
> "Yes, it came yesterday."
>
> "Great. Can we get together sometime to talk about the possibility of you renewing your gift?"
>
> "You don't need to visit me for that. I'll be happy to renew."

In this exchange, even though he is planning to renew his gift, Frank may still feel pleased that he was given this attention; again, the interaction is very brief. If Frank does want to meet, he will be drawn even closer to the organization and you will have a chance to see how your group appears to someone who is thoughtful about how much money to give you.

Many major donors, particularly those who live far away from the group, are willing and even prefer to conduct business by e-mail. You will still send a letter the old-fashioned way and offer to call or call and meet, but you can add a note to your letter that says, "Feel free to e-mail me at jim@goodgroup.org if that is easier for you." Be sure to print out copies of e-mail correspondence for the donor's file and note on the donor's record if he likes to use e-mail.

When to Ask for More

Two questions often arise: How many times should you ask donors to renew their gift at the same amount before asking for an upgrade? And similarly, once the gift is upgraded, how long is appropriate before asking for another upgrade? The answer to both questions is simple: know your donor. The sooner you meet the donor and learn more about him or her, the sooner you will have a sense of whether they like to be visited, whether they are giving to their capacity and cannot give more right now, whether they would rather make up their own minds about when and how to increase their gift, and so on.

Of course, you can't know all your major donors right away and some you may never meet. When you don't know, follow this formula: get the gift, the following year ask for a renewal, the third year ask for an upgrade. If you receive a larger gift after asking for an upgrade, ask for a renewal of that gift the following year and the next year ask for a gift that is one-third again as much. Then repeat the cycle: for a couple of years ask for a renewal and then another upgrade, and so on. If the donor stays at the same level, keep asking for more unless you get information that the donor is giving as much as he or she can afford.

In addition to this formula, use common sense. If someone gives you $5,000, you may need to ask for a renewal for several years before asking for more. If someone gives you $250, then ask them to double their gift. On the other hand, think twice before asking someone giving $10,000 to double. You can always add the phrase "or more" onto any request you make if you really don't know how much more to ask for.

Of course, your organization must be able to justify needing more money, and that need must be expressed to the donor in a compelling way by putting it into programmatic terms. Hiring another staff person, for example, is not compelling; serving twenty more children (what the additional staff person is needed for) is.

THE HARDEST YEAR

In planning to add a major gifts component to your fundraising, keep in mind that the first year of recruiting major donors may be the hardest. Do not set your goals too high; you don't want volunteers to be demoralized by failing to reach an unrealistic goal. Major gifts solicitation can be done in the form of a campaign—that is, with a formal beginning and ending time, specific materials, and a special committee, as described in Chapter Twenty-Three, or it can be an ongoing program, with different volunteers helping at different times.

The most important step to take in a major gifts program is to start. Even if you have only one prospect, ask that prospect. If the largest gift you can imagine someone giving is $250, start by asking for $250. A major gifts program builds on itself; simply establishing the groundwork for the program will begin the process of getting major gifts.

Setting Up and Maintaining Pledge Programs

Pledging is possibly the oldest form of thoughtful giving. It is found in almost every religious tradition in the practice of tithing, in which a person pledges a certain amount of income, usually 10 percent, to their house of worship. Since few can afford to give the entire 10 percent at once (if they could, they should be giving more), most donors give the amount promised over some period of time. In an annual giving program, they give it over the course of a year; in a capital campaign, a pledge may stretch over as many as five years.

A pledge is a legally binding contract in which a donor commits a certain amount of money and then fulfills the commitment with regular payments. Although few organizations would sue a donor who did not fulfill her or his pledge, it is important for donors to understand that this is a serious commitment and under accounting law, the organization must count pledges as accounts receivable.

There are two great advantages of a pledge program to an organization: first, if payments are spread over a time period any donor can give more than they could give all at once, and second, a well-run pledge program means reliable monthly income.

There are also clear advantages for the donor. People who are committed to an organization can express that commitment with a bigger gift by pledging than they could with a one-time donation. Many working people who could not give $300 all at once could afford $25 a month. Further, people who give $100, $500, or even $1,000 in one-time gifts may be able to repeat that gift four times a year or even every month. Certainly, donors can't make this kind of commitment to every group, but they can and will make it to their favorite organization if the mechanism is in place for that organization to ask them.

Pledging is the simplest strategy with which to start the upgrading process. You will have the pleasant surprise of seeing some people increase their giving by 400 percent—or even 1,200 percent—as they go from giving $25 a year to giving that much every quarter or every month. Further, renewal rates for people who pledge are higher than for regular donors, particularly if those pledging are giving by direct debit or electronic funds transfer (explained below). Finally, donors who pledge are more likely to include your organization in their will; in fact, introducing a pledge program is often the first step in introducing a legacy giving program.

INTRODUCING A PLEDGE PROGRAM

Once an organization decides to institute a pledge program, it needs to introduce it in all its fundraising materials. First, send a special appeal to your current donors asking them to consider pledging. In the appeal letter, explain that the reader is a valuable supporter and that your organization wants to give him or her an opportunity to give more without undue hardship. Explain how helpful it is to your organization to have a known amount of money coming in every month and what kind of work you can do with these extra funds.

Second, use a small amount of space in your newsletter to discuss the pledge program. Third, include pledging on all your return forms as one of the choices, as in the following illustration:

I want to give $___ per month/quarter (circle one). My first payment is enclosed.

Please bill to my credit card: (card type, number, expiration date)

_____

Put information about pledging on your Web site and give people the option of signing up to pledge at the site if you have a secured area for giving. The idea of pledging sometimes takes a while to catch on, but when donors see this option in many different places and grow familiar with it, more and more of them will take advantage of it.

Make it as easy as possible for people to pledge by allowing them to put their pledge on a credit card or to fulfill it through direct debit from their bank account via electronic funds transfer. Your organization will have between 90 and

95 percent collection success with these methods, and the amount pledged will often be higher than if the donor were billed.

Organizations sometimes find it helpful to provide incentives for pledging by creating a special category for people who pledge, such as a Gift of the Month Club or a Sustainer Council. People who pledge can also be given a benefit not available to other donors and can be listed in a special category in newsletters or annual reports.

COLLECTING PLEDGES

Many pledge programs have failed because the organization did not put time into collecting the pledged amounts or did not have a system in place to keep track of payments. I have pledged to more than a dozen organizations over the years; with some of them I made one or two payments, then forgot about my pledge. Most of those organizations failed to remind me of my pledge or reminded me in such a sporadic way that my pledge was paid sporadically. In one case, after being asked to pledge $10 a month to an organization that I found appealing but knew little about, and after making payments for a few months, I received a letter from the group asking if I could pay the rest of my pledge in one payment because the group "found the process of depositing so many checks every month too time consuming." Since the reason I had pledged was to be able to make a larger gift than I could at one time, I found their request lacking in an understanding of the purposes of a pledge program. Further, I found my feelings a little hurt by the implication that losers like me and the other people pledging were taking up so much of the organization's valuable time with our endless donations. As a result, I stopped giving altogether. Perhaps not surprising, I never heard from the organization again.

Keeping Track of Pledges

It is easy to keep track of pledges in your fundraising database. Most databases have fields built in to record pledges and to make sending reminders simple, or you can buy a module specifically designed for managing a pledge program. If your database does not have this feature already or you do not want to add another component to your computer systems, set up fields in your existing database to record pledges and the payment due dates. As payments are made, record them. Send a pledge reminder each month or quarter so that it arrives right before the first of the month, when most people are paid. If people are billed regularly on this timetable, you will have the smallest number of dropouts. Send a form such as the one shown here, sized to fit the stamped return envelope that accompanies it. The forms can come right out of the database or they can be filled in by hand. Make sure to note how much has been paid and how much is still owing.

Sample Pledge Reminder Form

Organization Name and Address

Date

Dear *Donor Name,*

    Your monthly (quarterly) pledge of $_____ is now due.

Please remit in the enclosed envelope. We are very grateful for your ongoing support and for your commitment to our work.

                                      Director or other
staff name

Total amount pledged $_____
Total amount paid to date $_____
Make checks payable to: Your organization, address.
Your gift is tax deductible to the full extent of the law.

Although far more laborious, you can keep track of this information on a paper system. Record the pledge information for each person on a file card and keep all the pledges in a file box. Each file card should contain the donor's name and address, the amount pledged, the date the pledge was made, and how often payments will be made. Create a column noting the dates payments are due, and check off beside each date as payments are made. A quick glance will tell you whether the donor is behind in payment. Once a month go through the box, fill out preprinted pledge forms, and send them with a stamped return envelope. Pledge collection is an excellent fundraising task for a careful and thorough board member or volunteer.

Most groups find that they collect between 80 and 85 percent of pledges that require the kind of billing described here. If a person has been reminded three times without paying, assume that he or she is not going to fulfill the pledge. Some groups have found it helpful to call the donor to see if there is a problem that the organization can rectify. Usually it has nothing to do with the group, but instead that the donor's financial situation has changed for the worse or that the donor didn't realize what a difficult commitment their pledge would be for them. Don't hound people for payment. Simply roll them back into the regular donor program.

At the end of the year, send a personal letter with the final pledge note asking the donor to renew his or her pledge. Include a renewal form. The letter can be simple and straightforward, such as the following:

Dear_____,

This is the last payment on your pledge of $250. Your ongoing support has been tremendously important to us this past year. We have been able to use the extra funds provided by our Sustainer Council to do _____ and _____. Thank you very much for your commitment.

I hope that you will renew your pledge. We will continue to send you reminders, and you will receive *(name a benefit here),* available only to people who pledge. I enclose a form for you to fill out. Thank you again for all your support.

Sincerely,
Director or Board Chair

Collecting Pledges by EFT or Credit Card

There are two systems for collecting money from donors that require little paperwork on the part of the donor and ensure immediate collection of the pledged amount of money: electronic funds transfer and credit cards.

Electronic Funds Transfer.   Electronic funds transfer (EFT) allows the transfer of funds from one account to another via a computer network. For many people, electronic banking has taken the place of check writing, with people authorizing their mortgage, phone bills, health club memberships, and other debts to be withdrawn from their bank account automatically; others are paying most of their bills online (which is another form of EFT).

The advantages of EFT to an organization are many. When a donor authorizes a regular withdrawal from his or her bank account to the organization's bank account, pledge fulfillment is increased to nearly 95 percent. Donors must cancel the EFT arrangement in order to indicate that they are not renewing, which results in a renewal rate of between 92 and 98 percent. Organizations with established donor programs find that EFT is one-fifth as expensive as traditional pledge collection systems because there are no mail costs and fewer processing costs.

The main advantage for the donor is that EFT is very convenient—a one-time authorization takes the place of writing and sending a check each month or quarter. The donation is listed in the donor's monthly bank statement, so they are reminded of their gift.

You can set up an EFT account with your bank or with an EFT service provider. Most organizations find that using an independent provider gives better service because EFT is the provider's only business. You will need to investigate available EFT suppliers, get bids, and research them with the same care you exercise in looking for good printers, adequate databases, technical support, and so on. EFT works best with a high volume of users, which offsets the set-up fee and fees for each transaction, which usually decrease with volume. Talk with other organizations that are using EFT to get the best sense of what arrangement will work best for you.

There are a few federal requirements for signing someone up for EFT in the United States, which mostly serve to ensure protection for the donor. The donor must sign a form that authorizes the transaction, and the terms of the transaction must make clear the length of time the transactions are authorized for and that the donor is free to cancel at any time. Most organizations specify that transactions will continue until the donor requests they stop. The donor must receive a photocopy of the transaction form.

There are no disadvantages to EFT, but an organization must have a solid donor base and excellent bookkeeping and accounting systems in place to work quickly and efficiently with the EFT vendor or bank and with the donors. Your system must be computerized, and you will want to be able to project that at least one hundred donors will be using EFT in some period of time, usually a year, for it to be truly cost effective for your organization.

Here's an example of how one group advertised their EFT program to its donors.

SAMPLE AUTHORIZATION FORM AND INCENTIVE OFFER FOR EFT PROGRAM

Join People for Cultural Preservation's Simple Gift Program . . . and receive a cassette of early American hymns

The Simple Gift Program Is Convenient

Your gift is paid automatically each month by your bank, and you will never have to write us another check (unless you want to!). A record of your contribution will appear on your monthly bank statement. You can cancel at any time.

The Simple Gift Program Increases the Value of Your Gift

The cost of processing your donation is reduced, so more of your money can go right to work in our preservation research and publication efforts.

Here's How to Join

1. Fill in your monthly gift amount, name, address, and telephone number on the attached form.

2. Initial the Inflation Guard Box if you would like to increase your gift by 5 percent each year on the anniversary of your enrollment.

3. Sign and date the form.

4. Enclose your check payable to People for Cultural Preservation for this month's gift—transfers will begin in about six weeks.

5. Mail the form and your check in the enclosed return envelope.

Terms of Agreement

My authorization to charge my account at my bank shall be the same as if I had personally signed a check to People for Cultural Preservation (PCP).

This authorization shall remain in effect until I notify PCP or my bank in writing that I wish to end this agreement and PCP or my bank has had a reasonable time to act on it. PCP or my bank can terminate this agreement with ten days' written notice mailed to me.

A record of my payments will be included in my regular bank statement and will serve as my receipt.

My initials in the Inflation Guard Box authorize PCP to increase my monthly charge by 5 percent on each twelve-month anniversary of the initial charge.

Monthly pledge $___ Inflation Guard? __Yes___No

Signed _____ Date _____

Credit Card Charges.   If you decide to use a credit card option for donor pledges, set it up through your bank (if you haven't already). The bank will run a credit check on your organization to see how many checks you have bounced, whether you pay your rent and other bills on time, and what your assets are. If your organization uses credit cards for its own purchasing, your credit rating will be a help (or hindrance, if you don't pay your bills on time). Someone from the bank will also visit your organization, mainly to verify that the organization exists and seems to be what it claims.

Sometimes a bank will ask board members, in their capacity as trustees, to supervise the maintenance of a credit card program and to aver that, to the best of their knowledge, the organization is sound enough to undertake such a program. (Such management is part of board liability and is not an extra duty for board members.) The bank may also run a credit check on those individuals. (Such investigation is not part of board duty.)

The bank has a nominal set-up charge, a monthly fee whether or not anyone uses the service, and a transaction fee of between 2 and 5 percent, depending on your volume. You have to decide how to handle authorization and you have to factor in a small number of bad cards. Unlike EFT, you also have to ask donors to renew their pledge in the year their credit card expires because your authorization to debit their card only lasts until the expiration date on that card.

With a pledge program, the donor's credit card is charged every month with the amount of the pledge. There are services run by nonprofits, such as Ground spring.org and NetworkforGood.org, that will handle both credit cards and EFT donations for you. These are well worth exploring.

TWO DON'TS OF PLEDGE PROGRAMS

There are two warnings to heed in setting up a pledge program.

First, don't set up any pledge program unless you are confident that your record-keeping and accounting systems are adequate to handle it. You want to be particularly thorough in handling EFT and credit card collections, as banks have long and unforgiving memories. Ask board members and other volunteers to inaugurate your EFT or credit card pledge programs while you work out any glitches in your system, then move on to your donor base. Organizations often find that they upgrade their own infrastructure as they upgrade these systems to handle more sophisticated ways of interacting with donors. In that way they not only raise more money but they also run more efficiently and effectively overall.

Second, don't be tempted to cut costs on your pledge programs. For example, don't try to save the cost of mailing donors reminders of their pledges by providing a donor who has made a monthly pledge with twelve envelopes at one time, expecting the person to return one envelope containing a payment each month. People cannot be expected to remember to pay their pledges or to keep track of envelopes for an entire year. Even though churches give congregants a box of envelopes for an entire year, they have the advantage of reminding people weekly about their pledges. Further, for people who don't come to church regularly, the church will send a letter reminding the congregant of their pledge, and the minister or the chair of the finance committee will call.

In a similar vein, don't leave the stamp off of the return envelopes. Some organizations reason that if the donor can afford and is committed enough to pledge, he or she can afford a stamp. The purpose of the stamp is not to save donors money. It is to make it as easy as possible for them to pay their pledge in a timely fashion and to show respect for the commitment they have made. Do not set up a pledge program only to undermine it with poor record keeping or penny-pinching.

chapter
TWENTY

Segmenting Donor Lists to Build Loyalty

I hope it is obvious by now that having a donor is not like having a pillowcase or a table. Donors take maintenance. They are living, breathing beings with feelings and attitudes, and they are being sought by 1.5 million other nonprofits. Certainly, they gravitate to organizations they believe in, but if they have a choice between two organizations they believe in and one pays attention to them and the other doesn't, it is not hard to guess where they will send their money. Segmenting donors basically means figuring out how various cross sections of your donor base like to be asked for money and avoiding using strategies that they don't like or don't respond to.

If one donor says she or he hates to be phoned or wants to receive no more than one appeal a year, we tend to think that a huge number of our donors think exactly like this one. I have known organizations that stopped sending multiple appeals because one donor complained, even though fifty donors might have sent in an extra gift! Donors are not all alike. Some dislike being phoned, but others give only by phone. Some will never read an e-newsletter, others will ignore a paper newsletter. One thing donors do have in common is that everyone appreciates thoughtful, personal attention, so we give that to all donors as best we can.

Because people have individual likes and dislikes, we should accommodate these preferences when we can. For example, if someone sends your organization $35 with a note that says, "I only give once a year, so please only ask me once a year," code this donor's file in your database to suppress their name for any other mailing during the following twelve months. That person will not be invited to an event or get the spring appeal. Similarly, someone who writes on their reply card, "Absolutely no phone calls" should never be phoned because the information was

263

put in their donor record. In fact, even if you could take their phone number from their check, don't enter it into your database. If you don't have it, you are much less likely to make a mistake and call.

Most donors don't tell us directly what they want. They may still have desires, however, and they indicate their preferences by their behavior. Our goal is to make an informed guess about their behavior before they decide not to give us any more money. Segmenting, which means dividing your donor lists into smaller batches according to various criteria, allows you to take their preferences into account and saves your organization time and money because you are not using strategies with people who have never responded to them.

The first set of segments is very simple. Donors should be sorted by how long they have been giving your organization money (longevity), how big their gift is (size), and how often in the same year they make a gift (frequency). Let's look at each of these criteria.

Longevity. In many ways, the most important donors are the ones who have given you money for at least three years, regardless of the size of their gift. Create a category for those people. If your organization has been around for a while and your records are good, you may want to create categories for donors who have given for five or even ten or more years.

Size. Determine what amount of money is more than most people in your constituency can give, and create a list of donors who give that much or more. In some organizations, this may be $100, but for most it will probably be $250 and up.

Frequency. Although there are many donors who give only once a year, there are many others who give every time they are asked. Create a category for people who give two or more times a year.

Once you have grouped your donors according to longevity, size, and frequency, print out the following lists of donors:

- People who have given $250 (in one gift) more than once a year for three or more years

- People who have given $250 once a year for three or more years

- People who have given between $100 and $249 once or more than once for three or more years

In descending order, these donors are your best prospects for upgrading and are often good people to consider for volunteer opportunities. Your personal solicitation efforts should be directed to these groups. They care about you and have shown that caring for several years. These donors are signaling that they like your organization. Chances are they will respond favorably to personal attention.

Show this list to trusted board members, volunteers, and people who know your community and who have some discretion. Ask if they know whether any of the people on these lists are capable of giving a lot more. Perhaps Jane Smith gives you $250 twice a year and has done so for three years. A volunteer knows that Jane Smith gives $1,000 to an organization similar to yours and says that Jane always speaks highly of both organizations. Because as a general rule donors should be asked to upgrade their gift every third year, Jane is a little overdue. Your next solicitation to her can ask her to consider making a gift of $500 or even $1,000 (with a good reason for needing that much of an increase, and if the solicitation is done personally).

Donors who only give once a year should only be asked once or twice a year, whereas consider sending an extra appeal during the year to people who give every time they are asked; these are also people who should be asked to join a pledge program. People who always renew by phone should no longer get three renewal letters before being phoned; instead, send them one renewal letter and then call them.

By observing patterns among your donors, you can save yourself a lot of time and money and increase your fundraising income with little extra work on your part.

In addition to categorizing by size, longevity, and frequency, note which donors only come to events or perhaps only come to one event. These donors should not get regular appeal letters unless you have evidence that they respond by giving to those as well. If a donor only gives when she comes to your signature event, does so for three years or more, and does not give to any other appeals, that is a sign that she does not need to get the other appeal letters. If one year that donor does not come to the event, then you could send her a letter after the event telling her how well the event did and how she was missed and asking for a contribution. (Keep in mind that all the donors are getting the newsletter so they can know what is happening at the organization if they want to find out. Segmenting the donors does not mean that some donors never hear from you.)

Note which donors only give to appeals for specific things (playgrounds, scholarships, capital projects) but who never send money in response to general appeals. If you have a specific need, these are the donors to approach more personally for that need. These are often your best prospects for capital campaigns as well.

Identify the people who give several times a year and either send them one more appeal or ask them to become members of a pledge club to see if you can convert them to monthly or quarterly donors. All donors should be offered the chance to pledge on all your reply devices and as a suggestion in renewal letters, but donors who give frequently should be offered that option in a special letter about the advantages of pledging. (For more on setting up a pledge program, see Chapter Nineteen.)

Your goal in looking closely at how donors give to your organization is threefold:

- You give donors the kind of attention they want

- You save the organization from phone calls or letters from frustrated donors saying, "You send too much mail," or "I can't stand being phoned," or "You are using all the money I gave you to ask me for more money"

- You are able to focus your primary fundraising energy on donors who are loyal to the organization, as opposed to donors who are loyal to a person in the organization or to an event

STAYING IN TOUCH WITH DONORS

In times of economic downturn or world instability, loyal donors are not only the bread and butter but also the lifeblood, to mix metaphors, of an organization. Whatever work you can do to build their loyalty is critical. Matching strategies of asking with types of donors, as described in this chapter, is one way to help build loyalty.

Of course asking for money, even in a way the donor responds to, cannot be the only way you are in touch with donors. You need to make sure you are telling the donors what you do and helping them be ambassadors of your work with their friends. Examine all the ways you are in touch with your donors and put yourself in the donor's shoes. If all you knew about an organization was what donors receive, would you as a donor feel proud to be a member of this group? Puzzled? Excited? Would you have a sense of the consistency of your group's work or would it seem scattered?

For example, for three months in a row a monthly newsletter from an organization that works with students in the public schools has printed a number of pictures of young people in political demonstrations. The captions require knowledge that is not provided in the newsletter: "Elkmont High School students protest HR 2233," "Lakeshore Middle School students protest Harris Firing," and "Monument Parents Upset over Locker Room Decision." One has the impression that this organization works primarily through protests and walk-outs around issues that are not common knowledge. Moreover, their thank you notes are generated by computer and merely state, "Thank you so much for your gift of $___. It helps us do our important work improving public education." Although a handful of major donors are sent additional information, mostly because they are also serving in some volunteer capacity, what donors read in the newsletter is all most of them know about the organization's work. When it conducts a small survey of donors, the organization is surprised that no one knows about their tutoring program, or that they are sending ten students to internships in Washington, D.C. These are also exciting program activities that lend themselves to photographs and show much more of the range of the organization's work.

The organization rethinks its communications so that each newsletter features an in-depth story on one program area and smaller updates on other programs. The thank you notes are changed so that they also contain a one-paragraph description of one aspect of the work. Not surprisingly, more donations flow in and donors add notes to their reply devices, such as, "Great story about the importance of one-to-one organizing."

Read a years' worth of communication from your group and see what you would know and not know about the group's work if that was all you got. You will quickly spot problems and be able to fix them. Further, see if you can add any personalization to your thank you notes or contact donors with an occasional letter or phone call to show more personal appreciation of their efforts. A letter that begins, "This is the fifth year you have helped us. Let me list some things your gifts have helped make possible over the past five years" is a relatively easy letter to create when seeking renewals.

We appreciate all gifts and all motives for giving. But our best chance of getting a donation year in and year out is by building a relationship with the donor— a relationship that goes beyond any of the people in the organization. Segmenting, then deciding how to treat each segment of the donor list, is an easy and important step in building and keeping a broad donor base.

Considering Legacy Giving

Alegacy gift is any donation that requires a lot of thought on the part of the donor. However, we mostly use the term *legacy giving* (also called *planned giving*) to refer to arrangements made for a group to receive contributions from the estate of a donor. These gifts are generally made by long-time, loyal donors who believe in the need of the group to exist after their own life is over, and more important, who have faith that the organization will continue to do a good job for years and years to come. These are not necessarily major donors; many bequests come from donors who have given small amounts to an organization for a long time. When I look around at board meetings I attend, I often reflect that in fifty years (which is really very little time), people who aren't even born yet will be running the organization. I will be deceased. What would I need to know about this organization to trust that it will continue to attract people to its board and staff (people who don't exist yet) who will continue to do good and needed work? Whatever information that creates that confidence is fundamental to getting donors to consider legacy gifts.

Some organizations use legacy gifts for annual expenses, but since the gift is not repeatable, this practice is unwise. Others use legacy gifts for capital improvements. Most groups, however, use legacy gifts to build endowments. An endowment is a permanently restricted fund invested to generate interest. The principal, or corpus, is never spent but is added to as more legacy gifts come in. The interest income can be used as the organization wishes, unless the donor has created terms restricting how the gift can be used. Interest income is usually used to offset general operating costs, as these are the most difficult to raise money for. In the next chapter, I discuss endowments in more detail.

GETTING READY FOR A LEGACY GIVING PROGRAM

Many organizations think that getting ready for a legacy giving program involves going to seminars and memorizing complicated financial planning language, then identifying the organization's oldest donors, explaining what you have learned to them, and watching them sign on the dotted line. In fact, before anyone in the organization begins the process of learning the many different ways to word a bequest, a number of things have to be in place.

First, it is critical that your organization discusses and agrees on the need to exist far into the future and comes to grips with what that means for your overall mission.

Second, in addition to deciding how far into the future your group needs to exist, you need to look at whether people trust you to do your work now and understand your need for funds. Does your group have a good reputation—not just for work accomplished, but for stewarding resources, handling money responsibly, and raising money with integrity? Although many grassroots organizations could answer yes to all these questions, they may be surprised at the extent to which their donors have no sense of how their group deals with money. If you don't put out an annual financial report, if you don't publish the names of your donors from time to time, and if you don't regularly talk about how you raise money, your donors may have never thought much about your financial needs. For example, if someone asks where the local humane society or college or symphony orchestra gets its money, many people would answer that these institutions get a lot of money from individuals and bequests. Because of that, as people write their wills, many think of leaving some of their estate to the humane society or their alma mater or local arts group. You can start a legacy giving program without people being aware of how your organization raises and spends money, but it will not go very far until that information is more commonly known.

Third, and closely related to the previous point, you need a donor base that includes people who have given your organization money for several years and who think of your organization as one they will support as long as they can. Many groups need to develop their donor base before they begin a legacy giving program—not just in terms of numbers of donors, but also in terms of donor loyalty.

If one or more of these elements are not in place, skip this chapter and re-read the preceding chapters. Do what is recommended in those chapters and you will be ready to come back to legacy giving in a year or two.

PREPARING TO TALK ABOUT LEGACY GIVING

Many organizations that have the donor base in place to start a legacy giving program hesitate to do so because of the almost universal taboo about talking about death: not only do people feel awkward talking to anyone about their death, they feel doubly awkward raising the subjects of money and death at same time. Such a discussion may seem not only in bad taste but intrusive. However, it is important to remember that in the United States bequests, which are the most common form of legacy giving, account for nearly 10 percent of all the money given to nonprofits. In fact, the money given from bequests in most years is equal to the money given by foundations and always surpasses the money given by corporations. (An old joke in fundraising is that dead people give away more money than corporations.) If you want people to think of your organization when they are drawing up their estate plans, you will have to ask them in one way or another.

When you ask someone for a bequest you are not asking them to die—as inevitable as that will be for us all. You are instead making a statement about your organization and its need, complimenting the donor on their loyalty and commitment to your cause, and giving them another opportunity to act on that commitment.

THE IMPORTANCE OF A WILL

To give you a sense of the market, more than half of all people die without a will. Of people who make a will, only about 7 percent include a bequest. Even among very wealthy people, for whom a bequest would lower estate tax for their heirs, in the past few years, only 18 percent of estates included bequests. Nonetheless, the vast majority of legacy gifts, regardless of size, are bequests. Fully four out of five planned gifts are made this way, so for many organizations, particularly grassroots ones, establishing a solid bequest program is as far into legacy giving as they will ever need to go. The terms of almost all legacy gifts, even very complicated ones, are laid out in a will.

Everyone should have a will because no one knows when they are going to die and because everything you own during your lifetime you also own after your death. You have the authority to direct what happens to your property after you have died, but if you choose not to make a will the state will make that direction for you. Introducing your donors to legacy giving is thus a service to them because it causes them to think about making or updating their wills. Your nonprofit may get some money as a result, but the main service is that making a will protects the donor's family and other interests.

If a person dies without a will (called "dying intestate"), the law specifies who will receive the estate, as follows:

- If the person is survived by a spouse and not survived by a child or parent, their spouse receives all their property

- If a person is survived by a spouse and a parent and not a child, the spouse and parent share the property

- If a person is survived by a spouse, child, and a parent, the spouse and child share the property; the parent receives nothing

- If a person is not survived by a spouse or a child or a parent, then their brothers and sisters and the children of any deceased brothers and sisters share the person's property

MOTIVATING DONORS TO MAKE A WILL

In most grassroots organizations that have middle-class, working-class, and low-income donors, the first step in a legacy giving program is motivating donors to make a will. The second step will then be to encourage them to name the organization as one of their beneficiaries. A few case studies about what happens to people who don't have wills motivates most donors to create one. Names have been changed in the three examples presented here, but they are true stories.

THE IMPORTANCE OF A WILL

Mary Springhill, age fifty, died of breast cancer. She had no children and her parents were deceased. She was separated but not divorced from her husband. Mary was a fairly successful artist and her estate, including a house, a new car, and some savings, was worth a little more than $400,000. Mary had never gotten around to writing a will; during the time she had cancer, she was too sick to think about preparing one. Mary had left her husband three years prior to her death, after enduring his physical and emotional abuse for fifteen years. Now, as the surviving spouse and sole heir, he is the beneficiary of her entire estate.

Pro-choice activist Alice Williams, age thirty-three, was killed in a car accident. She and her parents had clashed about her pro-choice views as well as her progressive attitude toward many issues. Her parents were active in their fundamentalist church and had told their daughter on a number of occasions that she was "going to hell." Although they were all on speaking terms and Alice spent some holidays with her parents, their relationship was very strained. Alice believed she was too young to need a will and that her estate did not warrant the cost of going to an attorney to draw one up. (Like many people, Alice erroneously believed that only attorneys can make legally binding wills.) At twenty-one, Alice had inherited $100,000 from an aunt. She had never spent the money, although she often used the interest it generated to augment her salary. Without a spouse or children, Alice's estate of $100,000 went to her parents. Alice may not have objected; however, in the belief that the money could, as they put it, "nullify some of the evil work poor Alice had done," her parents gave it all to a variety of anti-abortion organizations.

Fay and Marianna were lovers for five years. Fay had inherited an apartment building and a handsome stock portfolio from her father. She and Marianna lived in a home Fay had bought before they got together. They were planning to add Marianna's name to the title of the house, as well as to create wills, when Fay was struck and killed while crossing the road by a drunk driver. Because Fay had no will, her parents became her legal heirs. They had never approved of Fay's relationship with Marianna. After Fay's death, they evicted Marianna from her house and told her that she would receive nothing from Fay's estate.

Most people underestimate the worth of their estate and overestimate the time or cost involved in setting up a will. They do not realize that when there is no will, whoever ends up dealing with someone's estate can be in for a tremendous amount of work. Finally, aside from the distribution of property, a will can carry wishes about how the person wants to be buried, whom they want looking after children or pets, and any other legal or other obligations the deceased wishes heirs to assume.

A warning before proceeding further: Nonprofits cannot be involved in the creation of someone's will. They can encourage people to create a will, offer workshops about wills led by attorneys or estate planners, and discuss what they know about wills with donors and in written materials, but they must not get involved in giving legal advice or in helping people to write their wills. The only advice anyone in a nonprofit should give current or potential donors is that the donor consult their own attorney or financial planner. The reason for all these cautions is that people who work for nonprofits are subject to being accused of "exerting undue influence," thus opening the way to legal challenge of a will.

THE BEQUEST

The simplest form of legacy giving to a nonprofit—and the most common—is the bequest. A person notes in their will what property they wish your organization to have: cash, stocks, bonds, art—anything of value. People who already have wills and don't want to change them substantially can add a "codicil" or amendment to their will to specify gifts to your organization.

One of the most famous and earliest bequests was given by Ben Franklin in 1790. He left the equivalent of $4,000 to be divided between the people of the state of Pennsylvania (76 percent) and the city of Philadelphia (24 percent) on the condition that it not be touched for two hundred years. (Franklin had great faith in the future of his state and city!) In 1990, when the two hundred years were up, Franklin's bequest was worth $2.3 million. A group of Franklin scholars given authority to recommend the best use of the money decided that the city's money should be kept in a permanent endowment at the Philadelphia Foundation and the state's money should be shared between the Franklin Institute and a consortium of community foundations around the state.

HOW SOMEONE MAKES A BEQUEST

Anyone can make a bequest. All that is required is that they are alive and of sound mind when they make their will and that they own something they can't take with them. Many people think bequests are only for wealthy people, but in fact, if all someone owns is a late-model Ford, they can leave that car to a nonprofit, which can then keep whatever amount they can sell it for.

All bequests are revocable during the life of the donor—a will can be changed any number of times. Your organization may be included in one will and left out of a later version. Thus, unrealized bequests (bequests promised to you by donors who are still alive) cannot ethically be counted toward a fundraising goal.

Wording of Bequests

Although nonprofits cannot direct people in the wording included in their wills, they can, in their newsletter or other printed material, let donors know the appropriate wording for various types of bequests they may wish to leave to your group.

The General Bequest. The general bequest is the simplest bequest, whereby a donor gives a stated amount to the nonprofit group without attaching any conditions. The bequest reads as follows:

> I give and bequeath to *(exact legal name and address of organization)* the sum of $____ *(or a specific piece of property)* to be used as the board of directors directs.

To be absolutely certain there is no confusion about which nonprofit organization the donor meant, it is a good idea to include the address of the group.

Similar to the general bequest in language and intent are two other types of bequests.

Bequest of a Percentage. With this type of bequest, the donor makes the following type of statement:

> I give and bequeath ___ percent *(a specific percentage)* of the total value of my estate to *(exact legal name and address of organization)* to be used as the board of directors directs.

Bequest of Residue. A bequest of residue is a provision that all wills should have. It leaves the remainder of a person's estate to an organization or a person after all other bequests are fulfilled. These bequests are often the largest ones; they read as follows:

> The rest, residue, and remainder of my estate, both real and personal, wherever situated, I give and bequeath to *(exact legal name and address of organization)* to be used as the board of directors directs.

The remaining three types of bequests have more strings attached or only come into play under certain circumstances.

Contingent Bequest.   A contingent bequest leaves a bequest to the nonprofit if any of the other beneficiaries are unable to receive their bequests because of death or other circumstances. Everyone should have a contingent bequest in their will in case circumstances have changed since it was drawn up.

> Should *(name of heir)* predecease me, the portion of my estate going to *(name of heir)* I give and bequeath to *(exact legal name and address of organization)*.

Income Only to Be Used.   This type of bequest carries the following wording:

> I give and bequeath to *(legal name and address of organization)* the sum of $____ to be invested or reinvested so that the income only may be used as the board of directors directs.

Designated Bequest.   This type of gift provides a sum of money for a specific or designated project or program.

> I give and bequeath to *(legal name and address of organization)* the sum of $___ *(or the property or percentage)* to be used for *(specific description of program, scholarship, building, and so on)*

Ideally, a designated bequest has some kind of contingency, such as the following:

> Should this program no longer be needed, or be fully funded from another source, the bequest may be used as the board of directors directs.

The most flexible bequests are those that are best for the nonprofit; it is the wording of those that you will wish to advertise.

You can see from these various types of bequests how a donor might change their will over time to make your organization more of a direct beneficiary. Some donors start with a contingency bequest, basically saying that if one or more unlikely things happen, your organization will benefit. They may move to a percentage or an actual amount for your group. Later, they may change their bequest to a residue bequest—anything they have forgotten about is yours. The fact that bequests are revocable works in favor of nonprofits as well as donors and should not be seen as a disadvantage.

GIFTS FROM INSURANCE AND RETIREMENT FUNDS

Any time a person owns an asset, such as an insurance policy or investment in a retirement fund, they will be asked to name a beneficiary. That beneficiary can be a nonprofit organization, or they can name an heir and then a nonprofit in the case that the heir dies first. Here are a couple of common examples.

Existing Life Insurance Policies

People generally buy life insurance to protect their survivors if sufficient assets have not been accumulated. The value of the life insurance policy may cover mortgage debt or protect a business. As a person gets older, they may not need that protection and can change the beneficiary of their insurance to a charity of their choice. With certain kinds of policies, the older the life insurance policy, the more cash value it builds up. Sometimes people realize that they don't need the policy anymore, and they donate its value during the policyholder's lifetime. (This, of course, is not as much money as the policy would pay as a death benefit.) The *Life Insurance Fact Book* (a real page-turner) estimates that there are some four hundred million life insurance policies in existence in the United States

Buying Life Insurance to Fund a Gift

For people wanting to make a gift to an organization that is far greater than they imagine they would ever be able to give from accumulated assets, buying a life insurance policy and making the charity a beneficiary may be a way to go. The premiums on such a policy may be tax deductible.

From an organizational viewpoint, this kind of insurance is problematic because it means the donor is paying out money to help your organization, but you will not see the results of this money until the death of the donor, perhaps far in the future. If the donor stops paying his or her premiums, the nonprofit has neither the insurance nor the donor.

IRAs or Other Retirement Plans

Most Americans are eligible to participate in some kind of tax-deferred retirement plan. You can encourage your donors to make your organization the primary, secondary, or final beneficiary of their plan or to name your organization as a recipient of a percentage of the proceeds. This money may come to you if the person dies before retirement or before they have used all the money in the plan.

The types of legacy giving I have described are the vast majority of planned gifts and will keep the average small nonprofit quite busy.

INTRODUCING YOUR LEGACY GIVING PROGRAM

You have probably thought, as I often have, "I don't how I would bring up the idea of leaving a bequest with anyone; even if I did, they would be completely shocked. These feelings are totally normal. I have known donors who had a favorite grassroots organization to which they made significant donations and for which they volunteered, only to make legacy gifts to their university or another much larger institution. They made this decision because they could not be sure the grassroots group would last long enough to benefit from a bequest or because they did not trust that the organization could manage an endowment. This is a vicious circle, and people in fundraising roles in small organizations need to break it by learning as much as they can about legacy giving and convincing some of our bolder donors to take the leap with us. Once a few do it, others will follow.

The best way to introduce a legacy giving program is also the easiest and most low-key: use letters, newsletters, and your Web site. In them, discuss your endowment and your vision for the future, and ask donors to think of you when they are making their estate plans. Then add a description of some of the kinds of bequests and an invitation to make your organization a beneficiary of a donor's will.

Start with the newsletter. Once or twice a year, include an article that focuses on the need for your organization to exist for a long time and therefore to have an endowment, and on the need for the donors to have a will that expresses their commitments. Use real-life stories and give people examples of language they can use to create a codicil (amendment) to their current will.

Once a year, send a mailing specifically focused on wills to your whole donor list, or if you want to segment, to donors who have given for three or more years in a row. You may wish to use a brochure explaining bequests and send it with the mailing. There are many planned giving professionals who will provide you with a generic brochure for a small fee that you can customize for your own organization, so there is no need to start from scratch on this. You can find reputable people by asking development professionals in universities and hospitals who they recommend, or by looking on the Web site of the Association of Fundraising Professionals or the National Council of Planned Giving Professionals.

Many people are happy to answer questionnaires, so one way to introduce your legacy giving program is to include a questionnaire in a mailing or newsletter, as in the following example:

Reviewing Your Plans

Do you have a will?	❏ Yes	❏ No
If the answer is no, would you like more information about how to create one?	❏ Yes	❏ No
Have you reviewed your will in the last three years?	❏ Yes	❏ No
Have you experienced significant changes since you last reviewed your will (such as moved to another state, had a child, bought a house)?	❏ Yes	❏ No
Have you included the organization you care about in your will?	❏ Yes	❏ No

---

Follow the questionnaire with the article in your newsletter described earlier or with a letter giving some of the answers to commonly asked questions about preparing wills and leaving money to charity. In the article or the letter, offer to meet with anyone who would like to discuss your organization's need for an endowment and how they might help.

In every newsletter and on your Web site, include a notice (like a classified ad) that your organization is receiving bequests and ask people making up their wills to remember you. Here is sample language for such ads:

> As you are making out your will, remember us with a bequest. Our full legal name and address are _____. For more information about bequest language, call or write: *phone number, postal and e-mail addresses.*

Or:

> If you have provided for *(name of your group)* in your estate plans, please let us know. If not, please let us show you how you can. Call or write: *(group's name and addresses).*

Givers can also be reminded that they can name your organization as the first, second, or final beneficiary for part of all of the proceeds from IRAs, insurance policies, wills, or any other estate-planning documents.

Present this information frequently and people will begin to notice. Once they begin to notice, they will remember your organization when they are making out their will. It generally takes about three to five years for a legacy giving program to begin to produce results (that is, that you actually begin receiving bequests or you know that some of your donors have provided for your organization in their will), so it is certainly not a quick fix to an immediate financial crisis.

Create a Legacy Giving Mailing List

As you do more mailings about legacy giving and as people contact you for more information, you will develop a list of people who have identified themselves as wanting information about legacy giving. This list includes some serious prospects who want to help your organization and may consider doing so with a legacy gift. It also includes people doing fundraising for other groups who want to see your material and people who love to get mail and write away for everything. You will have to sort out the serious prospects from the others in order to focus any personal attention you want to give to genuine planned giving prospects.

Many organizations create a "heritage society"—a named group of people who have included your organization in their will. This group of people get some special mailings from time to time, some of which can describe your organization's legacy giving options in more detail, using examples and stories. These people can be invited to receptions or lectures designed for them. These groups turn out to be of a nice cross-class makeup because to be part of such a group, a person simply notifies the organization that they have left it a bequest, which could be of any size.

People interested in legacy giving can also be encouraged to sign up for information sent by e-mail. Any e-mail notices you develop should also be posted on your Web site and reached through an icon, "Making a Bequest" or "Ensuring Our Future." Look at the Web sites of large organizations to get ideas for how to promote legacy giving using the Web.

Hold a Seminar

A good community service that can also generate some legacy gifts is a seminar on estate planning. Invite people who have indicated an interest in legacy giving and announce your seminar to the broader community, if you like. Have an estate planner there and plenty of materials both about your group and about estate planning strategies. If you can, have someone there who will discuss how they made up their estate plans to include your organization.

The purpose of the seminar is to help people think through what they are going to do with their estates, so you don't want to spend a lot of time talking about your organization. However, you will need to mention yourselves a few times to drive the point home that if a person includes a charity in their will, you hope it will be yours.

A seminar lets you meet people, making follow-up easier. One follow-up technique is for your group to be the impetus for forming groups of people who want to discuss estate planning or legacy giving options with the help of an expert. Each month or so, your group provides an expert for these prospects to meet with who presents one topic in depth. (The group can also discuss related personal issues, such as when children should have access to their inheritance, the kindest thing to do with pets at the death of an owner, living wills, and so on.)

Work Collaboratively

Many groups have found success in cosponsoring seminars such as those described above. More people attend and it is clear that no one charity is being emphasized.

Beyond bequests, there are other legacy giving strategies, some of which can benefit donors during their lifetime by paying dividends on money put in trust for the nonprofit after the donor's death. Some organizations have had good luck working with their local community foundation to hold and manage trusts such as these and related types of funds. Since community foundations are set up to handle complicated giving arrangements, they have the language and the knowledge of how to do so as part of their program. A foundation may also impart to a donor a sense of solidity and stability that reassures them that their investment will be well managed. Your organization receives the interest, just as you would if you were managing the asset, but without any of the headache.

Once you are able to move past your anxiety and awkwardness about talking about legacy giving, you will see that a legacy gift is probably the most mutually beneficial gift a donor can make. In any gift, the organization benefits from the donation and the donor benefits by knowing that work he or she believes needs to be done will continue. The bigger the gift, the more assurance the donor needs to have that this will be the case. An organization expresses its gratitude to these donors for moving the work forward through thank you notes, special events, and other kinds of attention. With a legacy gift, the donor may actually be thanked with income earned as well as taxes lowered

A gift given through a donor's estate is the final expression of commitment from a donor to an organization and the most profound opportunity the organization offers the donor to help. It is the ultimate exchange. It does not and cannot take place outside of a relationship that the person has with the cause and the mission of the organization.

An organization that wants a working legacy giving program will have in place everything that a group that wants a working fundraising program has: a desire to work with donors, the capacity to keep meticulous records, people willing to ask, plans and goals for the future, and a belief in the enduring value of the work.

Setting Up an Endowment

During boom years, even the smallest group can be found putting money away into an endowment, a reserve fund, or just a savings account. This money is invested in mutual funds or certificates of deposit and with a little tending, the principal grows, sometimes dramatically. Endowment income is a reliable part of an organization's annual needs, and for organizations with large endowments, the endowment gains can be a major part of income. During bust years and dramatic stock market downturns, putting money aside is less popular.

Just as a family or an individual saves for retirement or hard times, any organization that possibly can should put some money aside. Organizations that should be permanent fixtures in the nonprofit landscape need to start endowments. There are ways to invest safely and to ensure both long-term growth and some income.

ENDOWMENT DEFINED

An endowment is a permanent savings account for an institution. Money is put aside as principal and a small percentage of that principal (traditionally 5 percent) is used for the annual needs of the institution. In years when the principal increases more than 5 percent, the value of the overall endowment increases accordingly, which then increases the amount the organization can use while still staying at the 5 percent figure. In years when the principal does not increase by 5 percent, the organization can still take out 5 percent of the assets without truly eroding the original principal. On the other hand, during huge market downturns, even the original principal may lose value; taking out any of it for operating expenses is not as useful at those times, as doing so further lowers the endowment's value.

Using a mix of investments, an endowment can generally weather market instability and still be productive. Like any source of money, an endowment can lose value or even disappear, which is why organizations have to have diversified income streams so that the investment income from an endowment is not critical to survival.

BENEFITS OF ENDOWMENTS

Though the advantages of endowments may seem obvious, let's review them:

- Just like a savings account, an endowment provides a measure of financial security and takes some of the anxiety out of annual fundraising.

- An endowment allows, indeed forces, an organization to think in terms of long-range planning, because an endowment implies a commitment to exist in perpetuity.

- An endowment provides a vehicle for people to make larger gifts to an organization than might be appropriate as an annual gift, and an endowment allows people to make one-time-only gifts with the assurance that the gift won't be spent right away.

- An endowment gives people a way to express their commitment to an organization through their wills; few people will leave money to an organization that does not have some kind of permanent fund. (See Chapter Twenty-One for more on wills.)

- An endowment attracts donors who perceive it to be a sign of good planning and long-range thinking in an organization.

- Principal from an endowment can be used for capital expenses (such as a building purchase) and as collateral for loans, if ever needed. In extreme circumstances, the endowment can be used to keep the organization afloat until it can generate other income. (While what's called "invading principal" is something organizations try not to do, there are circumstances in which it might be the best or only recourse, and it is nice to know you have that possibility.)

DISADVANTAGES OF ENDOWMENTS

Believe it or not, endowments have some drawbacks, too.

- If an endowment is big enough, it allows an organization that should have gone out of business, or at least changed the way it works, to exist permanently and to stay the same.

- The income from a large endowment can allow organizations to become unresponsive to their constituency.

- Philosophically, money in an endowment has been diverted from the tax stream but is not being used directly for tax-exempt activities. Organizations that are troubled by decreasing support from government funding and increasing privatization of services they believe the government should be providing with tax dollars will need to grapple with this dilemma.

- As we have seen in the first years of this century, endowments can provide a false sense of security. Interest rates vary, stock markets crash, and of course, money can always be invested badly.

- The existence of an endowment may discourage some donors from giving who prefer to support organizations that they perceive to need the money more. On the other hand, some donors may choose to give to an endowment rather than to annual operating costs.

- As with any large source of money earmarked for a specific program, endowments that are linked to certain programs can cause the work of the organization to become driven by the donor's stipulations rather than by its own mission. Moreover, by the time it is clear that the program needs to be changed or abandoned, the donor is usually deceased and the terms for changing how the funds are spent may not be in place. If the endowment is large enough, lengthy and expensive court cases may result.

- Managing an endowment is an additional piece of work for board and staff. This management time can become the tail that wags the dog, particularly if there are problems with the investments or disagreement about how to use the income.

CONSIDERING AN ENDOWMENT OR RESERVE FUND

It is obvious that only organizations with strong annual campaigns are really in a position to start endowments. When thinking of starting an endowment, organizations often focus on the money: how much to raise, how to raise it, whom to ask for it. But there are two critical questions that must be answered before even one dollar is invested in your endowment.

Does Everyone in the Organization Agree That Your Group Should Exist Permanently? Most nonprofits involved in social change are formed with the idea that if their work is successful, they will put themselves out of business. The founders generally do not think of the group becoming permanent, and everyone may be surprised at how long it is taking to solve the problem the organization was created to address. Arts groups, independent schools, historic preservation societies, parks and wildlands conservation groups, and some social services are clearly permanent, with their work always needed or wanted. On the other hand, environmental, feminist, liberation, and advocacy groups, if they are successful, will cease to exist.

Sometimes the most interesting part of the endowment process is discussion of this question at the beginning: Should we always be here? "Permanence" in terms of endowment has shades of meaning. It can take its traditional meaning of "always and forever" or it can take the meaning of "fifty years from now." But endowments do imply existing well past the lifetime of anyone in the group, and they require the group to imagine the day when people who are not yet born are sitting on the board of directors and working as staff. Will your group be needed then? What is the evidence of that need?

It is important to make sure that everyone among board, staff, key volunteers, and donors agrees that permanence is a value. When people don't agree on that condition, the fundamental reason to have an endowment and the driving force of endowment fundraising are already in trouble.

What Will Endowment Income Be Used For?   Just as couples may have differing ideas about how and when to use savings, so may board and staff differ about using endowment income. Some will see the income stream as a relief from constant fundraising and will not expect the group's annual budget to grow substantially. Others will see the endowment income as paying for particular programs or doing things the group has not been able to do before.

What you use the income for is related to how big you want your endowment to be. An organization with a $250,000 budget simply looking for a little financial relief along with some financial security will be happy to start with a $100,000 endowment that yields both $5,000 a year and the knowledge that there is principal that can be borrowed against or added to. This money can be used to increase staff health care benefits, buy better equipment, or fix up the office. It is not enough money to change the direction of the group in any way, but it is enough to make life easier. A group looking for enough endowment income to open a satellite office or explore new program directions will need an endowment of $1 million or more from which they can safely draw $50,000 a year.

Once these two questions are resolved (which can take as much as a year of discussion), you are ready to begin the initial logistical steps. These steps involve authorizing the endowment, determining what gifts will be accepted, and deciding on investment policies.

THE AUTHORIZATION

First, the board agrees to create an endowment fund and to hold this money in perpetuity. This fund will be reflected in all financial reports as a separate line item. Once this decision has been made, the group should consider and decide on a series of policies about the endowment money.

Use Policy

Policies detailing how the interest income from the endowment will be used can be couched as broad statements, but they should not be so broad that they are subject to a variety of opposing interpretations. For example, one organization's policies stated, "Endowment income is to be used for operating costs." Later, that group opened a second office and added new programs. Some board members thought the endowment income should be spread to include all operating costs for all programs; others felt the income was limited to operation of programs in place at the time the policy was created and that new programs were therefore on their own to raise all the money they needed.

Use policies should also specify how the use of the endowment income could be changed. For example, if an organization that is using endowment income to fund their ongoing program and general operating expenses thinks it may in the future want to purchase a building, use policies would specify whether endowment income could be used for expenses related to the maintenance and improvement of the property. Or use policies that specify endowment income is to go to operating expenses could also discuss the circumstances under which such income could be applied to program expenses.

Invasion Policy

Are there any circumstances under which the organization would use (invade) the endowment principal? There are no right or wrong answers to this question, but in most cases endowment principal is only invaded under the most dire circumstance or in the years when the principal does not grow by 5 percent.

The group will need to decide on the categories of dire. Most board policies establish that endowment principal can only be used if the organization itself is in danger of closing and that the amount taken from the principal must be paid back within a given time period. Some boards rule that the principal cannot be touched even if drastic cuts are required, whereas others decide that the principal can be used to balance the budget.

These contingencies should all be spelled out in the authorization. There have been several circumstances in which a board of directors and staff worked hard to build an endowment, then years later, after all those people were gone, another board with too much latitude to invade voted to use endowment principal to balance the budget, gradually burning through the whole corpus.

A related question is who will have the authority to decide whether to use endowment principal. Most boards rule that the whole board would have to approve of such a use. Others stipulate that up to a percentage of the principal can be used on the vote of the executive committee; beyond that percentage, the decision must go to the whole board. At the full board meeting, some boards require unanimous agreement; others deem that a simple majority or two-thirds' vote is sufficient. Some of these procedures will be determined by how the group makes decisions on other matters.

Gift Acceptance Policy

Another broad category of decisions involves determining what types of gifts you will accept, who has the authority to accept them, who will draw up contracts with donors about them, and under what circumstances the organization will accept or decline a gift. (Most organizations should have some gift acceptance policy in place even if you don't have or never intend to have an endowment. As you can see from the examples that follow, any kind of fundraising effort could raise these types of questions.)

For example, will you accept the gift of a house? "Well, why not?" you ask brashly. One group discovered that a house was given to them because the owner could not sell it, even at a huge loss. Another group accepted a house with a lien on it. Another accepted a duplex with tenants, intending to convert the building into an office. When they sought to evict the tenants, they faced a public relations nightmare, including this headline: "Single mothers evicted for 'social justice.'"

Will you take jewelry, art, or antiques? You have to think about what you will do with this stuff. How will you sell it? Do you have access to appraisers and buyers of fine art? These items may be worth a lot of money, but you may not be able to sell them. You can spend hours of staff and volunteer time trying to getting a fair price for these items; at the end of the day they have cost you more than they were worth.

Will you accept stock from companies that make weapons, degrade the environment, or use sweatshop labor? (Because stock should be sold immediately, most organizations can accept stock from companies they disagree with without feeling that they are supporting the company.)

Will you accept endowment gifts that are restricted in use? For example, if someone wants to endow your children's program forever, will you accept that restriction? If they want to create a new program and endow it, will you consider that?

To keep things simple, at the beginning most grassroots organizations should accept only cash, appreciated securities (stocks and bonds), and life insurance—all with few or no use restrictions. Others kinds of assets can be negotiated on a case-by-case basis.

Your published gift acceptance policy can be quite simple: "The board of directors of People for All Things Good reserves the right to turn down any gift that it believes will not be in the best interest of our mission or that we cannot handle appropriately." What you publish is not as important as having this conversation with your board and staff and everyone understanding what you are getting into. The tendency of most organization is to accept all gifts ("Don't look a gift horse in the mouth"), but without spending an inordinate amount of time on it, you need to be clear that some gifts can be burdensome beyond their value.

If you have questions about the types of gifts you should accept and what is involved, hire a consultant with experience in creating endowment policies to help you. This may save you money and time later.

Investment Policies

Finally, your organization needs an investment policy. Will you invest entirely for income, or will you have a mix of investments that allow for growth of the principal and income? Will you require socially responsible investing and if so, what screens will be put in place? For example, some groups specify that they will not invest in certain kinds of products or businesses, such as tobacco, box stores, or logging. Others require evidence that the company does not engage in union busting, has a racially diverse staff and board, or offers health and other benefits for domestic partners. If you do social screening, you need to set priorities. If you try to screen for everything bad, you will have few places in which to invest.

Once the organization begins receiving endowment funds, the board will need to create an investment committee. This committee can include people who are not on the board. Friendly bankers, your biggest donors, and program officers at foundations can help with recommendations for candidates for this committee and sometimes may serve themselves. For many grassroots board members, their biggest investment is a new car; investing endowment funds requires learning a number of new concepts. Even if the board delegates responsibility for investment decisions to others, it must still educate itself in order to monitor the management of the endowment. It is not always easy to tell what is a good or bad investment, nor is it always easy to tell if someone is using your lack of investment knowledge to their (and not your organization's) financial advantage. Although you may want to hire an investment professional, don't ever trust your investment decisions to just one person or a group of people who are all friends with each other.

Here is a checklist to help you determine if you are ready to start an endowment:

Is Your Group Ready for an Endowment?

We currently have a strong individual donor program in place. Thank you notes, newsletters, and appeals go out on a regular basis. We regularly meet with our major donors, and a majority of our staff and board feel comfortable asking for money in person. Further, our annual income from individuals has been growing for the past three years, both in amount of money and in number of donors.   ❑ Yes   ❑ No

The entire board, staff, and key volunteers (hereinafter referred to as "We") agree that our organization needs to exist at least fifty more years.   ❑ Yes   ❑ No

---

We have considered the drawbacks of having an endowment and have decided the advantages to our organization merit the risks.	❏ Yes	❏ No
We have decided on the use of the income from our endowment.	❏ Yes	❏ No
We have decided on an approximate ideal size for the endowment (understanding that this may take several years to achieve).	❏ Yes	❏ No
Authorization to open an endowment has been given by the board and is reflected in the board minutes.	❏ Yes	❏ No
The board, in discussion with all appropriate parties, has created the following policies: a use policy, an invasion policy, a gift acceptance policy, and an investment policy.	❏ Yes	❏ No
We have a plan for creating an investment committee once we begin receiving endowment funds.	❏ Yes	❏ No
We are excited about moving into this next phase in our organizational development.	❏ Yes	❏ No

Do not short-circuit these steps in creating an endowment. They do not have to be monumentally time consuming, but they allow you to have some in-depth discussions about the future of your organization that you should be having anyway. Once you have agreed on a case for needing to exist far into the future and you have in place the policies you need, you can announce your endowment and encourage people to contribute to it as an ongoing part of your fundraising. You can direct your bequests and other legacy gifts to it, and then, if you want, you can conduct an endowment campaign, as discussed in Chapter Twenty-Five.

 **PART FOUR**

Fundraising Campaigns

Almost any aspect of fundraising can, and often is, done as a campaign. That is, it has a specified beginning and ending, it has a goal, and it has certain tasks that must be completed by a core group of people in order to be successful. The difference between a fundraising campaign and a fundraising program is mostly in the fact that a campaign is time-limited. Phone-a-thons, membership drives, major gifts, house parties, and the like can be run as fundraising programs—year round, with more intensity at some times and less others, and they can also be easily converted to campaigns.

In the following chapters, we look at three kinds of campaigns: major gifts, capital, and endowment. Of these three, capital is the only one that really must be run as a campaign and does not lend itself to a year-round program. In previous chapters I have described major gift and endowment programs and what has to be in place for those to succeed. In this section I discuss what changes when an organization decides to turn a program into a campaign. The last chapter in this section looks at feasibility studies: how to figure out whether a big campaign will be successful, how and when to do one, and very important, when not to. The principles for conducting a major gifts campaign can be applied to other strategies as well, and I encourage you to look at all your strategies through the campaign lens.

Sometimes organizations feel that they must be more sophisticated than they are or have more infrastructure in place than they do in order to conduct a campaign. I find that actually doing a campaign is a great way to get sophisticated in a hurry and to find out what you don't have in place. It's a great way because it's fun, it brings out the latent competitiveness in many of us, there is excitement and creative tension built into racing to meet the goal, and it often stimulates volunteers far more than an ongoing (and from the volunteer viewpoint, never-ending) program.

Certainly, a campaign run badly or sloppily is not a good idea and will damage the reputation of the organization, so we don't want to leap into campaigns just because they seem more exciting than our dreary day-to-day work. Campaigns are loaded with details, and like special events, many details build on others, so there is not much room for mistakes or not getting things done. Nevertheless, I encourage all organizations of any size to work with the campaign format and see whether it creates excitement and momentum in both staff and board.

Launching Major Gifts Campaigns

Once an organization has mastered the process of identifying prospects for major gifts, asking them for money, and developed a working major gifts program, it is ready to consider moving to a more formal major gifts campaign. The main differences between an ongoing major gifts program and a major gifts campaign are that a campaign is time-limited—it begins and ends on specific dates; the goal of the campaign is made public; and markers toward achieving the goal are announced frequently, as in thermometers showing how far the group has come toward its goal, announcements in the newsletter, and so on. Reaching or surpassing the goal in the time frame that is set becomes part of the excitement. Although a major gifts program has a goal that is part of the organization's overall fundraising plan, the program is in place all year and the goal is not necessarily public. You have a full fiscal year to reach the goal, and achieving it feels like no more of an accomplishment than the fact of meeting your budget. Because a major gifts campaign, on the other hand, is time-limited and public, you can use it to generate publicity about the overall needs of the organization.

During the time of the major gifts campaign, a few volunteers devote themselves intensively to meeting a specific financial goal, giving amounts of time and effort to the campaign that would be difficult to maintain beyond a short commitment.

A major gifts campaign requires nine steps, some of which are the same as for any major gifts program. The steps are listed below, then discussed in detail.

1. Set a goal
2. Prepare supporting materials

3. Identify and train solicitors

4. Identify prospects

5. Assign prospects and solicit gifts

6. Kick off the campaign with a special event (optional, though it can attract media attention and recognize donors)

7. Hold regular reporting meetings

8. Celebrate the end of a successful campaign with a special event (also optional, though it can attract media and recognize donors)

9. Thank donors, record gifts, and incorporate new donors into ongoing fundraising efforts

THE STEPS IN DETAIL

Step 1: Set a Goal

The first step in a major gifts campaign is to decide how long the campaign will last and how much money will be raised. For small organizations, a campaign of six to eight weeks is ideal because volunteers and overworked staff can maintain momentum and excitement for that much time fairly easily and a lot of money can be raised in this short period of time.

To determine a fundraising goal, first calculate how many prospects could be asked in that length of time. Generally, a volunteer can ask about one to three people a week for six to eight weeks without undue strain. A committee of five volunteers, then, could ask between 40 and 120 people during an eight-week campaign. Assuming the usual 50 percent rate of success, your group would have from 20 to 60 new major donors after such a campaign.

If you have a shortage of volunteers, you can ask each volunteer to solicit more people per week, but only volunteers with a lot of time and comfort with the process of asking will be able to do more than twelve asks in one month. Your better bet will be to lower the goal so that the major gifts campaign is something volunteers will want to do again, not something they gave their all to and burned out doing.

Knowing how many gifts you can get, now plot how many gifts of specific amounts you will need in order to reach your goal, using the following method. Select the lowest amount that will be solicited in face-to-face meetings. Most groups choose $500 as the minimum request for which they will seek a meeting; others start in-person solicitations for gifts of $250. Rarely would it be worth the time to make face-to-face solicitations for less than $100. Next, determine what your largest gift will be, which is usually 10 percent of the total goal. With the largest and lowest gifts decided on, you can chart what size gifts you will need and how many of each to meet the goal. (See Chapter Eighteen for how to create a gift range chart.) A gift range chart for a campaign to raise $30,000 might look like this:

Major Donor Campaign Gift Range Chart

Goal: $30,000

Gift Size	Number of Gifts Needed	Total	Number of Prospects
$3,000	1	$3,000 (×4)	4
$1,500	2	$3,000 (×4)	8
$1,000	7	$7,000 (×3)	21
$500	16	$8,000 (×3)	48
$250	36	$9,000 (×2)	72
TOTAL	62	$30,000 (×2.5)	155

Remember that you need fewer prospects at lower amounts because some of the people who say no to a higher amount will contribute a lower amount. Once you have asked four people for $3,000, you should have one gift of $3,000 and one gift of some other amount as well as two people who are not giving.

With your gift range chart complete, you can figure out how many workers you will need to carry out the campaign. To accomplish this $30,000 campaign, then, you would need approximately twenty people soliciting one person per week for eight weeks, or six to seven people soliciting three people a week for the same amount of time. Remember that all the people working on the campaign need to make their own gift first, so the first gifts are pretty easy.

Don't get bogged down in making your chart. There is no scientific way to do it. Basically, if turned into a figure, the chart would look like a triangle or pyramid, with fewer people at the top and more people at the bottom. The point of the chart is to recognize that not everyone will give the same amount and to set a limit on the number of people needing to be solicited. Share this chart with prospects and donors; it lets them know that your organization has planned the campaign and allows them to think about how they might like to fit into it.

If you are doing a major donor campaign for the first time, set your overall goal slightly lower than you think is achievable with good solid effort so that you are almost bound to make it. This will give an early sense of accomplishment and provide momentum to future campaigns. A good campaign goal feels like a stretch, but one that will be accomplished if the majority of workers do their share. If you have never done a campaign before, you will want to make sure your goal is realistic by making a list of all the prospects you have going into the campaign so that you feel confident that your organization actually has some prospects. Some organizations start Step 4: Identifying Prospects, at this point just to check the reality of their campaign. They then complete the step later. You do not need to have all, or even most, of your prospects identified right away, but you do need to have some of the biggest ones identified and feel confident that the rest are out there.

Step 2: Prepare Supporting Materials

A campaign needs a number of materials for solicitors to use, some of which will already exist in your organization and some of which will need to be created for the campaign. The supporting materials are of two types: materials that solicitors will give to donors, and materials that are for the solicitors' use only or that relate to the campaign committee.

For the solicitor to use with donors you will need the following materials: a campaign case statement, a pledge card, and stationary, envelopes, and return envelopes.

A Campaign Case Statement. The case statement can be in the form of a report or a brochure. It should be simple and inexpensively produced. It can be designed in-house and printed with a laser printer, then copied on a high-quality photocopy machine. The case statement spells out the goal of the campaign, the gifts that are needed, what the money will be used for, and a brief history of the organization. It invites donors to a celebration at the end of the campaign (if you are having one) and tells them what special benefits they get for their money (if anything). A book, their name on a plaque at the organization, or a specially created piece of artwork are all nice benefits. The benefit should not cost more than $10 or $20 per donor. While not imperative to give, special benefits have an appeal to many donors. Some donors will give more to get the benefit, some will give the same amount regardless of a benefit offer, and a few will tell you that the money could be better spent and will refuse the benefit. Whether to go to the trouble of having a special benefit will depend on your organizational culture, what benefits you have access to, and how the solicitors feel about the need for them.

A Pledge Card.   This is a small card on which the solicitor notes the donor's name, what he or she has agreed to give, and the method of payment. Once the solicitation is complete and the card filled out, it is returned to the office and kept as part of the permanent record on the donor.

Stationary, Envelopes, and Return Envelopes.   Have enough of these stationary items printed for all the prospects, with a few extras for mistakes. These materials are used for both initial letters and thank you notes. It is not necessary or useful to create special stationary or envelopes for a major donor campaign.

For the solicitors' or committee use only, the following materials will be needed:

- A timeline of the campaign steps
- A complete description of the campaign and some soliciting tips
- The organization's overall budget
- A list of difficult and commonly asked questions about the organization and possible answers
- A list of the other solicitors and whom to contact for more information

All of these materials should be put together in a "Campaigner's Notebook," which can be as simple as a manila folder, but which looks nice, has the name of the campaigner on it, and seems official. You should also send all this material by e-mail so volunteers can download what they need and reprint it if they lose something or if they want to give a prospect a copy of the budget. Solicitors should be encouraged to e-mail or call with questions or concerns.

Step 3: Identify and Train Solicitors

Invite people to be on the campaign committee as solicitors. Look for people who believe in the mission of your organization, who are well respected in your community, and whom you know have a sense of discretion, as much of the information that will be exchanged in the committee will be of a confidential nature. Ideally, invite one or two more people than the number of people you need to meet your goals. That way, if a solicitor has an emergency, or if two solicitors want to work together, or if someone just flakes out, you have back-up. Committee members should fulfill two simple commitments, with a third commitment optional. First, each member should themselves be giving a gift that is significant to them; the number of committee members and the total amount of their gifts are counted toward the goal and are an encouraging way to begin the campaign. Second, each member must agree to solicit a certain number of prospects each week for a certain number of weeks. Third, and optional, members of the committee can provide names of prospects for the master list. If your committee does not provide these names, you will need another way to get them, and if that is the case, you will need to do the next step—identifying prospects—before this step.

Some organizations have found that getting people to agree to be on the major gifts committee is the biggest hurdle to starting their major gifts campaign. People they approach may be afraid they won't be good at asking for money, or they feel they don't know anyone to ask or that they don't have time, or they put forth any number of other objections. To get people you think would be excellent but who show reluctance to consider serving on the committee, first ask them to come to a training session where they will learn what is involved and what their commitment would be. Tell them (and mean it) that there is no obligation to serve on the committee after the training, but that you would like them to be open minded. If the training is fun, the food is good, and the other people who might be on the committee are friendly, generally you will have no trouble getting the majority of people to agree to serve. Reassure them that they will not be asked to do more than their time allows and that if they don't already know anyone they feel comfortable asking, they will be provided with names of prospects. Be sure to emphasize that what is required for successful major donor work is commitment to the mission of the organization.

Once enough people have agreed to consider serving on the committee, set a meeting for the training at which they are briefed in more depth about the campaign and taught how to ask for money. After the training, ask who wants to be on the committee and either have them stay longer at the meeting and continue with the steps below or set another meeting to divide up prospects.

The meeting should last about three hours, with the following agenda:

- A review of the campaign and the organization's need for money (twenty minutes)
- Training in how to ask for money, including practice solicitation (two hours)
- Distribution of prospect names and supporting materials (fifteen minutes)
- Assignment of some prospects and discussion of a system for getting more prospects. (People only need enough prospects to get them through their first week or two. At their check-in meetings or by e-mail, they can be given new prospects as they finish asking their current list.) (fifteen minutes)
- Responding to final questions and setting the next meeting time (ten minutes)

The staff or fundraising committee of the board should conduct the meeting, but many organizations find it helpful to have an outside trainer lead the training in how to ask for money (see also Chapters Six and Seven). It is imperative that every person on the committee be at this training even if they have participated in fundraising solicitations before. The experience of people who know how to ask for money will be of great benefit to those who are feeling unsure. This initial meeting helps the committee develop a sense of itself as a team and should encourage a strong camaraderie from the very beginning.

Step 4: Identify Prospects

Review Chapter Seven, The Logistics of Personal Solicitation, for the basics on prospect identification. Ask members of the committee for names of people they know, and review your list of current donors to identify the following types of people: those who have given a major gift, those who have the ability to give a major gift, and those who should be asked to give more this year. For example, anyone on your list who has given the same large donation for two or more years ought to be asked to increase their gift; this campaign provides an excellent way for this upgrade to happen. Unlike an informal, ongoing major gifts program, in a campaign most of the prospects must be identified before the campaign can begin, although some will be identified as the campaign goes on, including some names that will be given to you by other prospects. Now prepare a master list of all the prospects as in the following master tracking form.

Major Donor Campaign Master Tracking Form

Prospect Name	Amount Asked For	Solicitor	Outcome	Thank You Sent

Everyone on the committee should receive a copy of the master tracking form. No one should be solicited who is not on this master list to ensure that no one is asked by two people. All of this information is highly confidential. On your database, keep the address, phone number, and other information needed for each prospect. While all committee members will have access to the giving history of every prospect, and what amount or range of gift the prospect will be asked for, any more personal information will only be given to the person soliciting the prospect.

Step 5: Assign Prospects and Solicit Gifts

At the meeting, after the solicitors are trained and familiar with the materials and the campaign, they are each given a copy of the master prospect list. Each member of the committee should read through the list quietly and note who they might be willing to solicit. Then the committee chair or facilitator should read each name out loud, with committee members identifying who they can ask. Should two solicitors be willing to ask the same person, they briefly discuss and decide right there which of them is going to do it. (They also have the option of going together to see the prospect.) As the names are read aloud and assigned, committee members should decide how much each prospect will be asked for and where they fit on the gift range chart. By the end of the meeting, everyone should have a list of prospects and the chair or the development director should be confident that no one prospect will be solicited twice. Doing this process out loud also helps to ensure that prospects are being asked for the right amount and that the right person is doing the asking. Solicitation can now begin.

Step 6: Kick Off the Campaign with a Special Event (Optional)

A kick-off event is not a gala affair, but the press might be invited as well as all the prospects and all the solicitors. Soft drinks and hors d'oeuvres can be served. Someone from the committee should give an impassioned, enthusiastic, and articulate but brief speech about the campaign, including its goals, the need for the organization, what donors will receive for their gifts (if you have benefits, hold them up for everyone to see). The event also provides a time for people to see who else is involved and who is being asked to give—this peer identification adds an important element to the desire to give. The speech ends with, "We will be contacting all of you individually in the next few weeks to see what questions you have and whether you can help in this important endeavor."

For campaigns covering large geographic areas, such as whole states or large rural areas, a series of small events would be appropriate.

Step 7: Hold Regular Reporting Meetings

Regular reporting meetings (or conference calls, if you are geographically spread out) to discuss progress and boost the morale of campaign volunteers should take place at least once every two weeks and preferably weekly during the campaign. The meetings need last only thirty minutes; many groups hold them over breakfast at 7:30 A.M. so people can attend them before work. The purpose of the meetings or calls is to give everyone a chance to report their progress, which forces everyone to have made some progress between meetings. They can share frustrations, fears, and successes. Biweekly—and toward the end of the campaign, daily—reports on the progress toward the goal should be e-mailed to all the solicitors.

Although solicitors will complain that the meetings are taking valuable time, you will notice a direct correlation between the number of meetings (or phone calls) attended and the number of solicitations made. A handful of people can be relied on to do their work without checking in—may your committee be entirely made up of them—but these people are so rare they could be a category on the Endangered Species List. Make the committee members check in.

Step 8: Celebrate the End of the Campaign with a Special Event (Optional)

Though holding an event to close the campaign is optional, it is an excellent way to recognize and reward the committee as well as the donors. A simple reception with soft drinks, fruit, and cheese from 5:00 to 7:00 in the evening, with a speech announcing the successful conclusion of the campaign, is fine. Some groups have formal dinners—or in the case of capital campaigns, ground-breaking ceremonies—but it is not necessary to be elaborate. This event is largely for the solicitors and something simple but gracious will help ensure that they will be willing to do it all over again next year.

Step 9: Recognize Donors and Incorporate Them into Ongoing Fundraising Efforts

Aside from raising money, a major donor campaign strengthens donor loyalty, brings in new donors, and upgrades current donors. As mentioned many times in this book, you need to be in regular touch with all these donors through a newsletter and occasional personal correspondence. Because major donors often do not get the regular mail appeals that other donors get, they must be kept abreast of the organization's work in other ways. Like all donors, major donors must be thanked promptly when their gifts arrive, and there has to be a method by which the solicitor is informed as her or his prospects send in money. All donors to the campaign should receive another thank you note at the successful end of the campaign, telling them the organization was able to reach its goal and stressing again the work you will be able to do with this money.

Major gifts campaigns must be done right to succeed. Don't try to take shortcuts or launch the campaign without proper preparation. A major gifts campaign should be both fun and lucrative, and its success will be a reward for good planning and good organizing.

Understanding Capital Campaigns

Acapital campaign is an intensive, time-limited effort to raise money for a project that presents a one-time need over and above the annual budget. Capital campaigns are traditionally used to finance buying, constructing, or refurbishing a building; more and more frequently, they are being used to begin an endowment. The financial goal of a capital campaign is often at least as large as the organization's annual budget and often many times larger. Most capital campaigns last two to three years; some go on as long as five years. Capital campaigns allow donors to pledge a large amount and take as many as five years (and for very large pledges, ten years) to pay it off. Donors are asked to give to the capital campaign in addition to their regular annual donations, and they are explicitly asked not to decrease their annual gift in order to make a capital gift. Capital gifts are usually so large that the donor cannot finance the gift from their income and must donate cash from savings or other assets (stocks, real estate, art).

In understanding a capital campaign, it is helpful to review the fundraising context, first presented in Chapter Three, in which a capital campaign would be the strategy chosen.

THE ORGANIZATION AND ITS FINANCIAL NEEDS

Organizations have three types of financial needs:

Annual Funding. The money they need every year. For most grassroots groups, raising this money consumes all their fundraising time.

Capital Funding.   From time to time, groups need something that they don't need every year. Items such as computers, a new phone system, or furniture; or maintenance, such as rewiring or installing carpeting are capital improvements. For these, additional money needs to be raised beyond a group's annual budget. For small capital needs, a group may just add money to its annual budget and raise it with an extra appeal, or it may submit a proposal to a foundation or an appeal to a generous major donor. When the capital improvement involves buying, retro-fitting, or renovating a building, the group usually needs to conduct some kind of campaign to raise the money from a number of sources.

Endowment Funding.   As discussed in Chapter Twenty-Two, organizations that think they will be needed forever, or at least as far into the future as they can project, will want to invest some of their money and use only the interest from the investment as part of their annual income. The principal that is set aside to be invested is usually referred to as an endowment.

Donors can provide income for these various funding needs through a few different vehicles:

Gifts of Income.   The majority of people earn money every year from a job, investments, a pension, or some combination of these sources. About seven out of every ten people give some of their earned income away. These gifts generally provide for the annual needs of the organizations they donate to. In other words, some of my income as a donor becomes some of your income as an organization.

Gifts of Assets.   In addition to their income, many people have saved or inherited assets that are in various forms of investments—stock, real estate, bonds, art, insurance policies, and so on. A donor can also give these assets to an organization, which generally uses them for capital. In other words, I give some of my savings—or my capital—to increase the capital of an organization.

Gifts from Estate.   Everyone eventually dies, but as described in Chapter Twenty-One, they control what they own even in death through the terms of their will. Through their will, a trust, or other estate-planning mechanism, a donor can arrange for nonprofit organizations to receive some or all of their estate. These gifts are most often used for endowment. In other words, the last set of gifts I will give, which form my legacy, are used for the group to exist long after I am gone.

Unless restricted by the donor, organizations can, of course, use gifts of assets and estate for their annual needs. In the case of very small gifts or when donors regularly give stock as their annual gift, this may be appropriate. But for the most part, using assets and estate gifts for annual purposes is unwise because these gifts will not recur.

Similarly, but probably less obviously, using gifts made from a donor's income for capital or endowment purposes is also ill-advised. First, you don't want to raid your annual income for funds to pay for capital costs (a practice that, unfortunately, many groups do), and second, any amount that a person can afford to give from income they should be encouraged to give every year and not just for a one-time event such as a capital or endowment campaign. I hope that it goes without saying (but I will say it anyway, just in case) that if a person wishes to give a gift from their income to a capital or endowment effort, a group should not turn that gift away; they should accept it and thank the donor appropriately.

When contemplating a capital campaign, many groups will say, "Our donors don't earn that kind of money." However, your donors' earnings are less important than their savings. I have seen groups mount successful capital campaigns with lead gifts from older donors living on fixed incomes who have some highly appreciated stock or a piece of property they are willing to give. Because the donor can deduct the fair-market value of their gift, they avoid the capital gains tax on that part of their savings, enabling them to make a much greater gift than they might have thought they could and at considerable tax savings.

Keep in mind, then, that with a capital campaign you are not asking donors to make extra gifts from their income; you are asking them to go to a whole new level with your organization—giving assets and often paying their gift as a pledge over a period of several years. Some organizations elect to conduct a feasibility study before embarking on a capital campaign. Such a study will look at, among many other things, your donor's ability and willingness to access assets. (See Chapter Twenty-Six for more information on this.)

BEST USE OF CAPITAL CAMPAIGNS

Some grassroots groups have conducted what they called capital campaigns to buy new computers or to send staff to fundraising workshops, which meant their goal was $5,000 or less, their time frame was a few weeks, and people were simply asked to put in a few extra dollars. However, capital campaigns are best used to seek gifts of assets from a wide pool of people and institutions, not just to seek "something extra" from the annual incomes of current donors. Capital campaigns should be seeking people in your donor base who may own property or securities and who would not help you in this way every year, but might give you a big gift once in a while. For this to be your intention, your capital campaign goal needs to be at least $100,000. If you need to raise less than $100,000, consider structuring your campaign as a major gifts campaign as described in Chapter Twenty-Three and run the campaign for a short time during one year, or seek two or three foundation or corporate grants to meet the goal and don't run a campaign at all.

Although your most loyal annual donors will also give to a capital campaign if they can, there are many other types of people who give to capital campaigns who are not regular annual donors. For example, three years ago a local attorney helped a small community organization in Alabama file a lawsuit against their city. The attorney admired the group's feistiness and their willingness to take risks. She was impressed that the sole staff person would work for a low salary and that the volunteers put in many hours at the organization beyond their own jobs elsewhere. She did not charge for her assistance with the lawsuit, and she donated $100 after it was over. Because she did not wish to become a regular donor to this group, she did not respond to their subsequent annual appeals. However, she did have lunch with the executive director from time to time, and she continued to provide legal advice when asked. She bought a table at their annual event for $1,000 for two years in a row, and she gave the group $2,000 when asked to help send a number of their constituents to a conference. When, a few years later, the organization decided to buy a building to house their organization, they asked her for a lead gift of $20,000. The work she had done pro bono on the lawsuit had been worth about that much, and the staff figured she still admired them. She did, and she admired their boldness in asking her. She gave $10,000 outright and pledged an additional $10,000 as a challenge to be met by other lawyers.

Universities and private schools often have the experience of receiving a one-time gift to a capital campaign from an alumnus or alumna who had been a minimal donor prior to the campaign. Some people like the idea of contributing to something as substantial as a building.

To ask donors to stretch their own giving and to seek donations outside of the immediate "donor family" means having a goal that implies stretching will be required to meet it. It must seem to a prospect—including a corporation, government agency, foundation, or religious institution that might not support your annual program work—that the organization cannot get this money simply by asking a few people or writing a single grant proposal.

BEGINNING A CAPITAL CAMPAIGN

A capital campaign begins when the organization has identified a large one-time need. The board of directors must fully concur with this need and must support the idea of conducting a capital campaign, which is a lot of extra work for everyone and may require an initial outlay of money to hire extra staff and develop materials.

Key volunteers who are not on the board along with long-time major donors should also be consulted about doing a capital campaign. Everyone who is important to an organization should have an opportunity to voice his or her concerns and feel part of the decision. There are dozens of buildings in the United States that are underutilized because key people in the organization were divided about the idea of constructing a new building and the people opposed to the capital campaign were outvoted. The organization may have had a few donors or funders who paid for the building, but without a lot of community support, the building is more albatross than asset. Sometimes the organization has enough money for the building, but exhausts all its donors in the capital campaign and doesn't have the money to run all their programs or sometimes even to finish furnishing the building. So the building becomes underutilized. In other instances, campaigns have had to be called off halfway through the process because so many volunteers and donors had left the organization to protest doing the campaign in the first place. A capital campaign is a highly visible enterprise; it needs widespread support within the organization.

Estimating Costs

After all the parties have been consulted and there is general agreement on the need, a goal needs to be set. Similar to the understanding that in a fancy restaurant the eventual cost of the meal will be double the entree (with drinks, dessert, and tip) the true cost of a campaign is far more than the cost of the project itself. One group learned this fact the hard way. They needed larger office space and decided that buying a building would, in the long run, be less expensive than continually paying rent. They found a building that suited them priced at $250,000. The group launched their campaign for $250,000, forgetting that there would also be closing costs, insurance, furnishings, the cost of the campaign, and so on. In the end, the true cost of the building was $310,000. The organization spent two years climbing out of a $60,000 deficit caused by their lack of understanding the full financial implications of the building purchase.

The following items need to be added in to the actual cost of buying or constructing a building or starting an endowment:

Fundraising Materials.   Materials to be used for the campaign include a case statement, brochures, pledge cards, background information for solicitors, pictures, architect's renderings, a special newsletter to capital campaign donors to keep them informed of progress, and a prospectus (see page 314).

Cost of Staff Time.   Someone has to handle pledges, write thank you notes, report to the board, work with the contractor, decide who has to approve paint color or carpet choices, know what to do when someone donates stocks, and handle emergencies.

Record Keeping.   A process needs to be set up to keep the campaign's income and expenses separate from the annual budget and to collect pledges (which may extend well past the end of the campaign). If you plan to use current staff to do that, then someone will have to do some of their work. In a multiyear campaign, it is unlikely that a group could get by without hiring extra staff.

Office Extras.   You may need to put in extra phone lines or buy more computers. If you hire staff, that person will need to sit somewhere, so you may need another desk and chair.

For the Building Project Itself.   Someone with expertise in this area will need to help you list costs related to the building, such as construction insurance, building permits, design costs, disaster preparedness, fire extinguishers, landscaping, plumbing, and wiring, and help you with how much to estimate for cost overruns or unforeseen delays.

Furnishings for the Building.   What are you going to bring from your current office and what else will you need? What will these items cost?

Debt Service on a Bridge Loan.   You will probably have to pay bills before pledges are fully paid, and you may have to borrow money to cover the gap between pledged income and received income. The interest on that debt needs to be factored into the goal of the campaign. Banks will lend money with pledges as collateral, but you have to pay interest on the loan.

Additional Costs.   Add 15 percent for people who pledge but cannot finish paying or decide not to pay. Add another 5 to 10 percent onto the grand total and you can feel reasonably safe that this will be the cost of the campaign.

In any fundraising endeavor, but particularly in campaigns with big-ticket items such as buildings, follow the adage: Plan expenses high and income low.

Preparing a Case Statement

Once the need is established and the costs are known and provisionally approved by the board, the next step is to write up a case statement for the campaign. This case statement is separate from the organization's overall case statement, although certainly it borrows from it. The capital campaign case focuses solely on the goal of the campaign and shows how this goal will help the organization meet all its other goals. The case statement implies or overtly states that the work of the group will be greatly enhanced by the addition of whatever the campaign is proposing to achieve and will be significantly slowed down or impaired by the lack of whatever is being proposed. The final page of the case statement is the financial goal displayed as a gift range chart.

The Gift Range Chart

The pyramid that is constructed by a capital campaign gift range chart is much shorter and narrower than that of an annual major gifts campaign (see Chapter Eighteen). In a capital campaign, the lead gift equals between 15 and 20 percent of the total goal, and 80 percent of the money comes from about 10 percent of the donors. The gift range chart follows this pattern:

One gift = 15 to 20 percent or more of the goal

Two gifts = 10 percent each or more

Four to five gifts = 5 percent each or more

So, 50 percent to 70 percent of the goal will come from about seven or eight gifts.

After these largest gifts, increase the number of gifts and decrease the gift size as makes sense for your group and number of prospects until the goal is reached. Here is an example:

Capital Campaign Gift Range Chart		
Goal: $1 Million		
Number of Gifts	**Gift Size**	**Cumulative total**
1	$150,000	$150,000
2	$100,000	$350,000
4	$50,000	$550,000
8	$25,000	$750,000
10	$10,000	$850,000
15	$5,000	$925,000
20	$2,500	$975,000
25	$1,000	$1,000,000

In this example, eighty-five gifts will be required. Whereas in an annual major gifts campaign, we assume that about three prospects will be needed for every gift that is given, except in the higher reaches of the chart, with a capital campaign we look for four times as many prospects as donors in each gift range in order to give the group a little padding for those people who give less than $1,000. In this example, then, the group will need to identify 340 prospects (85 × 4). All of these people will have to be asked in person, and some of them may have to be visited more than once. If any of these gift amounts are to be sought from foundations or corporations, proposals will have to be written.

Sometimes grassroots organizations feel that seeking only gifts of $1,000 or more will exclude too many people who may want to be part of the campaign. However, when they realize how many people it will take to reach their goal and how many people will have to be asked, they usually see the logic of focusing the capital campaign largely on people who can give big gifts. Further, by offering people the opportunity to pay their pledge over two or three years, a $1,000 gift becomes doable for many middle- and lower-income people.

Timing

The final decision the organization must make is about timing of the campaign. Try to find out what other organizations will be having capital or intensive fundraising campaigns during the time you wish to run your campaign and assess whether any of your prospects will be key prospects for those groups. It's best to launch your campaign during years when you expect your annual campaign to be doing well and to make sure you do not anticipate any shortfalls in annual income. Because during the capital campaign your annual income will probably not rise, do not plan major new programs outside of the capital project.

Final Approval

Once you have prepared the case statement, with costs, gift range chart, and timing, bring the whole package back to the board, key volunteers, and staff for reapproval. While these people may have approved the concept of the campaign, when faced with the realities of the money and time involved, they may wish to change their minds. Without full board and staff ownership, the campaign will fail. Taking the time to make sure that everyone understands the implications of the campaign is imperative because once the campaign is launched publicly, it must be seen through to the end.

FOUR STAGES OF THE CAMPAIGN

A capital campaign is conducted in four stages. The first stage is the "pre-campaign"; it starts when the case statement is ready and approved. The second stage is the "launching" stage, when the campaign is publicly announced and begins to seek support beyond the inner circle of donors. The third stage is often called the "intensive" stage; this stage continues for the longest time. This is the stage where solicitors are out visiting prospects and gathering commitments. When the campaign has reached between 85 and 95 percent of its goal, the "wind-up" stage (sometimes called the "topping off" stage) begins.

The Pre-Campaign Stage

Have you ever noticed how an organization will have an event to announce their capital campaign and declare, "We are proud to launch our $3 million building campaign today, and we are pleased to report that we already have $2.3 million pledged"? Do you wonder how they could have raised all that money in just one day? Of course, that money was not raised in a day; in fact, it may have been raised over a period of months or even years. The purpose of the pre-campaign is two-fold. The first purpose is to test the concept of the campaign on people who could actually pay for it. Everyone can feel good about the case and the need for this campaign, but the true test of its possibility for success is whether people feel good enough about it to give a big gift. Some campaigns have to be abandoned or seriously rethought at this phase if not enough people step up with early gifts, but no real harm is done at that point because the campaign has not been made public. The second purpose is to give a feeling of momentum at the public launching of the campaign. "Wow, that's great they have so much money already. My gift can move them forward," is the response one wants from the people at the launching.

The goal of the pre-campaign is to get 30 to 50 percent of the campaign's total from the top three to five donors. Most fundraisers feel that if you can get the largest gifts first you will be able to find all the remaining gifts needed. (The largest gifts are called the "lead" gifts, though they may not truly be the very first gifts, as those should come from board members.) The power of the lead gifts may sound like a superstition, but there is much anecdotal evidence to support it. Lead gifts provide momentum, instill confidence in the campaign, and inspire other big donors. Smaller gifts seem more helpful when they are put toward a goal already partly reached.

Conversely, starting a capital campaign without lead gifts is dangerous because the momentum lags. Furthermore, if a group doesn't know possible lead donors at the beginning of the campaign, where does it think it will meet them later? It is worth postponing a campaign for months or even years in order to ensure that the first gifts given are also the largest. At the risk of redundancy, let me repeat: an organization does not need to know all of its prospects ahead of time, but it must know those that are capable of making the lead gifts, and it must have a sense that it will ultimately know about as many donors as it needs for the whole campaign.

The Prospectus.   In order to solicit lead gifts, you will need to design a document called the prospectus, which is a brochure, booklet, or folder incorporating information from the case statement in a shorter and more artistic format. The prospectus will be given to all prospects and it must look good. The prospectus shows the prospect that you know what you are doing and that your group is able to handle large amounts of money and manage this large capital project. The prospectus can also be posted on your Web site, along with regular updates on the progress of your campaign, your gift range chart, and how donors can contribute. Few, if any, gifts will come from the Web site, but it is good for visibility and consistency of message.

The Lead Gifts.   The lead donor must not only be able to give a big gift, he or she must also be a person who likes to set the pace, to set an example, and to take a leadership role. These first large gifts come from people who will gamble with you that the campaign will succeed and who actually pride themselves on being risk takers. Obviously, they must care very much about your cause and be committed to the capital project. Frequently (and ideally), the lead gifts come from a few people who were involved in the planning and approval of the campaign. If those people are not able to give the biggest gifts, they need to know people or institutions that can.

Approaching the Lead Prospects.   The process of approaching people who could make lead gifts is the same as approaching any major donor—a letter, followed by phone call and request to meet, followed by a meeting at which the gift is requested—with one slight change. With requests for capital gifts, an answer almost never comes at the meeting; often the prospect wants more information that must be sent or brought to a subsequent meeting.

When prospects seem to be stalling or wanting more information, see it as a good sign. In fact, many fundraisers believe that if a person says, "I need to think about it" in response to a request for a large gift, they have asked that person for just the right amount. The amount was not one they could give easily at the meeting, nor was it an amount that was patently out of their range, but it was an amount they could give, albeit not very often. A person who says yes to a request for $10,000 in one meeting may be someone who has thought a great deal about the campaign and made their decision, but it also may be someone for whom $10,000 is not a stretch gift. Don't be discouraged by prospects wanting more information or needing additional meetings; making a capital gift is a big decision. Most people will make, at most, a handful of capital gifts in their lifetime. Even very wealthy people can't afford to give capital gifts very often and they want to make sure their gift will be well used.

These gifts should be solicited by teams of two people—usually a board member and a staff person or two board members. The board members must be giving what is a stretch gift for them and should be willing to share information about their gift with the prospect. For example, the board member might say, "I am giving ten times my annual gift to this campaign and paying my pledge over five years." Or "My partner and I decided this endeavor was as important as our car, so we are giving the same amount as our car payment over the next two years." If the solicitor feels comfortable, he or she may also share the actual amount of their gift. The point to make clear to the prospect is that the people asking are giving as much as they can possibly afford and that their gift has been made after a lot of thought. They are hoping the prospect will make a similar commitment.

The case statement can be shared with the lead donors; once they have agreed to a gift, they should be asked if they would be willing to help solicit other gifts. Some people find it flattering and sometimes emotionally moving to be asked for a gift by someone who has given the biggest gift.

Once the very top of the pyramid has been filled in with donors, the group is ready to move to the second stage.

The Launching Stage

The launch of a capital campaign should be marked with a special event. The press, donors, volunteers, and foundation and corporate staff should be invited. The press should receive a press release ahead of time with background information on the group and the campaign or they should be given one at the event. The invitation to the launch should be attractive because it is the first impression most prospects will have of your capital campaign. The event itself doesn't need to last very long. If you want to make it into a regular special event, you can add a dance or speaker, but this is not necessary. Large graphics on display should describe the overall goal of the campaign and show the gift range chart and how much money has been raised. A board member should describe to the gathered crowd how important the campaign is and invite everyone to celebrate the donations that have come in so far. Champagne, soft drinks, and hors d'oeuvres may be served.

The Intensive Stage

Immediately after the launch the intensive stage begins. During this time teams of two people are visiting prospects with as much speed as that process will allow. Most prospects are visited at least once during this time, and this stage is the longest. As each gift is received, the total still needed is revised and publicized at least to staff, board members, and solicitors, so there is a constant sense of movement toward the goal. During this stage, the two most important elements are maintaining good records and keeping in touch with volunteer solicitors. Thank you notes must go out promptly. When people pledge to pay over several years, they must sign a pledge agreement. It can be very simple, as in the following example:

SAMPLE PLEDGE AGREEMENT

I, *(name)*, pledge the sum of $_____ *(amount)* to be paid in monthly (or quarterly) installments of $____ for the next ___ years.

This document constitutes a legally binding agreement, and I know that plans are being made and money is being spent based on the expectation that I will pay this pledge in the way I have described. A copy of this pledge agreement has been placed with my will.

Signed:

_____

The system for collecting pledges (as described in Chapter Nineteen) must be in place.

Solicitors must be notified of new gifts as they come in; they should meet regularly (at least every three weeks) to report on their progress. Any problems they run into must be dealt with promptly. One such problem is conditional gifts. Prospects will often offer to make a gift on certain conditions: "I'll give if three other people match my gift," or "I'll give if the conference room can be named for my mother," or "I'll give if I can have a seat on the board." Conditional gifts, regardless of how benign the condition proposed, must go through an approval process, preferably at the board level. Solicitors can say to such prospects, "That's a very kind offer. Let me see what we can do about it. I don't have the authority to make those promises." Then the organization decides if it wishes to accept the condition or not. An organization should never take money on conditions that it doesn't wish to meet. People should not be able to "buy" board seats, for example.

The Wind-Up Stage

When more than four-fifths of the money has been pledged, the group goes into a wind-up phase. At this point you look for one or two people who can put the goal over the top: "Mr. Jones, we are $10,000 short of our goal—would you finish this campaign with a gift of that amount?" To find people who can close the campaign in this way, go back to your original prospect list for lead gifts and see if any of the people on that list were not asked because solicitors felt that they would not take a risk on being the lead gift, or see if any of them said, "Come back to me when you are further along." The wind-up phase is also a good time to ask for a lot of small gifts, because at this stage gifts of $1,000 are clearly helping to move the group toward its goal.

The end of the wind-up phase is a large celebratory special event. If you are purchasing or constructing a building, this is often a ribbon-cutting or ceremonial groundbreaking event, if that hasn't happened already.

THE POST-CAMPAIGN

Volunteer solicitors should be given their own party, such as dinner at a fancy restaurant, and should be presented with gifts of appreciation. These are often plaques. Though nice, the gifts should not be expensive. Staff should also be rewarded at this party, possibly with a certificate for a weekend away at a bed-and-breakfast or a gift certificate to a store they would like.

Staff and solicitors should review all the donor records for the campaign to make sure they are accurate and that all needed documentation is in place. A special report should be sent to all donors and funders describing the successful conclusion of the campaign and reiterating what wonderful work the group will be able to do in its new building.

Soon after the end of the capital campaign, you will need to increase the amount of money you are raising annually, since you will not have had an increase in two or three years while the campaign was active. A good capital campaign usually has the effect of helping increase annual income, as donors feel closer to the organization and realize they can afford to give more than they thought. Further, the high visibility of a capital campaign will often attract new annual donors.

As you can see, a capital campaign is a time-consuming project and one that requires keeping track of a lot of details. Only organizations with a strong working board of directors, a loyal donor base, and a well-designed major gifts program should undertake such a campaign.

Developing Endowment Campaigns

An endowment campaign has the same structure as an annual fund campaign, a major donor campaign, or a capital campaign in that it has a financial goal for which a gift range chart and time line have been developed to help the organization meet that goal. Many organizations conduct a feasibility study to determine what the goal of the campaign should be or even whether to commit to the campaign at all. (See Chapter Twenty-Six for a discussion of feasibility studies.)

As with a capital campaign, the tasks for launching an endowment campaign include forming a committee of solicitors, compiling a list of prospects, and developing creative materials that describe the campaign and its benefits. Once these tasks have been done, the prospects are prioritized and solicitation begins. Unlike other types of campaigns, an endowment remains open for new gifts even after the campaign has ended. The gifts sought during the campaign are from donors who will give over the next few years; gifts through estates are not the focus of this campaign.

For all the similarities of the steps, in each of them there are subtle and not-so-subtle differences between endowment campaigns and other kinds of campaigns.

STEP 1: SET A GOAL

To determine a goal for your endowment campaign, you need to decide how much interest income you want and what amount of principal will be likely to generate that amount of interest. A financial adviser will be able to help you with projections; these must also take into account whether you are investing only for income or for both income and growth. In addition, consider whether you want your endowment principal to keep pace with inflation, which will mean reinvesting some income back into the principal or investing at least some principal in growth stocks. Generally, an organization can safely assume that they can take the equivalent of 5 percent of the principal out every year and the principal will continue to grow. To generate $50,000 a year in interest income, then, will require an endowment of about $1 million; to generate $200,000 a year will require an endowment of $4,000,000. An endowment is not a quick fix to a cash flow problem!

There are two ways to get to your goal: one is to conduct a campaign for that goal. If you need $1 million, your campaign goal is $1 million. However, if that sum seems out of your reach right now but you think you could get to, say, $250,000, you can conduct a campaign to "seed" your endowment fund. With this type of campaign, you raise a decent amount of money and do not draw anything out the account it until it gets to the initial goal you have set. Once the campaign is ended, you keep raising endowment funds as part of your fundraising work, but without the intensity of a campaign. Having some money raised will help donors feel more assured that their endowment gift is joining existing money. The problem with the "seeding" approach, however, is that too often the endowment levels off at the small amount raised by the campaign. The endowment principal is too much money for the organization to spend, but not enough to generate the kind of interest that will really help with the annual fundraising crunch. If you decide to seed an endowment with a campaign, then, be sure that you have a plan in place for having the endowment grow after the campaign is over.

Sometimes groups just want "something to take the edge off"—the stiff drink approach to endowments. They want a pot of money that generates between $5,000 and $10,000 a year, so they only need between $100,000 and $250,000. An endowment campaign is not the best vehicle to raise this small amount of money. For any need of less than $25,000, an organization should consider increasing its annual fundraising goal, perhaps by diversifying to a new strategy or being more aggressive with current donors. Generally, it is not worth the effort of starting an actual endowment campaign if your goal is to raise less than $500,000.

Of course, however much money you decide to raise in your campaign, you should always be seeking and accepting additional endowment gifts. But keep your endowment moving by setting a large enough goal to be meaningful.

STEP 2: CREATE THE GIFT RANGE CHART

Once you have a goal, you need to create a gift range chart. A chart for a goal of $1 million is shown below. As with capital campaigns discussed in the previous chapter, an endowment campaign differs from an annual major donor campaign in that it seeks a lead gift that is generally 20 percent of the goal instead of 10 percent, and all the gifts are fairly large. The chart calls for one gift to equal 20 percent of the goal, two gifts to equal 10 percent of the goal, and three to five gifts to equal the next 10 percent of the goal. Six to eight donors, then, contribute 50 percent or more of the total goal.

Endowment Campaign Gift Range Chart	
Goal: $1 Million	
Number of Gifts	**Gift Size**
1	$200,000
2	$100,000
4	$50,000
5	$25,000
10	$10,000
20	$5,000
20	$2,500
25	$1,000
Total Gifts	87

Generally, gifts of less than $1,000 are not sought (although all gifts are gratefully accepted). Because donors have several years to pay off these gifts, $1,000 is affordable even for lower-income people. For example, a pledge of $27 per month, which is relatively affordable, carried out for three years totals $1,000. Organizations with a donor base of very-low-income people, however, need to think twice before launching an endowment. Even if such an effort could be successful, it means the organization will have a kind of financial security that few, if any, of its supporters have. This can exacerbate a danger present in all endowments: a perception on the part of donors that the organization doesn't need annual gifts and that, in fact, the organization has lost touch with its base. A further danger is that donors will give to the endowment instead of to the annual fund. As the saying goes, you will have robbed Peter to pay Paul.

STEP 3: CREATE THE TIMELINE

The timeline for an endowment campaign is generally not less than two years and definitely not more than five years. The timeline for the campaign does not include all the discussion involved in deciding to do a campaign or the feasibility study, but it does include the preparation time in terms of prospect research and materials. It usually takes the best part of a year just to solicit the lead gifts (because many of the lead donors will have to be talked with several times) and to create appropriate materials, and it may take another year to solicit all the other gifts. Three years allows for the unforeseen to be dealt with and the maximum number of donors to be solicited. Five years is the outside maximum amount of time an organization can sustain interest and passion for a campaign while maintaining annual fundraising. Usually two to three years is the ideal amount of time to conduct a campaign. A fourth year can be used as a "wind-down" period, and pledges can be paid over five or more years even if the solicitation phase of the campaign is completed in two years.

STEP 4: FORM A SOLICITATION TEAM

Traditionally, endowments are funded by gifts from estates. This is why traditional endowments cannot be conducted as campaigns, because the receipt of the gift usually depends on the death of the donor as well as the time it takes to settle the estate (which can be years). Some groups have counted the unrealized value of bequests as part of their endowment campaign goal, but this is both foolish and unethical. Bequests can be changed any time before the donor's death, so even when a donor has promised you a bequest, it may not happen if the donor has a change of heart or circumstance. Only irrevocable—unable to be revoked—legacy gifts (such as trusts) can be counted toward a goal.

In conducting an endowment campaign, organizations are asking donors for assets: gifts given during the donor's lifetime. (Because an endowment lasts forever, a gift from a donor's estate is welcome; many endowments are built mostly or entirely from estate gifts. However, a campaign format means that we seek gifts that are made in the donor's lifetime—in fact that are paid in the next few years.) Although gifts made from a donor's annual income are certainly welcome, they will never be as large as assets or estate gifts, because even the wealthiest donors reserve the bulk of their income for their own needs.

In forming a committee, then, you are looking for people who are comfortable asking donors for assets; usually, these are people who have made an asset gift themselves. The people on the solicitation team include members of the board and people who have made large gifts to the endowment. Although this is the ideal committee makeup for any campaign, for an endowment it is imperative that those who are asking know what it feels like to decide to give a gift that they cannot give very often. The role of volunteers in these campaigns cannot be overstated. Staff can ask, and they do, but even then a staff person will need to have made a endowment gift in addition to their annual gift.

To form the solicitation team, first identify the people closest to the group who can make the largest gifts. A team consisting of a board member and a staff member asks each of these potential solicitors for their own gift, then asks them to be on the team. Some members of the solicitation team are usually identified during the discussion about whether to have an endowment. They are the ones who argue in favor of it and say that they will give to such a campaign.

Conventional financial planning dictates that one should "never touch principal." Yet principal is what you are asking for. In a sense, you are asking people to transfer some of their "endowment" to your endowment. This is a process that requires thought, commitment, and careful consideration. All the solicitors must be people whom the donors trust to have gone through this process. Moreover, there is something very convincing when a person can say, "My husband and I have accumulated a nest egg of $100,000 over many years of saving. It is for our retirement and for emergencies. But the threat to reproductive rights (or environment, our children, or world peace) is bigger than our need for a nest egg. We want to make sure that Important Group is able to do their work and not have to struggle so with fundraising. So we are giving $10,000 to the endowment as our investment in our community's future."

Even someone with no real assets can make a good solicitor, as long as they have given a significant gift. In one organization, a board member postponed buying a new car. He described his gift this way: "My old car can be coaxed into a couple more years of use. In the meantime I am going to give the equivalent of a car payment on a new car for two years to the endowment campaign. That will bring my gift to $5,000. I don't have any real assets, but I can give by postponing getting an asset, and my gift will have far more permanence than a new car." In another instance, a solicitor described her gift this way: "I put some money aside every month and once a year I go away for two weeks. This year, I vacationed at home. I saw friends, I planted a garden, I read books, I went to free events at my library, and I gave the money I saved to the endowment. I had a great time, so although my gift was significant for me, it was not painful."

The solicitation team can be formed slowly. It can start with two or three endowment donors and as more donations are received, new donors can be asked to join the team.

STEP 5: COMPILE AND ORGANIZE THE LIST OF PROSPECTS

In all campaigns, the rule of "top down, inside out" is the way to organize your prospects. Ben Franklin, who was one of America's earliest and best fundraisers, advised, "Apply to all those whom you know will give something; next, to those whom you are uncertain whether they will give anything or not, and show them the list of those who have given; and lastly, do not neglect those who you are sure will give nothing, for in some of them you will be mistaken."

Franklin's advice is what we mean by "inside out." Start with the people closest to the group. Those will be board members (if they are not the closest people to the organization, then reconsider doing an endowment campaign), other major donors, volunteers, former board members and volunteers (assuming no ill will accompanied their becoming "former"), staff, and so on. Then, start from the top of that list and work your way down. The first gift should be solicited from the person closest to the organization who can give the biggest gift. This may not be the biggest gift you need, but it should be the biggest one you can get right now.

Sometimes it is hard to figure out which of the people who are closest you should approach first. Think through who on the list can give the biggest gifts. This exercise should narrow your list somewhat. Now think about who is most excited about the endowment. Remember there are going to be major donors who love your organization's work but who are not going to support the endowment. There will be some who simply don't agree that a grassroots organization should have an endowment. There will be some who have given to other endowments only to see the endowment funds spent on annual needs by a careless board. And there will be others who wish your endowment effort well but are only interested in funding more immediate needs. Finding donors who agree with all three premises of the case for an endowment—that the organization currently needs some financial stability, needs to exist indefinitely into the future, and is mature enough or sophisticated enough to handle this kind of money—and who also have the capacity to give is not simple.

Use common sense in identifying these prospects. Think about what else you know about the people on your list. For example, a person giving $50 every quarter might be close to the group, but she is probably far from the biggest donor. However, if her $50 gifts are derived from income earned from investments, then she definitely goes to the top of the list because perhaps she would give you the asset that is yielding that $50 each quarter. Someone who gave you $1,000 that he won in the lottery, whose gift prior to that was $25, and who actually ekes out a living as an artist, is not going to be high on the list, but he may be an excellent solicitor because he actually gave an asset that he could have used himself.

Many people will say that they have no idea what assets their donors have. If you really have no idea, then you are going to have to find out more about your donors before you begin asking them for gifts to your endowment. However, a general easy rule to follow in soliciting capital or endowment gifts is to ask for a gift that is ten times the amount of the donor's annual gift. You want to make it clear that this gift is in addition to their annual gift. You don't want your annual income to decline while you are doing the campaign. When you tell donors that you are asking everyone for the same thing—ten times their annual gift—people are not offended, even if the size of the gift is absolutely out of their range. The real risk you take in following this formula without other knowledge is that you would ask someone for too little.

The final step in compiling a prospect list is to be sure you have enough prospects. A prospect for an endowment gift is someone who has demonstrated a commitment to your group, usually by giving over several years and often through other than just financial involvement; someone who has the money; and someone whom you know or you have access to.

As with capital campaigns, you need about four times as many prospects as the number of gifts you seek because 50 percent of your prospects will say no and 50 percent of the group that says yes will give you less than what you ask for. In our $1 million gift range chart shown above, you would need about 348 prospects (87×4) to be certain that you could complete this goal. You don't need to have all the prospects right at the start, but you do need at least some of the prospects for the biggest gifts right from the beginning. You would be ill advised to launch a million-dollar endowment campaign with fewer than one hundred prospects for the gifts of $2,500 or more. Far worse than no endowment at all is an endowment campaign that sputters and moves slowly. The energy of the campaign is part of what makes it successful or not. A report that "Our campaign is going so well" makes people want to give. The news that "Our campaign is getting off to a slow start," or "We asked a bunch of people who said no" is not as appealing.

STEP 6: SOLICIT THE GIFTS

For a full description of the process of soliciting large gifts, please re-read Chapters Eighteen, Twenty-Three, and Twenty-Four on major gifts programs, major gift campaigns, and capital campaigns.

The primary differences between major gifts or capital campaigns and endowment campaigns is in the case. A person being asked for a major gift needs to be convinced that there is a pressing, immediate need that your organization can meet and that this need must be addressed with, among other things, some very large gifts. A capital campaign makes the case that the pressing needs of the organization cannot be met adequately in the facility you are in or with the equipment you currently have or without some other large investment. The case for the endowment goes one step further, explaining that the organization needs stability currently and into the future. It tells the donor that his or her commitment to your current programs is so important that you hope they want to help make your work a permanent feature of your community.

Even the most progressive person becomes a fiscal conservative when asked for capital or endowment gifts. They may well believe that your organization does wonderful things toward ending racism or providing creative learning opportunities for kids with disabilities or advocating for more just tax policies. But do these same donors believe you will be able to manage investing large amounts of money or be good at managing a building? Donors will have these questions, and organizations must be able to respond to them. When an organization wants to start an endowment, there will be an added question that no one can really answer: "What will happen when everyone who is currently involved in this organization is gone?" Taking seriously the right (and indeed, the obligation) of donors to raise these questions and doubts and preparing thoughtful and reasonable answers are the marks of organizations ready for capital and endowment projects.

Conducting Feasibility Studies

A feasibility study is a survey of people whose agreement and support you would need in order to succeed at a particular project. Usually, prospective donors, board members, community leaders, and program officers at foundations and corporations who might be approached to contribute to a project are asked to state anonymously what they think about your capital or endowment project and what level of support they or their organization might provide. Generally, the survey is done in two or three parts: a written survey sent to all the prospects who will be asked for major gifts, a phone survey to a smaller number of donors who will probably be asked for lead gifts, and an optional handful of in-person interviews or a focus group with key leaders.

WHO CONDUCTS THE FEASIBILITY STUDY

Most organizations hire a consultant to carry out their feasibility study. The reason for this is straightforward: in order for the prospects to feel that they can be as honest and candid as they want, their answers have to be truly anonymous. Maximum anonymity is ensured when they are asked by a consultant whom they don't know to fill out a form sent by mail that does not call for them to include their name and address and that they return to the consultant, not the organization. Although some people might be willing to say whatever they want to say to anyone, human nature is such that to spare someone's feelings or to avoid a confrontation, many people will not be as direct if they know that what they say is going to get back to someone they know.

327

The written survey consists mostly of structured questions presented in a multiple-choice format so that the results can be easily tabulated. A few open-ended questions can also be included to get more information about anything else the prospect might want to add about his or her confidence in the leadership of the organization or the program directions it is taking. Once those results are in, the consultant or other person doing the feasibility study looks for any pattern of response or issues that need to be clarified. The results of the written survey form the basis of the questions in the phone survey. On the phone, the surveyor can probe a little more, record anecdotes and examples, and even query respondents about whether they agree or disagree with some of the opinions or findings that came from the written survey. Many studies don't include in-person interviews. They are helpful if there is a need to clarify the case or probe further about any anomalies found in the phone or written surveys, but otherwise you might have enough information to go on without them.

A feasibility study is complicated and time consuming to conduct, which makes it expensive. The least-expensive study conducted by a professional will likely cost at least $5,000; many studies run as high as $25,000. The size of the income that can be expected from the campaign resulting from the feasibility study will not correlate directly to the cost of the study, because a campaign with a low goal will not necessarily involve fewer surveys or fewer phone calls. Because of the costs involved, these studies are usually reserved for large campaigns.

WHETHER TO DO A STUDY

There is no need to do a feasibility study in the following situations:

- If you intend to do the campaign no matter what the study shows. I have known half a dozen organizations that spent money on a study only to conclude that the results showing lack of support were wrong. They proceeded with their campaigns—some succeeded and some failed.

- If you are going to use the study simply to find out whether or not you can make your goal. You will discover easily enough whether you can raise the amount of money you need by asking for lead gifts from qualified prospects before the campaign is announced publicly. If they all say no or give much lower gifts than you needed, don't announce your campaign, and go back to the drawing board.

- If your goal is less than $2 million, the cost of a full-scale study is not justified. You can decide to do only a written survey or a limited phone survey if you have some specific questions, but what you really want is to go to the lead prospects and see what they say.

You will need to do a study under the following circumstances:

- The key leadership in your organization has a mixed reputation. I conducted a study for a capital campaign for an organization whose executive director had been there thirteen years. She was well liked, but as one key prospect said, "The organization has gotten too big for her and neither she nor her board can handle the responsibility of a building." The study showed that unless the group made significant changes in staffing, such as hiring an associate director who could handle a lot of the administrative and human resource issues the executive director was not good at, few were likely to contribute.

- Your building project may be controversial in some way. A proposed homeless shelter discovered that they would face major neighborhood opposition if they expanded in the way they envisioned. By slowing the process down, they were able to address neighborhood concerns with public education programs. Once that was done, the campaign proceeded successfully.

- You want to raise more than $2 million and you have never raised that amount of money before.

- You want to know exactly what the capacity of the people closest to the organization is before you ask them. The results of your study will not show you what any individual donor can give, but you will learn whether there are people in your sphere who have the capacity and willingness to give large amounts. You will need to figure out who those people are.

A feasibility study gives you an added measure of assurance and will help you define and counter big problems. When raising large amounts of money, a feasibility study will allow you to discover the capacity of your donors in a way that would otherwise be difficult, given our society's strong taboo about talking about how much money a person actually has.

In my experience, grassroots organizations that are able to raise the first third of their goal from five to ten people will be able to raise the rest of the money to get to their goal. I advise groups to use that guideline as the most reliable indicator of whether their campaign will succeed.

If you want more assurance without having to buy a feasibility study, you can talk to the people who would have to take the lead for your campaign to succeed. Tell them about the possibility of the campaign and ask what they think about it. Tell them you are "testing the waters," or "getting feedback on this idea." Make the conversation very casual, but pay close attention to what they say.

WHAT FEASIBILITY STUDIES TELL YOU

Feasibility studies often predict that a campaign will bring in a lower amount than it actually raises in the end. Many consultants prefer to underestimate the amount that can be raised, but the main reason campaigns exceed their goals is that it is impossible to factor in the effect of the excitement generated by the campaign on the prospects. It is one thing for a prospect to talk on the phone about what they might, theoretically, do for a campaign should it be launched, but quite another for them to be asked in person to give to a campaign by someone they admire. On the phone, a person is sober and serious and not wanting to mislead the questioner. They name an amount that is perhaps a stretch for them but that they feel confident they would be able to pay. Later, during the real campaign, when a friend or colleague comes with a staff person to ask for their gift, they are likely to become excited by the enthusiasm of the askers, and end up giving more than they told the interviewer they might during the phone survey. Perhaps on the phone a prospect said they would be unlikely to give, but faced with the reality of the campaign they may not want to be left out. Their objections, which seemed so big during the phone call, can fade in the light of the campaign. This does not mean you should add on a few hundred thousand to whatever the study suggests you can raise, but it does mean that you can be confident that a well-done study will present an amount that is at or below what you can really bring in.

ACHIEVING SUCCESS

Of course, there is no assurance that any plan will succeed. But you have a better chance of succeeding if you have a plan than if you don't. Moreover, evaluating your success will be easier if you have a plan—in fact a plan is what makes evaluation possible.

Another requirement for success is to make sure your board of directors is on board. If a board of directors does not want to work on the campaign, the campaign is going to go nowhere. People look to the board for leadership. Your board may well be made up of people who cannot make big gifts to a capital or endowment campaign. That's fine. But they need to make some gift, and they need to be involved in planning the campaign.

The best way to know if you are going to succeed is to take the time to plan properly, as discussed in the chapters on capital and endowment campaigns, then implement the quiet phase of your plan. The requests made during the quiet phase give you the most accurate information with the least amount of public risk.

PART FIVE

Fundraising Management

Fundraising for low-budget organizations generally falls apart because of one of the following three difficulties:

- Strategies are not used properly and so are rendered ineffective.
- The organization doesn't have a clear case or loses sight of its mission and goals in its search for funding.
- Fundraising is not managed properly—there are bad record keeping systems, the fundraising staff have more than their own jobs to do, and the organization cannot keep to its plans.

This section is meant to help organizations forestall the last difficulty. A colleague once observed that fundraising was like an iceberg—you don't see most of it. I would go further and say that what you don't see is often the most important part of it. Starting with the office and basic working conditions and covering finding staff, consultants, and volunteers for fundraising, this section explains what has to be in place for effective fundraising to happen and how even a small organization can work with those elements.

The Fundraising Office

Few offices of low-budget organizations are adequate in size, equipment, or support staff, but there are some basic office requirements without which fundraising staff and volunteers will be unable to carry out an effective program. Some of the requirements detailed here cost money, but because they will pay for themselves, these costs should be seen as front money. Other requirements cost time, which also must be seen as a front-end cost.

There must be a separate space in the office for fundraising staff, files, and materials—preferably, a room or at least a partitioned area. This space must be quiet and include a desk of adequate size with drawers, a chair, a filing cabinet with at least three drawers, a bookshelf, a telephone, and a computer. Certainly, a printer can be shared by many people, but the days of several people sharing the same computer are over. (Some of this equipment can be obtained for free from corporations.) The space must have proper lighting and ventilation, and it should not be used by people other than fundraising staff and volunteers—too much of the information here is confidential. Moreover, files, mailing lists, reports, letters, and the like need to be kept in order and should not be handled by anyone who is not dealing with them. The data in the database should be protected with a password.

The organization must take the fundraising process seriously. Both paid and volunteer fundraising staff should be seen as professionals needing certain tools to carry out their job. A computer, a decent database, a desk, filing cabinet, phone, and separate space are the tools of a fundraiser in the same way, and with the same importance, as hammers, saws, levels, and the like are the tools of a carpenter. Just as you can't build a building without construction equipment, you can't build a donor base without fundraising equipment.

In addition to an adequate office set-up, a fundraiser should have a basic library of fundraising books as well as a dictionary, thesaurus, and style manual to aid in writing and planning. (See Resource E for recommendations of books on fundraising.)

Obviously, fundraising staff should not have nicer office space or fancier equipment than everyone else in the office. The whole organization should examine its working conditions from time to time and make it a priority to improve them if needed. It is ironic that many social change or social service groups will work in conditions that include too much noise, dim light, ergonomically horrible chairs, and inadequate equipment when they would be outraged to read about such conditions for other workers. Good working conditions cost time and money, but poor working conditions cost more: lower productivity, stress, burnout, loss of creativity, loss of information, and finally, loss of income to keep the organization going.

Managing Your Information

A major part of fundraising is information—about people, about sources of money, about timing, about strategies. But fundraising is not just knowing things. The creativity to make fundraising successful is in putting together what you know: asking the right person at the right time for the right amount; scheduling the right event and inviting the people most likely to be interested in attending; using volunteers to the best of their abilities.

In order to use all the information available in the most effective ways, a fundraiser must know how to manage the information that is constantly coming in. Too often what one finds in the office of fundraising staff are piles of papers on the floor and windowsill interspersed with unlabelled CDs and multiple foundation guides. Desks are strewn with notes, Post-its are stuck all around the computer monitor, and a telephone is perched precariously atop the overflowing in-basket. The staff's e-mail inbox will contain hundreds of e-newsletters and messages from the many listservs they subscribe to.

Too often we mistake the message that such an office sends—the inability to get and stay organized—with being overworked. Since having too much work is often a major component of many fundraisers' lives, one compounds the other. A fundraiser confided to me recently that she was secretly relieved when her office flooded and her papers and hard drive were destroyed. Now she had an excuse for not getting work done she wouldn't have gotten to anyway.

What has been called for the past twenty-five years the "information age" is really information glut. In addition to the traditional books and magazines about fundraising, new Web sites, listservs, e-newsletters, and computer programs pop up daily, ostensibly to help you gather and sort information in ways you never thought of. Dozens of toll-free numbers provide more information or technical support for your must-have new module on your database. There is more to know

337

about everything than any human can process; moreover there are mountains of misinformation.

People in fundraising must always be clear about what they need to do and what they don't. This chapter will help you deal with the overload of information.

INFORMATION YOU NEED FOR FUNDRAISING

In order to know what to keep, what to throw out, what to delete, what to order, and what to file, you must make a list of priorities about your job. What information do you need to be on top of, what do you need to have access to from time to time, and what doesn't matter at all? While the answers to these questions will vary from person to person, most fundraisers must keep track of the following information that is the most important to their work:

• Information pertaining to current donors

• Information pertaining to prospects

• Information about the organization that will be used to get more donors and prospects

• Reference materials and records about past fundraising activities

Any papers that come across your desk or any e-mail that pops up on your screen that does not pertain to the categories listed here needs to be deleted, recycled, or at least put out of sight. Among other items that will get tossed are newsletters from other groups unrelated to your group, advertisements for seminars and classes, catalogues, annual reports of foundations your group will not be applying to, old annual reports of prospective foundations, old to-do lists, and reports on all causes unrelated to your group. Similarly, delete any files that are not related to current or prospective donors, past donors, or past fundraising efforts, as well as ancillary information about any of those items. In your physical filing cabinet, use the bottom file drawer for reference material about your group. Put in that drawer one copy each of your past newsletters, proposals funded, evaluations of direct mail appeals, reports on special events, board minutes and reports, and financial statements.

Every piece of paper and every byte in your computer should be held up to this test: Will this item help me get money from someone? If yes, who and how? Then put it in the appropriate place: the prospect's file or the reference drawer. If the answer for any piece of paper or computer document is no, throw it out or delete it or forward it to another staff person whose work it will help.

KEEPING TRACK

Once you learn a few simple rules about what to keep and what to save, keeping track of information will actually not be that difficult.

First, review the basics: What is your job? What do you have to know? What would people reasonably expect you to be able to lay your hands on quickly? Even if you are the only paid staff person, you still have a limit to your job. These are the types of information you must have and have easy access to:

- Records of official meetings of the organization and reports offered to the board, the public, or the IRS about the organization. Keep one (at most two) copies of board minutes, audits, 990s, newsletters, direct mail appeals, annual reports, and so on.

- Records on the donors: their names, addresses, and gift history, as well as information that would help you or someone else ask them for more money or for some other type of involvement. Most of this information is kept virtually in a database; it must be backed up every day on either a flash drive or backup disk. Once a week a copy of that back-up must be taken out of your office.

There are other items you probably should have if you are a one-person shop— you decide. But do you really need copies of newsletters from organizations you are not interested in? Dozens of samples of invitations? (Pick the best ten and throw the rest away.) The latest reports from the most prolific think tanks on every subject from ozone depletion to police brutality, from campaign reform to the role of women in rural Hindu communities? No. What is your organization? You will be kept busy enough keeping up with what pertains to you.

Having set priorities on the kinds of information you need—and limit yourself to five priorities at the most—sort all your papers into those categories and throw away anything that doesn't fall into them. Especially throw away the volumes of information you now keep that you feel you "should" read: the stuff that you bring home but never quite get to, the stuff you downloaded to read in the airport but always manage to ignore in favor of something else you have found. If you feel that you "should" read it, you won't. Lighten up. It's all right not to read everything; it's even all right not to read most things.

The final guideline about what to throw out is that if you haven't looked at it in six months and it is not needed for the IRS or as an archive copy, throw it out.

YOUR FILING SYSTEM

Next, think through your filing system for both your paper and your computer files. Create broad categories, then file within those categories. Categories might include board, donors, prospects, foundations, finances, programs, personnel, and publications. You may want to keep some of these items in files for each year. Within some of those categories you may want subcategories. For example, the board section might have the following subcategories: board members—current, past, potential; board reimbursements; board minutes; staff reports to the board. The files in some of these categories will be arranged alphabetically, in others chronologically. For example, board minutes and reports to the board should be filed chronologically.

To test your filing system, ask a friend or another staff person to come into your office and start naming things for you to find. It should not take you more than two minutes to lay your hands on or bring up on your computer any piece of information you are in charge of. If you can't do that, reassess your system. Once your system passes this test, see how well it works for someone else. Suppose you were hit by a train—how obvious is your information set-up? If it takes someone else more than five minutes to figure out where something is, your system is too mysterious.

Many otherwise neat people have sloppy virtual files, so give this problem extra attention. I know, because I am one of these people. Virtual files fool you because you don't often notice how much room these are taking up—the "clutter" is invisible, so it is easy to let the information on hard drives get out of control. I, who rarely handle a piece of paper more than once, will spend an hour scrolling through my files with the intensity of a mad scientist—did I save it under "November" because it happened in November, or under "Special Events-Ideas-Fall Plans" or in "Docs-Fundraising-Special Events-November"? Why would I even have a filing system like that?

The same standards apply to computer files as to paper files: Will you need it again? How can you name the file and the subfile so their contents are obvious?

As you save documents on your computer, think about what you name them. There are people who name their files after the day of the week or even an abbreviation of something in the file, but all of this makes the files obscure even to the one who named them. Again, apply the standard, "If I were hit by a train, could someone else find this?" Give it a name that makes some sense. Spend time clearing out your computer files.

STICKING WITH IT

To help you stay on top of your papers and computer files once you get organized, post a 3 × 5 card with the one, two, or three things that will most help you stay focused on what to keep. One person has this on his card:

Is it a donor?

Is it a prospect?

Could it lead to a donor or a prospect?

Another has this:

When in doubt, throw it out.

After all, what is the worst thing that can happen?

Another's says:

If this were my last day at work and I was sorting through my stuff, would I give it to the person succeeding me?

In our business, information is like food: we eat it, we serve it to others, we save it for a few days, but we don't keep it permanently. It is useful for what it does for us, but is not really useful beyond being converted to energy, enjoyment, or in this case, donors. Seeing information in that light will let you be in control of it so that you can use it to do your work.

Managing Your Time

Effective time management often marks the difference between a good fundraiser and someone who is never going to make it in this field. First, remember that the fundraising job is never done and you are never caught up on your work. Also, Murphy's Law says that expenses rise to meet income. The more successful the fundraising plans are, the more plans the organization will make to spend that money. Consequently, no amount of money raised is ever enough. Fundraising staff (paid and unpaid) must set their own limits because no matter how supportive the organization may be of your work, it is still relentless in its need for more money. Here are some guidelines for using your time to best advantage.

GUIDELINES

There are certain tasks that must be completed either every day or every week.

Every Day

Reserve Time When You Cannot Be Interrupted. For one (and sometimes two or three) hours each day, let someone else or your voice mail answer the phone. Do not talk to other staff, and do not reply to e-mail. Use that time for research and writing.

Write To-Do Lists at the End of Each Day. Spend fifteen to thirty minutes at the end of the day writing up a to-do list for the next day. At the beginning of the day, review your to-do list. Unless something comes up that really can't wait, do only those tasks already on your to-do list. Put new things on tomorrow's list.

Make Sure Thank You Notes Are Getting Written. Ideally, a board member or volunteer is coming into the office to write thank you notes on a regular basis, or the executive director is adding a personal note to a thank you generated by your database program. You must stay on top of this process.

Update Your Database.   This task often happens when you are entering the information that will enable you to generate a thank you note, but don't get behind on it.

Every Week
Review Your Fundraising Plan for the Month.   Go over your plan to make sure you are on target. Don't put off tasks such as getting a letter to the printer, calling a foundation, setting up meetings of the major gifts committee or the special events committee. Do these tasks on time.

Watch for Time Sinks.   How many times have we looked up at a clock and in total disbelief said, "How could it be four o'clock?" or "Where did the day go?" Sometimes this is a sign that we have been absorbed in important work, but sometimes it is a sign that we have used up our time doing a lot of stuff that seemed important but wasn't, or that is important but could have been handled in a fraction of the time. Here are the most common time sinks:

The Telephone.   Limit the length of your calls by standing up while you are on the phone. If you know the telephone is a big temptation for you, move it off your desk so that you actually have to move to answer it or to make a phone call. Because you know that for most of the calls you make you will get voice mail, spend a few seconds before you call thinking about the exact message you are going to leave. We all hate to get rambling or disjointed messages, yet many of us leave them. This wastes our time and the time of the person we are phoning. While friendliness and warmth are wonderful, limit yourself to one expression of either of these: "Hope your day is going well" does not have to be followed by, "And I hope your weekend was fabulous," or "And I hope you are feeling good and having time to enjoy this wonderful weather." Ditto with "OK, take care. Look forward to talking with you. Great to hear your voice." Pick one of those, preferably a short one.

E-Mail.   What could have been a great time-saving device has become the greatest time sink ever. Get off of listervs that you don't find useful or that are unrelated to your work. Delete without reading anything that has been forwarded to you that you know is simply a list of jokes or a petition. Don't feel obligated to answer every e-mail, particularly if you get e-mail from people who are not and are never going to be important to your group or who would never have paid the money to call you. Limit yourself to looking at your e-mail three or four times a day. Check it first thing in the morning, at the end of the morning, in midafternoon, and right before you go home. Don't check your work e-mail in the evening.

Chatty Coworkers.   Learn to sort out what kinds of conversations are important for maintaining morale and showing interest in other people, and what conversations simply occur because you or your coworker is procrastinating getting work done. Schedule social time with coworkers you like so that you will not have to steal time away from work. When you spend time talking with someone when you know you should be working, you are neither really enjoying the conversation nor, obviously, getting your work done.

People Who Drop By.   If someone comes by whom you don't need to talk with and you don't have time to talk, try the following tactics: tell them that you will call them later, or set a lunch date right then, or stand up and remain standing while talking to them (they will not sit down if you are standing). Another tactic is, at a moment when you are the one speaking, look at your watch or your calendar. This will remind your visitor of time without you being rude. You never need to act hurried or rushed with spontaneous visitors so long as you don't get panicked about how you are going to get rid of them.

CALENDARS AND ACTION PLANS

Understanding that information is time-related is integral to running an efficient office. Once you have organized your office, paper, computer files, and desk in a way that allows you easy and quick access to the information you need and provides a sensible system that someone else can follow, assign a time by which you will have used or acted on the information you are keeping track of so effectively. There are two principal methods: calendars and action plans.

Calendars

Buy or make the following three calendars or use the calendar function in your computer or on your PDA:

- A "Year-at-a-Glance" wall calendar. This calendar shows all twelve months at once, with boxes for each day within each month.

- A "Month-at-a-Glance" calendar. Some people get these calendars as desktop blotters. You can also buy a smaller, desktop calendar from a worthy group so you have uplifting stories or fabulous nature photos to look at. Just be sure that the box for each day has enough room to write a few lines.

- An appointment calendar to carry with you in your purse or briefcase. This is a simple daily calendar with all the days of the year laid out two or so to a page.

You can get all of these functions on your PDA and then sync them with your computer, which provides a useful back-up system. Don't, however, feel you must go to an electronic system to be efficient. What is best is what works best for you and what you can use most easily.

Although you can certainly invest lots of money in fancy calendar systems or calendar functions that allow you to record your expenses, birthday reminders, car mileage, meeting notes, priority to-do lists, meeting agenda items, tax information, and the like, I have yet to meet anyone who actually used all those systems. Further (and this is not a judgment of these systems, simply an observation of people who use them), in my experience, the fancier and more expensive the system, the less reliable the person. I always know when someone pulls out the ten-pound calendar with multicolored tabs or turns on their super slimline state-of-the art PDA and begins pecking at it, that whatever they just said they would do will probably never happen. On the other hand, when someone takes the free calendar they got from their insurance agent or an inexpensive one bought at an office supply store and writes what they have committed to on the day the commitment is to be fulfilled, I am reasonably certain it will get done. In terms of calendars, then, the simpler the system, the more workable it is likely to be.

Now take your "Year-at-a-Glance" calendar and cross out the following days:

- Major holidays and one or two days before and after those holidays
- Your vacation
- Your birthday (don't work on your birthday)
- The day (or two, if you wish) after any work meeting or conference that you know will be grueling or for which you have to travel a long distance

What you have left is close to the true number of days you could get work done.

Now put a large dot on the dates of board meetings, the annual meeting, special events, proposal deadlines, newsletter deadlines, and any other meetings or deadlines that you can anticipate. With a marker, draw a line from each deadline back as many days as you think it will take you to prepare for it; if work will be generated by the event, extend your line for one or two days after the event. Whatever work days don't have lines, dots, or crossouts are days you can do the rest of your work.

You now have a clear visual picture that allows you to assess quickly, "Can I take on this commitment?" "Does it make sense for me to attend this conference when I will be exhausted from our annual retreat?" "Should we conduct our major donor campaign during our audit?"

Remember also that some of the days of the year will be used up by illness (yours, your partner's, your children's, and so on), by goofing off or not working efficiently, and by work emergencies that take precedence.

Now take your "Month-at-a-Glance" desk calendar or your PDA task function and note the major task areas that have to be taken care of each day in order to keep on schedule, such as thank you notes, the tasks related to a special event, newsletter production, and so on. This calendar does not take the place of a to-do list. However, most people do not keep the relationship of their to-do list and their calendar clear enough. For example, someone calls you and asks for an appointment. You look at your appointment calendar and seeing a clear day, make the appointment, only to realize later that the day was kept clear because of the approaching deadlines covered by the to-do list. Whenever possible, set your meetings, appointments, lunch dates, and so on by referring to your yearly or monthly calendar. A day does not stand alone. Do you really want to have a 7 A.M. breakfast meeting with a major donor the morning after a board meeting that will run until 10 P.M.?

Use the daily calendar that you carry with you for tracking current appointments, keeping addresses and phone numbers, making future meetings and appointments when you are not in your office, jotting notes from meetings, and so on. However, every two or three days (some people do this at the end of every day), move all relevant information from your daily calendar onto your to-do list or onto your hard drive. Note in your daily calendar the deadlines and days that are filled with writing or preparation, including all that you have already noted on your yearly calendar.

Finally, make appointments with yourself. My friend Bill, who has a hard time saying no to anything, assigns meeting times to HH in his calendar. Then, when someone trying to set up a meeting with him leans over to peer at Bill's calendar and says, "Bill, looks like you have an open afternoon," Bill will have protected a hard day of work, even though it involves no appointments, with a long appointment with HH (HH stands for "ha-ha"). These fake appointments jar him into not saying yes. He can say, "I have a meeting," which for him, as for most people, is easier than saying, "I have to write the campaign brochure." It also spares him the frustration of having to respond when someone says, "This will only take twenty minutes—it will be good for you to have a break from your writing."

Here are some things to avoid in using calendars and scheduling your time:

Avoid Having a Home Calendar and a Work Calendar.   People who maintain two calendars (one for work and one for social appointments) almost always miss their Monday morning appointments (because they don't have their work calendar with them) and are constantly trying to recall whether they can make an evening meeting on Thursday, because they think that's the night of their daughter's soccer match—or is that Wednesday? Your daily calendar shows your whole day, from home to work and back home. Put your important home-life appointments and activities in your single daily calendar.

Avoid Bemoaning Your Busy Life.   When you say to yourself or others, "I am so busy," or "I don't know how I'll get everything done," you tend to set up a self-fulfilling prophesy. Further, comments such as these don't accomplish anything except to use up time. Most people are busy and few people get everything done. Tell yourself instead, "I can get this done. I have enough time."

Skip Unnecessary Meetings or Conferences.   Conferences, trainings, Webinars, workshops, and seminars are the order of the day. They are both expensive and time consuming and rarely worth either the time or expense. Choose the events where you will really learn something or see people you truly want to see. Then go and be there. Too often we decide to attend a conference half-heartedly and spend most of the time during the plenaries and workshops making notes or to-do lists for when we get back, sending text messages, or slipping out to answer our cell phone. If you choose to attend a conference or seminar, be there. Do not answer your cell phone during the sessions and do not call your office unless absolutely necessary.

Avoid Scheduling Too Many Meetings.   Although we have work to do in meetings and admittedly, a certain amount of the work we do at meetings is socializing and building camaraderie, many meetings are not essential, and almost every meeting lasts too long. Question every meeting: Is this meeting necessary? If it is, do I need to be there? Can I be there for part of it and not all of it? If you have any say in the meeting, make sure there is an agenda with times beside each item. People tend to talk for the amount of time that is listed. People can negotiate the need for extra time as it comes up.

Action Plans

One of the difficult things about working with individual donors is that this work has no externally determined deadlines, so you have to create your own. Once you have your calendars set up, you are ready for the next step in organizing your fundraising office: creating action plans.

Whenever you work with a donor or a prospect, make a note in their record of what you intend to do next. This is called your "action plan" or more simply, the "next step." This information should be recorded in a separate field under their name in your database. An action plan is brief, such as, "Invite to Marian's house party," or "Call with outcome of organizing effort in Roane County," or "Send report on toxic waste dumping as soon as available." Then add a date by which you plan to take the action. Put this date in your calendar. Note the donor's last name or some identifying phrase that will remind you to check what you were going to do on that date. Contact-management software is very helpful for keeping up with these plans, but the built-in calendar and task function in most PDAs also do a great job, and simple paper and pen have worked well for decades. Find a system that works for you and use it.

If you are systematic about your donors, for each major donor or major donor prospect you will have a date on which you are going to do something to move the process of building their relationship with the organization along. By spreading these dates out over the year, you can give more personal attention to donors and not get jammed with unrelated donor meetings during a campaign or at the end of the year. If you have thousands of donors, you will obviously have to decide which ones you want to work with personally, but the action plan concept can be used for group activity also, such as, "Oct. 1: All $50–$249 donors receive news alert mail appeal."

A fundraiser's job is often compared to that of the circus performer who balances plates on sticks by keeping the plates twirling and runs from stick to stick to keep the spinning going. If she misses, a plate falls and may break. The calendar is the stick, and the action plans are the plates. This is how you keep your plates spinning and not falling. The overall idea is to have as little to remember as possible. You shouldn't have things in your memory that you could write down or enter in your computer. This system frees you to use your mind to be creative or to learn new details about new people and write those down later.

The wide variety of tasks involved in fundraising are both exciting and one of the many difficulties of the job. You can minimize some of the difficulties by relatively simple procedures to keep your office running efficiently. A calendar and action plan system allows you to use the information you accumulate to raise maximum dollars for your organization.

Keeping Records

Accurate, up-to-date, and thorough records that are easy to access are the most basic necessity for an ongoing fundraising program. Without such records, you have little capability to ask donors for more money, target projects to specific donor interests, track response to appeals, set goals, evaluate your progress against your plan, or any of the other requirements for maintaining and increasing your base of individual donors.

Obviously, the most important thing to keep track of is information about your donors. The vast majority of even the tiniest organizations do this on a computer database. If you use a paper system, you still need to keep good records; most of this information will be the same for a paper system as for a computerized one. (At the risk of revealing myself to be a Luddite, I need to say that a paper system that works is preferable to a database that doesn't. People raised billions of dollars before there were even memory typewriters, let alone computers. However, a database that works well for you gives you a lot more options than any paper system and allows you to sort information in many useful ways, so I recommend getting one if you don't have one now.)

Your database needs to be able to do at least the following five functions:

- Hold a lot of names (preferably an infinite number)

- Hold a lot of information in many fields about each name

- Sort fields quickly and easily

- Produce reports by compiling information (such as total number of gifts from the summer appeal, amount pledged versus amount received, difference in direct mail costs and income between this year and last year)

- Merge with a word processing program for individualized letters and format labels of different sizes for mailings

PURCHASING A DATABASE PROGRAM

Although some off-the-shelf database programs can be customized to meet all of the requirements listed here and more, I strongly recommend getting a program designed for fundraising. All computer programs will have bugs that have to be fixed, and all people using computer programs will run up against the limitations of their own ability to understand a function and the inability of the manual to explain it. When you purchase a program designed for fundraising, there should be a technical support person you can call. If you have a customized database program, on the other hand, you have to hope that the person who customized it is available. Just in the last year, people have told me the following sad stories about using their customized database programs: "We can't get that database to do a mail merge for our major donor campaign and John, who designed it, is in Nepal for six months." "The database has freaked out! It won't sort anything and it freezes every five minutes. Mary, who customized it for us, is mad at us and won't help." "Fred, the guy who put this program together, decided that we need all new computers and refuses to fix this until we agree to buy them. Meanwhile, it seems to have lost all current information. I know it's in there, but I can't figure out how to restore it."

Your database should be as useful as having another staff person. If it takes a staff person to keep it working, something is probably wrong.

A big myth about computer programs for fundraising is that they are all terribly expensive. You can pay a lot if you want, but there are some very effective programs that are priced at well under $2,000, and there are even some free programs that can be downloaded from the Web, although the technical support for these tends to be spotty. Several commercial database vendors will let you pay over time with low or no interest, and several have versions you can "grow into"—that is, you buy a program that has fewer functions or holds fewer names and as you grow and need more sophistication, you apply the cost of your previous program to an expanded version that serves you better. The final reason to buy a database program designed for fundraising is that you will get upgrades to the program, usually for free. (Visit techsoup.org or grass rootsfundraising.org for software comparison charts.)

Before you buy a fundraising database program, try it out—many have demonstration versions available for download at their Web site. This preview will show you what the program can do and give you a sense of how user friendly it is. Before buying anything, be sure all your questions have been answered and that you understand the answers. Don't be afraid to ask elementary questions and don't let salespeople make you feel stupid or old fashioned. Finally, find out what kind of support the company provides once you purchase their program: Is there a toll-free telephone number? Can you call as often as you need to? How difficult is it to get through to a tech support person? How are charges for this support figured? What kinds of training programs to help you understand the program does the company have, where are they held, and what do they cost?

Think through what information you will want to gather and keep up to date so that you have consistent information on each donor. You don't need to know as much about someone who gives your group $25 as someone who gives $25,000. You will want to know more about someone who has given you money several times a year for ten years than about someone who gave one gift and then didn't give again. For all donors, however, you need to know the following information:

Name, Address, and Phone Number.   Get this information off of the photocopy of their check, if they give using a check, rather than from their reply device. Information on people's checks is generally accurate, particularly the spelling of their names. People are offended when their name is misspelled, and they don't take into account that their handwriting may have made their name impossible to read.

Form of Salutation.   If you don't know whether your donor wants to be referred to by their first names or using an honorific, use a formal salutation that is not sexist: Dear Ms. Smith is preferable to Dear Mrs. Smith. For couples, try "Dear Friends."

Gift History.   Date of gift, size of gift, and what the gift was in response to (such as board member request, direct mail, canvass).

Renewal Date.   In many cases this will be in the "Gift History."

Correspondence Record.   Note "thank you sent" with the date, and make a note of any other correspondence you have. Actual copies of the letters will probably be in a paper file or in another file in your computer.

Other Information.   This category, or field, may remain empty if you have no other information, but it can be used to note anything you know about this person that is pertinent to him or her being a donor or a prospect for a bigger gift. For example, "Sister of board president" would go here. Or suppose a gift of $30 comes in from Joe Cumberland, but his check says, "Joe Cumberland; Janice Ruark, MD." First, you can check to see if Janice Ruark is also a donor. If she is not, make a note: "Check was in his name and Janice Ruark, MD." This information may be useful or it may never lead anywhere. Sometimes a reply card will carry the name of a person, such as "Lydia S. Turner," but the check says, "Sampson Family Foundation." Make a note of that. Probably the "S" in Lydia's name is for Sampson. In the "action plan" field for this donor, make a note to look up the Sampson Family Foundation at the Foundation Center Library.

Special Requests.   If you trade lists with other groups and you have given donors the chance to check a box on your reply device asking not to have their names traded, this information would be coded in another field so their names are suppressed when you trade names. People who indicate they only want to be asked once a year or never want to be phoned will have that information coded on their database record.

This is all the information you keep on people who have given only once so far or who have given less than $100 for fewer than three years and whom you don't know anything else about. For people who give more than $100 or have given some amount for more than three years, or for people who give several times a year or whose gift does not reflect how much they could give considering how much they seem to care about your cause, start keeping the information outlined in Chapter Eighteen on prospect identification.

Most databases designed for fundraising will have a number of built-in categories to help you think through what you need to keep track of, and you will be able to add fields for your particular situation. There are two useful categories that can be easily added: "Missing Information" and "Next Step." It often happens that you know some details about a donor but not enough to include them in the upper ranges of your gift range chart, for example, or to ask them to give an extra gift for a capital improvement. It is helpful to focus on what you would need to know to feel comfortable asking them for more money or extra money. Possibly you need to know more about their friendship with a board member. Are they very close or simply acquaintances? Perhaps you need to know what other charitable commitments the donor has made. Maybe you need to know more about what the donor thinks about a particular issue that your group is working on. Or maybe it is something simpler, such as their phone number. Make a note of whatever you need to learn under "Missing Information." Once every month or so, sort your records to find those with notes in the Missing Information category. The result will give you a complete list of what you need to do to get your donor records in better order.

The other useful category is "Next Step." Obviously, one logical next step may be to find the missing information, but this category can be used more proactively. The next step is often not to ask for more money, but to be sure to send some article of interest that you promised the donor. Maybe Sally, your board member who lives down the road from this donor, needs to invite the donor to a house party or a meeting. Maybe this donor has a lot of contacts and you want to ask her to give you a list of them right before the spring major donor drive. Note what the next step is and a date by which it should be done. Then you can sort by dates and give yourself a current to-do list for next steps with donors.

THE IMPORTANCE OF DONOR RECORDS

People sometimes feel that gathering this information so systematically and writing it all down or entering it on a computer is an invasion of the donor's privacy and feels nosy and manipulative. They fear they will begin to see other people only in terms of money. To gain some perspective on the reasons for keeping donor records, keep the following three facts in mind:

If You Don't Record This Information, You Will Forget It.   Without this information, you will not be able to raise money as effectively as you could with it. Many people have "birthday books" where they write down all the dates of the birthdays they want to remember. No one thinks this is an invasion of privacy—in fact, they are pleased to get a card on their birthday. You are trying to use donor resources to the best advantage, which is what donors want and deserve. There is no point is asking someone for more money who only gives once a year, but it is a shame not to ask someone who likes your organization and would gladly give more often if asked. Further, how will the organization know that your long-time loyal donor, Tania Lopez, hates to be called at work if someone doesn't record that fact? Or that Steve who owns the deli said he would cater your annual meeting for free if you get back to him by March?

Don't Record Anything You Don't Need to Know.   Your goal is to get every donor to be as loyal to your group as possible and to give you as much money as they can afford because of their loyalty. Everything you record about a donor should be information that helps you toward that goal. So, no matter how interesting it might be that Max was once lovers with Fred, don't record it. If a donor who is also a friend confides to you that she spent time in prison and is having trouble with the parole board, don't write it down. Think of this: If a donor asked to see his or her record, would you be embarrassed to show it? Why? What's in there that shouldn't be? You should be recording only information that is easily obtainable or that people would not object to your knowing, such as how many children they have or where they work.

This Information Is Highly Confidential.   Only a few people, such as the executive director, the development director, the treasurer of the board, and sometimes the bookkeeper or administrator, should have access to all the information in your database. (Commercial databases include a password system. One password allows access to the fields for name, address, and phone; a second password accesses the gift history field; a third allows one to see all the information. Only a few people should have all three passwords.) Donor records, such as paper files, back-up disks, correspondence, and so on should be kept in a locked file cabinet with access limited to a few people. People who can see this information must understand its delicate nature and use the same discretion in revealing it as is used in recording it. Even though this information is not secret, it is not to be shared carelessly.

KEEPING YOUR LIST IN SHAPE

Update your donor records on a regular basis. Don't let more than ten names go unrecorded or you will get careless with numbers and spelling. Many small, understaffed groups put off updating their records until the night before they need their mailing list for the newsletter mailing. Then a staff member and a volunteer frantically try to get everything in order. That kind of list is inevitably full of errors.

Watch for duplicate entries, particularly when you are going to use the list for a mailing. Donors dislike getting more than one copy of your newsletter or mail appeal. A database program will not know that J. P. Miller and John Miller are the same person, or that Sally Jones doesn't live at 22 South St. anymore, but is now Sally Moondaughter on 44 North St. Every so often, print out your whole mailing list and go through it looking for duplicates, spelling errors, incomplete addresses, and so on.

Don't keep people on your mailing list who have never given and whom no one knows. I have known many organizations that have mailing lists of 4,000 but donor lists of 700. When I ask what the other 3,300 people are doing on their list, they will say, "This is our outreach program." But most groups have no evidence that these people gain from this outreach, or even that all of these people are alive or at the addresses on their records. Considering that it costs from $3 to $10 per entry every year to keep someone on a mailing list—presuming you send at least two newsletters and at least one appeal—you could be spending hundreds or even thousands of dollars keeping people on your mailing list about whom you know nothing. That same money could be invested in a mounting true outreach or direct mail program to drive traffic to your Web site and using an electronic newsletter for outreach.

Because as many as one-third of the people on a list move in a year, it's important to know when the address you have is no longer accurate. You can get address corrections from the post office by printing "Address Correction Requested" on all your bulk mail. You pay a certain amount for each piece returned to you, but the returns will have any forwarding address on them, which helps keep your list clean. Request address corrections at least once a year.

SAFETY FIRST

You should save your work constantly as you go along, and you should back up your hard drive at the end of each day. Once a week, take a copy of your back-up files to another location, such as a safe-deposit box at a bank or the home of a board member or staff person (each week this flash drive or CD will be replaced with the newly updated files). In addition, you should keep copies of legal documents and any records that it would be difficult to replace in a location away from your office. That way, if your hard disk crashed or your building burned or if there was a flood, vandalism, earthquake, hurricane, or any number of other disasters that have ruined nonprofits' offices the same way they have ruined residences and businesses, you will have copies of your most important records.

For many fundraisers, record keeping is the bane of their existence. But keeping records takes less time if you do it regularly and don't get far behind than if you wait until the last minute and do it badly. Then you have to spend time cleaning up your mess. Record keeping needs to be seen as being as necessary and habitual as brushing your teeth.

Managing Volunteers

I have been criticized for recommending strategies that rely too heavily on volunteers; some people have said that the number of volunteers that are required to implement a grassroots fundraising program is unrealistic in these times, when so many people are working so hard at one or more paid jobs. As I travel, I see that many organizations' fundraising programs rely heavily on staff. In very large organizations, the solution to fundraising problems is often to "staff up." I know that there are far fewer volunteers available than there were twenty years ago and that many organizations find it harder to recruit and keep volunteers than they used to.

On the other hand, I also see grassroots organizations that have twenty, thirty, and even one hundred regular volunteers. They have volunteers who have full-time jobs, children, and other volunteer commitments. They have volunteers who are on welfare, who are single parents, who travel half of the time for work, who are elderly and not able to come to meetings at night, and so on. In other words, we can still recruit and keep volunteers. What we need to do is focus on how, rather than how hard it is, to have a successful volunteer program.

There are many fine books on volunteering; some are listed in Resource E and will be helpful for you to consult. Put briefly, there are five things you need to know to get volunteers productively involved in fundraising.

Take the Time Necessary to Orient Volunteers to Your Fundraising Program.   A two-hour in-service program in which you go over your budget, your fundraising goals, and your progress to date will set a good example of transparency and allow people to ask any questions they have or voice concerns. Such an in-service meeting can also set the context in which your fundraising plan is developed, as described in Chapter One, including where money comes from, how many nonprofits there are, who gives money away, and so on. Use this in-service especially to focus on your case statement; have volunteers practice describing your organization to each other and answering questions about it.

Volunteers need to feel "in the know" and they need to feel competent with regard to describing mission, goals, and objectives of the organization. We often think a volunteer is unwilling to ask for money when in fact he or she may feel insecure about discussing the organization. I have often had volunteers say, "I didn't ask for the money because I thought I might do more harm than good in trying to explain what the organization is doing."

Help Each Volunteer Choose the Fundraising Strategies They Will Feel Most Comfortable Doing. In this way, you play to volunteers' strengths. In their book, *The Accidental Fundraiser,* Stephanie Roth and Mimi Ho describe three broad categories of activities that volunteers will prefer, depending on their personality and confidence. First, there are those who prefer to raise money by entertaining. They happily host house parties and they are good at organizing other special events. They know how to make people feel welcomed, and they are good at thinking through what would be fun or interesting for a group of people. These volunteers often like to work in groups; they are the one you will find on special event committees. The second type are those volunteers who prefer to sell things: these volunteers are good at selling products or events. They are excellent people to staff a booth selling T-shirts, mugs, books, and so on that your organization produces or distributes. They will sell products to friends, neighbors, and family, and they can be relied on to sell tickets to events. However, they are less willing to ask for money directly, which brings us to the third, and smallest group. These are the people who prefer direct asking to doing other fundraising tasks. People in this group are likely to have a little more experience with fundraising; they know that if you ask enough people you will get the money you need. Many of these people are or have been in sales or real estate and have overcome their own psychological barriers to asking. Some of them come from countries where taboos about money are not as strong as in the United States. Both the sellers and the direct askers have stopped taking rejection personally.

Of course, some people are good at all three approaches, whereas a minority of volunteers are not comfortable with any strategy that requires talking to people about money. This latter group can be put to work writing thank you notes, entering names and addresses into a database, researching foundation funders—anything that you need in fundraising that is not people oriented.

To create a list of tasks such volunteers can do is simple. With each task you begin each day, think to yourself, "Could a reasonable, intelligent person accomplish this task with a minimal amount of training?" If the answer is yes, ask yourself why you are doing it. Paid staff should as much as possible focus on doing things that an organization really could not expect a volunteer to do. Tasks that require technical knowledge, that are tremendously time consuming, or that involve a lot of sequencing should take up the bulk of a staff person's time.

Remember That Good Enough Is Good Enough.   Staff-volunteer tension can come about because the staff person wants the job done perfectly according to their own definition of perfect. For example, in a small nonprofit, two volunteers took on the task of writing and sending the e-newsletter, scheduled to go out on the third Thursday of each month. Over six months, three newsletters went out on time and three went out two days late. Most of the newsletters had a few typos. These lapses were too much for the staff person, and she took the job back from the volunteers. Obviously, if the volunteers had usually been a week late with the newsletter and if it were riddled with typos, her action would be justified. But these volunteers were for the most part both reliable and thorough. Far too often in dealing with volunteers, the best becomes the enemy of the good.

Show Genuine and Frequent Appreciation.   Remember Cesar Chavez's dictum for organizing: "People are far more appreciative of what they do for you than of what you do for them." Thank them often. Thank you notes, thank you calls, and brief mentions at meetings go a long way. Flowers, plaques, and ribbons are fine, but they are not as important as the occasional grateful word.

Give Volunteers Time Off.   People need time off for good behavior. Many volunteer fundraisers have found that their reward for doing their work is more work. "Ruby, you did such a great job with the auction. You are a natural! Once you catch your breath, do you think you could chair the membership drive?" Such a comment is a sure way to guarantee that Ruby will run, not walk, away from your organization as soon as she can.

Make sure that, unless the volunteer insists otherwise, volunteers have at least two or three months between intense fundraising activities and that they are encouraged to get involved in other aspects of the organization beyond fundraising.

Keep in mind, then, that what is most efficient for getting a job done thoroughly and quickly is rarely most effective for building an organization and developing new leadership. As you work on managing your volunteers, remember that you are ultimately trying to ensure that the organization could continue even if a key person were suddenly not available. By keeping your eye on the prize of longevity and stability of the organization, you will structure your volunteer management efforts much differently and will find that, even today, there are plenty of people who want to be active, engaged volunteers.

PART SIX

You, the Fundraiser

The Association of Fundraising Professionals (AFP), the international trade association for development directors and other fundraising professionals, has conducted a number of studies over the years that show that development directors leave their jobs every eighteen to twenty-four months. Many move on to other development positions, but sadly, many leave the profession altogether. The cost of replacing any employee—including searching for, interviewing, selecting, and then training a new employee—is estimated to be at least $5,000, an exorbitant amount to small nonprofits. Many theories are put forward about why there is such high turnover, including salaries not being high enough, the development staff not having enough involvement in program work, too much pressure on the job, and so on.

These may well be reasons that some people leave their fundraising jobs, but they are not the two main reasons people leave development jobs:

Development is a job of great responsibility and little authority.

There is a lack of understanding on the part of everyone involved as to exactly what the job of a development director is.

This section seeks to address and proactively prevent the second of these reasons. Many grassroots organizations have hired enthusiastic but inexperienced first-time development directors, and neither the organization nor the new staff person really has a clear idea of what the job involves. High expectations followed by huge disappointment either generate some badly needed clarification, possibly saving the person and the position, or in less functional organizations (which are most of them), lead to the person leaving.

This section reviews the job of the development director, the role of a development consultant, and the field of development as a career. It also addresses the two things that even experienced development directors often find difficult to deal with: their own anxiety and working with their executive director.

When everyone is clear on what they can expect from whom, many more people will make social justice fundraising their career—a career I have found to be eminently fulfilling for more than thirty years.

Hiring a Development Director

As small organizations grow, they grapple with the ongoing need to raise more and more money as well as manage the infrastructure (databases, volunteers, Web site, research, communication, reporting, and the like) required to do so. Inevitably, they must consider hiring someone to take charge of the fundraising function. This is a difficult decision. A group is gambling that the investment of salary—money they often barely have—is going to generate much more money than they are currently raising. The gamble will pay off if the person they hire is effective, the board already accepts its role in fundraising, and the organization has its basic infrastructure in place—that is, adequate record keeping systems and a fundraising plan with clear goals and objectives. However, there is little margin for error. What if the person isn't skilled enough or isn't a good worker? What if everything is in place, but the fundraising program takes longer than planned to bring in the needed funds? How will the organization support itself in the meantime?

To avoid these problems, three issues need to be clarified before your organization decides to hire a staff person to manage fundraising. These are the role of the fundraiser or development director, the tasks this person will carry out, and whether hiring a development director will actually solve the problems you have. Let's consider each of these issues in more detail.

The Role of a Fundraiser or Development Director

First and foremost, everyone must understand that the person whose primary responsibility is fundraising does not run around bringing in money. Instead, a development director's job is to work with the board and staff to develop fundraising goals and sensible, easily understood plans to meet the goals. This person spells out the strategies that will be used and helps everyone figure out their tasks and stay on task. In addition to creating workable fundraising plans, the development director either does or supervises the following activities:

- Keeping accurate fundraising records
- Maintaining the mailing list
- Sending out thank you notes
- Reporting to foundations or large donors on specific projects
- Conducting prospect research
- Sending mail and e-mail appeals, renewals, and other fundraising letters
- Helping write the annual report
- Overseeing the Web site
- Going on major donor visits as needed

Of central importance, the development director works closely with the board, helping them make and then fulfill their fundraising commitments. The development director may also research the grantmaking programs of foundations and corporations and write grant proposals, if that is a part of the organization's plan, and there may be other fundraising strategies that he or she must oversee or implement.

The development director primarily works behind the scenes establishing a structure for effective fundraising by volunteers and ensuring that when volunteers do solicit donors, the volunteer is confident that the donor will be thanked promptly, names will be spelled properly, and information will entered into the organization's records accurately.

Many board members and paid staff imagine that hiring a development director will save them from further fundraising tasks. "Let's pay someone to do this so we can do the real work" is a common and potentially fatal suggestion. First it must be remembered that fundraising is real work, and it is work that should be integrated into the day-to-day functioning of your program and organizing efforts. Second, while the paid fundraising staff obviously relieves the load of other staff and may relieve the board of some tasks, everyone's consciousness of fundraising and their involvement in it must stay the same or increase for the expanded fundraising program to be successful.

The Tasks of the Fundraiser

Many people wonder why the task of fundraising has so many different job titles attached to it, such as "fundraiser," "fundraising coordinator," "development director," or "resource developer." In many social change organizations, the person is called the fundraising coordinator in a reflection of a nonhierarchical structure. In other, usually larger, organizations, this position is called the director of development. Beyond the terminology, there are actually important differences between fundraising and development.

Fundraising is the process of bringing in the amount of money an organization needs in order to carry out its programs from year to year. Development, in addition to raising an operating budget, includes most of the following activities:

- Creating a strategic plan and updating it on a yearly basis (augmenting the case statement)
- Instituting a planned public relations program
- Maintaining a planned and frequently evaluated process for bringing on new board members
- Providing fundraising training for board, staff, and volunteers
- Planning and evaluating the financial needs and fundraising plans for the organization's future
- Developing the group's capability to conduct capital campaigns and start planned giving programs

One development director characterized the difference between fundraising and development this way: "In fundraising you make do with what you have. You keep the organization going and out of debt. In development, you start with what you have and you help it grow."

Solving Your Problems

Before you hire anyone, analyze your situation to see whether your problems actually lie in fundraising or whether it just looks as though they do. All problems in an organization show up in their funding, and often they show up there first. However, fundraising may only be a symptom of other problems, in which case hiring someone to do fundraising will not solve the problem and may in fact make it worse.

To begin this analysis, answer the following questions:

Is your board active in fundraising? Does almost every board member participate in fundraising in some way, whether organizing special events, opening doors for you to other people, asking for money face-to-face, or helping in more behind-the-scenes but still useful ways?

Does it sometimes seem that the board and perhaps the staff spend more time planning for fundraising than actually raising money?

Do board members and other volunteers involved in fundraising seem to suffer from a lack of knowledge of what to do rather than a lack of enthusiasm?

Is the executive director or other staff constantly pulled away from program development and organizing to do fundraising? Do the staff feel torn about setting priorities for use of their time?

Is your budget more than $250,000 or do you need to raise more than $100,000 from sources other than government or foundations?

If your organization answers yes to three or more of these questions, you should seriously consider hiring a development director. This person would direct and kindle the fundraising energies of the board, plan for fundraising, train others in fundraising tasks, and enable program staff to get on with program work.

If, on the other hand, you need a better and more involved board, then you should strengthen your board and provide some motivational training for them before you hire a development director.

If what you need is help with data entry, writing the annual report, compiling financial reports, answering the phone, dealing with the mail, handling checks, processing credit cards, sending thank you notes, and the like, then you should consider hiring support staff, such as a secretary or office manager.

If what you want is someone to help you plan and carry out a time-limited fundraising project, such as a large event or a major gifts campaign, consider hiring a consultant.

PAYING THE FUNDRAISER

Imagine this scenario: An organization is debating whether to hire a development director. They have little front money, and they worry about both finding the right person and meeting a salary. As if in answer to a prayer, a handsome stranger shows up and offers to raise $250,000 (their budget) plus a 20 percent commission. He will only take his commission from money he raises, he explains, so if he raises nothing, they pay nothing; of whatever he does raise, he will be paid 20 percent. He predicts he can raise the full budget, plus his commission, in six months; if successful, he will earn $50,000, then go on his way.

There are several reasons that no organization should accept such a deal (whether the stranger is handsome or not). First, no one else in the organization is paid on commission. People are paid a salary in recognition that their work is part of a process; they may be very good at their job without showing a lot of immediate progress toward ending racism, stopping pollution, or whatever the group is working on.

Second, a commission tends to distort salaries. In this case, this fundraiser would be earning the same salary in six months that the executive director makes in a year.

Third, this person will not bring his own list of contacts. He will be working with the organization's donors. He says he has some contacts from previous jobs, but you don't know whether they are appropriate for your work. Moreover, do you want this person taking your donor information to his next job? Further, his whole livelihood depends on donors saying yes to his requests. Even a totally honest fundraiser working under these conditions would be tempted to distort information, seeing his rent check in the eyes of each prospect. In addition, many big gifts take cultivation, which can mean several visits with a donor. This fundraiser may be willing to settle for a smaller gift in order to get it quickly rather than take the time to carry out proper cultivation for the size gift a donor is capable of making.

Fourth, what will the donors think if and when they find out that 20 percent of their gift went to this temporary staff person? Few things make donors angrier than learning that a significant part of their gift was used for inappropriate fundraising expenses.

Fifth, as was stressed earlier, one person should not be in charge of actually raising money for an entire campaign. Even if he is both honest and successful, when he leaves, the group will be $250,000 richer, to be sure, but no wiser in regard to fundraising.

Finally, the person coordinating the fundraising should absolutely believe in the cause and be a part of the team of people putting the campaign together.

For these reasons, paying on commission is highly frowned on in fundraising. All the trade associations for fundraisers, including the Association of Fundraising Professionals, the National Association of Hospital Developers, and the Council for the Advancement and Support of Education, have issued statements advising organizations against commission-based fundraising. The only recognized exception to this policy is with canvassing (see Chapter Fifteen), where people are often paid a base salary and a commission. However, the nature of canvassing means the canvassers rarely deal with soliciting major gifts. Even so, the commission-based nature of canvassing has presented some of the problems presented above and is a gray area in fundraising.

Rather than being based on commission, the development director's salary should be based on other staff salaries. If you have a collective salary structure, then that person's salary would be the same as everyone else's. If there are pay differentials, then the development director's salary would be less than the executive director's but more than the office manager's. In a hierarchical structure, the development director is a management staff person, usually reporting directly to the executive director.

Organizations often think they have to pay a lot to get a capable development person. This is not true. A good person for your organization is someone who, first and foremost, believes in your group and wants to be part of it. This person will express his or her belief through fundraising, just as someone else is expressing their belief by doing direct service, organizing, or policy development. If someone who meets the criteria of believing strongly in your work has fundraising skills but can't afford to work at the salary you are offering, you may need to reevaluate everyone's salary. Chances are you are losing out on good staff people for other positions as well.

HOW TO FIND A CAPABLE DEVELOPMENT DIRECTOR

Once you have decided that you need a development director, the first step in hiring one is to create a fair and accurate job description. Many job descriptions fail to attract candidates because the job has been structured to encompass too many responsibilities. Avoid the temptation to add components to the job that are not related to fundraising or public relations. It is fair to ask the development director to edit and oversee the publication of the newsletter; it is unwise to ask that person to also be the accountant.

You should be able to describe the job in one page (see example). Think about what skills are essential, as opposed to those that are desirable but not imperative. Ask applicants to send a writing sample, since writing will be a large part of almost any fundraiser's job.

Advertise in publications geared to nonprofits. Unless you are in a small town, avoid advertising in the newspaper—you will receive a lot of resumes of unqualified people. Ditto for advertising on Web sites that post all kinds of jobs. Post your job description in places and on Web sites that activists visit. Send the announcement to other nonprofits and call directors and development directors you know and tell them the job is available. Don't rely only on e-mail to get the word out. Everyone receives far more e-mail than they can handle. Follow up your e-mail with a call.

Don't get bogged down in trying to find someone with all the "right" qualifications and experience. If you find such a person, hire her or him immediately. But if you don't find such a person, look for other sorts of qualifications that are evidence of experience related to fundraising, such as running a small business, teaching, or managing personnel. Any job that required that a person be a self-starter and that called for planning, working with diverse groups of people, and good organizational skills is a good background for fundraising.

Look closely at volunteer experience and encourage applicants to describe their work as volunteers. Many people know more than they realize about fundraising from having volunteered. People with little or no volunteer experience are not good candidates because they will have little idea of how to work with volunteers.

In addition to broadening your criteria in hiring someone, it might be easier to imagine a capable, but untrained, person in the job if you are willing to hire a consultant for a few days to help your new staff person get a running start on their job or to send the new development director to some of the many classes and courses that are offered on fundraising. The theories and how-tos of fundraising are not particularly difficult to understand, even though they take a lot of work to implement. Getting someone who is underqualified but bright, committed, and eager to do a good job is almost as good as getting an experienced person with the same attributes.

SAMPLE JOB DESCRIPTION—DEVELOPMENT DIRECTOR

The Peace Consortium is a twenty-year-old organization that supports the creation of a just society through nonviolence training, public policy development, and organizing on issues of peace and war in local communities. The Peace Consortium works in three states to strengthen grassroots efforts in the broad-based movement for progressive, systemic social change.

Organizational Structure

There are currently four full-time employees: executive director, program director, IT manager, and office manager. The Peace Consortium is offering a full-time position (1.0 FTE) of development director, reporting to the executive director. Current annual budget is $750,000. Board and staff—particularly the executive director—are highly engaged in the organization's fundraising.

Function Summary

The Development Director will work closely with the executive director, fundraising committee, board, and ad hoc committees to coordinate a comprehensive resource development program that includes the annual membership campaign, expanding major donors, and enhancing public relations outreach to increase the visibility of the Peace Consortium and its work.

Hours

Full time, forty hours per week. Some weekend and evening work is required as well as occasional travel within the region.

Responsibilities

Management and administration: Work with board and executive director to develop overall strategies, goals, and outcomes and to track progress toward goals

Major Gifts Campaign:

- Implement overall major gifts strategy
- Oversee cultivation, solicitation, and stewardship of all major donors
- Identify and implement strategies to attract new major donor prospects

Donor Recruitment and Renewal:

- Develop and implement a plan for activities to attract new donors (working with the marketing committee), particularly establishing an online presence
- Monitor and refine annual renewal fund: direct mail appeals (two per year); phone campaign (two per year); e-mail solicitations

Events

- Work with volunteers and board members to bring in major donors through house parties, annual fundraising dinner, and other fundraising events as needed

Skills, Talents, and Experience Needed

- Minimum three years of fundraising experience with a nonprofit organization
- Experience in managing individual donors, events, cultivation, and major gifts work
- Ability to create, build, and maintain strong relationships with major donors
- Ability to plan and implement successful fundraising strategies and programs with major donors
- Knowledge of the basic components that make up successful fundraising strategies and programs
- Broad knowledge of progressive issues and organizations both locally and nationally

- Strong organizational and management skills, including program planning, budgeting, facilitation, time management, team building, training, and supervising
- Excellent written and oral communication skills
- Ability to work with diverse populations, including people of color, immigrants, women, lesbian/gay/bisexual/transgender communities, people with disabilities, low-income people, people in rural communities, and people with wealth
- Strong demonstrated commitment to working to undo systems of oppression, including racism, sexism, classism, and heterosexism
- Ability to work flexible hours, including some weekends and evenings
- Ability to travel throughout the region
- Proficiency with MS Word, Excel, Access, and Outlook

Salary

DOE; benefits package includes health care, vacation, and sabbatical after five years.

How to Apply

E-mail your resume and an explanation of why you want to work for the Peace Consortium, along with a writing sample and three references to Constancia Hernandez, Executive Director, at ch@peaceconsortium.org.

The Peace Consortium is an Equal Opportunity and Affirmative Action Employer.

Hiring a Consultant, Coach, Mentor, or Trainer

There are times in the life of almost every person or organization when hiring an outside person to help you think through or get through a certain time or situation can be very helpful. For a nonprofit organization's fundraising program, these times are characterized by one or more of the following situations:

- Your organization needs advice on how to improve its overall fundraising or some particular aspect of fundraising. You need someone with skill and knowledge who cares about the issues your organization is concerned with but is far enough removed to be able to "see the forest."

- You need help deciding on a course of action: Can you really launch a capital campaign now? Would a monthly donor program be a good strategy to explore?

- You need someone to do a time-limited piece of work: run a special event, train the board in fundraising, plan a major gifts campaign, design a Web site, research funding sources, or write a proposal.

- You need someone to help design the fundraising staff's work plan, provide guidance, and answer questions, especially when a bright and energetic but inexperienced staff person needs help getting up to speed.

- You need someone to run the development function of your organization temporarily until staff can be replaced.

- You need help with fundraising as you make a transition from a founder to a new executive director or during a major change in direction, goals, and structure, or during a name change.

- Your organization has relied on government or foundation funding sources that have now cut back and you need help getting out of the funding crisis these cutbacks have created.

The skills of consulting, coaching, mentoring, or training are all similar; sometimes one person is able to perform all of these functions. However, knowing the differences among them may help you decide which you need, and as we say in consulting, knowing what you need puts you 90 percent closer to being able to get it. Here is how these helping functions apply to fundraising.

Consultant.   A consultant works in partnership with an organization (usually working closely with one or two people in the organization) on a specific, time-limited project. How much that person does, as opposed to what he or she advises you to do, will depend on the consultant and on the project, but the job of a consultant is generally to get out of the organization as quickly as possible without the group becoming reliant on the consultant. A consultant is an expert who dispenses advice and has answers. The consultant is hired primarily for their knowledge and their ability to impart that knowledge. Consultants focus on what will improve effectiveness and increase success.

Trainer.   A trainer provides a workshop, seminar, or in-service presentation that can last from twenty minutes to several days to a group of people who all need to know the same thing and ideally, who are about to embark together on a fundraising task. Trainers will often provide training to boards, major donor committees, or other subsets of an organization. Trainers will also work with many organizations at once.

Mentor.   A mentor works with one person and serves as that person's guide, wise older sibling, and role model. Someone with several decades of fundraising experience is teamed up with someone who is learning on the job. The person being mentored sees attributes, qualities, or abilities in the mentor that he or she wishes to learn or emulate. Whereas a trainer or consultant is hired for a specific amount of time and a particular piece of work, a mentor is usually a volunteer, and she or he may work with a person for years. Mentors are often in work situations with the people they are mentoring, which makes access to each other easy.

Coach.   A coach can work with one person, several people, or an entire organization to help with the process of making decisions, imagining the future, and creating a plan to get there. In coaching, the starting point is the client's desire for personal and professional success. Coaching is not about how you came to be in the situation you are in, but rather about getting you from where you are now to a future that you want. Coaches clarify goals and help people through difficult or large transitions. Coaches are not generally used for how-to information or practical training, just as trainers generally don't help organizations deal with the death of a founder or help an executive director be a better manager.

Clearly, the lines among these roles are malleable and permeable, and the types of people who work in these fields will vary a great deal one to the other. This chapter deals mostly with how and when an organization should use a consultant; however, knowing the definition of coaching, training, and mentoring may help you realize when what you need is not a consultant but one of the other types of helpers.

Working with a Consultant

A consultant's work with your organization will be characterized by three things: it is time-limited (lasting either a few hours a week or a few days a month, or based on a contract for a specific number of months), the consultant is not involved in day-to-day operations, and there is more emphasis on advice and guidance than on doing hands-on fundraising work.

Partly because the services of a consultant are time-limited, the concept of employing someone in that capacity carries a negative meaning for many people. The jokes, "A consultant borrows your watch to tell you the time," or "A consultant gives free advice for a price," are said only half in jest.

The problem of finding a reliable and competent consultant is compounded by the sheer number of consultants working around the world. As with nearly any profession, there are sleazy and unreliable consultants in the fundraising profession, but a more common problem with consultants is that many have little knowledge of their professed subject. Sometimes people ask me how they should go about becoming a consultant. When I ask what experience they have, they respond with a list of the books they have read and the trainings they have attended. They think consulting would be exciting because one can travel a great deal and they imagine they can charge a lot of money. They are also enthusiastic about the fact that consultants do not carry the ultimate responsibility of the fundraising success or failure of any organization.

What my inquirers fail to see, however, is that consultants carry a different level of responsibility: the advice we give must be correct. If implemented, it must work. Further, consultants must trust others to carry out plans that the consultant designed. This means that the plan must be communicated clearly and be appropriate to the level of skills and resources the people carrying it out have or have access to. Moreover, consultants must know the difference between what can be learned by teaching, guiding, and giving advice, and what can only be learned from experience. They must know what they can do for an organization and what an organization can only do for itself. If they fail in these aspects, they will not be consultants for long.

What Fundraising Consultants Can Do

Fundraising consultants can do the following tasks:

- Create fundraising plans and help implement and evaluate those plans
- Research prospective donors (individuals, corporations, foundations, religious sources) and write proposals if needed
- Set up a database for keeping track of donor information
- Conduct feasibility studies
- Conduct direct mail campaigns
- Design an online fundraising strategy or serve as webmaster, or both
- Create a communications plan or public relations campaign
- Study and recommend structural changes in an organization to improve functioning and fundraising efficiency
- Help hire fundraising staff, including writing job descriptions and advertising for and interviewing candidates
- Organize special events
- Set up any other fundraising strategy that an organization has decided to use
- Manage mailing lists and donor information, including sending out pledge reminders, thank you notes, and renewal letters (generally, it is not cost effective for small organizations to use a consultant for these activities)

If the consultant is also a trainer, he or she can do the following:

- Train and motivate people in all aspects of fundraising
- Help board members understand their responsibilities, and help organizations recruit and train good board members

What Fundraising Consultants Cannot Do

Fundraising consultants should not be expected to do the following activities:

- Actually solicit money from individuals, unless they go as part of a team with someone from the organization
- Use their personal contacts to raise money. Consultants often know a great deal about wealthy givers in the community; with discretion, they can share that knowledge in prospect research. However, consultants do not go from job to job with their own list of prospects.
- Actually raise money. If a consultant offers to do all your fundraising for you, run the other way. This is not an effective solution because, at best, it postpones the necessity of getting the board, staff, and volunteers involved in fundraising.
- Guarantee their work. There are no absolutes in fundraising. There is a body of fundraising knowledge, largely based on common sense, and there are many applications of this knowledge. No strategy will work every time for every group.

HOW TO CHOOSE A CONSULTANT

Once you have decided that your particular situation may be helped by a consultant, here are the kinds of things to look for in that person:

Track Record.   Ask how much fundraising he or she has done and with what success. Find out if the person has worked with organizations similar to yours in both purpose and strategy and in similar locales. A successful consultant for social change groups in Manhattan may be less useful for rural advocacy groups in North Dakota than someone familiar with rural fundraising. Superb consultants for large institutions may not be good for all-volunteer operations with budgets of less than $25,000. If questions of gender, sexual orientation, race, class, or disability are very important in your organization, ask the consultant what experience he or she has had working on these issues or with diverse groups of people.

Recommendations.   If you don't know the person by reputation, ask for a contact person at the last three groups she or he has worked with. Then call those groups and ask about the consultant. Was the person helpful? Did the consultant listen well and really understand the situation? Would this group hire this consultant again? You can also check references, but you may get a more candid evaluation from groups the person hasn't listed as references.

Compatibility.   If you envision a relationship with the consultant involving more than a one- or two-day training, you may wish to meet the person. The consultant should offer a preliminary half-hour meeting without charge. In the meeting, you get to see if you like the person and if you would feel good accepting his or her advice. It sometimes happens that an excellent fundraising consultant is not the right person for your group because the personalities will not mesh. If the organization dislikes the consultant, both the consultant's advice and your money are wasted.

Confidence.   Ask what the consultant will do for you or what they recommend. Avoid asking for long written plans. Elaborate workplans or proposals are often standardized; each one is essentially the same as the next, with the name of your organization substituted for the name of the previous organization. You can ask for a resume, if you find that helpful. By the time of the first meeting, you are not looking so much for proof of fundraising knowledge as for ability to put that knowledge across. Ask yourself, "Is this person believable?" "Does she or he convey confidence, enthusiasm, and goodwill?" "Will the people who will be working with this person like him or her?"

Belief.   Finally, the consultant must be able to articulate the mission of your organization and believe that your group should exist. The consultant does not have to be a donor to your group, and she or he does not have to think that your group is the greatest idea since sliced bread, but the person needs to care about what you stand for and want to help you out of conviction as well as needing a job. This belief is particularly important if your group is controversial or one that challenges the status quo. Avoid consultants who advise you to "tone down" your message or broaden your goals "to make everyone feel included." A fundraising consultant's job is to help your group raise money—not to water down the group's message or philosophy and then help a newer, lightweight group raise money.

PAYING CONSULTANTS

There are no standards or guidelines for how much to pay a consultant. A high price does not necessarily mean better performance or more accountability, but a price that is too good to be true probably is. By hiring a consultant, you are investing in the present so you will have more money in the future.

Most consultants charge by the day or the hour, but some charge by the job. A person's daily rate should work out to be a lower fee per hour than their hourly rate; several days' work should average out to a lower fee per day than just a one-day job. Consultants also charge for all their expenses: hotels, meals, telephone, photocopy, and travel are the most common. You can cut some of these costs by offering to house the consultant in someone's home and by providing their meals, but if you do that, make sure the consultant is comfortable and can get a good night's sleep. I have often agreed to stay with someone only to discover that I was sleeping on a fold-out couch in the living room, which would be invaded by small children wanting to watch the cartoon channel beginning at 6 A.M. When you cut costs on comfort, you decrease the consultant's ability to be helpful by increasing their exhaustion.

Establish clearly what you are paying for. For example, you pay for the consultant's time, but when does that time start? In some cases, the time starts when the consultant reaches the office of the client or the training site. Even if it takes a day to get there, some do not charge until they are there. Other consultants start charging the minute they leave their house or office. Find out, too, if the consultant charges for phone calls and at what rate.

If you are hiring a consultant for several days or months of work, build in evaluation points. For example, you might say, "At the end of one month, we will evaluate progress and decide whether or not to continue or if the plan needs to be modified." This practice is best for the consultant, too, who may need to re-estimate the time involved or who may have run into some unforeseen obstacles. It is important to have a written statement that you both sign spelling out your understanding of the consultant's role, fees, and expenses.

For the same reasons as discussed in the last chapter on hiring a development director, never hire a consultant on a contingency or commission basis.

NO MIRACLE WORKERS

Consultants play an increasingly important role in helping organizations increase their fundraising ability, solve problems, and get board members and volunteers to understand all the ways they can help raise money and why they should be involved in fundraising. However, like the results generally reported from personal psychotherapy, it seems that one-third of the groups do better, one-third do worse, and one-third stay about the same. Consultants cannot create motivation and cannot force people to change bad habits. Timing is key: Is the group willing to change? Is it willing to try something new? Or does it merely wish it were willing to change but not really ready to do so? Does the group only want to hear what it wants to hear, or is it willing to hear what the consultant has to say? Are there major personality conflicts that need to be addressed before fundraising can begin? Are there other hidden problems?

During the first meeting with your group, a good consultant should be able to help you figure out if consulting is what you need. If it is, he or she can also help you determine what the best use of their time would be. In the end, for a consultant's time to be truly useful, your organization has to be willing to hear what the consultant has to say.

Making Fundraising
Your Career

What would you say if you could have a career that paid you a salary from $25,000 to $200,000? Gave you work with fairly measurable outcomes? Where talking about your values and writing about what you believe are part of the job? Where all the people you work with agree that what you do is really important?

Sounds like a great career, doesn't it? It is: it's a career in fundraising.

I have had many goals in my life, but now my goal is to have more people make fundraising their career. I have three major reasons for wanting to expand the number of fundraisers:

• I have too much work, much more than I can handle. In another few years, I want to retire knowing that there are many other people able to do the work I was doing.

• I want fewer phone calls from headhunters, desperate executive directors, and friends who sit on boards all saying, "Do you know anyone who can take our development job? We've looked everywhere. We've extended the deadline for applications indefinitely."

• I want to see good organizations succeed in their fundraising, and one thing many organizations need in order to succeed is someone who is paid to coordinate the organization's fundraising efforts.

Of course, my goal is more specific than simply bringing new people into fundraising. What I really want is to bring a new generation into fundraising for progressive social change, which is at the lower end of the salary scale I mentioned earlier.

"But fundraising isn't a cool career," many will say. "Not like actually doing advocacy or service or maybe even being a public interest attorney—being on the front lines of changing society." I've heard this before. For example, a woman I once worked with recently wrote to tell me that she had left her fundraising position to take a job as an advocate in an agency serving homeless mentally ill adults. "I'm glad to have had this fundraising experience," she wrote, "but it will be good to be out on the front lines again." Her letter came on the same day as a phone call from another colleague who said, "I just have to get back into doing the real work. I can't do this fundraising anymore."

I know that we need organizers and attorneys and social workers. But none of these positions needs to be exempt from fundraising, and someone needs to be the main person in charge of that fundraising.

Before you dismiss a fundraising career as for wierdos only, consider two facts:

- Fundraising allows you—in fact, requires you—to talk about what you believe in to people whom you would probably never otherwise meet and to discuss the difference their money will make in implementing those beliefs.

- Fundraising gives you the chance to experiment with strategies. Will this letter work? How can your organization get maximum mileage out of your Web site? Would people pay to come to this kind of event? While some strategies are formulaic—you follow a recipe and you can predict the result (comforting with so much uncertainty all around us)—others will require your full attention, creativity, and intelligence. Most fundraising is a combination of good luck, good people, and good thinking.

Of course, fundraising does have its drawbacks. As with any difficult job, you have to be able to handle lots of tasks at the same time. In most organizations the fundraising staff has a lot of responsibility with very little authority. People tend to blame the fundraising department for everything that goes wrong in the organization. People who have no knowledge of fundraising have unrealistic ideas of how much money can be raised in short periods of time. And worse, they tend to believe that all the organization's problems can be solved by finding previously unknown but very large foundations to give them grants or by meeting lonely, generous, and previously unsolicited rich people who will lavish them with funds.

FUNDRAISING'S BAD RAP

Let's admit it, fundraisers are regarded with the same mixture of admiration, suspicion, and awe with which we in America regard money itself. This attitude explains some of the problems in attracting people to fundraising positions. As I have pointed out several other times in this book, money is one of the great taboos of our culture. We are taught not to talk about it or ask about it, except with a limited number of people in a limited range of circumstances. As with the subjects of sex, death, mental illness, religion, politics, and other taboos, people say little about their experiences with money. With people so carefully taught that it is rude to talk about money, it's certainly not an easy task to ask for it.

Yet, as philanthropist and fundraiser George Pillsbury points out, "Although money cannot buy social change, no significant change can happen without it." Organizations cannot do their work without money. An organization that does not have enough money to accomplish its goals winds up wasting the time of its volunteers and staff and possibly hurting the constituency it claims to be working for.

When I decided to make fundraising my career more than thirty years ago, it wasn't because I liked fundraising. In fact, I was studying to be a minister. I thought the church was a great place from which to do community organizing and advocacy, and I saw myself in that role as well as pastoral care. But I found that no work could happen unless someone brought in money. If I wanted to do important and useful work for the movements that I cared about, there was no way to avoid being involved in fundraising.

I also chose fundraising because it meant that I would have to talk about money, which, in a small way, could begin to break down the taboo that surrounds it, and that, as I discussed in Chapter Six, helps to maintain the status quo.

WHY FUNDRAISING IS COOL

In addition to helping overcome the mysteries of money, here are some other reasons fundraising is exciting and cool.

Fundraising Teaches You About Money. Fundraising brings you face-to-face with the good, the bad, and the ugly about money, and about people. Fundraising allows you, perhaps even forces you, to confront basic issues of class in yourself, in your organization, and in the people you raise money for and from. If you are serious about social change, this is a good thing.

Fundraising Does Not Require Years of Education.   Although there are technical aspects to fundraising, the three main requirements for success as a fundraiser can be found in people of all educational backgrounds: common sense, a basic affection for other people, and a passionate belief in a cause.

Fundraising Requires You to Learn New Things All the Time.   While perfecting the set of basic skills you bring, you will learn plenty of new skills: I have learned basic accounting and budgeting, strategic planning, data entry, project management, prospect identification, and facilitation, just to name a few things. Sure, some of this I would have learned anyway, but much of it I wouldn't have or I wouldn't have learned as thoroughly.

Fundraising Connects Donors to an Organization.   Many donors have little relationship to the organizations they support aside from giving money: they don't have time to volunteer or they are not part of the constituency. A fundraiser helps them continue to feel connected and useful so that they will want to continue to give.

Fundraising Is Organizing.   Good fundraisers organize teams of volunteers to help with fundraising, and they should be teaching organizers how to ask for money. Organizers usually ask people only for time—go to a meeting, plan a strategy, come to a demonstration. Good fundraisers teach people skills and increase their confidence that they actually can raise money. By combining fundraising and organizing, people are asked for both time and money—as much of either or both as they can give. A much wider range of gifts, talents, and abilities can be brought out in our constituents by adding fundraising strategies to the mix.

BECOMING A FUNDRAISER

You can enter the field of fundraising in a variety of ways. One of the best ways to learn fundraising is to volunteer, and fundraising is one of the few jobs for which volunteer experience qualifies you. Being on the fundraising committee of a board of directors or helping to put on a special event have launched many a fundraising career. Interning with the fundraising program at an organization is another form of volunteering that can be instructive.

You can also learn about fundraising in college classes and courses, but this method only has merit if you have a way to apply what you are learning in a real-life setting. Working in a large organization as an assistant to the development director will give you a range of experience without requiring you to take on a lot of responsibility.

If you are serious about fundraising as a career, find a mentor. Many development directors enjoy mentoring people new to the field, and they can help you find your way through the difficult times.

Don't hesitate to jump in at the deep end. Take a job that you are not totally qualified for, then read, take classes, use your mentor, and wing it. As I described in Chapter Thirty-Two, I have often encouraged organizations seeking a staff fundraiser to stop looking for the person with perfect skills who may not exist and instead to find a bright, hard working, quick learner. If you can start in a job that has a solid team of volunteers to work with and that will give you funding to attend some basic fundraising trainings, with enough support and a little latitude, you are likely to be successful.

JOIN THE FRONT LINES

As you can see, when I say I want people to make fundraising their career, what I really mean is that I want people to say, "My role in working for social justice will be to help generate money." Fundraising cannot be separated from its context. It is a necessary and central part of developing an organization and fulfilling its mission. It is real work, and although it takes place on a slightly different set of front lines than organizing or advocacy, they are front lines all the same. The more fundraising is integrated into the rest of an organization, the more successful that organization will be and the more people will be drawn to fundraising in the future. The sooner that happens, the sooner I can retire.

Dealing with Anxiety

During the thirty years I have been in fundraising, I have observed that the greatest factor causing people to leave fundraising or to burn out is not the work itself or even the challenge of having to ask for money. It is the constant, gnawing anxiety that the money won't come in and the knowledge that once you have raised money for one month or one quarter you must simply begin fundraising for the next period of time. There is never a rest, success is short-lived, and lack of success shows up immediately. Fundraising can also be an isolating job, with the burden of producing money too often placed on one or two people.

Many paid fundraising staff have told me that they wake up in the middle of the night worrying and that they never really feel free to take a weekend off, let alone a vacation. Fundraising staff often watch their enthusiasm and self-esteem eaten away by the constant pressure of a job that by its nature can never be finished.

Aside from psychotherapy or quitting one's job, there are five ways to deal with this anxiety.

Recruit Volunteers and Delegate.   Saul Alinsky, one of the most important figures in community organizing in the twentieth century, had an iron rule for organizing that also applies to fundraising: "Never do for someone what they can do for themselves." People like to help. When you are doing something that a reasonable, intelligent person could do with minimal training, find such a person and get them involved. This will decrease your isolation and increase your productivity. Having volunteers help you will not save time, as the time you save by having them do the task is used in recruiting, training, supervising, and then thanking them, but the goal of having the work spread over a larger number of people is accomplished, and the feeling that it is all up to you is diminished.

Keep Your Priorities Clear. If your primary responsibility is to raise money, then every day that you come to work set your priorities around that goal. Ask yourself, "Of all the tasks that I have to do today, which one will raise the most money over the longest period of time?" Do that task first, then do the task that will raise the second-most amount of money, and so on. These decisions will call for some judgment on your part. For example, if you have the choice of writing a grant proposal for $10,000 or approaching a major donor for an additional gift of $1,000, you may decide to go to the donor because she is more likely to give year after year than the foundation. Or if you follow the advice to get others involved, you will try to get a board member to go to the prospective donor, freeing yourself up to write the grant proposal. Just remember that no one ever gets their whole job done. Make sure that the things you don't get done are things not related to fundraising. Here's an example.

In one organization, the director was the only staff person. Feeling responsible for everything, she did those things she knew how to do and that she could finish. She kept accurate and excellent books, paid bills on time, got out minutes and agendas for meetings, and wrote, edited, and produced the newsletter. The board did a lot of program work under her direction. Soon, the group had little money and was in danger of going out of business. This director quickly learned to change her priorities. Now she works on fundraising at least four hours every day, the organization has outsourced the bookkeeping, board meeting minutes and agendas are handled by the board secretary, and at each board meeting, the director has a fundraising to-do list for the board. While some board members object that they would rather be working on program than on fundraising, the director is teaching them that without money there is no program and no group. The primary responsibility of the board and staff of any organization is to keep the group going, which usually means active, ongoing participation in fundraising.

Detach from the Results of Your Work. Not being able to do everything is not a condemnation of your worth as a person. A request turned down or an unsuccessful mailing does not mean that you are a failure as a person or as a fundraiser. If you make a mistake, it doesn't mean you are a mistake. Ask yourself whether it will be important in ten years whether you got the newsletter out today or next week. One person can only do so much. Do what you can do in the time allotted, and let the rest go. Too often, groups have fundraising goals that no one could reach. Instead of trying to live up to impossible expectations, evaluate your goal setting.

Recognize That There Are External Forces Beyond Your Control. You can do your job flawlessly and your organization can be effective and well regarded, and you still may not be able to raise the money you need. The rising gap between rich and poor, which every year reaches another record, and the depth and breadth of government cutbacks mean that more and more organizations scramble for money. In the United States particularly, there is plenty of money, but it is very unevenly distributed. Without a major restructuring of social policy that places people ahead of corporate profit and a priority on peace rather than military might, nonprofits of all sorts will continue to struggle. This state of affairs is not your fault. Dealing with these larger forces means opening up the time in your organization to join and work in coalitions of organizations addressing tax policy, the preservation of "the commons," and the role of the nonprofit sector in general. Your organization has to work on issues beyond its own mission. Getting perspective on the larger picture will help reduce your anxiety.

Some people have found it helpful to form support groups with others doing similar types of work—either informal gatherings over happy hour or more formal, structured meetings at a specific time and place. If you do use a support group, make sure it supports your work and helps with strategies. Do not use it as a gripe session to compare notes on how awful everyone's job is. That will only make you more dejected.

Take Care of Yourself. Don't always work overtime. Take vacations. Ask for help. Delegate tasks. The overall work of social justice is the creation of a humane and just society where, among other things, work and leisure are balanced. If the culture of your workplace does not encourage balance, it is unlikely that your organization can have a positive role in creating social change.

There is a pervasive form of contemporary
violence to which the idealist fighting for peace by
nonviolent methods most easily succumbs:
activism and overwork. The rush and pressure of

modern life are a form, perhaps the most common form, of its innate violence. To allow oneself to be carried away by a multitude of conflicting concerns, to surrender to too many projects, to want to help everyone in everything is to succumb to violence. More than that, it is cooperation in violence. The frenzy of the activist neutralizes one's work for peace. It destroys the fruitfulness of one's work because it kills the root of inner wisdom which makes work fruitful.

Thomas Merton

Working with Your Executive Director

For many people reading this book, this chapter could be called "Working with Yourself," because as the only paid person, the title "executive director" describes you, as does the all-encompassing title of "staff." Nonetheless, even if you are a sole staff person, you may find this chapter helpful in avoiding mistakes once your organization is big enough to hire someone in the development role. If you are a development director working with an executive director, this chapter speaks directly to you.

As development director, the executive director can be your greatest ally or your biggest challenge, but rarely anything in between. The job of the development director is an odd one in the sense that you report to and are accountable to the executive director, yet your job includes organizing the executive director's time efficiently with regard to fundraising—which means telling your boss what to do. To work effectively with an executive director requires discussing early on in your tenure how the executive director wants you to present the fundraising tasks that he or she is to carry out and how the executive director intends to be accountable to that work. Here's how an ideal working relationship between an executive director and a development director would play out.

At the beginning of the year, the executive director and the development director create a draft fundraising plan. Perhaps the development director does most of the work on the plan and then brings it to the executive director to discuss, but the executive director is familiar with it and believes it is the appropriate plan for the year. These two staff go over the plan in great detail with the board leadership, such as the fundraising and finance committees. Board members' suggestions for changes are incorporated, then someone from the board presents the plan to the full board, ideally receiving enthusiastic buy-in (or at least willingness to do the job) from the full board. The development director feels supported by the executive director in all her efforts to work with the board and with the executive director. The executive director sees the development director as a partner in the financial future of the organization—a junior partner to be sure, but still someone she turns to for advice and whose counsel and instincts she trusts. The development director, in turn, sees the executive director as someone she learns from and whom she likes and respects. If not friends, at least these two see themselves as strong colleagues, interested in each other's opinions on a wide variety of topics related to running the organization.

Some coworkers develop this relationship naturally. They are usually people who are competent, not competitive, and not controlling, more committed to the mission of the group than to their own ambition and able to delegate tasks and share information. These people are not without their struggles or disagreements, but they are able to be straightforward in conversation and listen to each other, and they are willing to take the time to work things out.

People who do not naturally subsume themselves to the work of the organization can still have a strong working relationship if they work at it a bit. These are usually people who are competent but can be controlling, committed to the mission of the group but wanting personal recognition, so overwhelmed with work that they have trouble sorting out what can be delegated and what cannot, and who keep information to themselves more out of sheer inability to find the time to share it than any real intent to conceal. Again, honesty in communication will help this be an effective working relationship.

Unfortunately, there are far too many situations in which the relationship between the executive director and the development director does not work. Although some of these poor relations may be primarily the fault of the development director, the majority have their roots in the work style of the executive director. Here are the most common reasons a productive relationship between executive director and development director fails to occur:

- The executive director's successes eventually mean that the organization grows past her ability to run it. Rather than admit that she has reached her limit of competence, the executive director becomes more and more controlling and may actually shrink the organization back down to a size she can manage.

- The executive director has been at the organization too long. He feels tired and has lost enthusiasm for the work, but he stays in the job because he can't imagine what to do next. Mediocrity becomes the standard of work.

- The executive director is sensitive to criticism, even defensive. She creates a work environment in which only total loyalty to her is acceptable and questioning her decisions or directions is perceived as insubordination. Creativity is squelched.

- The executive director is afraid to ask for money and will not help with fundraising from individual donors. Often this fear is disguised as "I can't deal with a bunch of little gifts. Let's just get a foundation grant."

- The executive director doesn't trust the board members or wants to retain power, so does not share decision making with them. Few if any boards will actively engage in fundraising if they are not involved in policy making and other board activities, so the board is of no use in fundraising.

- The executive director is threatened by the development director's knowledge of fundraising and feels that his own lack of knowledge will be perceived as incompetence. He constantly belittles the development director's ideas or ignores them altogether.

- The executive director's job is too big. She works between sixty and seventy hours every week, which means she is often at the office on weekends; she rarely takes a vacation (and then is checking e-mail and phone messages several times a day); and she expects the same effort from the other employees. Such people do not realize that they simply disguise the cost of doing business and they wonder why they have high employee turnover.

- The executive director believes that the development director's job is to get the money. He wants the development director to bring in the cash, no questions asked. He is slightly embarrassed that the organization needs money at all.

There are many other variations on these themes, but these are the most common. If you are already working for an executive director who has some or all of these characteristics, it is possible to make a change in the staff dynamic, but it is more likely that you will need to find another job. To guarantee that you don't take a job where these dynamics prevail, make sure that you know what you have the right to expect from an organization and an executive director and what they have the right to expect from you.

One of the best ways to develop good working relationships is to be absolutely clear about your job. Your job is to coordinate the fundraising function of the organization. You are to make sure that all fundraising tasks are completed, one of which is to help the executive director complete his or her tasks. You lead by pushing others into doing the work, and your job is to get as many people involved in fundraising as possible so that the organization can raise as much money as it needs from as many sources as you can manage.

Given that these are your responsibilities, the executive director should expect that you and she would work closely together to create the executive director's fundraising task list and that you would have the authority to remind the executive director about her tasks and to hold her accountable for completing them. She, in turn, would expect you to provide the support she needs, such as materials, thank you notes, reports, and so on. Keep in mind that the executive director is the front person for the organization. Many donors will prefer to meet with that person rather than anyone else in the organization. The development director has to appreciate that the executive director balances many tasks, of which fundraising is only one—even if it is very important.

Sometimes the executive director will know a lot more about fundraising than the development director. In that case, the executive director should mentor the development director. More frequently, the development director knows more about fundraising than the executive director. The executive director should welcome this knowledge, recognizing that an organization hires staff partly because the executive director doesn't have the time—or necessarily the skills—to do the whole job.

Your job is also to coordinate the fundraising efforts of the board of directors and other volunteers. You should have access to all board members and be actively supported by the executive director in your efforts with the board. Both of you should work closely with board members, particularly on personal, face-to-face solicitation.

Both parties should know how the other likes to work. Questions of working style should be talked out early in the relationship. Such questions include whether interruptions are OK; how each feels about editing the other's writing (because the executive director needs to feel good about everything that comes out of the office, all written materials should be read and edited by other people); how much nagging about getting a task done is bearable, methods of dealing with conflict, the best way to hear criticism, and so on.

The way to have a good working relationship between development director and executive director is to be clear from the beginning what each of you thinks the executive director and development director jobs are and are not—and to agree on those job descriptions. In the end, the people in these jobs need to work as much as possible as partners in fundraising and to see the board as an asset to be developed. As development director, be mission-driven and know that your main loyalty has to be to the good of the organization. Know that you are not always going to see eye-to-eye with the executive director and that final decisions rest with the executive director. Above all, be honest and demand honesty in return. Your relationship needs to mirror the kind of relationships we want to see in the world: respectful, caring, nurturing, genuinely interested in the other, and joined in a mutual belief in something bigger than yourselves.

The Ethics of Fundraising

Whether as professionals or volunteers, we fundraisers run up against a number of ethical dilemmas in the course of our work. An ethical route is often quite obvious. For example, it is not OK to tell a funder or a donor that you are engaged in a certain kind of program if you are not, no matter how much money that donor might give you if they thought you were. Similarly, it is not a good idea to take on a program area or a piece of work just because someone has or might offer to fund it. "Following the money" in this way quickly results in mission drift. It is not OK to agree to hire your donor's worthless son-in-law to be your organization's program director or bookkeeper in exchange for a major gift. It is also not OK to keep two sets of books—one for the public and a different, truer accounting that remains internal to the organization. Many of these ethical or moral issues are addressed in standard accounting procedures and in the excellent Association for Fundraising Professionals' Code of Ethics (see Resource D).

Although these are all fairly obvious ethical strictures, there is a subset of ethical issues that fall into more of a gray area and that are usually the development director's job to navigate. These dilemmas often arise because the right thing to do is not completely clear and because the development director has conflicting loyalties. Let's look at some examples.

THREE MORAL DILEMMAS

A Question of a Small Fib

A think tank with a staff of five people is offered the opportunity to buy their office building. Their landlord suggests a reasonable price, but the building will need a great deal of work and the organization has never thought about owning property. The board chair is enthusiastic about buying the building, but the rest of the board is not and neither is the executive director. They feel the building needs too much work and that owning and rehabbing the building could take staff away from the actual work of the organization. As development director, you agree with the majority; in addition, you know it would be hard to raise funds for something that so few people are enthusiastic about. You share your thoughts with the executive director. At the next board meeting, the executive director announces that one of your biggest donors, who works in real estate, has expressed concern about nonprofits owning buildings. You know that no such conversation has taken place. The board chair graciously agrees to defer to the donor's knowledge, and the matter is dropped.

A Question of Whether Checking a Box Is a Big Deal

Your organization is awarded a foundation grant for $50,000; the grant agreement asks you to check a box that reads, "Our organization has taken appropriate steps to ensure that none of our employees or board members support terrorism or are involved in any organization that knowingly or unknowingly supports terrorism." You are faced with two facts: first, your organization has not taken any steps in this direction, and second, the organization feels that signing on to this antiterrorism language is unconscionable and that being asked to do so is possibly unconstitutional. You call your foundation program officer who says, "Just check the box—it is all a facade anyway. Obviously, we wouldn't fund you if we thought you were terrorists."

A Question of the Whole Truth

The chair of your board introduces you to her elderly aunt, who is interested in your organization's work. On the advice of the board chair, her aunt has decided to offer the lead gift for a program your organization has wanted to launch; moreover, the donor is willing to give this generous amount for three years. You and the board chair are thrilled. As your meeting with this woman is winding down she says, "I just have one question for you: Does your staff go to church regularly?" You do go to church, but your executive director is an atheist, and the two program staff who will run the program are Jewish. One is religious and one is not.

In these examples, there is one easy way out: just let it go. So what if the executive director made up a conversation in order to end the discussion about buying the building? That was the probably the right decision anyway; certainly, it was the one you agreed with. So what if you check the antiterrorism box on the grant agreement? It will just sit in a file anyway. Clearly, the funder doesn't care that much. So what if you make it sound as though your staff are active in houses of worship? The donor probably won't pursue the question further. On a scale of one to ten, with ten being a big lie, these are all twos and threes.

However, as the saying goes, giving in to any of these "So whats" leads you down a slippery slope. Each of these examples bears a deeper examination to ferret out the ethical and practical complications and to see if there is another way to respond.

THREE TOOLS

There are three tools that can help you avoid feeling the need to deceive, demur, or lie in any fundraising situation (and possibly in any situation). First, follow the Quaker adage, "Assume good intent." That is, assume that all the people you are having problems with are acting out of positive motivation. Second, follow a main principle of assertiveness training by making only "I" statements. "I felt," "I wonder," and so on. Third, use a "gut check." Does this feel bad or weird? What if this whole story were in the newspaper—would I feel proud of my role in the outcome? Using these three tools, let's look at the dilemmas in two ways: good endings and more difficult endings.

Good Endings

First, a look at how these situations could have easy, good endings.

In the first instance, a gut check says, "This is weird." Deceiving a board member is not a good idea. You need to talk with the executive director about his story. First of all, the board member may well know the donor whose name was invoked, and if she runs into him and thanks him for his clarity, your executive director will be found out and your board chair will be embarrassed and hurt. Second, if the board chair is a good person and good worker, why not see if she understands the fact that a capital campaign cannot succeed without total enthusiasm from everyone? However, assuming good intent, you ask the executive director why he thought his story was the best way to solve the problem. Regardless of his rationale, you can then use "I" statements to make your position clear. For example, if the executive director explains that he didn't want to hurt the board chair's feelings and is quite certain she doesn't know the donor in question, you could say, "I would rather see if she understands the need for full staff and board support for a big project. Otherwise, something else may come up that she supports and others don't and we'd be in a similar situation."

Here's how such a scenario might play out: the executive director agrees to have a meeting with you and the board chair. He tells the board chair that he exaggerated a conversation with a donor to avoid hurting her feelings and now feels bad about it. He realizes she is perfectly capable of understanding why pursuing the building did not seem like a good idea to him. You offer support for his position, including telling the chairperson how important she is to the organization and how no one ever wants to dampen someone's enthusiasm. She is understanding and, as is her nature, gracious. She does say lightheartedly as the meeting ends, "Don't worry about my feelings in the future. I'm tougher than I look."

In the second instance, the situation is clearer. Your "gut check" tells you the situation is wrong. Your organization is opposed to this antiterrorist language, as, apparently, is the funder. However, the funder seems comfortable with complying with the letter of the law while not pursing it further. You, the grantee, are asked to deceive in two ways: to check a statement that you don't agree with and to aver that you have complied with something that you have no intention of complying with. You are not going to interrogate staff and board about their affiliations outside of work. That would be no better than checking a box that said, "We make sure that everyone on our board and staff has citizenship papers," or "We make sure that no one on our board and staff has ever had an abortion."

As the development director, it is your job to bring this agreement to the executive director and the board, as they are ultimately responsible for these contracts. If even after you present the situation thoroughly they say, "Check it and forget it," then you have a bigger decision to make: whether you can in good conscience stay in your job. In this case, however, it doesn't come to that. The organization asks the funder to challenge this language in their own professional associations. They do, and they learn that other organizations have also been unwilling to check the box. As a result, they allow your group to turn in the agreement with that statement crossed out and you become part of a coalition of funders and organizations publicly opposing this kind of intimidation.

The third example is one in which "assume good intent" is the primary authority for your actions. You have no idea what the donor wants to know when she asks if you and other staff go to church. Perhaps she is just making conversation and in her circle of friends, this is a common question. You would answer, "I am active in First Methodist. The two people running the new program are Jewish. One goes to Temple Emmanuel and I don't know so much about the other's life. Are you involved in a church?" You might be surprised when she answers, "I'm an Episcopalian. I think churches and synagogues might be interested in this program, and some of them might be able to provide some money and volunteers. Perhaps one of the program people can talk to my women's group and to their own religious groups once the program is up and running."

More Difficult Endings

Of course, all three of these situations could have gone another way. Let's look at how we might work with more difficult endings.

In the first circumstance, the executive director becomes quite defensive when you discuss his fabrication and refuses to talk to the board chair about it. He says that he has made up things before in order to "get things done" and that you need to be more practical. Your dilemma now moves to a different level: Do you want to work with someone who you know will make up stories (possibly to you) in order to get his own way? This would not be an easy decision, particularly if you like the organization or if jobs are hard to come by. Over time, however, the price of supporting someone who regularly exaggerates or fabricates to get his own way may be too great. In addition, the executive director's defensiveness makes it even harder to discuss the issue. Everything is taken way too personally, and there is a limited ability to separate action from personality. "I disagree with you" is heard as "You are wrong and stupid." In this instance you will have to decide what you are going to do about the executive director's tendency to make things up, as well as his unwillingness to be confronted.

In the second situation, the funder says that if you don't check the box and stop making a big deal out it, they will be unable to make the grant. What's your price? Find out more about what the law says and stay in a negotiating posture with your funder. Generally, funders do not like to pull grants any more than organizations like to give up the money.

In the third case, a more difficult ending would be if the donor says she prefers to give money to organizations in which all the staff are involved in a church. Invite her to meet all the staff and hear from them personally before she makes a final decision. If this donor demands that people be active, church-going Christians in order for her to make her gift, you must politely decline her offer.

By continuing to negotiate in any situation, you stay in a place of integrity but not self-righteousness. Having been in many serious moral and ethical quandaries with regard to fundraising, I have always felt best, and felt that the best outcome resulted, when I told the truth—that is, what was true for me—without insisting this was the only or complete truth or even necessarily was the truth. (In other words, I was willing consider that I was wrong.) Offering options and asking to stay in conversation usually resolved the problem amiably.

As you can see, some of your willingness and ability to operate completely ethically will come out of having a diversity of funding sources so that no one person or source is so important to you that you are even tempted to give up your values for money.

It is also true that some things can't be resolved. Then the question is, What is the price of your own integrity?

 **PART SEVEN**

Budgeting and Planning

Lily Tomlin once said, "I always wanted to be somebody. I guess I should have been more specific." I think of this quotation whenever I think of planning. All nonprofits want to have enough money to do their work, but few can name what amount that would be. They certainly want to use the time and money of volunteers and donors wisely and make progress in accomplishing their goals, but the work of defining exactly what that would mean often doesn't get done. The founder and her friends are often working from a thorough plan kept in their heads and revealed to others on a "need to know" basis. This is not an effort to be secretive so much as a failure to take the time to talk it through, write it down, and get everyone in the group to own it. The budgeting process is "We need money—whatever we can get. We'll spend what we have, but it won't be enough." The fundraising plan is "Help! Write a grant, quick! Let's do an event—what's fast? Does anybody know anybody they can ask for a big donation?" If you thrive on this chaotic, crisis approach to budgeting and planning, then don't read the following chapters. But if you think, "There has to be an easier way," you are right.

Because time is our most precious nonrenewable resource, all efforts that use time respectfully, efficiently, enjoyably, and with the greatest results accomplished for the time put in ought to be our top life priorities. Developing a financial plan—a budget—and a fundraising plan will let you use your time to maximum effectiveness. When you think that taking the time to plan will just slow you down, remember the Buddhist saying, "We have so little time, we must proceed very slowly."

Developing a Budget

The first step in developing a fundraising plan is to develop a working budget. In its simplest form, a budget is a list of items on which you plan to spend money (expenses) and a list of sources from which you plan to receive money (income). A budget is balanced when the expenses and income are equal; an ideal budget projects more income than expenses. Budgets are usually prepared from year to year, although organizations doing strategic planning usually prepare three-year budget projections.

There are many ways to prepare a budget. As groups grow, they may change the way they prepare their budget a number of times before finding one that gives them the most accurate projections. In some organizations a single staff member prepares the entire budget and presents it for board approval, but this is a large burden for one person. Therefore, the method presented here assumes that a small committee will undertake the budget-setting process. This committee can be a standing finance committee of the board, which would then be in charge of monitoring the budget, or it can be an ad-hoc committee of two or three board members and a staff person. Many grassroots organizations lack expertise in developing budgets, so they recruit someone who has that experience onto their budget committee to help them create the budget. It is particularly helpful to have someone with financial expertise if you are switching systems or fiscal years or if you want to plan for more than one year at a time.

If you work with a committee, it should be limited to five or six members. Each should have some knowledge of the organization and be willing to put in the time it will take to do the job as thoroughly as possible.

There is a simple, two-step process for preparing a budget that most small non-profit organizations can use effectively. The process takes into account the largest number of variables without requiring extensive research or elaborate spreadsheets.

STEP 1: ESTIMATE EXPENSES AND INCOME SEPARATELY

The budget committee should first divide into two subgroups: one to estimate expenses, the other to project income. When these tasks are completed, the subgroups will reconvene to mesh their work in the second step.

Estimating Expenses

The group working on the expense side of the budget should prepare three columns of numbers representing "survival," "reasonable," and "maximum" expense figures, as shown in the example. The "survival" column spells out the amount of money the organization needs simply to stay open. If you are not able to raise this amount of money, you would have to shut your doors. Items here generally include office space, minimum staff requirements, postage, printing, telephone, and equipment. This column does not include the cost of new work, salary increases, additional staff or consultants, new equipment, or other improvements.

Next, the group prepares the "maximum" column: how much money the group would need to operate at maximum effectiveness. This is not a dream budget; it is a true estimate of the amount of funding required for optimum functioning.

Finally, the committee prepares the "reasonable" column: how much money the organization needs to do more than survive but still not meet all its goals. These figures should not be conceived of as simply the middle of the other two columns. For example, an organization may feel that in order to accomplish any good work, the office needs to be larger or it must upgrade its computers, or that in order to maintain staff morale, the organization must raise salaries. Because higher rent, better equipment, and increased salaries aren't necessary to a group's survival, they will not be included in the group's "survival" budget; however, they are important enough to the organization's work to be included in the "reasonable" budget.

The "survival," "reasonable," and "maximum" columns, then, give the range of finances required to run the organization at various levels of functioning. If you have a year or two of financial history, you can use the line items and costs from previous years to help in creating your budget.

The process of figuring expenses must be done with great thoroughness and attention to detail. For example, to estimate how much you will spend on printing, think through all the items you print and how many of each you will need. A simple mail appeal has at least three printed components—the letter, the return envelope, and the envelope the appeal is sent in. The budget for maintaining a Web site will need to include a webmaster or the cost of staff time for the person who will keep it up to date, a marketing plan for driving traffic to the site, and the staff time required to respond to e-mail or to download donations or orders generated by the site. When you don't know how much something will cost, do not guess. Take the time while creating the budget to find out. Be sure to include expenses for fundraising in the total expenses of the organization. In the first year that you prepare such a budget, your estimates of fundraising expenses will be educated guesses at best, but if you keep careful and detailed records and evaluate your strategies as recommended throughout this book, every year after the first will be much more accurate.

To ensure completeness and accuracy in budget-setting, many organizations have found it helpful to send board and staff members to training sessions on financial planning.

Projecting Income

At the same time that the expense side of the budget is being prepared, the other half of the committee is preparing the income side. Crucial to this process is a knowledge of what fundraising strategies the organization can carry out and how much money these strategies can be expected to generate. Much of this information will come from records kept in previous years. As shown in the example below, the income side is also estimated in three columns, in this case representing "worst," "likely," and "ideal."

To calculate the income projection labeled "worst," take last year's income sources and assume that with the same amount of effort the group will at least be able to raise this amount again, unless you know that the effort expended was more than can be expected in future years or you were given some one-time-only gifts. In the case of foundation, corporate, or government grants it may be wise to write "zero" as the worst projection unless you have been promised or strongly led to believe that your grant will be renewed.

Draw up the "ideal" income projections next. These figures reflect what would happen if all the organization's fundraising strategies were successful and all grant proposals were funded. Again, this is not a dream budget. It does not assume events that will probably not occur, such as someone giving your group a gift of a million dollars. The ideal budget must be one that would be met if everything went as well as it possibly could.

Sample Expense Projections

Item	Survival	Reasonable	Maximum
Salaries			
Director			
Fundraising Coordinator			
Support staff			
Program Coordinator			
Benefits and taxes			
Professional development (that is, seminars, classes, coaching)			
TOTAL PERSONNEL			
Travel			
Office rent			
Office equipment			
Lease photocopier			
Computers (desktop and laptop)			
Printer			
Fax machine			
Other (specify)			
Office supplies			
Telephone			
Equipment			
Monthly charges			
Internet service provider			
Photocopy			
Design			
Printing			
Brochures			
Annual report			
Mail appeals			
Newsletters			
Stationery			
TOTAL PRINTING			

Sample Expense Projections *(Continued)*

Item	Survival	Reasonable	Maximum
Other			
Board of Directors			
Meals			
Retreat costs			
Mailings			
Other (that is, trainings, board orientation, thank you gifts)			
Postage			
First class mail			
Bulk mail			
Bulk mail permit			
Other (specify)			
TOTAL POSTAGE			
Additional fundraising expenses (such as for events* and other outreach)			
Bookkeeping (contract)			
Other consultants (webmaster, fundraising) (specify)			
Training for board and staff			
Other (specify)			
Miscellaneous			
GRAND TOTAL			

*Each event should have its own income and expense budget; when totaled these expenses and income lines can be added to the total budget, or just the net income can be added to the income side of the budget. Again, good record keeping is critical here.

The "likely" column is a compromise. It estimates the income the organization can expect to generate with reasonable growth, hard work, most people keeping their promises, and by expanding old fundraising strategies and having success with some new ones, yet with some things going wrong.

All income categories are figured on the basis of their gross income: that is, the amounts you expect to earn from each strategy before expenses are subtracted. The expenses must be included in the expense side of the budget.

Sample Income Projections

Source	Worst	Likely	Ideal
Major Gifts			
New			
Renewals/upgrades			
Monthly donors			
Membership (or donors giving less than $250)			
New			
Renewals			
Special appeals			
Sale of products			
T-shirts			
Booklets			
Other (specify)			
Special events			
House parties			
Dance			
Conference			
Board donations			
Fees for service			
Foundations (specify)			
Other (specify)			
TOTAL INCOME			

Both the income and expense sides of the budget are presented in columns of numbers, but each subcommittee should also include a narrative that explains some of the rationale behind the numbers and outlines goals other than money that some fundraising strategies will be seeking to accomplish.

When the income and expense sides of the budget have been figured separately in this way, there is less chance of giving in to the temptation to manipulate the figures to make them balance. The committee should follow the old fundraising adage, "Plan expenses high and income low." If you follow this advice and your numbers are wrong (that is, if your expenses are lower or your income higher than projected), you will be pleasantly surprised. If you do what many groups do, which is to boost income estimates to make the budget balance, you will soon be in financial trouble.

STEP 2: MEET, COMPARE, NEGOTIATE

When the entire committee reconvenes, you hope to find that the amount in the "reasonable" expense column and the "likely" income column are close to the same. In that happy circumstance, those figures can be adopted as the budget with no more fuss. Occasionally, groups are pleasantly surprised to discover that their "likely" income projections come close to their "maximum" expense projections. However, compromises usually need to be made. Most of the time the expenses need to be adjusted to meet realistic income potential, not the other way around.

When no two sets of numbers are anywhere near alike, the committee will have to find solutions. There is no right or wrong way to negotiate at this point. If each committee has done its job properly, there will be no need to review each item to see if it is accurate. However, with more research, each subcommittee may discover other ways to delete expenses or add income.

As shown in the following illustration, there are nine possible ways income and expense projections can match up.

As an example, here are two case studies that illustrate different ways of reaching a workable budget using compromise and research.

Ways Income and Expense Projections Can Match Up

EXPENSES	INCOME
Survival	Worst
Reasonable	Likely
Maximum	Ideal

EXPENSES	INCOME
Survival	Worst
Reasonable	Likely
Maximum	Ideal

EXPENSES	INCOME
Survival	Worst
Reasonable	Likely
Maximum	Ideal

THE MAKING OF A BUDGET

Neighborhood Advocacy

Neighborhood Advocacy was founded in the early 1990s. For the first ten years, it functioned as a small organization of mostly volunteers. Then it applied for county funding and for the past five years has received a county grant of $50,000 annually. Last year, however, the group was informed that county money was no longer available. Of their total budget of $125,000, this shortfall represented more than 40 percent. Their budget committee developed the following estimates:

EXPENSES		INCOME	
Survival	$65,000	Worst	$45,000
Reasonable	$85,000	Likely	$75,000
Maximum	$130,000	Ideal	$100,000

All of their income projections were below their parallel expense projections. Furthermore, their "reasonable" expense projection was their budget from the past five years minus the county money and containing fixed increases in line items. Their "survival" budget represented significant cutbacks in service, which several board members felt were so deep there would be little point in even staying open. After much discussion among the board and staff, the group decided that they wanted to continue operating at the current level to avoid undermining morale completely and curtailing the program. Therefore, the board asked the budget committee to develop a budget in which expenses would fall between the existing "survival" and "reasonable" options and to research further some expanded fundraising programs, including getting a loan.

The expense half of the committee then created a budget called "Survival Two," which called for renting part of their office to another group and reducing a clerical position. The income half of the committee investigated hiring a consulting firm to help implement a large membership-recruitment drive using a direct mail and online strategy. The strategy was projected to pay for itself the first year and begin making money the second year. The front money required for this whole package would be $20,000. The budget committee returned to the board with these figures:

EXPENSES		**INCOME**	
Survival One	$65,000	Likely	$75,000
Survival Two	$75,000	Ideal	$100,000
		Loan	$20,000

When the full board met they first adopted the "Likely" income projection and the "Survival Two" expense budget. Board members all realized and agreed that their level of involvement in fundraising had to increase over that of previous years. They then committed themselves to the loan, which they arranged as a line of credit. This was a move of considerable risk, foresight, and courage. They planned to pay down the line of credit in the second year, when their new fundraising strategy begins to make more money. With some luck and a lot of hard work, Neighborhood Advocacy would never be as dependent on one source of money again.

North Fork Watershed Protection

North Fork Watershed Protection had been functioning for only two years. The first year the program was run entirely by volunteers, most of them residents living near the watershed area. In the second year, in conjunction with the group incorporating as a nonprofit, some volunteers agreed to form a board of directors. They were able to raise enough money to hire a staff biologist. With this person's expertise, the organization proceeded to document the sources of the pollution entering their watershed, which generated a good deal of publicity and attracted the attention of the public health department. To keep the pressure on and to ensure that appropriate steps were taken to mitigate this pollution, the staff member now needed a half-time assistant to help with fundraising, administration, and dealing with the press. The board's initial successful fundraising resulted from a few people making significant financial contributions, but no one was certain that these gifts would be repeated. It was also difficult for the board to make fundraising projections based on past experience because they had so little to go on. A budget committee estimated these figures:

EXPENSES		INCOME	
Survival	$58,000	Worst	$60,000
Reasonable	$75,000	Likely	$75,000
Maximum	$120,000	Ideal	$90,000

The only difference between the "survival" and "reasonable" expenses was the cost of an assistant. Even though the "likely" income could cover the "reasonable" budget, the board elected to adopt the "survival" expense for the first six months, along with the "likely" income. They reasoned that although their track record for fundraising was good, their fundraising program was not well enough established for them to draw conclusions about the future.

Because the program had grown rapidly, the board felt that taking on another staff person was ill-advised until they were sure of meeting their income goals. They decided that they would review their income after six months and hire the assistant if they had raised at least half of their "likely" goals. This strategy gave the board some breathing time and assured the staff person that the issue of her workload was being addressed and could be solved in a short time. In the meantime, board members and other volunteers committed themselves to helping out in the office and handling more of the media calls.

These case studies illustrate that budgets are designed to be flexible, to serve as measurements of progress, and to provide structures for the way money is spent and raised. Using a budget this way makes it a helpful document rather than a club hanging over an organization's head. Small organizations cannot know exactly how much money they will raise or spend beyond certain fixed costs, such as for rent or salaries, but they need the parameters that a budget can provide.

ONGOING MONITORING

Once the budget is developed and adopted, it must be monitored. There are many inexpensive accounting software programs that can help track expenses and income. Every month, you note what you have spent or raised in each category of your budget. Every quarter, you note what your expenses and income are for the quarter and what they should be if your cash flow were exactly even. (In other words, you divide your budget into fourths; each quarter you compare the extent to which your real expenses and income correlate to your planned ones.) Many software programs (Quickbooks is the most common) will do these calculations for you, including figuring a percentage of the total budget to show your current financial situation compared to the budget you projected. You can then make adjustments as needed and catch problems fairly quickly. Do not change your budget—use it as a learning tool. Compare what you projected would happen with what did happen and discuss the differences. This way, as the years pass the budgets you create will become more and more accurate.

Creating a Fundraising Plan

Veteran fundraiser and organizer Gary Delgado says that there are four steps to successful fundraising:

1. Plan

2. Plan

3. Plan

4. Work your plan

Because there is so much truth to this formula, it may surprise readers that this planning chapter is relatively short. That's because planning for fundraising is not difficult to explain, nor is it difficult to do. Not only is planning fully three-fourths of what makes fundraising successful, is it also true that one hour of planning can save three hours of work. But the final and most important truth is that planning does not take the place of doing.

Given that an organization is going to have to work its plan in order to raise money, how can a workable plan be created? There are five steps.

Step 1. Set a Goal. This figure will come from your budget, which you can create using the principles outlined in Chapter Thirty-Eight.

Step 2. For Each Income Strategy, Note the Following Details:

- Tasks required to complete the strategy

- Due date for each task

- Who is in charge of each task

- How much the strategy is going to cost and how much it is going to raise

You can put these pieces of information on a spreadsheet or write them up as a narrative with a budget attached.

Now put the plan on some kind of "Year-at-a-Glance" calendar so you can make sure that you have spread the work out over the course of the year as evenly as possible and that you have not made unrealistic plans.

Step 3. Plot Out Your Plans for Raising Money from Individuals.   From the amount of money the budget shows you must raise, subtract the amount that will be raised from strategies not involving individual donors, such as product sales, foundation grants, government grants, fees for service, and interest income. The amount that remains will form the basis of your individual donor fundraising plan. Analyze the types of gifts the money will need to come from and the types of donors you have now, as explained in the following steps. This analysis will help you develop a clearer sense of what individual donor strategies you need to focus on to meet your financial goals.

Given the amount of money that must be raised from individuals, determine how much will be raised from each group of donors discussed in Chapter Three: newly acquired donors, repeat donors, and donors upgrading their gifts. Following the formula described in Chapter Eighteen on major gifts programs, figure that 60 percent of the money will come from 10 percent of your donors, 20 percent of the money will come from 20 percent of your donors, and the remaining 20 percent of the money will come from 70 percent of your donors. The first number (60 percent of the total) is your goal for major gifts; the second number (20 percent of the total) is your goal for habitual donors responding to retention strategies, particularly from those donors who give several times a year; the last number (another 20 percent of the total) is your goal from first- or second-time donors giving through acquisition strategies.

Analyze your current donor base using the following questions:

- How many donors do you have now in each category—major gifts, habitual donors, first-time donors?

- What is your conversion rate? That is, what percentage of first-time donors give a second gift? (It should be at least 30 percent.)

- What is your retention rate? That is, what percentage of donors who have given at least twice keep giving? (It should be around 80 percent.)

- What is your renewal rate? That is, what percentage of all donors who give in one year give in the next? (It should be about 66 percent.)
- What are the organization's strengths in working with donors:

  - Do you do a good job of acquiring donors but have a lower-than-normal retention rate? Or do you have a strong base of very loyal habitual donors, with a higher-than-normal retention rate?
  - Do you do a good job of identifying the top 10 percent of donors and regularly seeking upgraded gifts and major gifts from them?
  - Has the number of donors to your organization grown, decreased, or stayed the same in the last three years? (If it has decreased, you are not doing enough acquisition and may also have a problem with retention of donors. If the number of donors has stayed the same, you are doing a good job with either retention or acquisition, but not both; otherwise, you would see an increase.)

Step 4. Decide on Numbers of Donors and Match Them to Strategies. Based on your analysis in the previous step, decide how many donors you need to meet your goals and match them with the strategies that work best for reaching those donors.

Step 5. Put the Plan onto a Timeline and Fill Out the Tasks. Voilà! A fundraising plan is born. (Two examples of fundraising plans are given in the case studies that follow.)

By using these steps, the planning process can be both simple and accurate. Once a plan is developed, working the plan should bring in the money you need.

FUNDRAISING PLANNING AT WORK: TWO CASE STUDIES

Artworks

Artworks is a community theater serving a city of 500,000 people. The theater performs works of local playwrights and works aimed at raising consciousness about or demonstrating the talents of children, seniors, and disabled people. It has a budget of $500,000 a year and four full-time staff: an artistic director, a development director, a program and marketing director, and an administrator. The administrator also helps with fundraising. The group has an active board of directors of thirteen people. This year they plan to raise $300,000 from ticket sales, small government grants, and fees from their acting classes. They will raise the remaining $200,000 from community donations, including making up for the loss of a foundation grant that has provided $50,000 for each of the last three years.

Using the formula in the third step of the budget-planning process, the group sees that they will need to raise $120,000 from major donors, $40,000 from small, habitual donors, and the remaining $20,000 from their current fundraising program of three special events and direct mail, focused mostly on acquisition.

The theater is highly visible in their community. The group currently has one thousand donors, more than eight hundred of whom give less than $100, and one hundred of whom give between $100 and $249. Many of these gifts are given at the end of performances, when a board member comes out to the stage and asks people to make a gift above the cost of their ticket. The biggest gifts overall are $2,500 from a long-time major donor, five gifts of $1,000 each from board members and former board members, twenty gifts of $500 each and forty gifts of $250 each from regular patrons, and two gifts of $5,000 each from sisters who support all the arts programs in this community. Total giving from all their donors is $100,000.

The group's donor attrition rate is more than 50 percent. For the past three years, they have steadily lost donors, going from 1,500 to 1,250 and now to 1,000. Some board members have blamed this decline on the artistic director's choice of productions. In the last two years, the group has put on a play about disability rights that some people complained was too strident, two avante-garde plays that some people found too obscure, and a play about an aging priest and his struggle with and eventual expulsion from the Catholic Church because of his views on sexuality, which some found anti-Catholic, others found antigay, and others found too pro-gay. Because the director mixes these productions with works appropriate for families and plays written and largely produced by children, other board members feel that the range of works is appropriate and suits the variety of people in the community. These board members also feel that since their mission is to raise consciousness, the plays that are chosen will necessarily raise hackles as well.

The board and staff have spent countless hours discussing these plays and audience reaction to them; by and large they have found these conversations helpful. However, fundraising has lagged. Now they have decided to focus first on fundraising and then to determine whether the plays they are producing are the cause of the decline in their donor base, since their audience numbers have not declined.

Applying the formula to their donor base of one thousand donors, they come up with the following figures:

- One hundred donors should give $250 or more, for a total of $120,000 (currently sixty-eight people give $250 or more for a total of $37,500 in major gifts)

- Two hundred donors should give $100 to $249, for a total of $40,000 (currently one hundred give in this range and their gifts total $20,000)

- Seven hundred donors should give less than $100, totaling $40,000 (currently eight hundred donors give small gifts that total $42,500)

- In addition, they must acquire at least three hundred donors to make up for a normal attrition rate of 30 percent just to maintain their base at one thousand donors.

Moving to Step 4, they draw up this outline:

Goal 1: Increase the number of donors giving more than $250 to one hundred and increase their total giving from $37,500 to $120,000. This will require asking for significant increases in current major donors' gifts and in moving some people up to major donors. This seems quite doable.

Goal 2: Double the number of people giving between $100 and $249. This will require a big effort both to acquire donors at this higher giving level and to ask about three hundred current donors to increase, and in many cases, double their current giving. This seems ambitious, but necessary.

Goal 3: Attract three hundred first-time givers and strengthen retention strategies to ensure that seven hundred of their current one thousand donors renew (many of whom will be also increasing their gifts). Achieving this goal, they will maintain their base of one thousand donors and not experience any more shrinkage. To reach this goal will require an intensive effort to convert single-ticket buyers to be regular donors.

To accomplish these goals, the group will conduct two donor campaigns, one in the spring focused on major donors and one in the fall focused on getting current small donors to move into the $100 to $250 range.

Spring Campaign. They will create a gift-range chart for major donors and seek to renew or upgrade their current donors as well as find thirty-two new donors, for which they will need one hundred prospects who could give gifts in the range of $250 to $1,000 (projecting both a 50 percent refusal rate and that 50 percent of the positive responses will give less than the amount requested).

Fall Campaign. A well-written and attractively printed personalized letter, with a personal note from a board or staff member, will go out to all donors who have given between $50 and $249 for three years or more. The letter will ask for an increase in their giving and will be followed up with phone calls. All other donors who have given more than twice and who are not in these categories will be asked to increase their gifts with a personalized letter. The Web site will be upgraded to emphasize giving and offer the ability to give online.

To retain donors, they will write to current donors three times during the year, describing different projects and aspects of their work. They will also introduce a pledge program and offer special receptions for donors who increase their gifts, regardless of the original gift or the amount of the increase.

Finally, they will continue with the acquisition strategies that are working: asking for donations at the end of their theater shows and their three annual special events.

Moving to the fifth step, they are ready to put their plan on a timeline. On a master calendar, they mark off when their plays are running. They note when their government grant proposals are due to be submitted, when their special events are scheduled, and when their quarterly newsletter goes out. Next, they schedule their extra appeals so that they go out just after the first three plays but at least three weeks before or after each special event. Finally, they schedule their major gift campaign in two small remaining windows of time: January 15 through February 15 and November 1 through Thanksgiving.

With this plan approved, the Artworks board divides into three committees: acquisition, retention, and major donors and upgrades. With the help of the organization's administrator, each committee prepares a task list and divides up the work.

Affordable Housing for Working People

Affordable Housing is located in a small town about an hour away from a major urban area. Because the town is in a beautiful rural location surrounded by parkland, many of its homes have been bought up as weekend and vacation places by the nearby urban residents. This influx has both driven the price of housing up and created a shortage of housing for people who actually work in the town. These people not only provide many of the services the second-homers rely on when they are there, they also help maintain the rural and diverse flavor of the town that is one of its drawing points. Affordable Housing seeks to purchase existing houses throughout the town and resell or rent the homes at affordable rates to local working people while holding the value of the land in trust for the community, as in the nationwide community land trust model.

After five years of building the organization, Affordable Housing has acquired its first property, which will ultimately house two families. Although it has launched a successful campaign to finance the purchase beyond what the rental income will cover, the group needs to expand its member base in order to maintain its small operating budget of $42,000 for the current year. This budget supports two part-time staff people and a small office. The plan is to meet the budget with a repeat (final year) operating grant of $10,000 from the county, another grant of $10,000 from a local foundation, $500 from local businesses, and $500 from events. The remaining $21,000 of the operating budget is designated to come from membership income.

Last year the group raised $12,000 in membership donations from 130 members. The renewal rate was low at about 50 percent. The group realizes it needs to increase its efforts to recruit new donors and retain old ones. Following the formula, it plans to raise $21,000 in individual donations as follows:

- 60 percent in major gifts from 10 percent of donors: $12,600 (average gift of about $500 from twenty-five donors, including board members)

- 20 percent from 20 percent of donors in midlevel gifts (both new and renewing), especially those giving more than one gift per year: $4,200 (average total annual giving of about $95 each from about forty-five donors)

- 20 percent from 70 percent of total donors in small gifts: $4,200 (average gift of $27 each from about 158 new and renewing donors)

The organization creates a fundraising plan for operations that includes goals, strategies, and actions, who will lead the effort, when each strategy will be implemented, and expenses involved (see chart).

Affordable Housing Fundraising Plan, 2006 Operations—Goal: $42,000

Constituency	Goal	Strategy and Action	Who Leads	When	Expenses
Individuals:	$21,000				
Major Donors (includes board members) ($250 or more)	$12,600 (25 at $500 avg)	Board members pledge and make gifts. Clarify major donor contact people and make regular contact. Develop and implement special program for informing, interesting, and involving current and new major donors.	Fundraising committee	All year	
Mid-Level Gifts (new members and renewals)	$4,200 (45 at $95 avg)	Renewals: Send up to three renewal notices. Monthly e-mail communication. Newsletter — 2x/year	Staff	Feb/Mar, May, Sept, Nov	Printing, mailing

(continued)

Affordable Housing Fundraising Plan, 2006 Operations—Goal: $42,000 *(continued)*

Constituency	Goal	Strategy and Action	Who Leads	When	Expenses
Small Gifts (new members and renewals)	$4,200 ($158 at $27 avg)	To recruit new members: • Each board, fundraising committee, and staff member recruit five new members = 55 • 20 new members from: 2 house parties with follow-up contacts = 10 1 annual event • Outreach at Farmers Market, Town Fair • Presentations to 2–3 community groups	Fundraising committee; hosts; staff and board	Nov/Dec	Printing and mailing; thank yous; outreach
		• Boxholder mailing after completion of 2nd unit construction		July/Aug/Sept	Printing and mailing
Institutions: County Comm. Fdn. Businesses	$20,500 $10,000 $10,000 $500	Awarded, to be received Feb. Solicit 2nd grant Solicit local bank; consider 2–3 other banks/businesses	Staff Staff		
Events:	$500 $100 $400	Convert annual lunch to pie bake Fall event with local historian	Staff Staff	July Sept	Advertising Advertising

What to Do in Case of Financial Trouble

First, don't panic. Like most people, organizations get into difficult financial straits from time to time. Panicking, searching for who is to blame, and whining will not solve your problem. What you must do first is carefully analyze the nature of the financial problem and how you got into it. This will help create a strategy for getting out of it.

There are several kinds of financial troubles, ranging from simple cash flow problems to serious mismanagement or even embezzlement of funds. I discuss each of these major types of financial problems below. However, it is important to recognize that financial problems are usually symptomatic of deeper management difficulties. These difficulties usually show up first, and often most seriously, in the areas of fundraising and spending. The root cause may be the failure of the board of directors to plan the year thoroughly and thus anticipate the financial crisis, or it could be the reluctance of a staff person to discuss the finances of the organization honestly and fully with the board, leading the board to approve an unrealistic budget. Sometimes the deeper problem is that fundraising projections are inaccurate because not enough research was done to make reasonable estimates of income. Whatever the problem turns out to be, it must be addressed and solved. If only the financial problem is solved, however, and the underlying organizational issues remain unaddressed, the financial problems will recur, each time with increasing severity.

There are four main types of financial problems: cash flow problems, deficit spending, serious accounting errors or mismanagement of funds, and embezzlement of funds.

CASH FLOW PROBLEMS

A cash flow problem occurs when anticipated income is not coming in fast enough, creating a temporary lag in income in relation to spending. A cash flow problem has an end in sight. You know that when a certain major donation or grant payment comes in, or when a reimbursement from the city, county, or state is received, you will be able to pay your bills and say goodbye to your problem. Until that time, however, the organization has to draw on its reserves; once the organization exhausts any savings it might have, then it is in a bind.

You have several choices at that point. You can try to put a freeze on spending and even up your income and expenses by ceasing to incur expenses. You can attempt to stall your creditors by paying bills in installments and by postponing paying as many bills as possible. In that case, call creditors and explain your situation, giving them a date by which you will pay the bill. Many times creditors will allow you to postpone payment if they believe you will have the money soon. Another option is to borrow money to cover your expenses and repay the loan when your cash flow improves. Depending on the size of the loan, you may be able to borrow the money from a loyal board member or major donor who will charge little or no interest and create no publicity. Foundations and corporations in some communities have emergency loan funds to help groups through cash flow difficulties when those problems are not the organization's fault. A final option is to set up a line of credit at a bank and draw on it to cover expenses. Depending on interest rates, however, this could be an expensive move.

A cash flow problem is largely a logistical one and often can be avoided in the future by setting aside money in a reserve account in anticipation of such times.

DEFICIT SPENDING

A deficit is a chronic cash flow problem or more accurately, a situation in which you are spending more than you are raising with no end of this discrepancy in sight. Irresponsible or short-sighted organizations finance their deficit with money from their savings, if they have any, or with money earmarked for special programs, a practice that is then problematic for the special program and may cause distress to the person or grantmaking source for the program. At some point, however, the organization will run out of money and no longer be able to finance the deficit.

There is only one solution to deficit spending: create an ongoing way to raise more money or permanently cut down on spending. Examine where you are overspending and put a freeze on those areas. Designate one staff person or board member to authorize all expenditures of more than $250. In a low-budget organization, careful attention to money spent on photocopying, postage, and office supplies can make a big difference.

Obviously, the organization's fundraising plan and income reports will have to be carefully examined and strengthened. Raising more money, however, is a long-term solution. Deficits require immediate attention because the longer they continue the worse they get. Once you are out of the deficit, avoid the situation in the future by spending only as much money as you raise.

SERIOUS ACCOUNTING ERRORS, MISMANAGEMENT OF FUNDS, OR EMBEZZLEMENT

In cases of even more serious financial errors, mismanagement, or embezzlement, the entire board must be notified immediately and the people responsible for the error or crime must be dealt with swiftly. If embezzlement has occurred, the person committing the crime must be fired; the board will have to decide whether to take legal action against the person or people responsible. In the case of serious error, some mitigating circumstances may be taken into account, such as if the person had never made an error before, the person admitted it immediately and took steps to remedy it, or the error was clearly a mistake and not indicative of carelessness or deception. Nevertheless, the person should probably be suspended until the situation is resolved.

Board members should prepare a brief statement on what happened and what the organization is doing about it. This statement can be sent to funding sources and used as a response should the story get into the newspapers or other media. Honesty and swift action are the best ways to ensure the fewest repercussions.

The more difficult problem to solve is how to make up the loss of money that such an error or crime has caused. Options include asking major donors who are close to the organization for extra gifts, seeking loans, and instituting spending freezes, vacation without pay, or pay deferments for staff. As a last resort, staff layoffs may be necessary.

If the financial situation cannot be improved by any of these means, the organization should consider closing. An organizational development consultant or a facilitator will be helpful in leading the board to a proper decision.

The most debilitating problem in the case of serious mismanagement or theft is the decline in morale of all the people involved. Very little work goes on when everyone in the organization is depressed and shocked. Morale will be boosted when the staff and board have decided on a course of action. If the organization is to stay alive, this must be done quickly and the plan implemented immediately. A crisis of this magnitude can pull people together and strengthen the organization as long as those who stay with it agree that keeping the organization going is of the utmost importance. (For more on this topic, see my book, *Fundraising in Times of Crisis,* which provides much more detail about how to handle and survive a crisis.)

 **PART EIGHT**

Special Circumstances

I f I had a dollar for every time I have been told, "You don't know what it's like to raise money for _____," followed by a description of the place where the group works, or the issue they work on, or the people they encounter, or some other variable, I could endow every group I ever cared about. Of course, it is true I don't know what it is like, but I can ask questions and learn, and that is usually why an organization is paying me to be there. What people mean when they tell me that I don't know what it is like is that I don't know how hard it is. No one says, "You don't know what it's like to have an easy time raising lots of money." People in nonprofits often imagine that it would be easier to raise money for a different group than the one they are in. People in the arts think social service fundraising is a cinch, people in advocacy imagine that providing free legal services would really loosen the purse strings, environmentalists covet the fundraising jobs of labor rights activists, and so on. For the most part, people kid themselves that fundraising would be much easier in another setting, but occasionally special circumstances make fundraising more difficult for certain kinds of organizations or at certain times in an organization's life. An accurate analysis of your fundraising situation is essential for planning long-term fundraising.

All problems in an organization will show up in their income, and they will often show up there first, leading groups to think that funding or fundraising is their problem. However, it is worth a few moments of time to understand that fundraising is sometimes a symptom of a different problem, one that must be solved before fundraising (or even fundraising problems) can be addressed. This topic is so big that I devoted another book to it—*Fundraising for the Long Haul*. For readers who think fundraising may not be their true problem, I advise them to check out that book.

Here are just a few ways organizations mistake what their real fundraising problems are:

- A group that feels an inadequate board hampers them from raising money may in fact be hampered because their executive director is not well liked or well respected.

- A group may feel that they can't raise money because no one agrees with their program, when in fact they have failed to articulate a clear case as to why they deserve support or their work is not generally known.

- An organization has drifted away from its mission. The programs it is engaged in don't really match what people think the organization is about.

- A founder has built the organization past his or her ability to run it. Instead of stepping aside and taking pride in their creation, the founder stays and unconsciously shrinks the organization back to something he or she can manage.

Aside from how an organization's own myopia may affect its fundraising, external factors also play a much bigger role than organizations realize. An organization's fundraising may be diminished for any of the following reasons:

- When the local economy is in really bad shape people just don't have that much money to give.

- A scandal in a large, well-known nonprofit can cause distrust of all nonprofits and decrease revenues temporarily. A series of scandals, as we have had in the first part of this century, can cause an overall decline in public confidence, which takes a toll on fundraising.

- The sheer number of nonprofits asking for donations can contribute to donor fatigue.

- Natural disasters take attention and sometimes funding away from the day-in and day-out work of service agencies. In recent years, we have had so many natural disasters (compounded by poverty and racism) that organizations are in an almost permanent state of raising money for themselves while being supportive of efforts to address major crises.

- Wars take a bigger toll than is generally acknowledged. Financially, they suck up money that needs to be spent elsewhere, but they also wreak psychological damage, as the scale of wounded and killed becomes so large that it is hard to make a case for a small group doing a piece of needed work in a local area.

- Issues come into style and go out of style; long after it has ceased to be popular to fund solutions to a particular problem, the problem will still exist.

I have chosen five of the more common special circumstances that an organization may find itself in, either temporarily (being brand new) or permanently (being rural). The fifth circumstance is one that all organizations face at different times, in which a question arises about whether to seek (or take) funds from a particular funding source—in other words, the question of clean and dirty money. An entire book could be devoted to special circumstances, but these five should give you a sense of how to think through special circumstances of your own and make fundraising plans that overcome the adversity and take advantage of the opportunity the special situation presents.

Raising Money in Rural Communities

A long-standing belief in fundraising is that it is much harder to raise money in rural communities than in urban or suburban settings and that you probably won't be able to raise the money you need. This belief has some logic: there are fewer people in these communities, which means fewer people to ask, and although those people have fewer local nonprofits to give to, there are still basic services that must be supported. A rural community has the same need for a clinic or schools or a library as an urban area but has fewer people from whom to raise the money or provide the needed tax revenue. Nevertheless, it is not only possible to raise money in rural communities, it is sometimes possible to raise large amounts of money.

Imagination and hard work are the key elements to raising funds in rural communities. But there are also seven factors that must be taken into account in doing nonprofit work in a rural community, each of which is considered here.

Everything Takes Longer.   There are two ways in which it takes longer to get things done in rural communities: the obvious time involved in getting from one place to another when great distances can separate homes or towns and the less quantifiable but equally important factor of rural hospitality, which tends to be more extensive than that of city dwellers. For example, suppose you decide to visit a major donor on his or her ranch. You make an appointment then drive one to three hours to the ranch. Once there, you do not chat briefly, ask for the gift, and leave in forty-five minutes, as you might in a city. The graciousness often customary in rural areas may lead your host or hostess to give you a tour of the ranch, invite you to stay for lunch or dinner, and perhaps encourage you to spend the night. This graciousness is wonderful but time-consuming; you disregard it at the cost of the relationship with the donor.

The Necessities of Ranch or Farm Life Can Limit a Donor's Availability.   There will be times, such as planting, harvesting, lambing, or calving, when contact with donors will be limited because people are working almost around the clock. When none of those activities are going on, the weather may make driving conditions so hazardous that volunteers cannot get to meetings, people cannot attend special events, and prospects cannot be visited.

Fundraising Costs Are Higher.   The city dweller's idyllic notion that everything is inexpensive or free in a rural area is false. Almost all supplies and equipment have to be shipped in, adding freight to their cost; lack of competition among businesses can add another layer of cost. Consultants to help repair your computer or handle your bookkeeping needs are fewer and may be more expensive. Although office space may be less expensive than in a city, there may not be any available. The distances between people and places make driving costs high, and there is rarely adequate public transportation.

Logistics Are Complicated.   If you wish to print a newsletter, mail appeal, or flier in bulk, you may have to send it to (and then pick it up from) the nearest city. If you need something sent or received quickly, there may be no overnight mail service from or to your community. Fax machines and e-mail have helped to solve this problem to some extent, and the world of virtual communication is changing rural life a lot. However, in communities where electricity often goes out in storms and few cell phones can get a signal, these twenty-first-century conveniences may not always solve the problem.

Relationships Are Often Complicated.   In rural areas, people often have known each other for many years; sometimes families have known each other for generations. The same people are often involved in more than one organization. For example, the development coordinator for one organization was puzzled that her two most reliable volunteers were reluctant to ask local businesses to purchase ads in their ad book until she realized that all the business owners were close relatives of these volunteers and that these same volunteers had asked these same businesses (sometimes over the dinner table) for an ad earlier in the year.

In rural areas, people depend on each other for help in hard times or for assistance in emergencies. This makes them cautious about doing anything that might cause offense—including fundraising assertively or asking people for money directly. Rural people do not wish to seem pushy in their requests to a neighbor partly because they know that if they have a medical emergency in the middle of winter and can't get their car started, they may need to call that person.

The Pace of Life Is Not Necessarily Slower or the People More Reflective Than in a City.   Rural communities have been seeing a lot of things change in how they operate, and nonprofits working in them must be able to adapt quickly. Many locally owned businesses have been forced to close as superstores like Wal-Mart have opened nearby or as competition from Web-based stores has lured customers with cheaper prices. Whole downtowns have been abandoned in favor of outlying malls. Many family farms have been bought up and put out of business by agribusiness concerns, and suburbs and exurbs have replaced farmland altogether in many places. All of these developments will have repercussions in fundraising.

Not Everyone Has Equal Loyalty to the Area.   Not all rural communities consist entirely of people who have lived in the same place all their lives and make their living from farming or ranching. Though this is a common situation and these people usually have deep and abiding loyalty to their area, other circumstances often bring people to rural communities who do not develop such loyalty. For example, some rural areas have grown into retirement communities, with many of the people living there having come from elsewhere and having developed little loyalty to the larger concerns of their new surroundings. Some of them do have money and, being retired, they may also have time to volunteer. Many will eventually develop a sense of belonging through these activities.

Other rural communities, such as those within a few hours of major cities, are bedroom communities for commuters who work in those cities. The increasingly common use of computers for business enables other people to live in rural communities hours from their workplace and still carry on their business, going to a city only as needed. Their loyalty to their local community may depend on whether they are raising a family there and how strongly they wish to be accepted and involved. "Back-to-the-land" small farmers, vintners in boutique wineries, owners of bed-and-breakfast inns, and the staff of retreat centers are some of the many types of people that can comprise or contribute to rural communities. The finances and values of these people are extremely varied, but many of them have developed a deep and abiding loyalty to their community and want to fit in and help make it a better place.

There are also many rural communities where people have made their living from mining or timbering (many of these people are now unemployed). Others work on other people's farms or ranches, in some instances as sharecroppers. There are rural communities primarily built around a college or a prison. There are many rural communities whose population varies seasonally, as part-timers—tourists or people who own cabins or timeshares at resorts—come and go. Many towns in popular areas will see fifteen thousand people on a weekend who don't live there. Tourists are the main economic driver in many rural communities, and local folks are often engaged in providing services at tourist destinations. Increasingly, there are rural communities where the majority of the population are non-English-speaking immigrants or refugees from Mexico, Latin America, Cambodia, and other countries. These varied populations and conditions add layers of complexity to any rural fundraising effort.

YOU CAN RAISE THE MONEY YOU NEED

The first step in fundraising in a rural community is to reflect on the nature of your particular rural community. How big is your permanent population, and what do most of those people do for a living? What other nonprofits are you competing with? If you have a part-time population, who are they—weekenders, tourists, students, farm workers? What is their giving potential, and how might you capture their gifts?

The second step—or more accurately, a simultaneous step—is to set a goal. How much do you need to raise? People have told me, "We can't raise millions of dollars here in Green Valley like you can in a city." If you don't need millions of dollars, then it doesn't matter that you can't raise it. Know your need. Even organizations in rural communities can raise substantial amounts of money. For one thing, there are people in every community who have the means and will understand the need for larger gifts.

Here's an example. There are a number of communities called "colonias" that span the border between Mexico and the states of Texas and New Mexico. These communities often lack running water or electricity. Their community facilities—schools, roads, and local government—are poor or nonexistent. The people in these communities tend to work in factories or farms nearby. Many people have lived in these communities for years. Raising money for nonprofit work is not easy in a place where so many people have so little, but some organizations have done well. In addition to setting up food booths and collecting small amounts of money from residents, these groups have identified a few people who care about the community and who can afford to give more. In one instance, a staff person of an organization working with teenagers identified a small farmer who they thought could give $100. When they asked him for that amount, he misunderstood the question. "Yes, I can give that every month," he said. This donor has been helpful in identifying other people who can also give substantial monthly or yearly contributions. Further illustrating the relationship between fundraising and organizing, he has helped several community groups petition the local government for roads, sewage systems, and public schools. He has helped people living in his community understand that since they pay taxes, they have the right to services that taxes are meant to provide.

Second, even relatively small communities can raise large amounts for a variety of big projects over time. In a town of two thousand people in northern California, for example, the Friends of the Library decided to raise $35,000 to rehab a small house so they could move their public library out of a converted garage. Everyone involved in the nonprofit part of the community agreed that such an amount would drain the community and make other large fundraising drives impossible. Nonetheless, with the support of many in the community, the Friends of the Library decided to proceed because the library would be so well used. Over the next eight months, they met their fundraising goal. Soon after, the community center in town decided they desperately needed a new space and set out to raise $750,000 to build a new community hall. They, too, raised the money they needed, this time in a three-year campaign. Now it was commonly agreed in the community that there certainly was no more capital money to be raised. Two years went by; the health clinic needed to modernize and expand and had no choice but to launch a capital campaign. That fundraising effort was also successful.

Each of these fundraising drives took place over a number of years and used several different strategies in their campaigns: special events, major donor solicitations, direct mail, and some grant funding. They all took a lot of hard work and the volunteer efforts of dozens of people. To be sure, this community has a number of wealthy retirees, many of whom made significant gifts to these campaigns.

But the entire community participated, and some money was even raised from tourists. A poorer town with no tourism and facing these kinds of needs would need to raise a greater percentage of the money from government or foundation grants, but it would still need to be open to the idea that a few people in their community could make significant gifts and that the rest of the community could give significantly with a number of smaller gifts.

The lesson here is that in any community, but more obviously in a rural community, fundraising is not a zero-sum game. There is always more money, and it is not diminished or used up by big campaigns. Organizations in rural communities will want to coordinate the timing of their campaigns—for two organizations to run a capital campaign at the same time will rarely be as successful as running them sequentially. The need has to be well established, and the community has to agree with the goal of the campaign; but it must be remembered that money grows back and produces more money.

PROSPECTS

There are three populations from whom an organization can raise money: locals, part-timers or tourists, and people in nearby towns and cities. Let's begin with the last group.

If you are located near larger towns or cities with populations of ten thousand or more—and where there is not another program like yours—focus attention on raising money in those areas, where the financial base is stronger. Most groups already have donors in nearby communities; they can be asked to host a small party for you. You can also contact sympathetic churches, synagogues, service clubs, and the like. You may be able to get an article in the local paper that reaches the larger community. Hold special events in these larger towns, and use direct mail and your Web site to recruit donors there. If local people have contacts in these nearby towns and cities, use those contacts to introduce your local needs to this population and to cultivate potential major donors.

Next, try to discover ways to raise money from people who pass through your community, particularly tourists and visitors. Some communities mount events just to attract tourists. For example, many communities have county fairs or various kinds of festivals, such as the Garlic Festival in Gilroy, California, Ramp Festivals in many Southern communities, and the National Storytelling Festival in

Jonesboro, Tennessee. These events attract tourists who spend money to attend the event and who also buy things that are sold there.

If you live in a place where tourists come to see the natural beauty or to vacation (such as along the coasts or near national parks or monuments), consider developing products that tourists will buy. Local crafts and homemade jellies and jams are always appealing. Photography books and calendars, guides to the local sights, and collections of stories or recipes of people who live in the community have all provided steady income streams for rural organizations.

If you live near a freeway or a frequently traveled road, set up a rest stop where truckers and tired drivers can buy coffee, doughnuts, fruit, or other treats. Such a rest stop can be especially lucrative in the cold winter months, particularly at night. It is also a community service that helps keep people from falling asleep at the wheel. In many instances people from rural community groups simply stand with buckets at busy crossroads and ask drivers to drop in spare change. Three hours at a crossroads on a shopping day can bring in a few hundred dollars.

At the local level, focus on finding a few people locally who can give larger gifts. Every community has generous people; a few of those will be able to give major gifts, if asked. Whenever possible, ask current donors for the names of other people who could give as well. People tend to be friends with people who not only share their values but are also in a similar economic situation. Someone who gives your group $100 will know two or three other people who could give $100 and one or two people who could give $250. They in turn will know people who could give $500.

You can also raise money from the community at large. Even in the poorest and most remote areas, churches, volunteer fire departments, rescue squads, and service clubs are supported by local residents. Even the smallest, poorest towns in the Bible Belt, for example, support at least two churches. Even if they do not have paid clergy, the congregants manage to support a building.

Money can be raised locally through special events. This helps counter the reluctance of many rural people to ask for money directly by providing something in return for a donation. Events such as raffles, auctions, and bake sales can be good moneymakers. Flea markets are also popular. It is often easier for rural people to donate items rather than cash, and people always seem willing to buy each other's castoffs. On the island of Sitka in Alaska, there is a thrift shop run by volunteers called the White Elephant. Between purchases from locals and, in the summer months, tourists, the store averages $100,000 in profit every year, which they donate to a variety of other nonprofits in the community. Often a prom dress or fancy suit will be sold two or three times before being retired to rags.

STRATEGIES FOR RAISING MONEY

Keeping in mind the seven factors described earlier, let's look at the most common fundraising strategies available to rural communities and the similarities and differences in carrying them out in rural communities versus urban ones.

Special Events

Everyone is familiar with the large golf tournaments, award luncheons, and black-tie dinner dances that raise $100,000 or even $1 million in urban areas. They cost thousands of dollars to put on and require paid staff and dozens of volunteers working for months to be successful. Generally, a rural community can't pull off something that elaborate. However, special events often form the basis of the social life of small towns and rural communities.

A rural organization can raise $1,000, $5,000, or even more from a special event with three or four months' lead time and a handful of volunteers. Start with an event that people would like to come to and might even travel to the nearest town for, and do your best to put it on in your community.

Take, for example, a dinner dance. The dance can be held in the community center or the school gymnasium, places that can often be used for free or a minimal fee. The food can be provided by members of your organization, but to make it more fun, turn it into a competition. Community cooks pay a small fee to enter the food competition in various categories, such as main course, salad, and dessert. Each is asked to bring enough food so that 100 people could each take a taste of the dish and a few people could have a full portion. People coming to the event get a sample of each entry and then vote on which they think is the best. They can then pay a little more for a larger portion of the courses that they liked. In reality, most will be full after the sampling, so the group will not run out of food. A cash bar serving smoothies, soft drinks, or juice can provide extra income. (Be cautious about serving alcohol to people who have to drive home, and be sure to get permission to have alcohol if your event is in a publicly owned building and that you have adequate insurance.) Later, dance music can be provided by a local band that is trying to become more well known and will perform for a small stipend or for free. Or recorded music can be provided by a DJ who is a friend of one of the members. Marketing and advertising the event can be done largely by word of mouth, public service announcements on local radio, and posters hung in the post office and general store. Each board member can be expected to sell ten tickets at $10 to $25 each. If your event is the only thing going on that Saturday night, getting one hundred people to attend should be easily done. At $10 to $25 per person, and with many people paying on average $10 or $15 more for extra food or drink, added to the entry fee of the food competitors who each pay $5, an organization can easily gross $2,500 to $4,000. If you have T-shirts or other items to sell, you can add a small income stream there with little effort. Expenses will include buying drinks to sell, printing nice-looking certificates or ribbons for the winners of the food contests, and mailing thank you notes after the event to volunteers and participants. Of course, some drinks can be solicited as donations and perhaps a member of the organization knows how to print the certificates from their home computer. Even with expenses as high as $1,000, the group could still net $2,000 to $4,000 from a "good time had by all." As the years pass, more and more people will want to enter the food contest and more people will want to come to the event.

A Chocolate Lovers Festival put on by an organization in a college town of eight thousand people—including students—was organized along the lines indicated above. By the fifth year, it netted $40,000, providing more than half of the organization's budget! Eventually, it attracted top chefs from restaurants in nearby towns in addition to lay people entering their favorite brownies or best hot chocolate.

The dinner dance is just one example of how malleable events are. Each aspect of the event should be conceived of as a separate component, and components can be added or subtracted according to the number of volunteers and the amount of time available. A silent auction can be added to the dinner dance, or a live auction could replace the dance or be added to it. An afternoon barbecue at the beach could replace the dinner, and games could replace the dance. That kind of event would focus much more on families with young children. Tea and dessert followed by a lecture would appeal to a more academic or older crowd.

The secret to these kinds of events is to do as much as possible for free or very low cost and to charge for as many things as you can without having people feel that they are having to pay for something at every turn. Advertising must be effective so that the maximum number of the right people are attracted to the event for minimum cost. Word-of-mouth is the cheapest and most effective advertising and marketing vehicle, and the organization's board should talk up the event everywhere they go; but public service announcements (PSAs) on community TV and radio stations and articles in the weekly paper are important as well.

Raising Money by Mail

Soliciting donations by mail provides another avenue for rural groups. Board members and volunteers can bring in ten to fifteen names each and the organization can send out two hundred letters by first class mail, with personal notes from a board member on each letter. This costs more for postage than using bulk mail, but there are no expenses for list acquisition. A group can even use a rubber stamp for the return address on the return envelope, thus saving printing expense, and they should hand-address the carrier envelope.

This highly personalized approach can easily bring in a 10 percent response. The secret here is the source of names of prospects. Board members' friends are good but finite. People who use the service your group provides or who come to your group's events may provide dozens or even hundreds of potential prospects. As is true with big direct mail appeals, not every appeal will be successful.

As described in Chapters Ten and Eleven on direct mail, the long-term success of a mail program is in the quality and consistency of renewals and extra appeals. Once a donor has been acquired, that donor must be kept informed about the doings of the organization and the worthiness of the projects their money is being used for. And that donor must be asked both to repeat their gift and to give extra gifts during the year. Ultimately, that donor should be asked to increase their gift.

Personal Solicitation

Personal, face-to-face solicitation is the most effective strategy for all organizations, big or small, rural or urban. Your rural organization may not have a lot of name recognition outside your immediate community, and you may not have famous people on your board, but your board members and volunteers have integrity. Donors are likely to give $500 or $1,000 because their friend, Terry, is on the board and affirms that the group does good work.

Personal solicitation is both the easiest and the hardest strategy for almost anyone. It is the easiest because volunteers just have to talk to their friends, who are presumably easy to find and comfortable to talk with. There is no real cost involved, except for the time of the volunteer and perhaps the cost of taking a friend out for coffee or lunch, and the meeting can be set at the convenience of the volunteer and his or her friend. At the same time it is the hardest because it requires asking for money and running the risk of rejection or of offending the friend. Because you will see your friend often, you don't want to do anything that will harm the relationship. Your request may be more low-key in a rural than in a more urban culture. Instead of saying, "Will you help with $500?" and waiting for a response right then, the approach might be, "I'd love it if you gave in the $500 range. Take some time and think about it." Follow-up will be important, but giving the prospect some room to turn you down without having to tell you no directly will help preserve your relationship.

Whatever strategy you choose, make the time to thank donors, volunteers, colleagues, and anyone else who supported your project. It's not only the right thing to do, it's the best public relations available. Thank people in person. Write a brief note by hand. Make a quick phone call. Remember how good you feel when someone thanks you.

When all is said and done, the essence of rural fundraising is the essence of all fundraising: building relationships. Successful fundraising of any kind requires ingenuity, commitment to the cause, love of people, common sense, a willingness to ask for money, and an understanding and deep appreciation of human nature—especially of the natural desire of people to be appreciated.

Fundraising for a Coalition

There are hundreds of organizations whose board members are representatives of nonprofits that have joined together for the benefits that a coalition of groups can bring. In campus ministry, for example, churches that are close to the campus appoint members of the board. In federated funds, members of the federation hold the majority of seats on their board. Almost every state has a coalition against domestic violence, for which directors of local battered women's programs serve as board members. Most regional associations and national organizations operate the same way, with most of those on the board of directors drawn from the member organizations.

There are obvious advantages to this type of board. A regional or national organization whose mission is to strengthen local groups and to raise overall visibility for an issue will be best governed by those most affected and involved in the decisions made. Sharing resources, working collaboratively, developing joint projects, and seeking to expand the reach of the work will all be done best by a coalition made up of people with power at their local level. A board or staff member of a local chapter will be in the best position to represent the concerns of the local organization to a regional or national group. This person will also well understand the need for a regional or national umbrella, engendering a commitment to the coalition as well. Ideally, this person will be the best qualified to make policy and help plan for the umbrella group and to translate the work of the umbrella group to the people at the local level.

From a fundraising point of view, however, this arrangement is difficult for the umbrella group because its executive director or development director is working with board members whose primary loyalty and main fundraising commitments lie with the organization they are representing. Sometimes people have not actually chosen to serve; they may be appointed to a coalition board by their organization and such service may be a part of their job description. In that case, with a job that is often more than full time, tasks related to coalition board service can get short shrift. Getting such a board to raise money requires patience, perseverance, and a degree of maneuvering. However, if you are the person in charge of that fundraising, keep in mind that it can be done.

EXAMINE THE PROBLEM

The first step is to examine the problem. Evaluate the excuses coalition board members offer for not being able to raise money. Most will say they can't participate in fundraising because they have to raise money for their local group. They can't ask the same people to give money to the umbrella group as well as to the local group, and the local work has much more immediate appeal to donors. Next, they will point out that strategies other than face-to-face fundraising are difficult for a coalition to carry out. Special events, for example, require a local presence to generate interest in the event. Direct mail is not a good way to sell an umbrella group because the service is too complicated and local representatives are reluctant to provide names of possible donors. An aggressive online fundraising approach will confuse the donors to the local groups. Many times when I have worked with board members of coalitions, they were able to offer cogent, sensible explanations as to why every strategy I suggested would not work. Yet they would claim that they were committed to the coalition—they just couldn't do anything to help with fundraising.

I puzzled over this conundrum for many years, until I happened to work with a local organization that was part of a coalition. In a casual conversation, the board chair of the local group said, "Part of our problem is that the executive director does so much fundraising for the coalition that he doesn't have enough time to do the fundraising he needs to do here." I was surprised to hear this, as I had worked with the coalition of which this executive was a part and knew him to be one of the most strenuous objectors at the coalition meetings about how fundraising responsibilities at his organization kept him from raising money for the coalition.

When I looked more closely at the people who complain most about how difficult it is to raise money for an umbrella organization, I realized that many were like this executive director: not effective at raising money at the local level or for the coalition. In fact, perhaps not so surprisingly, people who are very effective at their local level, with active fundraising committees and well-executed fundraising campaigns for their local organization, often make the best fundraisers at a regional or national level.

The reality of fundraising is that some people, foundations, or corporations prefer to give locally, others have no preference and will give locally, regionally, and nationally, and still others would rather be part of a national picture. To determine if a donor to a local organization would also give to the regional association requires asking that person.

Local organizations are in the best position to identify sources of funding that are based in their communities but who might be more interested in regional or national work. Those sources should be solicited for the umbrella group. It also happens that a donor will find and donate to an umbrella organization but is in fact more interested in supporting local work. The coalition should let all their donors know of all the local affiliates. Further, some donors will give to both the local group and the larger coalition, understanding the importance of both organizations.

Another common excuse from local people is that they don't have time to raise money in addition to all their other responsibilities for the umbrella board and their local group. This is a legitimate problem; however, these same people will spend hours debating personnel issues, discussing policy and program problems, and poring over the budget to see what can be cut. By shaving a few minutes off of each of those tasks, they would have some time for fundraising.

To be frank, you will fight an uphill and pointless battle if you spend all your time trying to get executive directors or active board members of local groups to raise money for the umbrella group. It is better to spend time recruiting and developing other board members who will raise money specifically for your umbrella group.

SOME SOLUTIONS

There are a number of ways of approaching fundraising for a coalition or umbrella group. First, every board of an umbrella group should have at least three slots reserved for at-large members—people who are not associated with a local group. These can be former staff or former board members of local groups, or simply people committed to the cause who don't happen to work for a local version of the cause. Their primary loyalty should be to your umbrella group, and their primary task should be fundraising. They should be recruited for this purpose.

Second, umbrella groups usually call for a representative of each local group to be on the umbrella board. This person does not have to be a staff member or an active board member at the local group. A person can represent his or her local organization who has previously been a staff person or a board member or who is a key volunteer but not on the board. These people will have more time to devote to the umbrella board.

One federated fund requests that member groups send as their representative someone who "does not have major responsibility for the health and well being of the local organization." Their board is active in fundraising and their board members do not have the problem of divided loyalties. Board members are clear that they represent their local group, yet their primary task is to promote the umbrella organization. Further, they understand that they work best for their local group by being part of a strong umbrella organization.

Third, coalitions perform a vital service for their members and need to create a dues structure that reflects the value of the work they are doing. In several coalitions I have worked with, the member groups paid no more than $50 per year, and in some groups no membership fee was charged. These token payments reinforce the idea that the money for coalition does not need to be produced by the members. Dues can be structured so that bigger groups pay more than smaller affiliates, but dues should comprise at least 20 percent of the income of the coalition unless there is some compelling reason that is impossible. (In thirty years of fundraising, I have not yet heard such a reason.)

Finally, it is critical to look closely at fundraising strategies and give all your board members tasks they can do.

Working closely with individual board members, lobbying with member groups for the most appropriate people to be nominated, and creating an organizational culture where everyone participates in fundraising will enable an umbrella organization to get maximum use of its board for fundraising. The following case study provides one example of a successful coalition's fundraising effort.

A LOCAL ARTS COALITION RETHINKS ITS FUNDRAISING

A statewide coalition of thirty-five arts and culture organizations has struggled for years to get the funding they need. The board is made up of one representative from each of the local groups; very few people on the board have ever helped with fundraising. The coalition has three staff. The executive director spends most of her time on the road giving speeches, talks, seminars, workshops, interviews, and the like on the critical importance of arts and culture to the quality of life in any community. She is an inspiring speaker and does an excellent job promoting the arts. Her deputy director does most of the fundraising as well as providing technical assistance to local affiliates on financial management, evaluation, marketing and promotion, and fundraising. The affiliates appreciate both of these staff and are quite loyal to the coalition. The third staff person does the administrative and financial management for the coalition.

These three women are stretched to the brink. They work far more than full-time, and the deputy director has developed a number of stress-related health problems. They can raise the money they need to maintain their budget, but they desperately need at least two more staff people. They are so short-handed that there have had to turn down several arts organizations that want to join the coalition because they can't provide services to them. They have also turned down an invitation to be part of another coalition of public schools and related programs that is lobbying for more state funding for art and music programs, libraries, and sports in schools, even though everyone agrees this work would be helpful in fulfilling their own mission. The staff and board agree that they are missing a number of opportunities and that the workload is far too big. However, most of the board members maintain that they cannot be involved in fundraising in any serious way because of their fundraising responsibilities in their own organizations.

With the help of a consultant, the coalition rethinks its entire fundraising approach. First, they institute an annual dues structure on a sliding scale from $100 for the smallest arts groups to $2,500 for the largest. All members agree on the necessity for dues and concur that what they get back is well worth the money. Next, the group sets fees for technical assistance to member groups. Because most of the thirty-five members use about four hours per year of technical assistance, the coalition continues to offer four hours without charge; hours after that are billed at $125, which is at or below the prevailing consulting rate.

The board then decides to shrink itself to eleven members from the current thirty-five, with a quarterly meeting to bring all the members of the coalition up to date and to elicit their concerns. This much more manageable board not only saves the coalition the expense of carrying a larger board (in travel, communication, and time spent), it is also better able to focus on fundraising and governance.

The thirty-five-agency membership now divides itself into five groups of seven representatives each; each group chooses one or two months in which it will be active in fundraising, focusing on one of five strategies. The five strategies they agree to are a corporate honorary membership drive; an art show; an online directory of artists, art supply vendors, galleries, classes, teachers, and the like called "ART: Art-Related Things," in which anyone who wishes to be listed pays a yearly fee (later this is taken over by a staff person); a major donor campaign; and a phantom event appeal.

The coalition hires a development director to work with the deputy director and a membership coordinator to work more closely with the member groups, as well as another support staff person. There are rough moments, as some of the five groups do better than others, and the staff still have a lot of work, but after two years the workload is more manageable and the organization has grown a great deal The point is that there are many ways to structure fundraising, and some of the most creative ones will also be the most successful. As T. S. Eliot said, "Only those who will risk going too far can find out how far one can go."

When Everyone Is a Volunteer

Thousands of successful organizations are run entirely by volunteers. Most service clubs, volunteer fire departments, PTAs, and neighborhood organizations have no paid staff. Many of these organizations have run effectively for years. They are designed by volunteers and designed to be run by volunteers. Other organizations may prefer to have paid staff but cannot afford them, so they, too, run on the energy of volunteers. If yours is such an organization, here are some pointers to help you function smoothly and effectively.

In an all-volunteer organization, the volunteers should think of themselves as unpaid staff. The goal for any organization, but especially one run entirely on unpaid energy, is an environment in which people do what they say they will do and do not take on any more than they can do. An organization should not tolerate incompetence and lack of follow through from a volunteer any more than it would from a paid person.

Like staff, volunteers have lives beyond the organization and should be encouraged to set boundaries. Suppose you know that Sally Jones would make a great treasurer but she says she hasn't got the time. Finally, after you implore her several times, she agrees to do it. Don't be surprised when Sally turns out not to be as good a treasurer as you had expected. As part of showing respect for each others' time, it is imperative to create and support an organizational culture that allows people to take on fewer tasks if it also encourages them to finish the tasks they do agree to. Moreover, some people have more time than others and may be able to take on more work than others. These differences need to be accepted in the group; people with less time must not be made to feel that they are not doing enough if they don't put in as much time as others. Ironically, one of the best ways to create this type of supportive work environment is to make sure that no one or two people take on most tasks. When you have "uber-volunteers" who get everything done, accomplishing more work than anyone else, it dampens everyone's else's enthusiasm.

Volunteers should use their own and other people's time respectfully. Meetings should start and end on time. There should be an agenda. A facilitator, the chair of the meeting, or the group as a whole should agree on how long each agenda item will take and try not to take longer than agreed on. There is usually more that can be said on any item and one more way of looking at things, but unless you are an academic think tank, don't try to explore every possibility.

People should take on particular responsibilities. Someone should be the treasurer, someone should prepare the agenda for meetings, someone should be the chair. Organizations working in a collective model can rotate these responsibilities (which need to be rotated occasionally in any structure). No one in the group should have to wonder, "Who is in charge of filing our 990 tax form?" or "Who has the checkbook?"

Think of your organization as a team. On a team, everyone has a place and they play their place. Everything is time-limited, rules are clear, and violations of rules have penalties. At any given time, some players are out on the court or in the field and others are resting on the bench. No one plays all the time and no one rests all the time. Discuss this team metaphor from time to time in your organization; examine how your organization is most like a team and where it needs to improve.

For an all-volunteer organization to succeed over time and over generations of new volunteers, people should be particularly careful to write things down. Every event, mail appeal, campaign, and so on should be evaluated so that next time it can be done better and more easily, even by new people. Any systems used should be documented. Err on the side of keeping track of too much rather than too little information. Imagine a graduate student in one hundred years reconstructing your organization from a box of dusty files, real or virtual. Would it be possible? It should be. Turnover in all-volunteer organizations is often high, and knowledge easily gets lost, particularly if there is no office or central place to keep files. If you do a special event, send a direct mail appeal, or write a proposal, keep track of everything someone else might want to know about it in order to do that same fundraising task faster and more easily the next time. If several people are storing this information on their individual computers, it can be compiled onto a Zip drive or a flash drive so that it is in one place and can be easily accessed next time. Preparing reports and narratives for the use of people who will come after you is the best way to ensure that your organization can continue to function well using volunteers. In fact, developing such a history helps to ensure that your organization can grow.

Volunteers should constantly seek to expand the number of volunteer workers. There is so much work to be done that a few initial dedicated volunteers will burn out quickly. You should be drawing new people into the organization all the time who can help share the work and broaden the organization's thinking and its access to funds.

All-volunteer organizations are not that different from many grassroots organizations that have one or two paid staff people. In fact, in many grassroots groups there are two kinds of staff: low-paid and unpaid. In all other grassroots groups there is one kind of staff: unpaid. The work is still valuable and people's time is still invaluable. Keeping these points in mind will ensure that your organization is able to do the useful and important work it has set out for itself.

The following case study examines some of the pitfalls for all-volunteer groups.

HOW MARY MORPHED FROM TEAM CAPTAIN TO ONE-WOMAN SHOW (AND BACK)

A PTA starts out with twenty active parents. Mary, the chair, is a full-time volunteer. Everyone else has a paying job; some of the parents have two jobs in order to make ends meet. When the PTA first starts meeting, everything seems to go well. Mary does more because she has more time, and neither she nor anyone else seems to mind. However, after a short time, Mary starts to volunteer to do things that others could easily do. For example, someone always brings snacks to the meetings, which are held right after work. José offers to bring them to the next meeting, saying, "I'll grab some stuff at the supermarket right after work." Mary says, "You don't need to do that. I have time. I can bake something healthy and delicious." After that, Mary always makes the snacks.

The meetings are always at someone's house. People can bring their children, who play with each other while their parents meet. Sharon offers her house for the next meeting as long as no one is allergic to dogs, as she has two friendly mutts she adopted from the Humane Society. No one is allergic, and several people say that they love dogs, but Mary says, "Why don't we just have the meetings at my house?" Mary does have the nicest house, with a playroom for kids and no pets. No one ever volunteers their house for a meeting again, and from then on they are at Mary's.

The PTA decides to have a "white elephant" sale to raise money. Bill and Tiffany are excited and offer to chair. They find a space, send out e-mails inviting people to donate stuff, and create a fun flier advertising the event. Bill stores the items in his garage. At the meeting two weeks before the event, Bill and Tiffany announce that they have gathered a lot of really good stuff, including a place setting for six with only one fork missing, some wonderful antique bookshelves, some interesting fabric, and two quilts. Tiffany has invited some antique dealers who she thinks will pay top dollar for some of the items. Bill has set aside time the evening before the sale for people to come over and put prices on things, which he knows is often a fun task. Mary says, "Oh, no. We need to research prices and I think it should be done this week. I can do all that—just give me a key to your garage." Bill reluctantly agrees that a more thoughtful approach might be better. The sale goes well. The antique dealers pay the prices Mary has set, and almost everything sells. Afterward, Tiffany, Sharon, and Bill volunteer to count the money, write a report, and make the bank deposit. However, Sharon and Bill can't do it until Tuesday, which is three days after the sale. Mary steps in. "Tiffany and I will do it today and get it in the bank right away." Sharon reluctantly agrees that getting the money in the bank sooner might be better. Although Bill is beginning to find Mary's controlling ways annoying, he doesn't feel he can criticize her, as she does get a lot done.

At the next meeting, Mary has baked a lovely cake that says, "Thank you Bill and Tiffany." The five parents who come to the meeting are grateful to Bill and Tiffany, who feel appreciated. However, the cake is so excellent and extravagant that ironically, the focus goes back to Mary and everyone thanks her profusely for her thoughtfulness. Bill announces that he can't come to meetings for a while because of work.

At the next few meetings, a new parent, Mimi, is present. She has just moved into the district and her son is starting school halfway into the year. She is an organizational development consultant by trade and notices immediately the dynamic between Mary and the rest of the parents, now down to eight others. She soon hears grumblings from other parents—a mixture of admiration for Mary's indefatigable energy and resentment of her seeming need for control. Mimi invites Mary to dinner and asks her how she feels about doing so much for the PTA. Mary admits she is getting stretched thin, but points out that she is the only one without another job. Mary says she tries to make up for the fact that she's the only one not working by doing as much as possible to make it easier for the other parents to participate. She also expresses puzzlement that so many parents have dropped out over time.

Mimi tells her that she imagines many of the parents feel that Mary is such an incredible volunteer that nothing they do can come close to matching her accomplishments, so they just give up. "Kind of the way kids will stop cleaning their room altogether if a parent never praises the attempts that they make," Mimi explains, "even if those attempts do not result in a perfectly clean and tidy room." Mary understands that metaphor immediately. "What can we do to get people back?" she asks. "You have to do less, and you have to ask some people to do more," Mimi advises. "For example, ask José to bring snacks next time."

A year later, the PTA is back up to twenty active parents. Mary is still the chair and still does a lot, but she is careful not to volunteer for everything. With Mimi's help, the parents have had some honest conversations about how they work together and have adopted much more of a team model.

Being Brand New and Starting Out Right

Organizations that have just been started are often operating on the donations of their founding members and the energy and enthusiasm these members bring to the cause that has propelled them to action. Soon, however, they realize that they must reach further for support or they will burn themselves out both financially and emotionally. Someone goes to a fundraising class or reads a book such as this one. Newly inspired to develop a membership base or raise money through any of the strategies presented, they can also be newly baffled. "But where do I start?" is often the next question. There are many possible starting places for raising money, but there is little money to meet start-up costs. They now know something about what will attract money, but there is not much room for making mistakes. This chapter provides some tips on where to start.

Or course, your group will make some mistakes. Challenge yourself to make new mistakes and not to fall into predictable and avoidable traps.

Figure out how much money you need for your organization to begin functioning smoothly. Once you have drawn up a budget for a year, break it down into what you need for this month and then the month after. See everything in the smallest possible time frame so that you don't get discouraged. If you can raise this much money for one month, then you can continue for that month. Then go on to the next month.

You have probably started by raising money from the founders of the organization—yourselves. Each person should pledge a certain amount per month or per quarter and should bring their pledge money to meetings or mail a check to someone designated as the treasurer. This practice will begin the important habit of developing a culture of giving money among all who work with the group. Next, each founder or core volunteer should assess how much money he or she can raise from friends, family, and acquaintances.

Each person should make a list of all the people he or she knows without regard to whether these people believe in your cause or give money away. Just list the names of people who would recognize your name if you phoned them. Next to that list, mark all the people who you know believe in the cause your new group represents. If you don't know, put a question mark. Next, for all the people who you know believe in the cause, mark all those who you know for a fact give away money. Now, for all the people on the list who you know believe in the cause and who you know give away money, note how much you are going to ask each of them for. If you are not sure what to ask them for, keep it small. Is it $50? $100? $35? Keep in mind that some family members and friends will give you money just to be supportive of you. Finally, note what method you will use to solicit this money. Will you hold a house party? Send a personal letter and follow up by phone? Set up a personal meeting? If a meeting, will you bring someone else from the new group with you? (See Chapter Seven on personal solicitation for detailed information on identifying and approaching prospects for gifts.)

Here's what your list might look like:

Potential Donors to Our Group

Name	Believes in Cause?	Gives Money?	Amount to Request	Method
Francisco	yes	yes	$100	meeting
Edward	yes	?	?	invite to house party
Marianne	?	yes	$35	mail appeal
Gloria	no			
Charmaine	yes	yes	$50	phone call

People sometimes object to raising money for a brand new group in this way by saying, "You can't just ask people for money without giving them something. We don't have a newsletter or a program or even an office. What are they giving to?" At this point, people are giving to an idea and to the people involved in making the idea an organization—you. They will give for the same reasons you are giving time and money—they agree with you and they think you are the people who can do this job. Some people enjoy—even prefer—to give money to new groups. (In fact, many organizations find that the people who gave them money in their first five years do not continue to give—they move on to other new groups.) Those who prefer to give to more established groups won't give to you right now, but that will not be everyone's response.

The next step is to identify a few people or foundations that will give larger amounts of money ($1,000 or more) for start-up costs. Use the methods described in Chapter Seven for this step. For information on approaching foundations, go to your local Foundation Center collection (see Resource F). You will need to develop a case statement, including a preliminary budget. Although your organization has no history, the people who are forming it have history. Each of the founders should be briefly described in order to show that knowledgeable and experienced people are behind this idea.

From the beginning, appoint someone to keep records and ensure that they are accurate. Always write thank you notes, even before you get organizational stationary. Keep founding donors posted on your progress by sending brief updates or occasional e-mail newsletters.

Being a brand new organization gives you a chance to do your fundraising the right way from the very beginning.

The Perennial Question of Clean and Dirty Money

Over the years, I have received dozens of questions about a problem that surfaces at some point in the life of almost every organization. The problem was nicely laid out in the following e-mail:

Dear Kim:

My group is struggling with what I understand to be a perennial problem: dirty money. We have two questions: Should we take dirty money, and how do we decide? A corporation has offered us a large grant for operating expenses, but several people in our group have problems with this corporation because of the way they treat their workers (badly). On the other hand, we need the money and not many places give money for operating expenses. What shall we do?

I responded that this group had stumbled on the subject that has probably taken up more time in progressive groups than almost any other topic one could name. In fact, had some groups held a "dirty money discussion-a-thon" and sought pledges for each minute they spent discussing the very questions the writer raises, they would be handsomely endowed by now and could change their discussion to "dirty and clean investment policies." However, the writer raises serious questions that are not easy to answer, which is why this debate is perennial.

Let's divide the questions into two parts: the idea of "dirty" money and the consequences of taking such money.

I don't subscribe to the idea that there is "dirty" money and "clean" money. Money is a tool. Similarly, a hammer is a tool. A hammer can be used to help build a house or it can be used to bludgeon someone to death, but we never talk about clean and dirty hammers. Because we don't credit hammers with power they don't have, we are able to see just what a hammer is and to separate the hammer itself from what it might be used to do. We need to get that kind of perspective on money. Money can be used wisely or squandered. It can be raised honestly or dishonestly. It can be earned, inherited, stolen, given, received, lost, found—and many combinations of all of these ways of getting money. It is not in itself dirty or clean.

If you let go of the idea of dirty and clean money, you can focus on the real questions in accepting money, which are these: How does it make you feel to accept money from a corporation whose labor practices you find appalling? How does it make you look to others to accept this money? What will be the cost in goodwill, faith in your organization, or even actual money given to your organization if you accept this money?

I have seen organizations answer this question in various ways. The most sensible one I've seen was adopted in 1980 by a group in San Francisco called the Coalition for the Medical Rights of Women during a marathon discussion about accepting free printing from the Playboy Corporation. The Playboy Corporation had always been a strong supporter of civil liberties and reproductive rights groups. In those days they offered to print stationery, envelopes, invitations, newsletters, and the like for nonprofit groups working for those causes. Any group using such money simply had to put the statement "Printing donated by the Playboy Corporation" somewhere on the printed piece.

The Coalition, which was the first place I worked as a development director, had occasionally accepted Playboy's services to get some of this printing. Although this was a big help financially, the group, which by definition was fighting against sexism in many areas of society, always had great uneasiness about taking advantage of Playboy's program. As a collective, we discussed whether to continue taking the free printing. We argued back and forth, with those in favor saying, "Playboy made their money off of women and we're simply putting that money to good use; we deserve it." Those against argued that Playboy exploited women and promoted sexism and we would help them in their sex-for-money pursuit by taking their free printing. Late one night, after we had made and remade every argument several times, one person finally said, "I don't know whether it is right or wrong to take this money. All I know is that the idea of taking Playboy's money or their free printing makes me want to vomit."

From then on, in questions about taking money, we applied the "vomit test." If a person who was important to the organization—staff, board, volunteer, longtime friend—said, "Taking money from such-and-such would make me want to vomit," we wouldn't take it, because that person and her continuing contributions to our group were more important than any money.

I have never found a more rational approach to the question, "How does it make us feel to accept money from a source whose practices we do not condone?"

The second question, "How does it make us look to the outside world to take this money?" is a more practical one. Sometimes a source of money will pass the vomit test but fail this second test. For example, a board member of a tiny health center in rural New Mexico was a fraternity brother of the vice president of a large uranium-mining operation that is polluting the entire area around it with radioactive uranium tailings. Through his contact, the board member secured a grant from this mining corporation, which so outraged several major donors to the health center that they stopped giving. The ensuing bad publicity and loss of donations was a major factor in the demise of that group the following year.

When an organization accepts money from a source that is controversial, it needs to think about how its other donors or contributors might react. Of course, others' reactions are sometimes hard to judge, but people are likely to be shocked or offended if an organization accepts money from a source that is perceived to be in conflict with the values or goals of the organization. So when a mining corporation whose irresponsible practices are causing serious health problems donates to a health center, accepting such a donation can be predicted to cause outrage. Had they donated to the public library, there might have been less of an outcry.

The other factors in accepting money from a controversial source are the amount of money relative to the budget of the organization and what kind of recognition the source wants for their gift. Though this may have happened, I have never heard of an organization spending hours debating whether to accept a $50 gift from a corporation with even the most foul practices or from one of that corporation's employees, because that amount of money cannot buy any influence. Similarly, I rarely hear of an organization refusing to accept even a large gift from an individual who may have made their money from a corporation with horrible practices, because the corporation will not receive any glory for that gift.

Sometimes an organization will accept money from a corporation if they do not have to publicize that gift, but they will refuse the gift if it requires public acknowledgment. Examining the hypocrisy of that position can be helpful to groups sorting out whether to take that money or not. Ask yourself, "If this gift from this source were to be headline news in our local paper tomorrow, would we be happy, would we feel embarrassed, or would we be nervous about the consequences?" If happy, take the money. If you would rather people didn't know about the gift, then don't take it.

The issue of clean and dirty money generally comes up in relation to corporations. Since corporations are only responsible for about 5 percent of all the money given away in the private sector, and only 11 percent of corporations give away any money at all, organizations are simply better off focusing their fundraising efforts on building a broad base of individual donors. When an organization receives most of its funds from individuals and those individuals ask no more than to be thanked for their gifts and kept abreast of the work, there is no need to worry about clean or dirty money.

Resources

A Potpourri of Special Events

This resource section presents a collection of twenty-two special events and the details of what is needed to put on each event. This sampling represents the major types of special events that small nonprofit organizations hold. Most other events are variations on these.

The events are divided into three categories according to the time required to accomplish them: those that can be done in one month, those that can be done in three months, and those that require five or more months of preparation. Needless to say, some of the events that can be done in one month with several people working on them would take much longer if only one or two people were available, or they could be much bigger if more time were taken. Conversely, some of the events requiring more preparation could be done in a considerably shortened time with the help of paid staff or more volunteers.

Each event listing is followed by a brief description of the event, the number of planners and other volunteers needed, and the principal costs of the event. All of these descriptions assume little or no involvement of paid staff, unless the organization has hired an event planner or unless working on special events is part of the job description of a staff person. In this scenario, "planners" are generally the volunteers in charge of the special event who then delegate as many tasks as possible to other volunteers. (It can be challenging to find the volunteers needed to do the jobs described here and to structure their tasks so that they are likely to get them done. See Chapter Thirty-One for a discussion of managing volunteers.) The important point here is that following events can be done entirely or almost entirely by volunteers, except where I have indicated that an event planner might be a wiser choice.

One more thing to think about as you consider these events: whether or not to serve alcohol. In many of these events you can create a lucrative income stream by serving alcohol. If you do serve alcohol, you will want to be familiar with liability laws in your community, have a way to prevent anyone driving away from the event who has become drunk, or have a designated driver program as part of the event. You will also want to think about whether your reputation will suffer as a result of serving alcohol. Public reaction will vary a great deal from community to community and by type of organization. It is increasingly common for groups not to have any alcohol at events, and although you lose that income, you also lose that worry.

EVENTS THAT CAN BE DONE IN ONE MONTH

Summertime Barbecue

Choose any weekend or holiday, find a park or beach, and invite as many people as you want to an all-you-can-eat barbecue. Volleyball, softball, and games for children round out this afternoon event.

Planners: One or two.
Tasks: Reserve a space for the barbecue (city parks generally need to be reserved through City Hall or the park commissioner); prepare and distribute advertising fliers or invitations; plan the food and table items needed.

Other Volunteers: Two or three.
Tasks: Help with publicity; cook and clean up on the day of the barbecue.

Main Costs: Permits for the barbecue; plates, cups, utensils, and so on; advertising fliers. Food can be an expense, but often one or more stores will donate some or all of it if you promise that a large sign at the picnic will note their donation.

Charge: Adults, $12; children under twelve, $6; children under five, free.

Dinner in a Private Home

A board member, staff person, or volunteer who lives in a nice or unusual home or setting or is a gourmet cook invites ten to twenty-five people (depending on what the house will hold) to a sit-down dinner.

Planners: One or two. The person doing the event may be the only planner.
Tasks: Compile guest list; send the invitations; cook the food for the event or recruit a cook, if that is part of the come-on for the event.

Volunteers: Two or three.
Tasks: Address invitations, tabulate RSVPs; help prepare the house, serve, and clean up the night of the event.

Main Costs: Invitations, which should look fancy or elegant (but can be produced with a computer and color printer), and postage. Generally, the person putting on the event donates some or all of the food and drink; if not, food and drink will be the only other large cost.

Charge: $35 to $100 per person; $50 to $200 per couple (depending on how fancy the food or venue is). Children are not generally included in such an event.

Garage Sale

On a small scale, garage sales are easy to organize and reasonably lucrative. Simply ask five to ten people to clear out their closets and bookshelves and bring their donations to a garage or yard located on a street with a lot of foot traffic.

Planners: One or two.
Tasks: Call friends, family, neighbors, board, and staff members to get contributions. You can also announce the sale in your e-newsletter, but be very clear as to whether you will pick things up, what kinds of things you can handle (many groups indicate that they cannot handle large items, such as furniture, appliances, computers). To make it as simple as possible, limit the outreach for stuff. Determine the location of the sale.

Volunteers: Four.
Tasks: Prepare signs noting the place and time of the sale; help price the items for sale transport and set up the sale tables and items, secure boxes for money and change for early large bills; staff the sale, collect money, refold clothes, answer questions of prospective buyers, and clean up, taking leftover items to a community thrift store.

Main Costs: None.

Charge: Price items below their actual worth and attempt to sell everything that has been donated. Be prepared to bargain with buyers to lower prices. In the last two hours of the sale, mark everything down 50 percent; in the last half-hour, sell everything for $1.

Pancake Breakfast

Serve an all-you-can-eat breakfast from 7:30 A.M. to 11 A.M. on a weekend morning at a public location, such as a school or service club.

Planners: One.
Tasks: Find a place, set a date, prepare advertising.

Volunteers: Three.
Tasks: Distribute fliers and help with any other invitations; cook, set up, and clean up.

Main Costs: Food, eating utensils, and advertising. The volunteers should seek donations or discounts on food.

Charge: Adults, $8; children, $5; children under six, free. Try for volume of people; make the charge low enough for a family to afford to go out for breakfast.

Progressive Dinner

This event starts at one person's house for drinks and appetizers, moves to a second house for dinner and to a third house for dessert. Two more stops could be added, one for soup and salad and a final stop for coffee and liqueur after dessert. The houses need to be near each other, and the guests should be able to walk or else carpool or be transported from house to house, then returned to the starting place.

Planners: Three.
Tasks: Line up the homes; help plan the menu; solicit food donations or cooking services of local chefs. Generally, the three planners are also the people in whose homes the various courses of the dinner take place.

Volunteers: Three to six.
Tasks: One or two people send invitations and help to set up each house. One or two people at each house help the host serve and clean up. Possibly one or two people drive the guests from house to house, if houses are not within walking distance.

Main Costs: Food, if the hosts or caterers do not wish to donate it; invitations and postage; any decorations or needed materials, such as rented wine glasses.

Charge: $50 to $100 per person; more if the food is very fancy or the homes particularly elegant or unusual or if entertainment, such as music, is offered at one or more of the homes.

EVENTS THAT CAN BE DONE IN THREE MONTHS

Book Sale

The same idea as a garage sale, but only books are for sale.

Planners: One or two.
Tasks: Collect and store the books; arrange a place for the sale; do publicity. Usually, a mailing to all local donors asking for books will bring in a large number. Ask people to bring books to a central location or offer to pick them up if you have volunteers to do that.

Volunteers: Six to twelve, depending on the number of books.
Tasks: Sort the books; secure and set up tables and books; staff the sale; clean up. Books should be sorted into hardbound and paperback and usually into broad categories such as fiction, travel, self-help, cookbooks, children's books, religion, philosophy, history, and so on. Someone familiar with books should pull out rare ones, such as first editions, old books, and out-of-print books. These should be displayed on a separate table and be sold at higher prices. Usually, a set price for paperbound and hardback books makes accounting easier and encourages sales. Set the price of not-rare books low (such as $0.50 for paperbacks and $1 for hardbacks) so that you sell as many as possible.

Main Costs: Advertising.

Charge: No admission charge; various prices for the books.

Crafts Fair

Give local artists a chance to display their wares while promoting yourselves to the public. (As an event like this gets bigger, you may want to use a paid event planner.)

Planners: Two to four.
Tasks: Identify a place to hold the fair; set the date; design the publicity. The place should be big enough for the number of crafts booths needed and in a highly

trafficked area, preferably with its own parking lot. A public park or community center is an excellent site. Attaching the fair to an existing farmer's market is common and helps both the market and your fair.

Volunteers: Five.
Tasks: Send out invitations to artists to display at the fair; advertise the fair to the general public; help set up the showroom and clean up afterward.

Main Costs: The place for the fair, the invitations, and publicity.

Charge: Varies. Generally, artists are charged a booth fee and there is a small admission charge for the general public. Artists can be asked to give a percentage of their sales for that day to the organization.

Halloween Haunted House

Convert a house, community center, or church activity hall into a haunted house. Supply cardboard or plastic skeletons, plastic spiders, and the like, and set up lighting and sound systems for appropriate scary ambience. Some volunteers should dress up as mad scientists, vampires, witches, and so forth, and make occasional unannounced appearances to groups touring the house. Two or more volunteers must lead group tours of the house, telling a scary story about the various parts of the house or objects in it.

Planners: Three or four.
Tasks: Find a site; plan the publicity and the house set-up.

Volunteers: Six to ten.
Tasks: Advance publicity; set up the house, including lighting and sound, dressing in costume to lead groups through the house; collect the entrance fees; return the house to normal at the end of the evening or the next day.

Main Cost: Publicity and sound and light systems, unless they can be hooked up to stereo and light fixtures already installed.

Charge: $3 to $5 per person, less for children under seven. The price should be low enough that children and their parents can take several tours through the house during the day.

Movie Benefit

A theater donates an afternoon or evening film showing to your group.

Planners: One or two.
Tasks: Find the theater and work with its staff to select a movie; design publicity in cooperation with the theater.

Volunteers: Two or three.
Tasks: Help get publicity out; depending on your arrangement with the theater, collect tickets or work the concession stand.

Main Costs: Publicity.

Charge: The same price as the movie theater normally charges, or more. Bill it as a donation.

Open House

Invite donors and prospects to your office to meet the staff and board. An open house is not technically a fundraiser, but you can prominently display donation cans and envelopes and sell your organization's products. You can also add a no-host bar.

Planners: Two.
Tasks: Set the date; prepare the invitations.

Volunteers: Two to four.
Tasks: Send the invitations; bring in refreshments (usually finger foods, soft drinks, and wine); set up; welcome guests; sign up new members; clean up before and after the event.

Main Costs: Food and publicity.

Charge: No charge at the door. Have things for sale (T-shirts, bumper stickers, publications, and the like) and encourage people who are not already donors to join. Have a lot of membership information available and a person whose only task is to answer questions and enroll new members.

Tasting

An exotic, sophisticated, or popular food or drink is offered in many guises or varieties for tasting. Wine, chocolate, liqueurs and cordials, fancy candy, and ethnic foods all lend themselves to this format.

Planners: Two or three.
Tasks: Find a place, decide on a theme, and prepare advertising.

Volunteers: Four.
Tasks: Solicit donations of the food or drinks to be tasted (manufacturers or distributors can gain a great deal of publicity through this event); distribute advertising; mail invitations; set up the place; keep the food and drinks replenished; collect money at the door.

Main Costs: Advertising. You may have to provide snacks at a wine tasting, or coffee and tea for a chocolate or candy tasting.

Charge: Varies depending on what you are serving, but usually $25 to $75 per person, $40 to $110 for a couple. Think carefully about whether to include children in such an event.

Tour

A guided tour of a historic part of town or architecturally interesting buildings (houses, churches, or other places), a garden tour, or a nature walk. Variations abound with this idea: ethnic tours, a tour of the history of a community at a certain time, toxic tours showing people the dangerous sites and what your group is doing about them, bicycle tours, and so on.

Planners: One or two.
Tasks: Find someone to lead an appropriate tour; design the advertising.

Volunteers: One or two.
Tasks: Greet people as they arrive, shepherd them along as needed, provide refreshments at the end of the tour, invite people to join your organization.

Main Costs: Advertising; possibly an honorarium for the tour guide.

Charge: $7 to $35 per person, depending on how exotic the tour is or how knowledgeable the tour guide.

Workshop or Class

Offer a learning experience on almost any topic that people want to know about for which you have a qualified teacher. Topics might include organic gardening, sewing, knitting, fundraising, tennis, judo, computer skills, designing Web pages, auto mechanics, aerobics, and so on.

Planners: One or two.
Tasks: Find the teacher; get a place; design publicity.

Volunteers: One or two.
Tasks: Help with publicity and registration; introduce the teacher at the start of the class; clean up after the class.

Main Costs: The place and publicity. Try to get the teacher to donate his or her time and try to get a free place.

Charge: The going rate for similar classes, usually between $25 and $150 per person. Depends on the class and how well known or in demand the instructor is.

EVENTS REQUIRING FIVE OR MORE MONTHS OF PLANNING
Auction

Planners: Three to five.
Tasks: Find a place; secure an auctioneer; design publicity; help get items to auction.

Volunteers: Ten or more.
Tasks: Get good items to be auctioned; get publicity; prepare a list of items to be auctioned to give to each participant, including value and minimum bid; the day of the auction, provide food and drink at the event, set up chairs, collect money, arrange for delivery of auctioned items, clean up.

Main Costs: The place and the publicity. You may also have to pay a professional auctioneer, although usually a volunteer can be found.

Charge: Charge a nominal admission price and charge for food and drink. The bulk of the money is made from the auctioned items.

Bingo

Your group may be able to be a one-night beneficiary of an ongoing bingo game. Check with your community's laws to ensure compliance.

Planners: One to four.
Tasks: Set up the bingo game, which generally means renting out an evening of an ongoing bingo game; advertise; recruit volunteers to manage the game. Some organizations prefer to pay the person running the game.

Volunteers: Two or three.
Tasks: Run the bingo game; collect money, set up, and clean up. However, if you are the beneficiary of an ongoing game, you may only need volunteers to do publicity.

Main Costs and Charge: Varies from community to community. Check with other groups doing bingo as a fundraising device.

Concert

One of the most common fantasies of a grassroots group is the idea of having a concert with a famous performer. This is one of the most difficult fundraising events to carry out successfully and one that I do not recommend organizing using only volunteers.

Planners: One paid planner and a small committee of four to five volunteers. You will want to pay a stage manager and a volunteer coordinator along with the planner.
Tasks: Find the performer (this can take months of research and cultivation); coordinate a time and place with the performer's schedule; prepare publicity.

Volunteers: Unlimited number.
Tasks: Distribute publicity, sell tickets; take tickets at the event; set up food and drink at the performance hall (if allowed); sell T-shirts, the performer's CDs, and any other items; clean up.

Main Costs: Rental of the performance space, publicity, and the performer's expenses (assuming that their fees are waived, you will still be charged for plane fare, local transportation, hotel, food, and incidentals. Many performers expect to fly first class, travel with an entourage, have specific food requirements, and so on, so the cost of a performer who is donating their time may nevertheless be quite high.)

Charge: Whatever the going rate is for similar performances, or more.

Conference

An expanded version of the workshop or class detailed previously. A conference of one or more days is held on a particular topic and can include a series of speakers and workshops. Ideally, offers some continuing education credits.

Planners: One paid person and four or five volunteers.
Tasks: Decide on the theme, arrange for conference space; contact speakers and workshop leaders; plan publicity; create packets for conference attendees.

Volunteers: Twelve.
Tasks: Advertise the conference, including creating a Web site for publicity and registration; monitor registration; pick up speakers at airport, escort them to their rooms; set up and clean up; register attendees on site; answer questions, solve problems, and act as runners for any items needed at the last minute.

Main Costs: Advertising and conference materials, honoraria for speakers, rental of conference space. (The total costs can be considerable.)

Charge: Depends on the number of days and the type of conference. Charge the going rate for similar conferences. Do not undercharge.

Dance

Planners: Three or four.
Tasks: Decide a theme, find a space, hire performers, and plan advertising.

Volunteers: Eight to ten.
Tasks: Promote the dance; arrange for decorations, food, and drink the night of the dance; get liquor license; take money at the door, staff the food and drink booths; set up and clean up.

Main Costs: The performers (unless donated), hall rental, security guard(s), publicity.

Charge: Depending on how popular the dance band is, charge at least $15 per person. Some groups charge $25 or $45 for a couple and include free munchies and one free drink. (Offering a free drink with a ticket encourages people to buy more drinks and is a lucrative strategy, but see previous discussion of alcohol.)

Decorator Showcase

A large, architecturally elegant home or one that is unusual or belongs to a famous person submits each room to be decorated by a different interior designer. People pay to tour the house.

Planners: One paid planner and five or six volunteers.
Tasks: Details seem almost infinite for this event. The main ones are to line up the house and the decorators and to plan publicity. There is a tremendous amount of work involved in coordinating the schedules of the homeowners and the decorators and giving the decorators time to do their work with minimum inconvenience to the homeowners (who usually move out during this time).

Volunteers: Unlimited numbers can be used.
Tasks: Promote the showcase; collect money; conduct the tours; arrange for parking for people coming to the showcase; assist the planners in coordinating the whole event.

Main Costs: Publicity and invitations.

Charge: $25 to $100 per person, depending on how fancy the house and decorations are.

Fashion Show

Put on a traditional fashion show—models displaying the latest fashions—or for more fun, do a take-off on that idea. Variations abound, such as a working woman's fashion show, which would show professional-looking but comfortable fashions for upwardly mobile working women, an around-the-world fashion show that would feature clothes from other countries, or a spoof on a fashion show that might feature clothing that is out of fashion, what never to wear in public, cyber fashion, military fashion, and so on. The models can be professionals or for fun, board members and other volunteers or politicians and well-known people in the community.

Planners: Two or three.
Tasks: Plan the theme; find appropriate models and clothing; find a place; plan publicity.

Volunteers: Four or five, not including models.
Tasks: Help with publicity; coordinate the show itself; write up descriptions of the fashions; announce the models and what they are wearing; set up and clean up. If food and drink are sold, volunteers need to staff those booths.

Main Costs: Hall rental and publicity. If the models are paid, that will be a main cost.

Charge: Depends on the theme of the fashion show and the intended audience— at least $10.

Tribute Luncheon

A fancy luncheon, usually held at a hotel, honoring one or more people and featuring a well-known speaker.

Planners: One paid planner and a committee of four or five.
Tasks: Decide whom to honor and why; find an appropriate speaker; solicit a sponsoring committee of thirty-five to one hundred people whose names will be used on the invitation as joining in inviting the community to the luncheon; design the invitation.

Volunteers: As many as needed, depending on how many other paid people you use.
Tasks: Reserve the hotel room; arrange the food; send out invitations, collate responses; solicit corporations and businesses to reserve tables at the luncheon; arrange the seating and see that things go smoothly the day of the luncheon. Many organizations produce an adbook for such a luncheon as an additional source of funds.

Main Costs: The hotel, food, and invitations, all of which are expensive. Like others in this section, this event is heavy on front money and must be planned with great care.

Charge: $50 to $500 per person, depending on how fancy it is and who the audience is. Encourage corporations or wealthy donors to buy whole tables for a set price, which is usually more than just buying that number of seats. The idea is that a corporation gets more publicity for reserving a whole table and all the people from that workplace can sit together.

Walk- Jog- Bike- Rock- Read-A-Thon

Participants collect pledges for units of accomplishment: every mile they walk, jog, or bike; every hour they rock in a rocking chair; every book they read; or for some other measurement of endurance or accomplishment.

Planners: Two or three.
Tasks: Plot the course of the event; get any required permission from the police department or City Hall for using the streets; attract dozens or hundreds of people to participate; design publicity.

Volunteers: Twelve or more.
Tasks: Help with publicity; monitor and mark pledge sheets of participants as they go by their checkpoints; collect money from participants (who must collect it from their pledges); provide beverages and perhaps snacks for athletes, First Aid in case of injuries.

Main Costs: Publicity, permits, and prizes (usually a T-shirt or certificate of participation) for those who participate.

Charge: There is usually no charge to enter, unless the -thon is done as a race among participants, in which case an entry fee is charged. Participants get pledges of whatever they can for each unit of accomplishment; usually a minimum pledge of $0.25 is suggested.

Variations on the Mail Appeal Package

Once you understand the purpose of direct mail as described in Chapters Ten and Eleven and how to put an effective direct mail package together, you can begin to think about variations on your appeals. The following suggestions will not work for every organization, and not all possible variations are explored here. But a number of options are suggested for using the principles of direct mail fundraising. Some of these may inspire you to create other variations on the theme.

A GIFT CATALOGUE

A gift catalogue is a mail appeal in which the organization lists items it needs and the costs of such items. People then either donate an item or—more usually—the amount it will cost the group to purchase an item. In the latter instance the donor's gift is "earmarked" for a particular item. (Note: There is an important difference between the terms *earmark* and *designate* in fundraising. An earmarked gift is to be used for the purpose indicated until that need is filled; after that, it can be used at the organization's discretion. A designated gift can only be used for the purpose for which it is designated, even if that need has been filled. Organizations are advised to stay away from the term *designated*.)

Gift catalogues work particularly well for groups such as shelters, land preservation organizations, clinics and other health services, and the like, whose shopping list can inspire donations more readily than can those of an organization that simply needs office supplies.

A land conservancy, for example, successfully uses the gift catalogue in their efforts to preserve ecologically significant land. A sampling of the items contained in their catalogue includes the following:

- Binoculars: four pairs, $200; one pair, $50
- Classroom visits: ten visits, $500; $50 each
- Scholarships for docent trainees: cost per docent, $100
- Gates for fences: one gate, $250; number of gates needed: ten
- Hand lenses: ten lenses for $25; number of lenses needed: two hundred
- Research grants for various projects *(which are described)*
- Weather-monitoring equipment: complete cost, $1,000

The catalogue itself may be only a few pages long. It should include an "order form" that is a variation on the direct mail reply device. People can then "order" more than one item.

Some organizations have used this concept to raise money for intangible program components, such as client care or provision of services. A nonprofit therapy collective listed these items in their gift catalogue:

- Scholarship for one family therapy session: $60
- Complete six-week therapy program: $360
- Parent effectiveness training

  Full scholarship: $200

  Partial scholarship: $50
- Day care for children of parents in therapy: $10 per hour (indicate number of hours you wish to donate)

The actual gift catalogue can be fancy or plain. It can include illustrations of the needed items or photographs of people using the services. It can be laid out like a regular mail order catalogue or simply list the needed items on a sheet of paper.

Using your imagination in layout and adding drawings and illustrations will make your catalogue more effective. Laying it out in the form of a newsletter or booklet will give it the air of a catalogue and make it stand out from regular mail appeals.

YOUR NEWSLETTER AS A MAIL APPEAL

If you have a newsletter or magazine that contains useful articles or information that people cannot easily obtain elsewhere, send a sample copy of portions of the publication to people not familiar with your organization and include information on how to subscribe. You can make up a special issue for promotional purposes that includes some of the best articles of your previous issues or you can use an issue that you think is particularly compelling.

In this variation, the cover becomes the mail appeal. The front or back inside cover includes a return form to be torn off, which is essentially a subscription form. A return envelope stapled into the newsletter will increase your returns. This appeal is not sent in an envelope.

If your newsletter is long (twelve pages or more) and expensive to produce, consider making up a special short edition. This piece might be four to eight pages and contain one or two excellent articles along with a listing of articles and information that people would receive by subscribing. Include a subscription form, either as part of the cover or somewhere in the newsletter.

Whatever style you use, make sure it is clear that this issue is complimentary and where to find information about subscribing.

Some groups have found it effective simply to stamp "Complimentary copy— Please subscribe" on their newsletter and send these free copies to people whose names they have acquired. These issues can go with their regular mailing of the newsletter or as a separate mailing. If the newsletter is good enough, that simple message can be enough to generate donations.

PHANTOM EVENT

In a phantom event, people are invited to a special event that is not going to happen. What will not happen is described in detail, and the prospects are invited to stay home and miss it. The appeal is sent in the style of an invitation, with the

RSVP as the return form. Phantom events work because they catch people off guard, they amuse them, and because they appeal to the many people who don't enjoy large social events. Here is an example:

> **THE BOARD OF DIRECTORS OF YOUTH ORGANIZING FOR PEACE** invites you to their first annual gala nonevent. We will not be at the event. We do not wish to look for parking and drink wine out of plastic glasses. We invite you to join us in staying home. You will not have to mingle with people you barely recognize. You will not have to eat soggy hors d'oeuvres, buy a fancy outfit to appear in, or travel after dark.
>
> PLEASE JOIN US IN STAYING HOME
> TIME: 6:00–10:30 P.M.
> DATE: You pick it
> COST: $59.95. Send us $50 and keep $9.95 to buy a bottle of wine to share with a loved one.
> We look forward to not seeing you.
> RSVP by June 1, using the enclosed card

THE BRIEF MESSAGE

Organizations working on issues that are familiar to most people or whose mission is totally self-evident can use the brief message format. Your appeal and return form are all on the same piece of paper and a return envelope is enclosed.

The brief message format conveys the following ideas: "I am not going to use a whole sheet of paper and precious minutes of your time. You know who we are. You read the paper and hear the news. Join us. We need you." Brief messages are effective when the organization or its work is well known and requires little explanation. The brief message must use the word "you" effectively.

Organizations working on specific health issues, such as arthritis, cancer, or asthma, or groups working on easy-to-understand programs, such as homeless shelters or stop-smoking clinics, can avail themselves of this method. An excellent example of the use of the brief message is an appeal from the UNC Fund (formerly the United Negro College Fund) that pictures a young African American man looking unhappy and contains this brief message: "His math got him into college. Economics may keep him out. Give to the UNC Fund." The reader is pulled in quickly and asked to decide. Further words are not needed.

USING PICTURES

Organizations that serve animals or people in distress can often express their message more poignantly through photographs or drawings than with words. A picture can take the place of many pages of text. Pictures can be part of a letter or a separate enclosure. For pictures to be effective they must be real and they must not be sentimental, maudlin, or patronizing. Photographs must not demean the people or animals in them.

Sometimes photographs are used to jar people's sensibilities. This tactic can be effective when done carefully. Showing an animal caught in a leg-hold trap, for example, is far more moving than a wordy description of the trap and its effect. A picture of mass graves or forest clear-cutting provides vivid evidence of situations that many people find hard to believe.

Drawings, such as an artist's rendering in an appeal for a capital campaign of a new building, are usually used to augment the text of a letter. Again, the drawing must depict something real and be well done. It does not replace as many words as a photograph.

USING PROMOTIONAL ITEMS

Many long-established organizations use promotional items to draw in donors. The method works because people open the envelope to get what's inside—stamps, bumper stickers, pencils, address labels, seeds, and so on. It also works by generating a feeling of obligation to reciprocate with a donation. Because these items are relatively expensive, it is generally better to use them as part of a thank you package, if it all. With the exception of organizations that have always used these items, using them does not seem to increase the rate of response relative to their cost.

Donor Bill of Rights

A DONOR BILL OF RIGHTS.

PHILANTHROPY is based on voluntary action for the common good. It is a tradition of giving and sharing that is primary to the quality of life. To assure that philanthropy merits the respect and trust of the general public, and that donors and prospective donors can have full confidence in the not-for-profit organizations and causes they are asked to support, we declare that all donors have these rights:

I.

To be informed of the organization's mission, of the way the organization intends to use donated resources, and of its capacity to use donations effectively for their intended purposes.

II.

To be informed of the identity of those serving on the organization's board, and to expect the board to exercise prudent judgment in its stewardship responsibilities.

III.

To have access to the organization's most recent financial statements.

IV.

To be assured their gifts will be used for the purposes for which they were given.

V.

To receive appropriate acknowledgment and recognition.

VI.

To be assured that information about their donations is handled with respect and with confidentiality to the extent provided by law.

VII.

To expect that all relationships with individuals representing organizations of interest to the donor will be professional in nature.

VIII.

To be informed whether those seeking donations are volunteers, employees of the organization or hired solicitors.

IX.

To have the opportunity for their names to be deleted from mailing lists that an organization may intend to share.

X.

To feel free to ask questions when making a donation and to receive prompt, truthful and forthright answers.

DEVELOPED BY
American Association of Fund Raising Counsel (AAFRC)
Association for Healthcare Philanthropy (AHP)
Council for Advancement and Support of Education (CASE)
Association of Fundraising Professionals (AFP)

ENDORSED BY
(Information)
INDEPENDENT SECTOR
National Catholic Development Conference (NCDC)
National Committee on Planned Giving (NCPG)
Council for Resource Development (CRD)
United Way of America

Source: Courtesy of the American Association of Fund Raising Counsel, Inc.

AFP Code of Ethical Principles and Standards of Professional Practice

AFP CODE OF ETHICAL PRINCIPLES AND STANDARDS OF PROFESSIONAL PRACTICE.

STATEMENT OF ETHICAL PRINCIPLES
Adopted 1964, Amended October 2004

The Association of Fundraising Professionals (AFP) exists to foster the development and growth of fundraising professionals and the profession, to promote high ethical standards in the fundraising profession and to preserve and enhance philanthropy and volunteerism. Members of AFP are motivated by an inner drive to improve the quality of life through the causes they serve. They serve the ideal of philanthropy; are committed to the preservation and enhancement of volunteerism; and hold stewardship of these concepts as the overriding principle of their professional life. They recognize their responsibility to ensure that needed resources are vigorously and ethically sought and that the intent of the donor is honestly fulfilled. To these ends, AFP members embrace certain values that they strive to uphold in performing their responsibilities for generating philanthropic support.

AFP members aspire to:

- practice their profession with integrity, honesty, truthfulness and adherence to the absolute obligation to safeguard the public trust;
- act according to the highest standards and visions of their organization, profession and conscience;
- put philanthropic mission above personal gain;
- inspire others through their own sense of dedication and high purpose;
- improve their professional knowledge and skills in order that their performance will better serve others;
- demonstrate concern for the interests and well being of individuals affected by their actions;
- value the privacy, freedom of choice and interests of all those affected by their actions;
- foster cultural diversity and pluralistic values, and treat all people with dignity and respect;
- affirm, through personal giving, a commitment to philanthropy and its role in society;
- adhere to the spirit as well as the letter of all applicable laws and regulations;

- advocate within their organizations, adherence to all applicable laws and regulations;
- avoid even the appearance of any criminal offense or professional misconduct;
- bring credit to the fundraising profession by their public demeanor;
- encourage colleagues to embrace and practice these ethical principles and standards of professional practice; and
- be aware of the codes of ethics promulgated by other professional organizations that serve philanthropy.

STANDARDS OF PROFESSIONAL PRACTICE

Furthermore, while striving to act according to the above values, AFP members agree to abide by the AFP Standards of Professional Practice, which are adopted and incorporated into the AFP Code of Ethical Principles. Violation of the Standards may subject the member to disciplinary sanctions, including expulsion, as provided in the AFP Ethics Enforcement Procedures.

Professional Obligations

1. Members shall not engage in activities that harm the member's organization, clients, or profession.

AFP CODE OF ETHICAL PRINCIPLES AND STANDARDS
OF PROFESSIONAL PRACTICE, Cont'd.

2. Members shall not engage in activities that conflict with their fiduciary, ethical, and legal obligations to their organizations and their clients.

3. Members shall effectively disclose all potential and actual conflicts of interest; such disclosure does not preclude or imply ethical impropriety.

4. Members shall not exploit any relationship with a donor, prospect, volunteer or employee to the benefit of the member or the member's organization.

5. Members shall comply with all applicable local, state, provincial, federal, civil and criminal laws.

6. Members recognize their individual boundaries of competence and are forthcoming and truthful about their professional experience and qualifications.

Solicitation and Use of Philanthropic Funds

7. Members shall take care to ensure that all solicitation materials are accurate and correctly reflect the organization's mission and use of solicited funds.

8. Members shall take care to ensure that donors receive informed, accurate and ethical advice about the value and tax implications of contributions.

9. Members shall take care to ensure that contributions are used in accordance with donors' intentions.

10. Members shall take care to ensure proper stewardship of philanthropic contributions, including timely reports on the use and management of such funds.

11. Members shall obtain explicit consent by the donor before altering the conditions of contributions.

Presentation of Information

12. Members shall not disclose privileged or confidential information to unauthorized parties.

13. Members shall adhere to the principle that all donor and prospect information created by, or on behalf of, an organization is the property of that organization and shall not be transferred or utilized except on behalf of that organization.

14. Members shall give donors the opportunity to have their names removed from lists that are sold to, rented to, or exchanged with other organizations.

15. Members shall, when stating fundraising results, use accurate and consistent accounting methods that conform to the appropriate guidelines adopted by the American Institute of Certified Public Accountants (AICPA)* for the type of organization involved. (*In countries outside of the United States, comparable authority should be utilized.)

Compensation

16. Members shall not accept compensation that is based on a percentage of contributions; nor shall they accept finder's fees.

17. Members may accept performance-based compensation, such as bonuses, provided such bonuses are in accord with prevailing practices within the members' own organizations, and are not based on a percentage of charitable contributions.

18. Members shall not pay finder's fees, or commissions or percentage compensation based on contributions, and shall take care to discourage their organizations from making such payments.

Amended October 2004

Source: Courtesy of the Association of Fundraising Professionals.

For Further Information

The following list of materials and information is not exhaustive. Every day new resources are being developed, published, sent over listservs, and so on. This list contains the books, magazines, and Web sites I have found most helpful or important for effective fundraising, as well as books and materials I have developed.

One of the most valuable ways to find out more about fundraising is to visit the Foundation Center Collection nearest you. The Foundation Center (headquartered in New York City) is a nonprofit library service supported by foundations, fees for service, products for sale, and other fundraising strategies. It collects and disseminates information about foundations, corporations, government, and all other types of fundraising and grantseeking. A list of Foundation Centers and their cooperating collections (that is, public libraries or other locations that have materials from the Foundation Center) is in Resource F. You can also find them online at http://www.fdnctr.org.

OTHER TITLES BY KIM KLEIN

Getting Major Gifts. (rev. ed.) Oakland, Calif.: *Grassroots Fundraising Journal,* 1999.

> *Collection of twelve articles on developing major gifts reprinted from the* Grassroots Fundraising Journal.

Fundraising for the Long Haul. San Francisco: Jossey-Bass, 2000.

> *For older social change organizations exploring their particular challenges. Case studies, personal experience, and how-to.*

Ask and You Shall Receive: A Fundraising Training Program for Religious Organizations and Projects. San Francisco: Jossey-Bass, 2000.

> *Easy-to-learn core competencies of fundraising presented in manuals for Leader and Participants.*

Ready, Set, Raise. Kim Klein and Russell Roybal. *Grassroots Fundraising Journal.*

> *Seven topics covered in twenty-minute sessions in a professionally produced video on DVD.*

Fundraising in Times of Crisis. San Francisco: Jossey-Bass, 2004.

> *How to identify, analyze, and solve problems in your organization, and how to plan for the short term and the long term and evaluate success.*

Coauthored with Stephanie Roth

The Board of Directors. (3rd ed.) Oakland, Calif.: *Grassroots Fundraising Journal,* 1999.

> *Collection of ten articles on creating and building an effective board of directors reprinted from the* Grassroots Fundraising Journal.

Como Recaudar Fordos en su Communidad, Grassroots Fundraising Journal, 2002.

> *Edicion especial del boletin para le recaudacion de fondos in comunidades de base.*

Raise More Money: The Best of the Grassroots Fundraising Journal. San Francisco: Jossey-Bass, 2001.

> *A collection of the best fifty-five articles on a range of topics from the first twenty years of the* Grassroots Fundraising Journal.

OTHER USEFUL FUNDRAISING MATERIALS
Periodicals

Grassroots Fundraising Journal. http://www.grassrootsfundraising.org.

> *Bimonthly how-to periodical. The Web site contains more than a dozen free articles and an archive of* Grassroots Fundraising's *e-newsletter column, "Dear Kim."*

Chronicle of Philanthropy. http://www.philanthropy.com.

> *Biweekly publication.*

NonProfit Times. http://www.nptimes.com.

> *National business publication focusing on nonprofit management. Free subscriptions to full-time nonprofit executives.*

Non Profit Quarterly. http://www.nonprofit quarterly.org.

> *Thoughtful, in-depth exploration of one or two current themes in the life of the nonprofit sector.*

Books

Allison, M., and Kaye, J. *Strategic Planning for Nonprofit Organizations: A Practical Guide and Workbook.* (2nd ed.) New York: Wiley, 2003.

> *A definitive resource on how to create a strategic plan for your nonprofit organization.*

Andresen, K. *Robin Hood Marketing: Stealing Corporate Savvy to Sell Just Causes.* San Francisco: Jossey-Bass, 2006.

> Applying the experience of corporate marketing to nonprofits; written in a humorous as well as informative style.

Burk, P. *Donor-Centered Fundraising.* Chicago: Cygnus Applied Research, 2003.

> What does and does not influence donor retention, increase donors' desire to give more generous gifts, and influence the pace at which donors maximize their generosity.

Burnett, K. *Relationship Fundraising.* (2nd ed.) San Francisco: Jossey-Bass, 1992.

> The techniques of effective communication with donors.

Carlson, M. *Team-Based Fundraising Step by Step: A Practical Guide to Improving Results Through Teamwork.* San Francisco: Jossey-Bass, 2000.

> How to build and maintain a fundraising team to diversify the number of people asking for money and strengthen the overall fundraising program.

Chait, R., and others. *Governance as Leadership: Reframing the work of Nonprofit Boards.* New York: Wiley, 2004.

> Useful analysis of why boards don't work and what can be done to change board structures so that being a board member is an attractive and interesting proposition.

Colvin, G. *Fiscal Sponsorship: 6 Ways to Do It Right.* San Francisco: Study Center Press, 2005.

> Written both for organizations seeking a fiscal sponsor and those thinking of sponsoring, this short book is easy to follow and thorough in exploring this often complicated agreement.

Drucker, P. *Managing the NonProfit Organization: Principles and Practices.* New York: HarperCollins, 1990.

> The tasks, responsibilities, and practices necessary to manage nonprofit organizations.

Festen, M., and Philbin, M. *Level Best: How Small and Grassroots Nonprofits Can Tackle Evaluation and Talk Results.* San Francisco: Jossey-Bass, 2006.

> A guide to using evaluation tools to help your organization stay mission-driven and to understanding how to measure your success.

Flanagan, J. *The Grass Roots Fundraising Book: How to Raise Money in Your Community.* (rev. ed.) Chicago: Contemporary Books, 1995.

> Excellent introductory book for small organizations. Out of print, but widely available used.

Flanagan, J. *Successful Fundraising: A Complete Handbook for Volunteers and Professionals.* (2nd ed.) New York: McGraw Hill, 2002.

> How to do large-scale fundraising events and campaigns.

Gary, T., and Kohner, M. *Inspired Philanthropy: Creating a Giving Plan.* (rev. ed.) San Francisco: Jossey-Bass, 2002.

A step-by-step guide on how to match your giving with your values.

Giving USA Foundation. *Giving USA: Annual Report on Philanthropy.* Indianapolis: Giving USA Foundation.

Annual analysis of giving and trends in philanthropy from the Giving Institute, formerly American Association of Fund Raising Counsel.

Grace, K. S. *Beyond Fund Raising: New Strategies for Nonprofit Innovation and Investment.* (2nd ed.) New York: Wiley, 2005.

Strategies for developing long-term relationships with "donor-investors" and volunteers.

Hogan, C. *Prospect Research: A Primer for Growing Nonprofits.* Sudbury, Mass.: Jones and Bartlett, 2004.

What you need to know about your donors and prospects, and how you can find it out, then manage this information and make it work for you.

Hitchcock, S. *Open Immediately! Straight Talk on Direct Mail Fundraising: What Works, What Doesn't and Why.* Medfield, Mass.: Emerson and Church, 2004.

Excellent and easy-to-read overview of direct mail, with many examples, by one of the leading authorities on the subject.

Hopkins, B. *650 Essential Nonprofit Law Questions Answered.* New York: Wiley, 2005.

Authoritative answers to important questions on business, tax, legal, and fundraising practices.

Hopkins, K., and Friedman, C. *Successful Fundraising for Arts and Cultural Organizations.* (2nd ed.) Phoenix: Oryx Press, 1996.

Fundraising strategies for arts and cultural organizations of all sizes.

Lakey, G., and others (eds.). *Grassroots and Nonprofit Leadership: A Guide for Organizations in Changing Times.* Philadelphia: New Society Publishers, 1995.

The nature of power and leadership, stages of social movements, and the social environment in which change organizations exist.

Landskroner, R. *The Nonprofit Manager's Resource Directory.* (2nd ed.) New York: Wiley, 2001.

Answers to questions about nonprofit-oriented product and service providers, Internet sites, funding sources, publications, and support and advocacy groups.

Quattman, V. *You Can Do It! A Volunteer's Guide to Raising Money for Your Group in Words and Pictures* (in Spanish and English). Maryville, Tenn.: Southern Empowerment Project, 2002.

Written especially for volunteers whose reading ability may be limited, this book is also useful for anyone in a hurry who wants to do effective fundraising. Also useful for group study and peer learning, and one of the few resources on grassroots fundraising in Spanish.

Robinson, A. *Grassroots Grants: An Activist's Guide to Grantseeking.* (2nd ed.) San Francisco: Jossey-Bass, 2004.

Hands-on guide to researching and writing grant proposals.

Robinson, A. *Selling Social Change (Without Selling Out): Earned Income Strategies for Nonprofits.* San Francisco: Jossey-Bass, 2002.

How to initiate and sustain successful earned-income ventures that provide financial security and advance an organization's mission.

Robinson, E. *The Nonprofit Membership Toolkit.* San Francisco: Jossey-Bass, 2003.

Step-by-step guide to building a membership organization.

Roth, S., and Ho, M. *The Accidental Fundraiser.* San Francisco: Jossey-Bass, 2005.

A detailed, easy-to-use guide to eleven fundraising strategies for people who have to raise money but do not intend to make it a career (or even a habit).

Salamon, L. (ed.). *The State of Nonprofit America.* Washington, D.C.: Brookings Institute Press, 2002.

Excellent analysis and historical overview of how we got here and what the future holds. This is the big picture.

Salzmann, J. *Making the News: A Guide for Nonprofits and Activists,* Boulder, Colo.: Westview Press, 1998.

An easy-to-use guide, with lots of examples, of how to get media coverage and what kind of media to seek out depending on your issue.

Sargeant, A., and Jay, E. *Building Donor Loyalty: The Fundraiser's Guide to Increasing Lifetime Value.* San Francisco: Jossey-Bass, 2004.

The factors that drive donor retention, how to keep donors committed to an organization, and suggestions for developing donor value over time.

Sen, R. *Stir It Up: Lessons in Community Organizing and Advocacy.* San Francisco: Jossey-Bass, 2003.

The steps of building and mobilizing a constituency and implementing key strategies for social change.

Stallings, B., and McMillion, D. *How to Produce Fabulous Fundraising Events: Reap Remarkable Returns with Minimal Effort.* Pleasanton, Calif.: Building Better Skills, 1996.

Step-by-step guide to a successful fundraising dinner.

Stanionis, M. *The Mercifully Brief, Real-World Guide to On-Line Fundraising.* Medfield, Mass.: Emerson and Church, 2006.

All the ways to use virtual technology in fundraising by a partner in DonorDigital, a pioneering firm in this area.

Tempel, E. (ed.). *Hank Rosso's Achieving Excellence in Fundraising.* (2nd ed.) San Francisco: Jossey-Bass, 2003.

> *The late Henry Rosso was one of the most famous fundraising consultants in America. This introduction to the theory and practice of fundraising is an invaluable tool.*

Warwick, M. *Revolution in the Mailbox: Your Guide to Successful Direct Mail Fundraising.* San Francisco: Jossey-Bass, 2004.

> *Step-by-step guide to writing a successful direct mail appeal by one of the nation's foremost experts on this topic.*

Warwick, M. *The Mercifully Brief, Real-World Guide to Raising $1,000 Gifts by Mail.* Medfield, Mass.: Emerson and Church, 2005.

> *Step-by-step advice on how to raise major gifts using the mail, with many real-life examples.*

Wendroff, A. *Special Events: Proven Strategies for Nonprofit Fundraising.* (2nd ed.) New York: Wiley, 2003.

> *A guide to producing large special events.*

Wheatley, M. J. *Leadership and the New Science: Learning about Organizations from an Orderly Universe.* San Francisco: Berrett-Kohler, 1999.

> *Using breakthroughs in biology, chemistry, and especially quantum physics, Wheatley paints a new picture of business management.*

Zimmerman, R. *Boards That Love Fundraising.* San Francisco: Jossey-Bass, 2003.

> *How to get your board members to embrace their fundraising responsibilities.*

WEB SITES

The following Web sites are not all specifically about fundraising or philanthropy, but they can help with the many other questions common to nonprofit organizations.

Association of Fundraising Professionals, www. afpnet.org.

> *Trade association for development professionals.*

Accountants for the Public Interest (API) http://www.geocities.com/api_woods/api/apihome.html.

> *Questions and answers as well as materials on accounting for nonprofits.*

Alliance for Nonprofit Management, http://www.allianceonline.org.

> *Professional association of individuals and organizations devoted to improving the management and governance capacity of nonprofits to assist nonprofits in fulfilling their mission.*

BoardSource, www.boardsource.org.

> *Formerly the National Center for Nonprofit Boards, a major resource for practical information, tools, and best practices, training, and leadership development for board members of nonprofit organizations.*

Building Movement Project, www.buildingmovement.org.

Helpful information on the nonprofit sector as a whole, particularly for organizations going through leadership change and social service organizations wishing to do more social justice work. A wide and varied range of articles and information. Check out the column "Jack's Corner," written by Kim's cat.

CompassPoint, www.compasspoint.org.

Training, consulting, and research on nonprofit management, concepts, and strategies. Also the site for nonprofit genie (http://www.compasspoint.org/askgenie/index.php), which provides answers to frequently asked management questions.

Groundspring, http://www.groundspring.org.

Handles giving for organizations; also has an excellent downloadable manual on online fundraising.

Internet Nonprofit Center, http://www.nonprofit-info.org.

Information, advice, and articles on numerous nonprofit management topics, including information on how to calculate program costs or fundraising ratios, or how to value donated goods.

Mal Warwick and Associates, http://www.malwarwick.com.

A wealth of information about fundraising using direct mail.

Network for Good, http://www.networkforgood.org.

Similar service scope to groundspring.

Technical Assistance for Community Organizations (TACS), http://www.tacs.org.

Good place to shop for accounting software.

Tech Soup, http://www. techsoup.org.

Great site for finding the latest information on fundraising software.

United for a Fair Economy, http://www.ufenet.org.

Works toward closing the gap between rich and poor with clear information about economics, taxes, and the relationship of the distribution of money to the quality of life of most Americans. Web site and newsletter are accessible and useful.

⌐Foundation Center Cooperating Collections Network

Knowledge to build on.

Free Funding Information Centers

The Foundation Center's mission is to strengthen the nonprofit sector by advancing knowledge about U.S. philanthropy. An authoritative source of information on grant-maker and corporate giving, we ensure free public access to a wide variety of services and comprehensive resources on grantmakers and grants through our five library/learning centers and a national network of Cooperating Collections. Cooperating Collections are libraries, community foundations, and other nonprofit agencies that make accessible a collection of Foundation Center print and electronic resources, as well as a variety of supplementary materials and educational programs in areas useful to grantseekers. The collection includes:

- Foundation Directory Online Professional or FC Search: The Foundation Center's Database on CD-ROM
- The Foundation Grants Index on CD-ROM
- The Foundation Directory, Part 2, and Supplement
- Foundation Fundamentals

- The Foundation 1000
- Foundations Today Series
- Foundation Grants to Individuals
- Foundation Grants to Individuals Online
- The Foundation Center's Guide to Grantseeking on the Web

- The Foundation Center's Guide to Proposal Writing
- The Foundation Center's Guide to Winning Proposals
- Guide to U.S. Foundations, Their Trustees, Officers, and Donors
- National Directory of Corporate Giving
- National Guide to Funding in . . . (Series)

505

FOUNDATION CENTER LIBRARY/LEARNING CENTERS

THE FOUNDATION
CENTER
79 5th Ave., 2nd Floor
New York, NY 10003
(212) 620-4230

THE FOUNDATION
CENTER
312 Sutter St., Suite 606
San Francisco, CA 94108
(415) 397-0902

THE FOUNDATION
CENTER
1627 K St., NW, 3rd Floor
Washington, DC 20006
(202) 331-1400

THE FOUNDATION
CENTER
Kent H. Smith Library
1422 Euclid Ave.,
Suite 1600
Cleveland, OH 44115
(216) 861-1934

THE FOUNDATION
CENTER
Hurt Bldg., 50 Hurt Plaza
Suite 150, Grand Lobby
(404) 880-0094

ALABAMA

BIRMINGHAM PUBLIC LIBRARY
Government Documents Dept.
2100 Park Place
Birmingham
35203

HUNTSVILLE PUBLIC LIBRARY
Information and Periodical Dept.
915 Monroe St.
Huntsville
35801

MOBILE PUBLIC LIBRARY
West Regional Library
5555 Grelot Road
Mobile
36609-3643

AUBURN UNIVERSITY AT
MONTGOMERY LIBRARY
Information Services
74-40 East Drive
Montgomery
36117–3596

ALASKA

CONSORTIUM LIBRARY
Acquisitions
3211 Providence Dr.
Anchorage
99508

JUNEAU PUBLIC LIBRARY
Reference
292 Marine Way
Juneau
99801

ARIZONA

FLAGSTAFF CITY-COCONINO
COUNTY PUBLIC LIBRARY
300 W. Aspen Ave.
Flagstaff
86001

PHOENIX PUBLIC LIBRARY
Information Services Dept.
1221 N. Central Ave.
Phoenix
85004

TUCSON-PIMA PUBLIC LIBRARY
Reference
101 N. Stone Ave.
Tucson
85701

ARKANSAS

BOREHAM LIBRARY
University of Arkansas, Fort Smith
5210 Grand Ave.
Ft. Smith
72913

CENTRAL ARKANSAS LIBRARY
SYSTEM
100 Rock St.
Little Rock
72201

CALIFORNIA

KERN COUNTY LIBRARY
Beale Memorial Library
701 Truxtun Ave.
Bakersfield
93301

ROONEY RESOURCE CENTER
Humboldt Area Foundation
PO Box 99
Bayside
95524

VENTURA COUNTY COMMUNITY
FOUNDATION
Resource Center for Nonprofit
Organizations
1317 Del Norte Rd., Suite 150
Camarillo
93010

FRESNO REGIONAL FOUNDATION
Nonprofit Advancement Center
3425 N. First St., Suite 101
Fresno
93726

CENTER FOR NONPROFIT
MANAGEMENT IN SOUTHERN CA
Nonprofit Resource Library
606 South Olive St. 2450
Los Angeles
90014

LOS ANGELES PUBLIC LIBRARY
Mid-Valley Regional Branch Library
16244 Nordhoff St.
North Hills
91343

PHILANTHROPY RESOURCE
CENTER
Flintridge Foundation
1040 Lincoln Ave., Suite 100
Pasadena
91103

CENTER FOR NONPROFIT
RESOURCES
Shasta Regional Community
Foundation's Center for Nonprofit
Resources
2280 Benton Dr.
Redding
96003

RICHMOND PUBLIC LIBRARY
352 Civic Center Plaza
Richmond
94804

RIVERSIDE CITY PUBLIC LIBRARY
Reference Dept.
3581 Mission Inn Ave.
Riverside
92501

NONPROFIT RESOURCE CENTER
828 I St., 2nd Fl.
Sacramento
95814

FUNDING INFORMATION CENTER
San Diego Foundation
1420 Kettner Blvd., Suite 500
San Diego
92101

COMPASSPOINT NONPROFIT
SERVICES
Nonprofit Development Library
1922 The Alameda, Suite 212
San Jose
95126

LOS ANGELES PUBLIC LIBRARY
San Pedro Regional Branch Library
931 S. Gaffey St.
San Pedro
90731

VOLUNTEER CENTER OF GREATER
ORANGE COUNTY
Nonprofit Resource Center
1901 E. 4th St., Suite 100
Santa Ana
92705

SANTA BARBARA PUBLIC LIBRARY
PO Box 1019
40 E. Anapamu St.
Santa Barbara
93101–1019

SANTA MONICA PUBLIC LIBRARY
Adult Services/Reference
1324 Fifth St.
Santa Monica
90401

SONOMA COUNTY LIBRARY
3rd and E St.s
Santa Rosa
95404

SEASIDE BRANCH LIBRARY
550 Harcourt Ave.
Seaside
93955

SIERRA NONPROFIT SUPPORT
CENTER
39 No. Washington St. #F
PO Box 905
Sonora
95370–0905

COLORADO

EL POMAR NONPROFIT RESOURCE
CENTER
Penrose Library
20 N. Cascade Ave.
Colorado Springs
80903

DENVER PUBLIC LIBRARY
General Reference
10 W. 14th Ave. Pkwy.
Denver
80204

PUEBLO CITY-COUNTY LIBRARY
DISTRICT
100 East Abriendo Ave.
Pueblo
81004–4332

CONNECTICUT

GREENWICH LIBRARY
101 W. Putnam Ave.
Greenwich
06830

HARTFORD PUBLIC LIBRARY
Reference Dept.
500 Main St.
Hartford
06103

NEW HAVEN FREE PUBLIC LIBRARY
Reference Dept.
133 Elm St.
New Haven
06510–2057

DELAWARE

HUGH MORRIS LIBRARY
University of Delaware
Reference Dept.
Newark
19717–5267

FLORIDA

BARTOW PUBLIC LIBRARY
2151 S. Broadway Ave.
Bartow
33830

VOLUSIA COUNTY LIBRARY CENTER
Reference Dept.-City Island
105 E. Magnolia Ave.
Daytona Beach
32114–4484

NOVA SOUTHEASTERN UNIVERSITY
Library, Research, and Information
Technology Center
3100 Ray Ferrero Jr. Blvd.
Fort Lauderdale
33314

LEARNING RESOURCES CENTER
Indian River Community College
3209 Virginia Ave.
Fort Pierce
34981–5596

JACKSONVILLE PUBLIC LIBRARIES
Grants Resource Center
122 N. Ocean St.
Jacksonville
32202

MIAMI-DADE PUBLIC LIBRARY
Humanities/Social Science Dept.
101 W. Flagler St.
Miami
33130

ORANGE COUNTY LIBRARY SYSTEM
Social Sciences Dept.
101 E. Central Blvd.
Orlando
32801

SELBY PUBLIC LIBRARY
Reference Dept.
1331 1st St.
Sarasota
34236

STATE LIBRARY OF FLORIDA
R. A. Gray Building
Tallahassee
32399–0250

HILLSBOROUGH CITY PUBLIC
LIBRARY COOPERATIVE
John F. Germany Public Library
900 N. Ashley Dr.
Tampa
33602

COMMUNITY FOUNDATION OF
PALM BEACH & MARTIN COUNTIES
700 South Dixie Highway, Suite 200
West Palm Beach
33401

GEORGIA

HALL COUNTY LIBRARY SYSTEM
127 Main St. NW
Gainesville
30501

METHODIST HOME
Rumford Center
304 Pierce Ave., 1st Fl.
Macon
31203

THOMAS COUNTY PUBLIC LIBRARY
201 N. Madison St.
Thomasville
31792

HAWAII

HAMILTON LIBRARY, UNIVERSITY OF
HAWAII
General/Humanities/Social Science
Reference Dept.
Honolulu
96822

IDAHO

FUNDING INFORMATION CENTER
Boise Public Library
715 S. Capitol Blvd.
Boise
83702

CALDWELL PUBLIC LIBRARY
1010 Dearborn St.
Caldwell
83605

MARSHALL PUBLIC LIBRARY
113 South Garfield
Pocatello
83204

ILLINOIS

CARBONDALE PUBLIC LIBRARY
405 West Main St.
Carbondale
62901

DONORS FORUM OF CHICAGO
LIBRARY
208 S. La Salle, Suite 735
Chicago
60604

EVANSTON PUBLIC LIBRARY
1703 Orrington Ave.
Evanston
60201

ROCK ISLAND PUBLIC LIBRARY
401 19th St.
Rock Island
61201–8143

NONPROFIT RESOURCE CENTER,
BROOKENS LIBRARY
University of Illinois at Springfield
One University Plaza, MS Lib 140
Springfield
62703–5407

INDIANA

EVANSVILLE-VANDERBURGH PUBLIC
LIBRARY
200 SE Martin Luther King Jr. Blvd.
Evansville
47708

ALLEN COUNTY PUBLIC LIBRARY
Reader Services
200 East Berry Street
Ft. Wayne
46802

INDIANAPOLIS-MARION COUNTY
PUBLIC LIBRARY
202 North Alabama St.
Indianapolis
46206

VIGO COUNTY PUBLIC LIBRARY
One Library Square
Terre Haute
47807

MOELLERING LIBRARY
Valparaiso University
1509 Chapel Drive
Valparaiso
46383

IOWA

CEDAR RAPIDS PUBLIC LIBRARY
500 1st St. SE
Cedar Rapids
52401

LEARNING RESOURCE CENTER
Southwestern Community College
1501 W. Townline Rd.
Creston
50801

DES MOINES PUBLIC LIBRARY
100 Locust St.
Des Moines
50309–1791

SIOUX CITY PUBLIC LIBRARY
Siouxland Funding Research Center
529 Pierce St.
Sioux City
51101–1203

KANSAS

PIONEER MEMORIAL LIBRARY
375 West 4th St.
Colby
67701

DODGE CITY PUBLIC LIBRARY
1001 2nd Ave.
Dodge City
67801

KEARNY COUNTY LIBRARY
101 East Prairie
PO Box 773
Lakin
67860

SALINA PUBLIC LIBRARY
301 West Elm
Salina
67401

TOPEKA & SHAWNEE COUNTY
PUBLIC LIBRARY
Adult Services
1515 SW 10th Ave.
Topeka
66604

WICHITA PUBLIC LIBRARY
General Reference
223 S. Main St.
Wichita
67202

KENTUCKY

HELM-CRAVENS LIBRARY
Western Kentucky University
Reference
Bowling Green
42101–3576

LEXINGTON PUBLIC LIBRARY
140 E. Main St.
Lexington
40507–1376

LOUISVILLE FREE PUBLIC LIBRARY
301 York St.
Louisville
40203

LOUISIANA

EAST BATON ROUGE PARISH LIBRARY
River Center Branch
120 St. Louis St.
Baton Rouge
70802

BEAUREGARD PARISH LIBRARY
Reference
205 S. Washington Ave.
DeRidder
70634

OUACHITA PARISH PUBLIC LIBRARY
1800 Stubbs Ave.
Monroe
71201

NEW ORLEANS PUBLIC LIBRARY
Business & Science Division
219 Loyola Ave.
New Orleans
70112

SHREVE MEMORIAL LIBRARY
Reference
424 Texas St.
Shreveport
71120–1523

MAINE

UNIVERSITY OF SOUTHERN MAINE
LIBRARY
Maine Philanthropy Center
314 Forrest Ave.
Portland
04104–9301

MARYLAND

ENOCH PRATT FREE LIBRARY
Social Science & History Dept.
400 Cathedral St.
Baltimore
21212

MASSACHUSETTS

ASSOCIATED GRANT MAKERS (AGM)
55 Court St.
Suite 520
Boston
02108

BERKSHIRE ATHENAEUM
1 Wendell Ave.
Pittsfield
1201

**WESTERN MASSACHUSETTS
FUNDING RESOURCE CENTER**
65 Elliot St.
Springfield
01101–1730

WORCESTER PUBLIC LIBRARY
Grants Resource Center
3 Salem Square
Worcester
01608

MICHIGAN

ALPENA COUNTY LIBRARY
Reference Dept.
211 N. 1st St.
Alpena
49707

**UNIVERSITY OF MICHIGAN
GRADUATE LIBRARY**
Reference Dept.
209 Hatcher North
Ann Arbor
48109-1205

WILLARD PUBLIC LIBRARY
Nonprofit & Funding Resource
Collections
7 W. Van Buren St.
Battle Creek
49017

HENRY FORD CENTENNIAL LIBRARY
Adult Services
16301 Michigan Ave.
Dearborn
48126

PURDY/KRESGE LIBRARY
Wayne State University
134 Purdy/Kresge Library
Detroit
48202

**MICHIGAN STATE UNIVERSITY
LIBRARIES**
Funding Center
100 Library
East Lansing
48824–1048

**FARMINGTON COMMUNITY
LIBRARY**
32737 W. 12 Mile Rd.
Farmington Hills
48334

**FRANCES WILLSON THOMPSON
LIBRARY**
University of Michigan-Flint
Library Reference Dept.
Flint
48502–1950

GRAND RAPIDS PUBLIC LIBRARY
Reference Dept.
111 Library Street NE
Grand Rapids
49503–3268

CORPORATE SERVICES
Michigan Technological University
ATDC Bldg, Suite 200
Houghton
49931–1295

**WEST SHORE COMMUNITY COLLEGE
LIBRARY**
3000 North Stiles Rd.
Scottville
49454–0277

TRAVERSE AREA DISTRICT LIBRARY
610 Woodmere Ave.
Traverse City
49686

MINNESOTA

BRAINERD PUBLIC LIBRARY
416 South Fifth St.
Brainerd
56401

DULUTH PUBLIC LIBRARY
Reference Dept.
520 W. Superior St.
Duluth
55802

UNIVERSITY LIBRARY
Southwest State University
N. Highway 23
Marshall
56253

MINNEAPOLIS PUBLIC LIBRARY
250 Marquette Ave.
Minneapolis
55401

ROCHESTER PUBLIC LIBRARY
Reference Division/FCC
101 2nd St., SE
Rochester
55904–3777

ST. PAUL PUBLIC LIBRARY
90 W. 4th St.
St. Paul
55102

MISSISSIPPI

**LIBRARY OF HATTIESBURG, PETAL
AND FORREST COUNTY**
329 Hardy St.
Hattiesburg
39401–3824

JACKSON/HINDS LIBRARY SYSTEM
Reference
300 N. State St.
Jackson
39201

MISSOURI

COUNCIL ON PHILANTHROPY
University of Missouri-Kansas City
PO Box 5813
Kansas City
64171–0813

KANSAS CITY PUBLIC LIBRARY
Reference Dept.
14 West 10th St.
Kansas City
64105–1702

**SPRINGFIELD-GREENE COUNTY
LIBRARY**
The Library Center
4653 S. Campbell
Springfield
65807

ST. LOUIS PUBLIC LIBRARY
1301 Olive St.
St. Louis
63103

MONTANA

FALLON COUNTY LIBRARY
6 West Fallon Ave.
Baker
59313–1037

LIBRARY-SPECIAL COLLECTIONS
Montana State University-Billings
1500 N. 30th St.
Billings
59101–0245

BOZEMAN PUBLIC LIBRARY
Reference
220 E. Lamme
Bozeman
59715

LINCOLN COUNTY PUBLIC LIBRARIES
Libby Public Library
220 West 6th St.
Libby
59923

MANSFIELD LIBRARY (MMLA01)
The University of Montana
32 Campus Drive #9936
Missoula
59812–9936

NEBRASKA

UNIVERSITIES LIBRARIES, UNIVERSITY OF NEBRASKA-LINCOLN
Reference Collection
Lincoln
68588–2848

OMAHA PUBLIC LIBRARY
Dale Clark Library, Social Science Dept.
Omaha
68102

NEVADA

GREAT BASIN COLLEGE LIBRARY
1500 College Parkway
Elko
89801

CLARK COUNTY LIBRARY
Reference Dept.
1401 E. Flamingo
Las Vegas
89119

WASHOE COUNTY LIBRARY
Reference Dept.
301 S. Center St.
Reno
89501

NEW HAMPSHIRE

CONCORD PUBLIC LIBRARY
45 Green St.
Concord
03301

HERBERT H. LAMSON LIBRARY
Plymouth State University
Plymouth
03264

NEW JERSEY

CUMBERLAND COUNTY LIBRARY
800 E. Commerce St.
Bridgeton
08302

FREE PUBLIC LIBRARY OF ELIZABETH
Reference
11 S. Broad St.
Elizabeth
07202

NEWARK ENTERPRISE COMMUNITY RESOURCE DEVELOPMENT CENTER
303–309 Washington St., 5th Fl.
Newark
07102

LEARNING RESOURCE CENTER
County College of Morris
214 Center Grove Rd.
Randolph
07869

NEW JERSEY STATE LIBRARY
PO Box 520
185 W. State St.
Trenton
08625–0520

NEW MEXICO

ALBUQUERQUE/BERNALILLO COUNTY LIBRARY SYSTEM
501 Copper Ave. NW
Albuquerque
87102

NEW MEXICO STATE LIBRARY
Information Services
1209 Camino Carlos Rey
Santa Fe
87507

NEW YORK

NEW YORK STATE LIBRARY
Humanities Reference, Cultural Education Center, 6th Fl.
Empire State Plaza
Albany
12230

BROOKLYN PUBLIC LIBRARY
Society, Science and Technology Division
Grand Army Plaza
Brooklyn
11238

BUFFALO & ERIE COUNTY PUBLIC LIBRARY
Business and Science & Technology Dept.
1 Lafayette Square
Buffalo
14203–1887

SOUTHEAST STEUBEN COUNTY LIBRARY
300 Nasser Civic Center Plaza
Corning
14830

HUNTINGTON PUBLIC LIBRARY
Reference Dept.
338 Main St.
Huntington
11743

QUEENS BOROUGH PUBLIC LIBRARY
Social Sciences Division
89–11 Merrick Blvd.
Jamaica
11432

LEVITTOWN PUBLIC LIBRARY
Reference Dept.
1 Bluegrass Ln.
Levittown
11756

ADRIANCE MEMORIAL LIBRARY
Special Services Dept.
93 Market St.
Poughkeepsie
12601

THE RIVERHEAD FREE LIBRARY
330 Court St.
Riverhead
11901

ROCHESTER PUBLIC LIBRARY
Social Sciences
115 S. Ave.
Rochester
14604

ONONDAGA COUNTY PUBLIC LIBRARY
Information Services
447 S. Salina St.
Syracuse
13202

UTICA PUBIC LIBRARY
303 Genesee St.
Utica
13501

WHITE PLAINS PUBLIC LIBRARY
Adult Reader/Information Services
100 Martine Ave.
White Plains
10601

YONKERS PUBLIC LIBRARY
Riverfront Library
One Larkin Center
Yonkers
10701

NORTH CAROLINA
PACK MEMORIAL LIBRARY
Community Foundation of Western
North Carolina
67 Haywood St.
Asheville
28802

THE DUKE ENDOWMENT LIBRARY
100 N. Tryon St., Suite 3500
Charlotte
28202–4012

DURHAM COUNTY PUBLIC LIBRARY
Reference Dept.
300 N. Roxboro St.
Durham
27702

CAMERON VILLAGE REGIONAL
LIBRARY
Wake County Public Libraries
1930 Clark Ave.
Raleigh
27605

NEW HANOVER COUNTY PUBLIC
LIBRARY
201 Chestnut St.
Wilmington
28401–3942

FORSYTH COUNTY PUBLIC LIBRARY
660 W. 5th St.
Winston-Salem
27101

NORTH DAKOTA
BISMARCK PUBLIC LIBRARY
515 North Fifth St.
Bismarck
58501–4081

FARGO PUBLIC LIBRARY
102 N. 3rd St.
Fargo
58102

MINOT PUBLIC LIBRARY
516 Second Ave. SW
Minot
58701–3792

OHIO
STARK COUNTY DISTRICT LIBRARY
715 Market Ave. N.
Canton
44702

PUBLIC LIBRARY OF CINCINNATI &
HAMILTON COUNTY
Grants Resource Center
800 Vine St.
Cincinnati
45202–2071

COLUMBUS METROPOLITAN
LIBRARY
Business and Technology Dept.
96 S. Grant Ave.
Columbus
43215

DAYTON METRO LIBRARY
Grants Information Center
215 E. 3rd St.
Dayton
45402

MANSFIELD/RICHLAND COUNTY
PUBLIC LIBRARY
43 W. 3rd St.
Mansfield
44902

PORTSMOUTH PUBLIC LIBRARY
1220 Gallia St.
Portsmouth
45662

TOLEDO-LUCAS COUNTY PUBLIC
LIBRARY
Business Science Society Dept.
325 N. Michigan
Toledo
43612

PUBLIC LIBRARY OF YOUNGSTOWN
AND MAHONING COUNTY
305 Wick Ave.
Youngstown
44503

OKLAHOMA
DULANEY BROWNE LIBRARY
Oklahoma City University
2501 N. Blackwelder
Oklahoma City
73106

TULSA CITY-COUNTY LIBRARY
Reference Dept.
400 Civic Center
Tulsa
74103

OREGON
OREGON INSTITUTE OF
TECHNOLOGY LIBRARY
Library Reference
3201 Campus Dr.
Klamath Falls
97601–8801

JACKSON COUNTY LIBRARY
SERVICES
205 S. Central Ave.
Medford
97501

MULTNOMAH COUNTY LIBRARY
Science & Business Dept.
801 SW 10th Ave.
Portland
97205

OREGON STATE LIBRARY
Reference Dept.
State Library Bldg.
Salem
97301–3950

PENNSYLVANIA
THE PAUL AND HARRIETT MACK
LIBRARY
Northampton Community College
3835 Green Pond Rd.
Bethlehem
18017

ERIE COUNTY LIBRARY SYSTEM
Reference Dept.
160 E. Front St.
Erie
16507

DAUPHIN COUNTY LIBRARY SYSTEM
East Shore Area Library
4501 Ethel St.
Harrisburg
17109

HAZLETON AREA PUBLIC LIBRARY
55 North Church St.
Hazleton
18201

LANCASTER COUNTY LIBRARY
Adult Services Dept.
125 N. Duke St.
Lancaster
17602

FREE LIBRARY OF PHILADELPHIA
Regional Foundation Center
1901 Vine St., 2nd Fl.
Philadelphia
19103–1189

CARNEGIE LIBRARY OF PITTSBURGH
Downtown & Business
612 Smithfield St.
Pittsburgh
15222

JAMES PETTINGER MEMORIAL
LIBRARY
Pocono Northeast Development Fund
1151 Oak St.
Pittston
18640

READING PUBLIC LIBRARY
100 S. 5th St.
Reading
19602

JAMES V. BROWN LIBRARY
19 East Fourth St.
Williamsport
17701

MARTIN LIBRARY
159 E. Market St.
York
17401

RHODE ISLAND

PROVIDENCE PUBLIC LIBRARY
150 Empire St.
Providence
02903

SOUTH CAROLINA

ANDERSON COUNTY LIBRARY
300 N. McDuffie St.
PO Box 4047
Anderson
29622

CHARLESTON COUNTY LIBRARY
Reference Dept.
68 Calhoun St.
Charleston
29401

SOUTH CAROLINA STATE LIBRARY
Reader Services Dept.
PO Box 11469
Columbia
29211

GREENVILLE COUNTY LIBRARY
SYSTEM
25 Heritage Green Place
Greenville
29601–2034

SOUTH DAKOTA

DAKOTA STATE UNIVERSITY
Nonprofit Management Institute
Nonprofit Grants Assistance
Madison
57042

SOUTH DAKOTA STATE LIBRARY
Reference Dept.
800 Governors Dr.
Pierre
57501–2294

E.Y. BERRY LIBRARY-LEARNING
CENTER
Black Hills State University
1200 University St. Unit 9676
Spearfish
57799–9676

TENNESSEE

CENTER FOR NONPROFITS
United Way of Greater Chattanooga
630 Market St.
Chattanooga
37402

KNOX COUNTY PUBLIC LIBRARY
Reference Dept.
500 W. Church Ave.
Knoxville
37902

MEMPHIS & SHELBY COUNTY
PUBLIC LIBRARY
3030 Poplar Ave.
Memphis
38111

NASHVILLE PUBLIC LIBRARY
615 Church St.
Nashville
37219

TEXAS

AMARILLO AREA FOUNDATION,
GRANTS CENTER
801 S. Filmore, Suite 700
Amarillo
79101

HOGG FOUNDATION FOR MENTAL
HEALTH
Regional Foundation Library
3001 Lake Austin Blvd. Suite 400
Austin
78703

BEAUMONT PUBLIC LIBRARY
PO Box 3827
801 Pearl St.
Beaumont
77704–3827

CORPUS CHRISTI PUBLIC LIBRARY
Funding Information Center
805 Comanche St.
Corpus Christi
78401

DALLAS PUBLIC LIBRARY
Urban Information
1515 Young St.
Dallas
75201

SOUTHWEST BORDER NONPROFIT
RESOURCE CENTER
1201 W. University Drive
Edinburgh
78539–2999

UNIVERSITY OF TEXAS AT EL PASO
Institute for Community-Based Teaching
and Learning
Community Non-Profit Grant Library
El Paso
79968–0547

FUNDING INFORMATION CENTER
OF FORT WORTH
Reference Dept.
329 S. Henderson St.
Ft. Worth
76104

HOUSTON PUBLIC LIBRARY
Bibliographic Information Center
500 McKinney St.
Houston
77002

LAREDO PUBLIC LIBRARY
Nonprofit Management and Volunteer
Center
1120 E. Calton Rd.
Laredo
78041

LONGVIEW PUBLIC LIBRARY
222 W. Cotton St.
Longview
75601

LUBBOCK AREA FOUNDATION, INC.
1655 Main St., Suite 209
Lubbock
79401

NONPROFIT RESOURCE CENTER OF
TEXAS
PO Box 15070
7404 Highway 90 W.
San Antonio
78212–8270

WACO-MCLENNAN COUNTY
LIBRARY
1717 Austin Ave.
Waco
76701

NONPROFIT MANAGEMENT CENTER
OF WICHITA FALLS
2301 Kell Blvd. Suite 218
Wichita Falls
76308

UTAH

GRAND COUNTY PUBLIC LIBRARY
25 South 100 East
Moab
84532

SALT LAKE CITY PUBLIC LIBRARY
Non-Fiction
210 E 400 S
Salt Lake City
84111

VERMONT

ILSLEY PUBLIC LIBRARY
75 Main St.
Middlebury
05753

VERMONT DEPARTMENT OF
LIBRARIES
Reference & Law Information Services
109 State St.
Montpelier
05609

VIRGINIA

WASHINGTON COUNTY PUBLIC
LIBRARY
205 Oak Hill St.
Abingdon
24210

HAMPTON PUBLIC LIBRARY
Reference Dept.
4207 Victoria Blvd.
Hampton
23669

RICHMOND PUBLIC LIBRARY
Business, Science & Technology
101 E. Franklin St.
Richmond
23219

ROANOKE CITY PUBLIC LIBRARY
SYSTEM
Main Library
706 S Jefferson St.
Roanoke
24016

WASHINGTON

MID-COLUMBIA LIBRARY
Reference Dept.
1620 South Union St.
Kennewick
99338

KING COUNTY LIBRARY SYSTEM
Redmond Regional Library
Nonprofit & Philanthropy Resource
Center
Redmond
98052

THE SEATTLE PUBLIC LIBRARY
Fundraising Resource Center
1000 4th Avenue
Seattle
98104

SPOKANE PUBLIC LIBRARY
Funding Information Center
906 West Main Ave.
Spokane
99201

UNIVERSITY OF WASHINGTON
TACOMA LIBRARY
1900 Commerce St.
PO Box 358460
Tacoma
98402

WEST VIRGINIA

KANAWHA COUNTY PUBLIC LIBRARY
Reference Dept., 1st Fl.
123 Capitol St.
Charleston
25301

WEST VIRGINIA UNIVERSITY AT
PARKERSBURG
Library, 300 Campus Dr.
Parkersburg
26101

SHEPHERD UNIVERSITY
Ruth A. Scarborough Library, King St.
PO Box 3210
Shepherdstown
25443–3210

WISCONSIN

MEMORIAL LIBRARY, UNIVERSITY OF
WISCONSIN-MADISON
Reference Dept., Grants Information
Center
Madison
53706

MARQUETTE UNIVERSITY RAYNOR
LIBRARY
Funding Information Center
1355 W. Wisconsin Ave.
Milwaukee
53201–3141

UNIVERSITY LIBRARY-FOUNDATION
CENTER
University of Wisconsin-Steven's Point
900 Reserve St.
Stevens Point
54481–3897

WYOMING

INSTRUCTIONAL RESOURCES
CENTER
Laramie County Community College
1400 E. College Dr.
Cheyenne
82007–3299

CAMPBELL COUNTY PUBLIC
LIBRARY
2101 4-J Rd.
Gillette
82718

TETON COUNTY LIBRARY
125 Virginian Ln.
Box 1629
Jackson
83001

SHERIDAN COUNTY FULMER PUBLIC
LIBRARY
335 West Alger St.
Sheridan
82801

PUERTO RICO

M.M.T. GUEVARA LIBRARY,
UNIVERSIDAD DEL SAGRADO
CORAZON
Reference Room
Santurce
00914

Participants in the Foundation Center's Cooperating Collections network are libraries or nonprofit information centers that provide fundraising information and other funding-related technical assistance in their communities. Cooperating Collections agree to provide free public access to a basic collection of Foundation Center resources during a regular schedule of hours, along with free funding research guidance to all visitors. Many also provide a variety of services for local nonprofit organizations, using staff or volunteers to prepare special materials, organize workshops, or conduct orientations.

A key initiative of the Foundation Center is to reach under-resourced and underserved populations throughout the United States who are in need of useful information and training to become successful grantseekers. One of the ways we accomplish this goal is by designating new Cooperating Collection libraries in regions that have the ability to serve the nonprofit communities most in need of Foundation Center resources. We are seeking proposals from qualified institutions (e.g., public, academic, or special libraries, community foundations, nonprofit resource centers, and other technical assistance providers) that can help us carry out this important initiative.

If you are interested in establishing a funding information library in your area, or would like to learn more about the program, please contact: Coordinator of Cooperating Collections, The Foundation Center, 79 Fifth Avenue, New York, NY 10003 (e-mail: ccmail@foundationcenter.org).

INDEX

Direct mail appeal package: brief description of, 149; brochure included in, 162; carrier (outside) envelope, 149–150; fact sheet included in, 162; incorporating mission into, 151; internal memorandum included in, 161–162; letter included in, 152–160; lift note included in, 160–161; newspaper article copy included in, 161; other ways to draw attention to, 151–152; reply device included with, 158–160; return envelope included with, 160; strategies for personalizing, 150; tips on preparing, 162–163; when to send the, 163–164

Direct mail letters: additional devices used in, 157; appealing to the readers, 153–154; closing paragraph of, 156–157; described, 152–153; length of, 156; opening paragraph of, 154–156; order in which letter is read, 154; postscript, 154; reply device included in, 158; short attention spans considerations for, 153

Direct mail lists: cold lists, 142; dos and don'ts of sharing, 146–148; hot lists, 142, 143–144; renting and trading, 145–146; types of, 142; warm lists, 142, 144–145

Direct mail reply device: design of, 158–160; psychology of, 158

Direct mail solicitation: appeal package sent for, 149–164; appealing to current donors, 171–172; benefits and premiums included in, 164–167; developing lists for, 142–148; evaluating your, 175–177; handling responses to, 175; one organization's results with, 139; overview of, 135–136; phoning after, 195–196; rural community fundraising using, 446; to seek renewal gifts, 167–171; three functions of, 137–138, 140; used on smaller scale, 140–142; what to appeal for in, 172–174

Dirty money: ideas of clean money and, 466; moral dilemmas regarding, 465, 467–468; "vomit test" for, 467

"Do Not Call" list, 179

Domain name, 201

Donor categories: benefits program, 165; direct mail, 159–160

Donor frequency segment, 264

Donor gift segment, 264

Donor giving: confidence in organization required for, 218–219; example of organizational strategy for, 33–34; getting comfortable asking for money from, 65–71; getting repeat, 138; Gina Generous story on, 28–31; matching organizational needs to, 32; three types of strategies for matching needs to, 32–33. *See also* Contributions; Giving

Donor giving charts: Capital Campaign Gift Range Chart, 312; Endowment Campaign Gift Range Chart, 321; Major Donor Gift Range Chart, 243; Major Donor Gift Range Chart and Prospects, 245

Donor list segmenting: benefits of, 263–264; criteria used for, 264–265; used to stay in touch with donors, 266–267

Donor lists: creating legacy giving, 280–281; database records on, 355–358; direct mail, 142–148; initial listing potential, 462; phone-a-thon, 180–181; regular updating of, 357; segmenting, 263–267; sharing and trading, 145–146. *See also* Information management; Prospect lists; Record keeping

Donor longevity segment, 264

Donor-Centered Fundraising (Burke), 167

Donors: action plans for contacting, 349; appreciation of thank you notes by, 232; belief in organization by, 74–75; bricks-and-mortar people, 171; characteristics of rural community, 437–440; database records on, 353–355; direct mail appeals to current, 171–174; e-mail correspondence with, 205–206, 249; getting them to renew their gift, 138, 140; getting them to repeat their gift, 138; Gina Generous story on, 28–31; logistics of personal solicitation of, 73–90; pledges made by, 253–254; three organizational goals for

renewal, 138, 140, 167–171; renewing major donor, 249–252; responding to your direct mail appeal, 175; segmenting donor, 264. *See also* Major gifts programs; Solicitation strategies

Gina Generous story, 28–31

Giving: as fee for service, 22; by foundations and corporations, 12–14; identifying individual and corporate sources of, 7–10; myth of foundation-corporate, 6–7; power of individual, 14–18; as "public-society benefit," 15; recipients of, 15–16; to religious sector, 16–18; self-interest motivation for, 21–22; the truth about, 10–12. *See also* Donor giving; Philanthropy

Giving USA (Giving USA Foundation): charitable giving patterns reported on by, 10, 15; philanthropic research reported on by, 6, 8; on sources of contributions (2004), 7

Goal statements, 38

Good intent assumption, 401, 403

Grassroots Fundraising Journal, 2

Groundspring, 202

"Gut check," 401, 402

H

Hanukkah direct mail appeal, 173–174

HH ("ha-ha") fake appointments, 348

High-speed Internet service, 201

History section (case statement), 39

Ho, M., 360

Holidays: cards sent to major donors on, 248; direct mail appeals during, 173–174

Honorary annual dinner committee, 117

Hosting house party, 108–109

Hot lists, 142, 143–144

House parties: choreographing the, 111–113; definition of, 107–108; evaluation and follow-up to, 115; example of two house parties for one group, 112–113; finding the host, 108–109; five steps in putting on a, 108; invitation to, 110; the pitch during, 113–115; who to invite, 109–110

I

Income projections: matching expense and, 414; procedures for, 409, 411–413; sample, 412

Indiana University, 8

Individual giving: identifying characteristics of, 7–10; power of, 14–18

Information management: using database for, 351–355; filing system used for, 340–341; identifying and tracking prioritized information, 339–340; of information needed for fundraising, 338–339; necessity of, 337–338; posting most important information on 3 x 5 cards, 341. *See also* Donor lists; Record keeping

Inner City Greenspace, 155

Internal memorandum (direct mail enclosure), 161–162

Internal Revenue Service (IRS): 501(c)(3) designation of, 43–44; number of tax exempt organizations recognized by, 5; "one-third rule" of, 20; UBIT (unrelated-business income tax) on adbooks and, 128. *See also* Legal issues

Internet: charity portals through the, 207–208; digital divide and, 200; nonprofit organization Web presence on the, 201–202; receiving donations and payment online, 202, 207–208. *See also* E-mail

Internet solicitation: driving traffic to your site, 203–204; overview of, 199–200; requirements and necessities for, 201–202

Invitation committee (annual dinner), 118

Invitations (house party), 110

IRAs (individual retirement funds), 278

IRS form 990, 7

J

Judgment issue, 95

"Junk mail," 136

K

Keeping records. *See* Record keeping

L

Launch (capital campaign), 316

Legacy gifts: described, 269; preparing to talk about, 271; wills and role in, 271–272

Legacy giving programs: creating mailing list, 280–281; getting prepared for, 270; holding seminar for, 281; importance of donor's will to, 271–277; introducing your, 278–282; making bequests, 274–277; working collaboratively with other groups, 281–282

Legal issues: fee-for-service income, 212–213; 501(c)(3) status, 43–44; setting up a canvass and, 219–220. *See also* Internal Revenue Service (IRS)

Letters (to prospect): direct mail appeal package, 152–160; following up phone-a-thon, 183–186; phone-a-thon reminder letters, 190; procedure after establishing contact, 85–86; thank you notes, 231–238; writing the, 82–83. *See also* Envelopes; Prospects; Stationary materials

Life insurance policies: buying to fund a gift, 277; existing, 277

Life note, 160–161

Lincoln's birthday direct mail appeal, 173

Lists. *See* Donor lists; Prospect lists

M

Mail list brokers, 146

Major Donor Campaign Master Tracking Form, 302

Major Donor Gift Range Chart, 243

Major Donor Gift Range Chart and Prospects, 245

Major gift campaign materials: case statement, 298–299; pledge card, 299; stationary, envelopes, and return envelopes, 299

Major gift donors: charting gift range and prospects of, 243, 245; keeping in touch with, 247–249; renewing gifts from, 249–252; solicitation of, 245–247

Major gifts campaigns steps: 1: setting a goal, 296–298; 2: preparing supporting materials, 298–299; 3: identify and train solicitors, 300–301; 4: identifying prospects, 301–302; 5: assigning prospects and soliciting gifts, 302–303; 6: kicking off the campaign with special event, 303; 7: holding regular reporting meetings, 303–304; 8: celebrating end of campaign with special event, 304; 9: recognizing and incorporating donors into ongoing fundraising efforts, 304; listed, 295–296

Major gifts programs: apportionment of gifts, 243–244; benefits of building, 241; expected response rate for, 244–245; first year challenges of, 252; setting a goal for, 242–243. *See also* Gifts

Major gifts solicitation: materials for, 245–247; solicitors used for, 247

Master Prospect List, 78, 79

Material committee (annual dinner), 118

Mathiasen, K., 55

MC (master of ceremonies) [annual dinner], 120

Media: phone-a-thon publicity through the, 191–192; sending major donors copies of coverage by, 248

Meeting (face-to-face solicitation): etiquette during, 87–88; objectives of the, 86; possible responses by prospects during, 88–89

Meetings: avoid scheduling too many, 349; for face-to-face solicitation, 86–89; saying "no" to, 347–348; skipping unnecessary, 348

Mentors: description and tasks of, 376; situations that may require hiring, 375–376

Merton, T., 392

Mismanagement of funds, 431–432

Mission statement: carrier envelopes reflecting the, 151; consultant belief in, 380–381; described, 36–38

Money: asking donors for their, 65–66; emotional conflicts over, 67–69; special events to raise, 92; specific fears about asking for,

your list in shape, 357. *See also* Donor lists; Information management

Refreshments. *See* Food and refreshments

Religious sector contributions, 16–18

Reminder letter (phone-a-thon), 190

Renewal gifts: database information on donors and, 354; direct mail solicitation of, 167–171; getting donors to commit to, 138, 140; from major donors, 249–252; phone-a-thon to solicit, 196–197

Repeatability issue, 97

Reply device (direct mail): design of, 158–160; psychology of, 158; return envelope included with, 160

Reserve fund, 28

Retention strategies, 32

Retirement plans, 278

Return envelope (direct mail), 160

Rio Del Vista, 156

Robert's Rules of Order, 46

Roth, S., 360

Rural community fundraising: approaches for raising money, 440–442; direct mail used for, 446; example of "colonies" communities, 440–441; factors to consider in, 437–440; personal solicitation used for, 446–447; prospects for, 442–444; special events used for, 444–446

S

Scripts (phone-a-thon): to determine interest, 193–195; following mail appeal, 195–196; sample, 182–183; training volunteers to use, 195. *See also* Solicitors

Seasonal direct mail appeals, 172

Segmenting donor lists, 263–267

September 11, 2001, 151

Serious accounting errors, 431–432

Services: cost of providing, 210; fees for phone-provided, 214–215; mandatory fees charged for, 211; voluntary fees paid for, 211–212. *See also* Fee-for-service income

Social justice: as fundraising context, 387; overall work of fundraising for, 391–393

Solicitation strategies: annual dinner used for, 115–121; direct mail, 135–177, 446; door-to-door canvassing, 217–223; endowment campaign, 326; house party as means of, 107–115; matching volunteers to, 360–361; materials for major gift, 245–247; personal, 73–90, 446–447; for rural communities, 444–447; special events, 91–134, 303, 304, 444–446; by telephone, 179–198; using the Internet, 199–208. *See also* Asking for money; Fundraising; Fundraising strategies; Gifts

Solicitors: canvassing by, 221–223, 370; major gifts, 247; matching strategies to, 360–361; training major gifts, 300–301. *See also* Scripts (phone-a-thon)

Special Event Report (Evaluation Form), 104–105

Special events: adbooks, 127–134; annual dinner, 115–121; choosing a fundraising, 93–97; described, 91; house party, 107–115; major donor campaign, 303, 304; planning, 98–105; raffle, 121–127; rural community fundraising using, 444–446; three goals of, 91–92; types of people who attend, 92–93. *See also* Fundraising

Special events committee: described, 98; evaluation role of, 103–105; planning checklist for, 102–103; tasks of, 98–102

Special events committee tasks: creating a timeline, 101–102; detail a master event task list, 99; preparing a budget, 99–101

Special events considerations: appropriateness of the event, 94; the big picture, 97; consistency and judgment issues, 94–95; energy of volunteers, 96; front money availability, 96; image of the organization, 95–96; repeatability issue, 97; timing issues, 97

Special events planning: checklist for, 102–103; committee role and tasks in, 98–102; evaluation as part of, 103–105